Sisters of the Raj

The Clewer Sisters in India

Valerie Bonham

Valerie Bonham

1997

1st published 1997

ISBN 0 9508710 3 6

Published by Valerie Bonham and the Community of St John Baptist, Clewer, and prepared by Thameslink, Windsor.

Copies of this and other volumes in the Clewer trilogy are available from:

The Community of St John Baptist,
Hatch Lane, WINDSOR, Berks. SL4 3QR

Also by Valerie Bonham:

In the Midst of the People (1983) (out of print)

A Joyous Service: The Clewer Sisters and their work (1989)

A Place in Life: The Clewer House of Mercy, 1849-83 (1992)

This book is dedicated to the greater glory of God,

and in thanksgiving for the life and work of the

Clewer Sisters in India, their

co-workers, and their successors.

And for Sister Eudora (1901–97),

last in a long line.

"Christ is the meaning of it all and the secret of it all" - *Sr Eudora.*

Frontispiece: The S.S. Capella *(Star Line), one of the ships in which the Sisters sailed to and from India.*

CONTENTS

C S J B

I N D I A

LIST OF ILLUSTRATIONS

Black and white plates are located between pages 146–147.
Colour plates are located between pages 274-275.

Colour photographs

Colour plates are located between pages 274-275.

ACKNOWLEDGEMENTS

I must reiterate my gratitude to the Community of St John Baptist for allowing me to write this trilogy. Over the years the Sisters have placed a tremendous trust in me by giving me unlimited access to their archives and by stoically agreeing to yet another volume! As a result the bond of love and trust has been mutual, and I have found this major task of writing the trilogy profoundly moving. My gratitude to Sr Eudora is recorded elsewhere, but I also wish to record special thanks to Mother Jane Olive who has seen this trilogy evolve, firstly as Sister Secretary, and latterly as Mother Superior. Individual Sisters have all played a part - it is above all, the Community's book, I have simply put the words together.

Elsewhere, I have written of the importance of my visit to India, but here I want to record my thanks to Canon Allchin for suggesting the visit, to Joyce Sampson for accompanying me, and to the Sisters for making it possible. And here too I would record my thanks to Mrs Chrestien and her staff at St John's Diocesan School for the welcome they gave us and for facilitating the rest of our time in Calcutta, and to Mrs Ghosh and Mrs Ghose at the Pratt Memorial and St Thomas' schools, respectively. Although I missed meeting Mother Susila, CSS, by about two hours, I was pleased to meet her at Wantage in the summer of 1996 and to hear her memories of the Clewer Sisters. Br Amit Biswas of the Oxford Mission at Behala, and Sr Florence, OMSE, gave us a welcome we will not forget.

Most of the research for this book was done at Clewer from the archive material there, but I have also received much help at different times from the staff of the British Library, India Office division. Former pupils of St Michael's, Darjeeling and the Pratt Memorial School have assisted me with their memories - Clare Walton, Joyce Keenan, Nancy Leslie, Suzanne Levi and Helen Wala, and I am grateful for their personal insights. I am also grateful to Miss Patricia Osborn for information about her aunt, Sister Blanche Annie CSJB. Mr Theon Wilkinson of the British Association for Cemeteries in South Asia, Mrs Bunny Gupta and Mr R Wright of Calcutta have helped locate the Sisters' burial site.

I also wish to record my thanks to Canon Vincent Strudwick for his perceptive foreword, fed by a deep knowledge of church history and Religious Communities. As Principal of the St Alban's and Oxford Ministry Course at the time of my visit to India, I was very grateful to him for giving me leave of absence.

Pam Marson has once again applied her expertise to the photographs and has also helped in the difficult task of making the final selection from the vast number at Clewer. Roger Cullingham of Thameslink has again taken my disks and transformed them into a book, and I am grateful for all his work on the whole trilogy. My family has continued to give me support - they have lived with the exploits of the Clewer Sisters for a long time now, although Fred, my husband, drew the line at going to India with me! I am grateful to my daughter Louise who has provided the logo for the chapter endings.

FOREWORD BY CANON VINCENT STRUDWICK

The first two volumes of Valerie Bonham's trilogy describe the extraordinary phenomenon of the revival of the Religious Life in the Church of England as it was expressed through the Community of St John the Baptist at Clewer. This final volume is about the work of the Clewer Sisters in India - but it is more than that, for through the work they created, and in the descriptions of their thoughts and experiences that appear in letters, we have precious insights for the social historian, and for all those interested in the complicated relationship between the people of the Indian sub-continent and the inhabitants of the British Isles.

The small band of Sisters set out in 1881, and in the words of their episcopal visitor, the Bishop of Oxford, John Mackarness, they were to share in, "the great - overwhelming - work, which it is England's duty and privilege to do in India."

In their hospitals and schools they were to be Missionaries of the Gospel *and* bearers of western culture and customs.

Such a "mix" is too easy to oversimplify and sneer at, and it is greatly to Valerie Bonham's credit that she has done neither - but nor has she falsified the account.

The Sisters were people with failings, and people of their time, but through her careful research and sympathetic evaluation, the author presents us with a story of courage, dedication and amazing energy, as the Community developed the work committed to it in what to the Sisters was a strange and dangerous land.

It was through this commitment that the Sisters began to discover the heartbeat of India. At first progress was modest - for example, singing *Onward Christian Soldiers* in Bengali, but gradually changes took place, as it did with the Sisters' attitudes to other religions. "Earthy, sensual and devilish," was Mother Jane Frances' judgement on a Hindoo festival, but she had the sensitivity and grace to add, "at least in its popular form." The Sisters withdrew before the enormous change in attitudes that took place in the West in the post World War II period, but as I read this text I am arrested by the commitment of the Sisters to the task as perceived, and their love for the people they served, which has been the basis for progression and fruitful change in every generation. The Sisters' pride in Mabel Singh (BA with honours, 1905), and their unswerving devotion to women's education in the subsequent years was the basis for the welcome Valerie Bonham received when she visited India to research the book, and found a contemporary and vigorous flowering of the seeds the Sisters had planted. This is a fascinating story, and a loving tribute to a Community facing cultural and institutional change today quite as enormous as that experienced by those Sisters arriving from Clewer in India at the closing decades of the last century.

Vincent Strudwick

PREFACE BY SISTER EUDORA, CSJB.

This book is dedicated to that period of time when the Sisters of the Community of St John Baptist were privileged to be sent to India to work among Indian girls and women. In Calcutta and Darjeeling it took the form of various types of schools, and in the Rice Country evangelistic work and witness. It is offered to the successors of their work, and to the present Principal and staff of the St John's Diocesan Girls' Higher Secondary School.

In the making of the book, many wonderful memories have come to light, and many devoted characters both Indian and European.

Among old students there must be some who remember the love and devotion of the then Mother Provincial - Dorothy Frances - her great contribution to the education of Indian girls for which she was awarded the Kaiser-i-Hind, but above all, her influence on so many - Sisters, students, staff - she loved all.

My own experience covers the years when "Young India" was alive and kicking - misplaced zeal at the time led to an attempt on the life of the Governor - which had repercussions in our own Christian Indian Girls' Boarding Hostel. In those days Mahatma Gandhi came to stay very near to our compound, and one could hope to catch a glimpse of him as one walked along the Elgin Road to the dentist!

Some of the pupils of St Michael's School Darjeeling will still have memories of Sr Georgina, so well known across the Continent. She meant so much to them in their school days.

But one must stop, for so many names come to the surface. It was an agonizing time yet very exciting to have lived in India in that era.

Eudora, CSJB.

C S J B

I N D I A

AUTHOR'S PREFACE

The publication of *Sisters of the Raj* marks the completion of the trilogy chronicling the life and work of the Community of St John Baptist, Clewer. It has been a mammoth task, but never a chore - the records have been too fascinating for it to have become a burden. It has been a labour of love stretching over many years, just as the work of the Sisters has been. I first started the research in 1984 when I was living in the parish of Clewer, just ten minutes walk from the convent. It soon became obvious that at least two volumes would be needed, and then the discovery of the Indian letters set the seal on the trilogy. Subsequently, two house moves and my embarking on ordination training, have not only resulted in my living much further away, but also in slower progress on the books than I had originally hoped.

Each volume of the trilogy has been totally absorbing in the research and writing, and the Sisters have awaited each one with great patience. My visit to India, the account of which forms the last chapter of this book, was tremendously important. It gave me a totally different insight into the Sisters' work there, as well as a positive means of ending the book. To have seen those schools in their present form would have delighted Sr Jane Frances and all who worked there in the days of the Raj. I shall never forget the welcome I received in Calcutta, nor the love which lay behind the hospitality. I can understand now why most of the Sisters who worked in India fell in love with it, and why they never quite left it when they came back to England. Fifty years later their influence is still there, and even more importantly, they are still remembered with an affection which I found deeply moving.

Sr Eudora, approaching her 96th birthday, has contributed so much to this book, not only in her preface and her chapter of memories, but also in many conversations, and always with an infectious enthusiasm. Whilst very frail, she would "light up" at the thought of Calcutta, and the intervening 60 years would slip away. Even as I write this, her health is failing rapidly, but her involvement in this book, the sharing of memories, and her meeting at Clewer in 1995 with Mrs Christien, Principal of St John's Diocesan School, Calcutta, and with Mother Susila in 1996, brought her much pleasure.

There are many critics of imperialism, and I too have little sympathy with the Victorian practice of imposing western culture on people whose civilisation is far older, and the depths of whose spirituality, though expressed differently, cannot be questioned. But my primary aim in writing this book was not to offer a critique of imperialism, but to chronicle how one particular Religious Community, worked in India within the imperial system, and despite having been invited by the Raj to work there, managed to maintain their own integrity throughout. And, as they became more familiar with India and its people and culture, so the Sisters' love for the people, and respect for their customs, deepened. That is why they are still so fondly remembered today in those schools where they taught Indian children. Their work amongst the English in India has gone - it ended when the last ship sailed away from Bombay, and is now only a memory cherished by former pupils, some of whom have contributed to this book. But the educational work amongst Indian girls lives and flourishes at St John's Diocesan Girls' Higher Secondary School, the Pratt Memorial School, and St Thomas' School, Kidderpore. This book stands not only as a tribute to the work of the Sisters, but also to those who continue that work both in the schools and in the Religious Life.

Valerie Bonham
Newbury. March 10th 1997.

Postscript: On March 11th 1997, the day after I wrote this preface, Sister Eudora died peacefully at Clewer. She had been well and active until the end of 1996, but a series of strokes had made her increasingly infirm. Her death marks the ending of an era - the last of the hundred or so Sisters to have worked in India. May she rest in peace and rise in glory.

A WORD ABOUT WORDS

Since beginning this trilogy, many of the words used in the original archive material have either changed meanings or are now socially unacceptable. This poses a dilemma for the historian who must be faithful to the sources, but must also interpret those sources in ways which are sensitive to the modern reader without altering the original meaning. A tightrope situation indeed! The problem in the first two volumes arose from Victorian attitudes to sexuality, the role of women in society, and how to address the social problems of the day. The linguistic stumbling block was the use from archive sources of the term "fallen women" which, given the subject matter of the two books, was unavoidable. But I endeavoured to put the phrase in its historical context, whilst trying to avoid being implicated in the slur! Now in this present volume other problems arise. Chief offenders are the words "native", "heathen" and "Eurasian", as well as attitudes towards racial origins and other world faiths. Regarding the word "Eurasian," I have only used it when directly quoting from source material; otherwise I have used the term "Anglo-Indian". I have applied similar rules to all other words which might be deemed offensive in modern parlance.

C S J B

I N D I A

-1-
FROM MERCHANT TO RULER

When in 1881 the Community of St John Baptist was invited to send Sisters from Clewer to work in Calcutta they knew they would be going to the hub of the British Empire. By that time British rule in India, the Raj as it was commonly called, was at its zenith. As a city Calcutta was second only in importance to London. But it had not always been so.

Britain had long had a foothold in India as a means to trade with the East Indies, chiefly Indonesia and the Moluccas. The East India Company began in 1600 on the initiative of a group of London merchants who had their sights set on gaining the monopoly of rich trading in spices and fabrics from the exotic East. Others too had similar ambitions, notably the Portuguese who had captured Goa as early as 1510, and the Dutch later in the century. Throughout the seventeenth century these rival powers vied with each other for trading rights, tentatively planting "factories" (i.e. warehouses) around the coast, and each looking for an opportunity to outdo one another and court favour with the ruling power. It was difficult to know who really did wield power at this time as the ailing Mughal Empire seemed to be assailed from all quarters.

The last great Mughal ruler was Aurangzeb who died aged 88 in 1707. Like his father, Shah Jehan builder of the Taj Mahal, he had ruled by tyranny and fanaticism. But the Mughal Empire was itself an invading force having largely ousted the Hindus in the mid 16th century, the latter living in a state of uneasy peace under their Muslim overlords to whom they paid heavy tributes in return for a degree of autonomy. Peace and tranquillity did not last long anywhere in this vast Continent and there were periodical uprisings against both Muslims and Europeans as the influence of the latter increased. Particularly rebellious were the Afghans in the north, and the Sikhs and the warlike Mahrattas (or Marathas) in the west.

At first the East India Company had confined itself to Surat on the north west coast, but in 1640 some land at Madras on the east coast was acquired from a Hindu ruler marking the real beginning of Company expansion. Politics and trade went hand in hand of course; thus the wedding of King Charles II with Catherine of Braganza in 1665 strengthened the Company's hand by the gift of Bombay as part of her dowry, and effectively staved off Portuguese rivalry, for the time being at least. A second inroad on the east side was made in 1690 when the Company established a colony on the Hooghly river not far from the shrine to Kali, most fearsome of the Hindu deities. From such an inauspicious beginning Calcutta was to grow. But slowly: for the time being it showed little promise, and the Company concentrated on trade.

Trade flourished, the Company (which had virtually been re-founded under its new Charter in 1661) grew in power and importance, and its officers grew rich. A growing fleet of sailing ships known as East Indiamen, new docks in the heart of London, and an impressive headquarters in the City of London told a story of prosperity. Trade began to give way to rule. Thus for administrative purposes the Company divided its holdings into three Presidencies: Madras, Bombay and Bengal (later Calcutta) each controlled by a President with a growing hierarchy of Company officials below him. In place of the old style merchant there arose a few powerful men who had pursued the Company's interests and made profit for themselves as well. Such success and prosperity heralded a new breed of Company official: the Nabob. Generally unpopular in England because they came from the merchant rather than the landed class, they rapidly bought their way into English society. Having got rich quick in India they returned home and soon built or acquired desirable country houses such as Caversham Park, Basildon Park and Bisham Abbey, not to speak of purchasing Parliamentary seats. (In the unreformed Parliament a pocket borough could be bought for around £4,000).

The growing power of the Company had to be defended and by the time Victoria became Queen, the Company army, first raised in the seventeenth century, was a well organised fighting force. The officers were all British, the men (sepoys) were Indian; all were servants of the Company and were paid by it. It was not just a question of defending Company interests against indigenous warring factions. Throughout the eighteenth century other European powers were still highly interested in India. The Dutch East India Company had long been a rival as had the French, and Portugal still maintained an interest. These rivalries were exacerbated by wars on the European front, and later in the century, by Anglo-French designs on Canada, and the British need to save face following the loss of the American colonies. When the War of the Austrian Succession broke out (1742-48) Britain and France found themselves on opposite sides (as indeed they were again in the Seven Years War 1756-63). Thus in 1746 the French fleet took Madras from the British who in return besieged the French settlement at Pondicherry - unsuccessfully. Diplomatic bargaining saw Madras restored to Britain, but when in 1750 two Indian rulers started a territorial dispute between themselves, Britain and France seized the opportunity for gain and supported opposing sides. The French army took Trichinopoly, the stronghold of the British-backed candidate, but with a master stroke which paid off, most of the British forces dashed to Arcot, the stronghold of the French-backed candidate, took it by force and withstood a 50 day siege, at the end of which British reinforcements arrived and secured the victory. This effectively ended French ambitions in India.

The hero of Arcot was Robert Clive who had gone to India as a minor

Company official and had applied for a commission in the Company army, rising to the rank of captain. After Arcot he resumed life as a merchant, made a small fortune and returned to England, the archetypical Nabob. But after 18 months he sailed for India again, as a Lieutenant-Colonel, to be second in command of the Company army in the south. If Arcot had brought brief fame to this depressive and suicidal man, his second tour of duty would secure his name in the history of India. In 1756 the new Nawab of Bengal, Siraj-ud-Daula marched on the British garrison in Calcutta with an enormous army. A number of captives were taken and imprisoned overnight in what became known as the Black Hole of Calcutta. Clive marched from the south and recaptured Calcutta without difficulty and went on to evict the French further north. Then he took an unprecedented step and deposed Siraj-ud-Daula putting in his place as Nawab a Mughal general named Mir Jafar. The deposed Nawab mustered his forces and the matter was settled in June 1757 with the British victory on the battlefield of Plassey.

Plassey was a turning point in the history of the East India Company, for Clive was a Company soldier and in deposing the Nawab he had taken the Company out of trade and into politics. The new Nawab, Mir Jafar, was now a puppet of the British: British rule was secure in Bengal. The way was now prepared for direct rule even though it did not come about immediately. In the meantime the Nabobs, not least Clive himself, continued to make their fortunes at the expense of India. Before his suicide in 1767 Clive had gained an Irish peerage. He also lived long enough to see widespread concern expressed in the English Parliament about the corruption of the once Honourable Company which had by now come very close to bankruptcy.

If the name Clive of India comes to mind first, then that of Warren Hastings must surely be next. An honourable man, Hastings went to Calcutta as a writer (clerk) in 1750 and slowly made his way until rising to the rank of Governor of Bengal in 1772. While he made money, he did not make a fortune in the manner of the Nabobs. His appointment to the Governorship was made with the intention of reform and one of his first was a Regulating Act passed by Parliament in 1773 which prevented Company officials who collected revenue or meted out justice, from engaging in private trade. Under the terms of this Act the Presidencies of Madras and Bombay were no longer to be autonomous, but would henceforth be answerable to the Governor of Bengal who would be known as the Governor-General. Thus all the Indian holdings of the Company would be under his jurisdiction in Calcutta. A few years later in 1784 the younger William Pitt, in response to Government alarm at continued Company corruption piloted the India Act through Parliament in an attempt to curb its powers. No longer would the Company Directors in London reign supreme: over their heads a Board of Control was now to supervise Company affairs. The Board was to consist of the Chancellor of the Exchequer, a Secretary of State for India and four Privy Councillors appointed by the Crown. All political matters relating to India would now be controlled by the Board, thus the Governor-General would now be much more subject to the Crown than the Company. The Company Directors were still to control all aspects of trade, but that was all.

Hastings' period in India was by no means one of uninterrupted peace. There were military campaigns and skirmishes at regular intervals, all of which helped consolidate the British foothold. But above all, Hastings concentrated on restoring trade which he did with marked success, and helped put the ailing Company back onto a sound financial basis. Another great achievement lay in his overhaul of the legal system. Courts were established with English judges but the existing codes of Hindu and Muslim law were maintained rather than imposing English law. Language difficulties and confusion over the interpretation of Hindu law (which was unwritten) made life very complicated indeed for the judges, but gradually a system was established whereby a Hindu or Muslim would accompany the judge and help interpret. Language was the greatest barrier, and encouraged by Hastings' own endeavours a new breed of Company man was coming to India with the intention of learning about Indian language and culture.

Warren Hastings returned to England in 1785 so that the full implementation of Pitt's India Act was left to his successor, Lord Cornwallis. He was the first British ruler of India who had not been a Company man: he was an aristocrat and a professional soldier who had fought in the American War of Independence. He did not seek to increase British territorial holdings, merely to consolidate those already under British rule. And he had no time for Hastings' philosophy of sharing administrative tasks with Indians. Under his auspices all Indians were removed from high office and were kept in subordinate roles. In effect Cornwallis laid the foundations of the Indian Civil Service, (though it was not known by that name for another 50 years), by extending the Regulating Act so that Company officials had to choose whether they served in the political or commercial sphere. Henceforth they would be prohibited from doing both.

Cornwallis and his successors consolidated British rule over the next generation so that by 1818 British power was firmly established. But the price was costly. There were innumerable border clashes with the Company army as one by one the small principalities, be they Marathas, Muslim, Hindu or Sikh, were subdued and became tribute-paying puppets. A small number of larger princely states notably Hyderabad and Mysore remained semi-independent whilst becoming hemmed in on all sides by British held territory. The last Mughal ruler, Bahadur Shah Zafar, living in his Red Fort at Dehli, stronghold of his illustrious forefathers, was all but a prisoner, hostage to the decline of his own Empire and the rise of the British.

By the middle of the nineteenth century much of the Indian map was coloured pink. But the days of the East India Company were numbered. In 1813 the Company Charter had been renewed for a further 20 years, but with certain conditions. Firstly, the Company's monopoly on all but the China tea trade was to end leaving the markets open to other commercial concerns; secondly, a sum of £10,000 was to be spent on education in India thus beginning an Anglicising process amongst the Indians themselves; thirdly, whilst there had been a Christian presence from England for some years, the Church of England was now officially sanctioned in India thus paving the way for missionaries, and later in the century, for Religious Communities. Henceforth the aim of the British would be not only to make the Indian map pink, but also Anglican.

The principal train of events which transformed English peoples' perception of India, and which was to alter the course of British rule there, finally ringing the death knell of the Company, was the series of incidents known collectively as the Indian mutiny. The pot had been simmering for some time as British power had increased and had taken on an ever more imperious tone. Gone were the days of trade as surely as the passing of the eighteenth century. Conquest had become the norm as the new century progressed and one war succeeded another - the Afghan War (1839), the conquest of Sind (1843), the Sikh Wars (1845 and 1848-9), the annexation of the Punjab (1849), and the annexation of Oudh in 1856. Sensitivity towards the feelings of Indians had not always been high on the British agenda, a trait which the mutiny would exacerbate. Despite their increasing dominance the British were vastly outnumbered, particularly in their fighting forces. In 1857 there were in the Company armies 34,000 European soldiers compared with 257,000 Indian sepoys. If security was breached or trust broken, the consequences would be disastrous. Those who wielded power failed to read the signs of the times because they had begun to distance themselves from the nation they sought to dominate. The "improving" instinct which sought to convert the heathen, to abolish suttee (widow burning), to stamp out thugee (armed bandits), and impose "Englishness" on far more ancient cultures, served only to add all these ingredients to a pot of discontent which was simmering in the background.

The singular factor which took the simmering pot to boiling point - cartridges greased with animal fat which was abhorrent to Hindu and Muslim alike - might have been averted with forethought. The use of hindsight and assurances that sepoys could grease their own cartridges with beeswax and vegetable oil proved worthless. Trust had been broken. The sepoys became convinced that it was a British plot to force them to break caste thus making it easier for the Christian missionaries to make converts. Unrest and isolated incidents of insubordination began to break out all along the Grand Trunk Road from Barrackpore near Calcutta, to Meerut near Delhi at intervals early in 1857. The public degrading and humiliation of 85 troopers from the 3rd Light Cavalry on the parade ground at Meerut provoked an unlooked for response. Next day, May 10th, armed sepoys rampaged through the garrison, released the sentenced troopers, and made their way through the town murdering and pillaging as they went. The pot had boiled over: the mutiny had begun.

In fact the area affected by the mutiny was relatively small, confined as it was to strategic points along the Grand Trunk Road. And there was no strategy or overall leader. It erupted along this major thoroughfare, begun by Bentinck in 1828 to connect Delhi with Calcutta. Where the mutiny made headway it was conducted with a vehemence which was ruthless and terrifying. The leaders of the Meerut uprising had sped to Delhi to the old King, Bahadur Shah II, whom they proclaimed leader of the mutiny; but it was a toothless and impotent leadership as all knew only too well.

Two events within the mutiny were to impress themselves on the imagination of the British to such an extent that they would become part of the folk-history of the Empire, and would serve to justify the new Raj as it emerged from the ashes of the old East India Company. And also to justify such British atrocities as firing captured mutineers from cannon. These were the massacre at Cawnpore and the siege of Lucknow.

Cawnpore was a large garrison town at an important strategic point on the Ganges. It had a highly respected commanding officer, Sir Hugh Wheeler whose wife was an Indian. The local tribute-paying Indian prince was the Hindu, Nana Sahib, adopted son of the last ruler of the Mahrattas(1), and his relationship with the British was guarded but friendly. As the threat of an uprising in Cawnpore itself grew ever stronger, Nana Sahib offered help to the British garrison which was gladly accepted. But when the trouble finally flared up on June 3rd the Nana's sepoys offered little or no resistance, and three days later the mutineers placed themselves under Nana Sahib's command and the seige of Cawnpore began. It lasted until June 27th when, exhausted, starved, injured and distraught after so many days of ceaseless bombardment, the garrison surrendered and accepted the Nana's terms. These included a safe passage to Allahabad for all who would lay down their arms. So it was that the survivors of the seige, (a large number of whom were women, children, and walking wounded) began the journey which involved a river crossing. As soon as the boats were loaded the watching sepoys opened fire killing the passengers; those who survived were taken ashore, murdered and their bodies mutilated.

Lucknow, capital of the Muslim province of Oudh was governed by Sir Henry Lawrence from an impressive range of buildings known as the Residency(2). Within months it would be a familiar name on the lips of all patriotic English people. The mutiny broke out in Lucknow at the end of June but Sir Henry had taken the precaution of moving the entire

European population (including the 1,700 strong garrison) into the Residency compound which had been fortified. The compound itself covered 33 acres and consisted of 16 buildings; nevertheless, overcrowding, shortages of food, drink and medical supplies, lack of privacy, and no sanitation became major problems. Lawrence was killed early in the seige, a crushing blow to morale. There were others: many of the loyal sepoys deserted; there were rumours of relief which never materialised. Then after 92 days a column of Highlanders arrived, but there were too few of them to effectively lift the seige, and they found themselves engulfed within it. Starvation and disease was rife and all the time the constant bombardment from the mutineers. A second relieving force did not manage to break through until the end of October. This time the strategy was better planned and the Residency was defended from outside whilst the battered and besieged occupants were enabled to leave. A legend had been born out of a terrible ordeal.

It was not until the summer of 1859 that the mutiny was finally crushed, though the heart of it had crumbled in the ruins of Lucknow. Compared with the size of the sub-Continent, the actual area affected by the mutiny was indeed small. But it had shaken the confidence of the British rulers and there was, perhaps inevitably, an outcry by the British for revenge. It was argued that Cawnpore and Lucknow demanded as much if only because of the terrible sufferings of the women and children. But clemency was the order of the day. Lord Canning, who become Governor-General just before the outbreak of the mutiny insisted that retribution by lynch-mobs was not the way forward and that Government policy would favour reconciliation. This did not further his popularity and he was disparagingly called "Clemency Canning."

The main change resulting from the mutiny was the abolition of the East India Company which had become an anachronism. Over the previous thirty years or so it had ceased to be a trading organization and now merely concentrated on administering India under the British government. Now it was all swept aside and the Crown became ruler of India. The Governor-General was renamed Viceroy and Calcutta remained the seat of power. The Indian princes were recognised, some of their ancient rights restored and their territories guaranteed, thus winning some powerful allies for the British Raj.

It was to be another twenty years before Victoria would be proclaimed Empress of India, but already the foundations were being laid: the Indian Civil Service brought all aspects of government under British control, and a whole way of life grew up around it. English society transplanted itself into the heat of Calcutta, relieved for a few weeks by moving to Darjeeling or Simla in the Himalayan foothills. English sahibs now brought their memsahibs and very formidable they could be. Servants abounded as in England, except that there were more of them. The English way of life was lived as closely as possible. And as part of the very fabric of that life there was the established Church - known until the mid 20th century as the Church of England in India. It was as part of that Church that the government of India requested the Community of St John Baptist to send Sisters to Calcutta. But first we must look at Calcutta: imperial city *par excellence*.

Footnotes

1. The Mahrattas or Marathas were warlike Hindus who fought both Mughals and Europeans for two centuries until they were finally defeated in 1819 by combined British and Gurkha forces.

2. Resident/Residency. During the days of the Company, the chiefs of its commercial establishments in the provinces, and also the European chiefs of districts, were termed Residents. In the days of the Raj the term applied also the official British representative at an Indian princely court. His official abode was termed the Residency.

C S J B

I N D I A

-2-
CALCUTTA: CITY OF EMPIRE

The centre-piece of the British Empire was India, and because it was the seat of government, the focus of India was Calcutta. There were other more ancient, stately, and spectacular cities than this essentially British creation; cities which were essentially *Indian*, which stood as monuments to past glories and faded splendours, to empires which had waxed and waned and had their day. But this latest empire was *British* and as it grew from a mercantile enterprise into a conquering and, (some thought) civilising power, so the trading post established by Job Charnock on the muddy banks of the Hooghly in 1690, became an imperial city on the grand scale.

Job Charnock had come to India as a junior official of the East India Company in 1655 but little is known of him except that he snatched his future wife from the funeral pyre of her husband, (the Hindu custom of suttee which was abolished by the British in 1829). Charnock's landfall claimed many victims in the early years, not so much from conflict as from climate, a trend which was to continue throughout British rule. The delicate constitution of the fair-skinned British was ill suited to the wet, humid conditions of Bengal, with its multiplicity of dangerous diseases, as a walk through the Park Street Cemetery will testify. Yet here around the stronghold called Fort William, begun in 1696 and named after William of Orange, the nucleus of the great city arose out of the mud and silt.

Fort William was largely destroyed in 1756 during the troubles with Siraj-ud-Daula, and was rebuilt on a complex plan over the next 20 years at the amazing cost of £2 million. Because it was meant to be an operational fort a large tract of swampy land was cleared and drained to give an unrestricted field of fire. This open space, called the Maidan, became a vast park and centre of recreation crossed by avenues and pathways, one of the oldest of which was known as the "Old Course". Until 1864 there were many fine trees on the Maidan, but in that year there was a cyclone and a large number fell victim to it. Parts of the Maidan evolved a character of their own, such as the racecourse in the south and the Eden Gardens in the north west overlooking the Hooghly. The latter was established by Emily and Fanny Eden, sisters of George Eden, Lord Auckland, who was Governor-General from 1836-41. Today it is better known as the home of the cricket stadium, shrine of Indian fast bowling. South of the Maidan the Zoological Gardens were founded in 1876 and soon became a tourist attraction in an age when the zoo was a novelty.

Owing to its fine outlook the Maidan became the most prestigious area of the fast expanding city, and both private housing and municipal buildings sprang up along the perimeter. Calcutta grew rapidly with English-sounding street names appearing on the new maps: Strand Road, Park Street, Dalhousie Square and The Esplanade, might equally have been found in any English watering place. And so too, the spread of great mansions which to all outward appearances would have been quite at home in Bath or Cheltenham, now found themselves in the fast growing, fashionable districts of Chowringhee and Alipore (part of Kidderpore).

All over India as British rule increased, great houses, civic buildings, gentlemen's clubs, and churches, were being erected. English architecture, (with a few concessions to the climate) was imposing itself on the Indian landscape. Calcutta was no exception in terms of rapid growth, but for the fact that it had grown from nothing. Bombay and Madras also expanded rapidly and grandly, each vying with the other, but in terms of prestige Calcutta outdid them all. However, these grand buildings were not always what they seemed. Sun-dried bricks (called *cutcha*) were the norm and these were fine until they became soaked by the monsoon rains; hessian ceilings, dried leaf thatch, and a veneer of lime plaster covering shoddy brickwork, all made for major structural problems. Indeed the word *cutcha* passed into Anglo-Indian parlance for anything second rate. Conversely, *pukka* bricks were kiln-fired and reliable - just like at home - so gradually anything trustworthy was similarly designated *pukka*.

Many of the greatest buildings in Calcutta were built well before the mutiny, in the days of the Nabobs and Company wealth. So Calcutta was essentially an 18th century creation, though building continued until well into the days of the Raj, and indeed one of the greatest landmarks, the Victoria Memorial, was not completed until 1921. Many of these great houses are now decaying, and most have either become institutions or have been demolished altogether. But one of the most well preserved survivors dates from 1820. Now the headquarters of the Royal Calcutta Turf Club, it was built in Chowringhee by a shipping magnate and looks every inch an English mansion. Nearby stands the Loretto Convent, once the home of Sir Henry Vansittart, Governor of Bengal from 1760-64. Warren Hastings had a number of houses, among which may be counted Hastings House at Alipore, built in 1777; Kidderpore House, which later became a school run by the Clewer Sisters; and Belvedere which became the official residence of the Lieutenant Governors of Bengal, and currently houses the National Library. Some way from the city centre there is the Tollygunge Club, founded in 1895 - Calcutta's only country club. The club house was built in 1791 as the residence of Richard Johnson, an indigo planter, and it later housed Prince Gholam Muhammad (whose father, Tipu Sultan, had been defeated by Wellesley in 1799 in the struggle to gain control of south India).

But grandest of all was Government House. The original Government House was a rented property on the Esplanade, and Richard Wellesley the Governor-General (brother of the Iron Duke), who had taken office in 1798, regarded it as totally inadequate. A new residence fit for a grandee of the highest rank was commissioned, and in 1799 work began on a replica of Kedleston Hall in Derbyshire. The architect Charles Wyatt of the Bengal Engineers, was a member of the well known family of architects, and he based his new building on Robert Adam's Derbyshire masterpiece. The result was a stately pile in a compound of 26 acres overlooking the Maidan, approached through imposing gateways with lions and sphinxes - it was a building just waiting to preside over an empire. With its grand ballroom, throne room and marble durbar hall, it proved a superb Viceregal dwelling. Even so, the building materials used were no better than in a good many other Calcutta houses. When in 1898 Lord Curzon of Kedleston became Viceroy it must have seemed like home from home, if not exactly home sweet home. Certainly Curzon wryly remarked that the pillars of one were of alabaster, and the pillars of the other of lath and plaster! But to all outward appearances (and to those who did not have to live in it) it was the most imposing of residences. Small wonder then that Calcutta became known as the City of Palaces.

There was another Vice-regal residence - Barrackpore House to the north of Calcutta, which Wellesley had planned to connect with Government House by means of a long, straight avenue. The house became a reality, the avenue did not. It was however, a welcome retreat from the grandeur (and the rigours) of Government House and was easily reached upriver. It was near enough to Calcutta to return in haste if need arose, yet far enough away to have a country feel about it, surrounded as it was by acres of pleasant parkland. During the hot season the whole Vice-regal entourage would remove to Simla for three months or so. In the meantime Barrackpore was an admirable compromise.

Back in Calcutta, the civic buildings were porticoed and collonaded in classical style - the Town Hall (which actually collapsed during construction in 1809 due to shoddy materials), the Mint, Metcalfe Hall (which housed the public library), were all built in the early 19th century in Greek revival style. A generation earlier in 1780, work had begun on Writers' Buildings, a large block which housed junior clerks of the East India Company. Originally designed like an austere barrack block, it was embellished at various times until 1880 when it was completely refaced in a pompous quasi-ecclesiastical gothic manner. The gothic style had progressed with the century just as it had at home and finally won the so-called "battle of the styles" against the classical revival. One of the most imposing civic buildings in Calcutta is the High Court, completed in 1872 overlooking the Maidan, and based on the 13th century Cloth Hall at Ypres. But the classical style had not died completely: the impressive looking General Post Office dating from 1870 has a Greek colonnade and is surmounted by a copper dome.

No great city is complete without statues, and as the days of trade gave way to days of empire so too the streets, squares and open spaces became filled with a clutter of statues erected to honour English dignitaries. All manner of conquering hero was depicted in various styles, from the great column on the Maidan known as the Ochterlony Monument but now called the Shahid Minar, (erected in 1828 in memory of Sir David Ochterlony who had fought in every campaign from the time of Clive until the conquest of Nepal in 1816); to the statue of Sir William Bentinck, the Governor-General who abolished suttee in Bengal and built the Grand Trunk Road. More controversial was the large obelisk erected outside Writers' Buildings in memory of the victims of the Black Hole of Calcutta. It was twice struck by lightning (in 1782 and 1810), and fell into such disrepair that it was demolished in 1821. A memorial to the victims was later erected in St John's churchyard.

And then there was the Church. The Church of England had received official sanction to enter India as a result of conditions imposed on the East India Company following the renewal of its Charter in 1813. Under these terms, which were largely the brainchild of William Wilberforce, a bishopric was to be provided for Calcutta together with three archdeaconries. Originally the Company had been adverse to any missionary activity and when William Carey and his colleagues from the Baptist Missionary Society arrived in Calcutta in 1793 the Company expressly forbade them to establish a mission. So hostile was their reception by Company officials, who threatened to deport them that they fled to Serampore, a small Danish colony 16 miles away and made their headquarters there. Meanwhile in England the Evangelical Revival was under way and many were influenced by the zeal of Charles Simeon. In 1806 a group of Evangelical Anglican clergy, notably Henry Martyn, came to India as Company chaplains. Together with their official Company work they also managed to work amongst the Indian people - but it was entirely unofficial and soon spread away from Calcutta. It was not until 1813 that the Company, in deference to the terms of the renewed Charter, relented over missionary activity, and the way was cleared for prosyletising amongst the Indian people. Thomas Fanshawe Middleton, first Bishop of Calcutta, arrived there in 1814.

There had of course been an Anglican presence in India long before 1813, but (except for Henry Martyn's unofficial prosyletising), its ministry was strictly confined to the English in the Company's employ. Thus the first churches were built within the forts in the Presidency towns where they doubled as garrison churches. In Calcutta the original church inside Fort William was destroyed during the troubles in 1756. The new garrison church inside the rebuilt Fort William was not built until 1822 - a many pinnacled and turreted extravaganza in the style popularly known as "Strawberry Hill Gothick". But the real successor to the old garrison church was St John's, designed by Lieutenant James Agg of the Bengal Engineers, and inspired by James Gibbs' classical design for St Martin-in-the-Fields. It was paid for by public subscription, and when it was completed in 1787 made quite an impression on the people of Calcutta from its imposing position just north of what became the Maidan. After the foundation of the bishopric St John's became the pro-cathedral until it was replaced by St Paul's.

The new cathedral of St Paul was begun in 1839 and consecrated in 1847. It looked just like an English cathedral which was exactly how it was intended; except that the location was not an English cathedral close but the corner of the Calcutta Maidan with Fort William just across the open space and Government House at the other end. Strawberry Hill gothick gave way to the Victorian version as the plain new building gradually became embellished over the years. The most striking external feature nowadays is the tower, a replica of the Bell Harry tower at Canterbury. But this is a modern replacement. The cathedral was originally built with a tall spire which sustained minor damage in the earthquake of 1897; it was repaired, only to be damaged again in the 1934 earthquake. Soon afterwards it was demolished and replaced with the replica of Bell Harry. Inside there are many features which reflect the "Englishness" of the whole building: a Clayton and Bell east window replaces the earlier one destroyed by a cyclone in 1864; the great west window by Burne-Jones dates from 1880 is a memorial to the Viceroy, Lord Mayo, who was assassinated in the Andaman Islands; the reredos behind the high altar is attributed to Sir Arthur Blomfield; and there is a Willis organ. The English congregation (who later provided a mission church elsewhere for the Bengali Christians), would have felt that this corner was indeed forever England - that is until they went outside into the penetrating heat or the seemingly never-ending monsoon.

But there were other corners which even now remain forever England: the burial grounds. St John's church owes its unconventional plan to the existence of a burial ground which could not be built over. Here in an octagonal tomb lies Job Charnock, founder of Calcutta, who died in 1693. The cathedral contains the memorial plaques to many British servants of both Company and Raj. But it is in the Park Street Cemetery near the Lower Circular Road where the mortal remains are enshrined of so many British men and women, young and old - but mostly young. And enshrined they are: it has been described as an Imperial city of the dead. Row upon row of great table-tombs, obelisks, and porticoed mausoleums stand like an exhibition of funerary ornament. Death, disease and disaster: tempest and earthquake; cholera and typhoid; childbirth and suicide. All found their way here; all remain until the last trump - and then what a day!

If St John's was the first Anglican church in Calcutta, it certainly was not the last, nor did Anglicanism have the monopoly. Just as imposing was the Kirk, dedicated to St Andrew, and completed in 1818. It succeeded remarkably well in upstaging St John's, both in the vista it commanded and in the avowed intention of Dr Bryce of the Kirk to have a steeple taller than that of St John's (despite the efforts of the bishop to thwart these plans). Ecumenism was still a forgotten Greek word.

The River Hooghly was important in the economy of Calcutta, the city having been established as a trading post, and its importance did not diminish in the days of Empire. Great docks developed at Kidderpore and further downstream at Diamond Harbour. Rich Bengali's built palaces along the waterfront, as did wealthy Nabobs, followed by servants of the Raj. But the Hooghly was more than a shipping and trade route: it flows into the Ganges and is therefore regarded as a holy river by the Hindu's. Great stepped jetties known as ghats are crowded with people at sunrise and sunset, performing the ritual ablutions sacred to them. At intervals along the waterfront there are the burning ghats where cremations are carried out and the ashes scattered on the waters. Until 1874 this great river was not bridged at all. Then a temporary pontoon bridge was erected which was not replaced until 1943 when the famous Howrah cantilever bridge was built. It is the largest in the world and probably the most congested! There is no rail crossing here despite the presence of Howrah station on the opposite side of the Hooghly. The railway bridge lies six miles upstream and is a more recent innovation. But most recent of all, is the great suspension bridge, a little downstream from the Howrah bridge, which was opened in 1992.

If the bridges are more recent than the Raj, one riverside feature which would certainly have been familiar to the sahibs and their memsahibs are the Botanical Gardens. Situated across the Hooghly in a south westerly direction along the Grand Trunk Road, the Botanical Gardens were founded in 1786 over an expanse of 269 acres. The chief landmark was the great banyan tree which still survives despite damage by lightning in 1925 which destroyed the central trunk. This vast tree, which is like a self-contained forest, still has around 1,500 subsidiary trunks all sharing the same roots, and originally all having sprung from the central trunk. The Victorians with their fascination for the curious found the banyan tree quite irresistible.

Calcutta was not all grandeur and palaces. It was also a city of poverty, of dirt, disease and death. In 1881 the population of this teeming place numbered 612,307; by 1901, the year of the death of Victoria, Queen and Empress, it had risen to 847,796. Just before the outbreak of the Great War Kipling was to write of what he called the Big Calcutta Stink. "It blows across the *maidan*; it comes in gusts into the corridors of the Great Eastern Hotel; what they are pleased to call the 'Palaces of Chowringhi' carry it; it swirls round the Bengal Club; it pours out of by-streets with sickening intensity, and the breeze of the morning is laden with it. It is first found in spite of the fume of the engines, in Howrah Station. It seems to be worst in the little lanes at the back of Lal Bazar where the drinking shops are, but it is nearly as bad opposite Government House and in the Public Offices."[1] It was indeed the City of Dreadful night though many of the British did not acknowledge this other Calcutta. But as will be seen, the Sisters of the Community of St John Baptist were soon painfully aware of it. By the time the Sisters arrived in Calcutta at the end of 1881 there were a large number of churches and missions established by all the main Christian denominations so that their presence there was by no means unique. What *was* unique was the invitation from the government of India to organise the nursing in the Presidency General Hospital, one of the oldest and largest of Calcutta's many hospitals.

Footnotes

1. KIPLING, Rudyard *From Sea to Sea and other sketches Vol.2. The City of Dreadful Night.* MacMillan & Co. 1914.

C S J B

I N D I A

-3-
ENGLAND'S DUTY AND PRIVILEGE

By 1880 the Community of St John Baptist, Clewer had won a respected place in Church circles. The numbers had increased rapidly during (almost) 30 years existence so that in 1884 there were 114 choir Sisters plus 27 novices, together with 36 lay Sisters and 13 lay novices. Women from all walks of life had joined the Community, and while it is true that many came from privileged backgrounds, it is equally true that many did not. The magnetic personality of Harriet Monsell, the Mother Foundress (whose humane approach to all who crossed her path proved an irresistible attraction), partly explains the success of Clewer in those early years. The buildings too account for much: a great flagship of gothic red brick. Such buildings, with their ambience of holiness, could not fail to attract many who sought to dedicate their lives to the service of God in the under privileged women, children, and sick poor whom the Sisters served at Clewer. But success breeds success, and after the initial hesitation felt in some quarters at the prospect of having Sisterhoods in the Established Church, their value and contribution was acknowledged. Mother Harriet, with her kindly common sense and her good connections, won souls for Christ and respect for Clewer.(1) Thus it is hardly surprising that when officials of the British Raj decided that the nursing in one of the main hospitals in Calcutta needed proper organisation, they should turn to one of the most respected and well established of Anglican Sisterhoods, the Community of St John Baptist, Clewer.

Anglican Religious Communities were beginning to establish themselves in India. In 1874 the Society of St John the Evangelist (popularly known as the Cowley Fathers), had landed in Bombay, and four years later they were joined by Sisters from the Community of All Saints whose work was to lie in nursing. 1877 had seen the arrival in Poona of Sisters from the Community of St Mary the Virgin, Wantage, initially to run mission schools, but later they also began nursing. In 1882 the Cowley Fathers also took up work in Poona.

Missionary societies were also flourishing by this time. Some of the Free Church societies such as the Baptist Missionary Society and the London Missionary Society (Congregational), had been in India for many years, as well as missions established by the Church of Scotland and the Jesuits, but Anglicans had been restricted until after 1813. The new East India Company Charter opened the door and enabled the Church Missionary Society to establish a mission in Kidderpore on the outskirts of Calcutta in 1815. Bishop Middleton, the first Bishop of Calcutta, established a theological college in 1820, which was placed under the control of the Society for the Propagation of the Gospel. In Delhi the

Cambridge Mission was established in 1877 with a Brotherhood dedicated to educational and evangelistic work, and the later development of women's work in conjunction with the S.P.G. In 1880 the Oxford Mission to Calcutta was founded as a missionary Brotherhood, and in December of the same year, four members arrived to begin their work.

Thus the presence of Religious Communities and Missionary Societies in India was already a reality when the Clewer Sisters were invited to Calcutta. The initial invitation to the Community to work in Calcutta had come in the autumn of 1880. The Sisters were enthusiastic and hoped to accompany the Oxford Mission Brothers, but complications arose and the Sisters had to hold things over for a time. A few months later under the direction of Sir Ashley Eden, Lieutenant Governor of Bengal,(2) Miss Milman, sister of a former Bishop of Calcutta(3) approached the Community with the specific request to supervise the nursing in the Presidency General Hospital and the Lady Canning Home for nurses which was attached to it. Although not a specialised nursing Order the Clewer Community had several English hospitals under its care, and the invitation seemed a good way of entering India with a view to taking other work later.

Negotiating the terms under which the Community was to go to India was a lengthy process and not without problems. The Sisters were not simply going to a different country but to an entirely different culture. It was not merely a question of understanding the Indian way of life, in many ways the Sisters coped with this aspect quickly and relatively easily. It was also the question of coping with the British Raj - the sahibs, and more especially their memsahibs, had built up a hierarchical structure which no one might transgress. Of course the Sisters were used to coping with the Committees and Councils which determined policy in their home-based institutions. These were male and usually predominantly clerical, but the Sisters knew how to handle them. But in India there was the phenomenon of the *Ladies' Committee* consisting of the wives of government officials, who had their own ideas about how the Sisters should do their work. Thus it took several months to negotiate a set of terms which the Sisters felt able to accept and work with.

The person delegated to negotiate with Mother Ellen at Clewer was Mrs (later Lady) Isabella Wilson, wife of the Hon. (later Sir) Alex Wilson, a wealthy tea merchant whose residence was in Chowringhee. Mrs Wilson was the honorary Treasurer of the Ladies' Committee of the Canning Home and her task was not always easy. Not only did she have to keep her own Committee happy, but also she had to explain to the Sisters some of the more ludicrous details of the work. Thus on May 2nd 1881 she wrote to Mother Ellen explaining that the Sisters would be given expenses for a servant/gatekeeper, a bearer, a table servant, a cook, a water carrier, a sweeper, a washerman, and a punkah coolie (the latter would pull the fan or punkah, as it was called). She was at pains to explain that the number of servants was not excessive: "It is impossible in this climate for Europeans to do as much for themselves as they do in a cooler one hence the amount of servants required. The only one that could be curtailed is the ayah [i.e. nurse maid]." In the same letter she went on to explain some of the difficulties of the work, and here the voice and the prejudices of the memsahib ring out: "Hospital work out here is very different to anything at home. First of all the Hospital is divided in three different blocks, each block containing two wards. There the Sisters have to do more superintendence and not so much actual nursing. Some of our nurses are very good and hardworking, but you must not expect the nice manners and very clean appearance of nurses you find in England, for though we have in the list two or three Europeans, they are merely Eurasians and they cannot be expected to be so refined as the pure Europeans. The doctors themselves prefer Eurasians as they consider they do not give themselves so many airs as the Europeans of that class do out here." This rather superior attitude towards both indigenous Indians and those of mixed race caused the Sisters great misgivings which was to be reflected in some of their letters home.

Mrs Wilson had a tentative connection with Clewer as she was at pains to explain in her letter of May 2nd 1881: "There are many ladies in India and [the] Sisters will [find] kind and true friends amongst them. It was Lady Garth who is, I believe, a cousin of 'Sister Gertrude'[4]. Although I have never been down to Clewer I have always heard so much about it from my aunt, Mrs Ed O'Brien[5], sister-in-law of your former Mother, Mrs Monsell. I have felt a great interest in the work so when Miss Wilson wrote and told me we might entertain hopes of aid from Clewer, I was indeed glad." Mother Harriet (Mrs Monsell) was still alive and living at Folkestone not far from several branch houses of the Community, though by now in failing health.

The Sisters had wanted to know exactly what would be required of them and consequently had sent a list of questions to Mrs Wilson which she had endeavoured to answer. Not least among these was the question of authority. Mrs Wilson replied that the Sisters would have all authority over the nurses in the wards: "seeing that they carry out the doctors' orders to the letter, and the nurses are responsible to the Sisters for each case." But the Sisters were concerned whether the head nurse of each ward would receive her orders from them or directly from the doctors. Mrs Wilson explained that: "the nurses go round with the doctors receiving their orders for each patient which are written down on a card and hung over the patient's bed and the Sisters see these orders are carried out. If the Sisters happen to be in the ward at the time the doctors are going round they can go with them if they wish. The nurses are entirely responsible to the Sisters."

Perhaps the Sisters were right to be cautious. They were after all, going to a strange country with an entirely different outlook regarding medical matters. Before making any firm commitment they wanted to be sure they were going on *their* own terms. They could not spare Sisters to go such a distance if their time and talents were going to be wasted or ill-used: there was quite enough work to do in England.

The Bishop of Calcutta, the Rt Revd Edward Johnson, wrote to Mother Ellen at Clewer on May 6th 1881, welcoming the prospect of Sisters coming to Calcutta. He was to be a firm ally throughout his episcopate (he resigned in 1898). But there was one note of caution relating to the Ladies' Committee: "I wonder whether you are willing to work *with* and in some respects *under*, such a Committee." Back home the Bishop of Oxford, the Rt Revd John Fielder Mackarness wrote warmly to Mother Ellen on June 14th: "As to India I can but rejoice in any prospect of your being able to take a share in the great - overwhelming - work which it is England's duty and privilege to do in India. Naturally for *your* sakes I hear of any new work with some dread of its being too large for your powers, and with some anxiety that you may be over-stretching your strength. I think too, of the losses which have befallen the good Sisters of St Mary's, Wantage in their Indian enterprise. However, I can but commend you to God's keeping and look for His blessing on your service to Him. I shall no doubt hear when you propose to send your little force out on its far off journey." Bishop Mackarness was Visitor to the Communities at Clewer and Wantage both of which were in his diocese. His letter reflects not only his pastoral concern for the wellbeing of the Sisters, but also the prevailing belief that the mission of the Church in spreading the Gospel to foreign parts was part and parcel of the civilising mission of Empire.

The Sisters' concern about the terms of their work turned out to be well founded. In her letter of May 2nd 1881 Isabella Wilson had concluded by saying that another hospital in the north of the city, (the Medical College Hospital) would also be under the Sisters' care and that it would involve a daily journey. Sir Ashley Eden was very keen for the Sisters to have this extra work, so much so, that he decided to sanction a further grant from the government to enable two Sisters to reside at the Medical College Hospital in addition to two at the Presidency General. In the event the grant would not stretch to funding four Sisters in all and so the plan to send out three was reverted to. But there were other problems: the head doctor at the Medical College objected to the Sisters, but Sir Ashley hoped to over-rule him. He wrote to Mrs Wilson (who passed the message to Mother Ellen in a letter dated June 29th 1881): "I have written to the Government of India and I propose they should give 120 Indian Pounds a month to the Canning Home to provide a fourth Sister who should reside in the Medical College... I will provide the necessary funds for her passage out. Please tell the Sisters I have this place in contemplation and I hope to settle it before the three Sisters start." In fact the matter was not resolved before the Sisters left England and so the initial contingent consisted of three, not four.

The Sister chosen to lead the small group from Clewer was Sr Lucy, professed in 1869 and by now 60 years old. She had experience as Assistant Superior and knew how to deal with people in a business like manner. So it is not surprising to find appended to Isabella Wilson's letter of June 29th 1881 the answers to a long list of questions submitted by Sr Lucy. The answers were signed by Sir Ashley Eden and the Bishop of Calcutta as Trustees of the Canning Trust Fund and represented the finalised terms under which the Sisters would work there. Clearly some hard bargaining had been done by all parties and concessions had been made on both sides.

The Sisters' outward passage would be paid by the Government of India together with their homeward passage at the end of three years, or sooner if they returned on account of illness. But if for any other reason a Sister wished to return to England, she would have to refund two-thirds of her outward passage money as well as paying her homeward passage herself. The Sisters would be provided with a furnished house consisting of three bedrooms, a drawing room and dining room, rent free, plus an allowance for expenses of 100 rupees a month for each Sister. This would be paid from the Canning Trust Fund. The Sisters had hoped that they might be able to accommodate extra Sisters in the House who would come out from Clewer in due course and take on different work, but they received a discouraging reply to this proposal: "The Canning Home, being an institution for training and providing nurses; it would be in breach of the power of the Trustees to permit any of the branches of a Sisterhood to be established in the house provided for the objects of the Trust." Even so, as will be seen later, other Sisters did come out to Calcutta to work elsewhere. But accommodation proved to be a problem until it was unexpectedly resolved in 1891.

The question of who was really in charge was hedged around in these questions and answers, and it was all very much a case of trial and error once the Sisters arrived. For instance, there was a matron who had been used to engaging and dismissing the nurses and generally being in charge of them. But the Trustees made it clear that henceforth she would be answerable to the Sisters and that the Sister-in-charge had power to engage or dismiss the staff: "The Sister Superior is to consider herself and be considered by others as being entirely in charge of the Canning Home Nurses Institution." But when Sister Lucy made the point that in English hospitals a Sister to each ward would be considered necessary, plus the supervision by the Sisters of the housekeeping, sick diets and laundry arrangements, she was told that the doctors consider two or three Sisters quite sufficient for the whole hospital. Furthermore, "the hospital being a Government institution, the doctors are responsible for the diet and laundry arrangements, and all orders or directions come through them. They will at all times be glad of suggestions from the Sisters." And then there was the question of the Indian servants who worked on the wards. Were they under the Sisters' control, and who paid them? The answer was the usual compromise - because they were "of a class difficult to manage," and because they were paid by the Government they were under the control and employ of the doctors: "They are however bound to carry out the orders and directions of the Sisters and nurses." So it seemed that the doctors' word was law in the hospital, and the Sisters' in the Canning Home, though the latter would always be subject to the Trustees who paid their expenses and to the Ladies' Committee which generally ruled the roost.

Despite this rather unpromising background Isabella Wilson wrote a very cheerful letter to Mother Ellen on August 22nd 1881 expressing her pleasure that all the difficulties seemed to have been overcome: "I am so very, very glad now I think that everything seems in satisfactory train for the Sisters' arrival." Nevertheless, it must have been with a good deal of trepidation that Sister Lucy and her companions left Clewer for their work in Calcutta in November 1881.

Footnotes

Unless otherwise stated, all the letters quoted in this book are to be found in the archives of the Community of St John Baptist, Clewer.

1. Harriet Monsell was Mother Superior at Clewer from 1852 until 1875; she died at Folkestone on March 25th 1883. Her successor at Clewer was Mother Ellen. For more about Mother Harriet and the growth of the Community of St John Baptist, Clewer see the first two books in this trilogy:

A Joyous Service: the Clewer Sisters and their work. 1989

A Place in Life: the Clewer House of Mercy, 1849-83. 1992

2. Sir Ashley Eden, 1831-87. Nephew of George Eden, Earl of Auckland and Governor-General of India 1836-41. After Rugby and Winchester followed by a spell at Haileybury College (the East India Company's own public school), Eden went out to India in 1852. In 1860 he became Secretary to the Government of Bengal and in 1877 succeeded Sir Richard Temple as Lieutenant Governor. He was knighted in 1878 and retired in 1882. He died suddenly of paralysis on July 9th 1887. The Eden Hospital for women and children was founded in his honour in Calcutta.

3. Robert Milman, Bishop of Calcutta 1867-76.

4. Sr Gertrude sailed for India on Jan 15th 1892 and returned on March 17th 1897. She worked at the Presidency General Hospital.

5. It is not clear to which of the O'Brien's Mrs Wilson is referring. Mother Harriet had a brother called Edward but he died in 1840. A more likely candidate is Edward, youngest son of the Revd Henry O'Brien of Cliffe Hall, Darlington. Henry died in 1895, but Edward lived into his 90's and cherished boyhood memories of Mother Harriet - "aunt Harriet" as he called her.

-4-
JACK'S COUNTRY HOUSE

"I shall no doubt hear when you propose to send your little force out on its far off journey." Thus the Bishop of Oxford had written to Mother Ellen during the negotiations. In fact he was able to see the Sisters before they left Clewer because the great new chapel which had taken three years to build was to be dedicated by him. It was a week of tremendous activity for the Community. On October 19th 1881 a service of blessing was conducted by the bishop in the old chapel for Sr Lucy, Sr Fanny Gertrude and Sr Anna Frances as a prelude to their voyage. Next day, in the presence of 104 Sisters and 90 clergy, the splendid new chapel was dedicated. A week later, on November 3rd, the three Sisters left Clewer for Liverpool on the first stage of their journey. They sailed on November 4th, and on the same day back at Clewer, Mother Ellen resigned office as Mother Superior. So by the end of 1881 the Community of St John Baptist not only had new work in India, but also a new Mother Superior - Mother Jane Frances, installed on December 21st. She was to lead the Community for the next eight years but, as will be seen later, her life's work was to be in India.

1882 saw the start of a regular journal for Associates and friends of the Community called the *St John Baptist Magazine*. It contained accounts of all the Community work, and many of the Sisters' letters from India were included. The first issue was published at Easter 1882 and contains Sr Lucy's account of the voyage to India, written on board the *S.S. Mira*[(1)]. It is dated November 4th 1881, the date of their departure from Liverpool: "We sailed at 11 o'clock from Liverpool which was soon out of sight. On Sunday we were in the Bay of Biscay, Monday off the coast of Portugal, and Wednesday the 9th we entered the Straights of Gibraltar - the air soft and warm, and the scenery grand on both sides. The beautiful old rock is five miles long. At 2 o'clock on [November] 16th we caught our first glimpse of Damietta and in about three hours were in front of Port Said. Ten years ago Port Said did not exist, [but] it has now a population of 12,000. We first saw it all glowing in the sunset, something quite different from what one had ever seen before."

"After dinner we went on shore in one of the boats. Our rowers were swarthy Nubians in loose white garments and turbans. They had a lantern in the middle of the boat. By daylight the town is wretched and dirty, but on a dark night, with only the stars and the lamps it is most picturesque - the streets full of people in every variety of costume, some very pretty, some grotesque, some very like evil spirits, but nothing at all European but ourselves. The shrieking, screaming and chattering, [are] just what one has read about. Several parties squatted in the streets at their meals, cooking over a little brazier in the midst of them. Others were doing business with a great deal of mutual abuse."

"The streets of Port Said are broad, paved with stone, over which grey sand is firmly pressed. We passed the Greek Church, and there are English, French, Greek and Coptic Churches. Public gardens, coffee houses etc., are all lighted with gas, the band playing vigorously in the 'El Dorado.' At last we returned to our ship as we came from it."

The Sisters had obviously enjoyed their time ashore and had made the most of their sightseeing. Port Said had grown rapidly since the opening of the Suez Canal in 1869 and the following description of the journey through the canal would have been of great topical interest to all Sr Lucy's readers back home. It was of course a marvel of modern civil engineering and shortened the journey to India by several weeks, saving the Sisters the perilous voyage round the Cape.

Sr Lucy's narrative continued: "The harbour was full of ships waiting to enter the Canal. It is too narrow for two to pass so there are stations every five miles where it is wider. As soon as a ship passes a station they telegraph to the next station to prevent another coming, and as they arrive they are moored to the bank if the way is not clear. We were most unlucky and had to wait four times. We left Port Said on November 17th at 9.30 and did not get through the Canal until the 19th. To the east was the desert of Shur, hot, loose and burning sand. We saw several mirages, principally mountains and water... There were several of the 'Children of the Desert' about [i.e. nomads], men and women, the women wrapped in long white veils only showing one eye. About 3.30 we caught our first glimpse of Suez - the spires and dome of a mosque, low and square houses. The hills round Suez are grand - the sunset was off Baal Zephon that night. Next morning (Sunday) we entered the Red Sea and had our Celebration in sight of Mt Sinai. It is a long range of high peaks, very grey and very grand. The waters of the Red Sea are the bluest we have seen, but very rough and choppy. The heat tremendous, day and night. It got cooler after we passed Bab-el-Mendab. Here we rose one day at four to see the Southern Cross - no words can describe its peculiar beauty. Venus was also rising out of the sea, as it were, and the Great Bear upside down!"

However interesting the journey may have been, the Sisters were very glad when they reached their destination. "On December 2nd we reached Colombo and left again next day, our one longing to reach Calcutta which we did on December 8th after the longest voyage the *Mira* has ever made. Two ladies of the Committee, Mrs Wilson and Mrs Peel, came to meet us but missed us." Fortunately the Sisters had been befriended on the voyage by a clergyman and his family who came to their rescue: " Meanwhile Mr Jackson most kindly left his own party to take care of us and brought us here where we were very heartily welcomed by the two ladies who have been in charge of the Home until now." Journey's end, but now the work began.

The Presidency General was one of Calcutta's oldest hospitals, having been founded in the 18th century and removed to its present site in 1766. It was enlarged by the addition of two wings in 1795 and by the time of the Clewer Sisters' arrival had about 200 beds, most of the patients being European. But it was by no means the only medical institution. The 1882 edition of the *Bengal Directory* also lists the Medical College Hospital, the Calcutta Ophthalmic and Aural Hospital, the Campbell Hospital, the Chitpore Lock Hospital, the European Lunatic Asylum, the Garrison Dispensary, the Howrah General Hospital, the Mayo Native Hospital, the Native Lunatic Asylum, the Sealdah Lock Hospital, the Sumbhunath Pundit's Dispensary, and Charitable Dispensaries at Alipore and Bhowanipore.

The Calcutta Hospital Nurses' Institution originated in 1859 through the suggestion of Lady Canning. A Ladies' Committee was formed to raise funds and provide four nurses and a matron for the European men's ward at the Medical College Hospital, there being no trained nurses there at that time. The success of this project led to the provision of more nurses both there and at the Presidency General Hospital, and also to serve patients in their homes. But the lack of organised training soon manifested itself, hence the need for the Sisters. The Nurses' Institution stood next door to the Presidency General Hospital and provided quarters for the nurses. In 1877 the Nurses' Institution was amalgamated with the Lady Canning Home. This had been built in the same compound two years earlier by public subscription as a memorial to Charlotte, Countess Canning, wife of Lord Canning, Governor-General at the time of the mutiny and first Viceroy[(2)].

Sr Lucy lost no time in writing home to Clewer describing her new surroundings. This letter, dated December 12th 1881, was published in the *St John Baptist Magazine* of Easter 1882 together with the description of the voyage. "The compound in which the hospital is built is very large," she wrote. "[There is] the hospital, then the Canning Home, and the nurses' quarters, besides which the doctors' have separate houses in which they live with their families. The compound is very well planted and the trees grow in tropical luxuriance. I never saw anything so lovely as some of the feathering palms, and I had no idea of their great size."

Going on to describe the Lady Canning Home she wrote: "Our quarters are in one corner of the compound. It is a very cosy building, well arranged and well built. All the rooms are large and airy, and there is a wide verandah looking south west, which in Calcutta is the correct aspect, for the only wind during the hot season blows from the south east. The nurses' quarters are close by - a nice building. There is accommodation for 24 nurses and a matron. The Canning nurses are those who go out for private nursing and receive higher wages than those in the hospital. At present there are five but the demand for more is great." The nurses' quarters and the Canning Home was indeed an impressive building with its large windows and open verandahs, so different from the Victorian gothic of Clewer.

Next followed a lengthy description of the hospital which of course was what everyone back home wanted to know about: "Now you must come across the compound and pay a visit to the hospital. The wards are divided into three large blocks. Number 1 block is two storeys high; the ground floor is not used and serves principally for ventilation, for presses to keep the men's clothes in, and other stowaway purposes. The first storey is the men's surgical ward, and the second is partitioned off into private wards where patients pay about 3 rupees a day and can have their relations, servants, linen etc., as they fancy. This arrangement is also allowed in the female ward where sometimes a whole family is admitted - grandmother, mother and grandchildren. Food is only given to the patient, the others either having their food from the hospital kitchen and paying so much per day, or else have it sent to them from their homes. It was perplexing at first, but now I grow accustomed to a whole family accompanying a patient, and really they are very good and amenable. Block 2 contains one men's medical ward, the library of the hospital (a very good one which is open daily for the patients' use), the dispensary, and a ward for observation cases. Each case as it comes in is put on one side for observation before being admitted into a ward, except the women who go straight to their ward. The lock-up room for 'delirium tremens' cases is also in this block. Block 3 contains another men's medical ward, the operation room, and upstairs, the female ward. In the ward there are also two patients' rooms and an operating room just curtained off only."

"Nearly all the patients are sailors and the hospital goes by the name of 'Jack's Country House.' I do not think I can describe the wards, they are so unlike any English hospital. It is all open arcades, each bed and locker is placed at the basement of the arches so that a current of air is between each bed. No windows are ever shut unless ordered by the doctor. The men sit out on the verandah to smoke and have their meals. It is the nicest part of the hospital, except that the coolies wash up here and make a great mess and untidiness. The patients are dressed up in bed or out of bed in white flannel drawers and jersey over which they have a shirt and a very flowery dressing gown patched up with any colour that can be found."

During the initial negotiations Isabella Wilson had warned the Sisters that Indian hospital work differed greatly from that in England. Now the Sisters, who had come out to Calcutta with no knowledge of Bengali and probably very little insight into Indian customs, began to understand exactly what she meant. But a sense of humour goes a long way and Sr Lucy certainly had one, as is evident from her description of a typical morning's routine: "You would be amused with the surgical doctor's morning round. He enters the ward with the house surgeon (apothecary, as he is called here), the native baboo or student, and the sergeant of the ward (each ward has a serjeant whose office I cannot yet make out). The Sister and nurse come after them followed by the native dresser who carries a spatula and stethoscope; the dressing basket native [follows] with a curious thing in his hand like a knife box containing an 'omnium gatherum' of useful things, instruments and greasepots; [then comes] the native basin, jug and soap dish holder, the native ink pot and pen carrier, the native mackintosh carrier who assists the native screen carrier in holding up a sheet when Dr Birch calls out 'Purdah'; the native dressing bowl carrier comes also, and the native poultice man. I think these are all, but if any extra is required an extra native comes with it. Sometimes the cook baboo also walks round in this procession and takes down any alteration in the diet. The nurses are Eurasians - half English, half Indian, most of them very dark... We hope that with patience and perseverance we shall get on. The doctors are very kind to us and I think will help us get things into some order. Our Eurasian nurses have such a fear of doing anything that would lower them in the eyes of the natives - they will scarcely put a bed tidy without calling for a coolie."

By February 1882 things were beginning to settle down although the weather was warming up. In a letter dated February 5th Sr Lucy remarked: "The weather is getting very warm - 120 degrees in the sun one day. Our wards are never below 80 degrees in the afternoon [even] where there is the greatest draught. The wards are not full - this is the healthiest season up to June when the rains begin. We seldom pass more than a week without a cholera case for which we have a special ward. They very seldom recover and have a very rapid end... One needs to be very strong here - the work is not so much doing things quietly, but you always have to be on the move first in one block, then in another, upstairs, downstairs, nurses and patients to be looked after, coolies to be kept going, wards to be made tidy, special cases to be seen. We have to be thoroughly up to the treatment used for each case and go round with the doctors who look to us to see that their orders are carried out."

By the end of 1882 the Sisters had begun to make their mark upon the hospitals of Calcutta. On Friday June 2nd Sr Eleanor Isabel and Sr Sophia had arrived from England after a long and stormy voyage thus making a total of five Sisters in Calcutta. Mid August saw the two new Sisters embark on their work - organising the nursing at the Medical College Hospital, the initial problems concerning this having now been overcome. They were to be based at the nurses quarters in the Medical College Hospital which was north of the Maidan in College Street near the district known as Bow Bazar (or Burra Bazar). The Medical College was opened in 1835 and the hospital in 1838 with 30 beds. In 1848 the foundation stone of the greatly enlarged hospital was laid by the Governor-General, Lord Dalhousie, and the new building which was constructed in an impressive Greek revival style was opened on December 1st 1852. It had over 300 beds and became one of the largest teaching hospitals in Bengal.

About three quarters of the patients were Indian, the rest being European. The senior doctors were European and the juniors were Indian. There were two categories of medical students: the military, who were mostly Eurasian and went to military hospitals after qualifying; and civil students who were usually Indians who proceeded either into private practice or into indigenous Indian hospitals.

The Government Report on Medical Institutions in Calcutta for 1882 paid tribute to the contribution of the Sisters and also underlined some of the problems they had met: "From the date of their arrival to the present time, improvement has made rapid progress. Having been accustomed in England to minister with their own hands to the wants of sick people, to prepare appliances, and use all the means required at the bedside, these ladies could not fail to notice *at once* faults which indicated difficulties before them greater than any they had anticipated. For they had to contend not only against defects arising from want of skill and knowledge, but against the fixed belief that manual work by the bedside, with few exceptions, was unworthy of the nurse whose duty it was to summon a native servant when a sick man called. The ladies however, though unused to this kind of pretentiousness, perhaps had been accustomed to organise and govern as well as to work, and did not shrink from the task of inculcating the dignity of nursing while they taught the skilful performance of it, and enforced order and discipline. How far they are satisfied with the results I cannot pretend to say, but I think they are much more hopeful of approaching to their own high standard than they were at the outset. And I know that the improvement they have already effected has exceeded all that had seemed possible to the Medical Officers whose patients have benefited by their exertions." Clearly the efforts of the Sisters were much appreciated, and the Report concluded: "The Lieutenant Governor's cordial thanks are due to these ladies for the unflagging care and devotion which they have brought to the performance of their self-imposed tasks."

As well as getting used to their new work the Sisters had to accustom themselves to the vast mixture of palaces and poverty which was Calcutta, to a totally new language, and to a culture which they found alien but rather fascinating. But although they regarded the non-Christian religions of India to be heathen and ungodly, yet they looked after their patients with complete impartiality. As Christians with a mission to unchurched India, they had much to teach and they looked for the opportunity to do so. But the letters home give the impression that they were also learning much from India, and that sometimes it was a humbling experience.

Footnotes

1. The *S.S. Mira* was a Star Line ship. The *St John Baptist Magazine* account spells the name *Mira*, but the manuscript list of Sisters in India in the Clewer archives spells it *Myra*.

2. Charlotte Canning, former Lady of the Bedchamber to Queen Victoria, came to India in 1855 when her husband was appointed Governor-General. Their six years covered the time of the mutiny and its aftermath. Like many other English people, Charlotte found the Indian climate very difficult, and her health seriously deteriorated. She finally succumbed to a fever and died at Barrackpore House on November 18th 1861. She was buried in the grounds the next day in a favourite spot overlooking the Hooghly.

C S J B

I N D I A

-5-
POOR BENIGHTED SUFFERING ONES

"I was delighted yesterday to find I had a new coolie who spoke and understood a little English," wrote Sr Lucy from the Lady Canning Home on February 5th 1882, in a letter published in the Easter 1882 *St John Baptist Magazine.* "He had been put to watch by a poor boy with typhoid fever and he reported to me with great glee: 'He plenty shout,' meaning he had been very delirious. When giving me a little account of himself and his home at Lucknow he added shivering, 'Calcutta plenty cold.' I must say I could not agree with him, but I can imagine the nights and early mornings strike cold to these poor creatures who have only a thin piece of muslin round them, and who like to lie out in the sun when the thermometer is at 120 degrees."

The Sisters' life was never dull, enlivened as it was by such scenes, and even in the saddest cases the comic element would often manifest itself. The grinding poverty which provided the backgrounds of many patients and hospital servants was ever present. Calcutta may have been called the City of Palaces, but it was also in Kipling's words, the City of Dreadful Night. With the onset of work in the Medical College Hospital the Sisters encountered many pathetic cases because there was a far higher ratio of Indian patients than in the European oriented Presidency General Hospital. There was always the conflict between what was best for the patient and the rules of their religion, and sometimes the Sisters felt quite powerless in the face of such rigidity. The following story related by Sr Lucy shows this tension:

"On Thursday in Easter week a little Hindoo boy of four years old [called] Muggra, or as the natives nickname him, Bundaro [meaning the little monkey], was brought into the hospital by the police having been found playing on the tramway lines and accidentally ran over. His left thigh and leg were fearfully mutilated, the right toes squashed, and his left arm much torn and wounded. But pain did not daunt Bundaro; he sat upright on the operation table playing with his wounded limbs, not a cry escaping him during the examination... The left thigh and three toes of his right foot were amputated, and as soon as he recovered consciousness he was brought up into the female ward. Shortly afterwards his mother arrived to take care of him. She is quite a young widow from Ghayah [Gaya] in Behar. Her husband, who was a bearer of the Chamar caste, is dead, and so to support her children she came up to Calcutta where she works as a charwoman. Bundaro was at first determined not to touch hospital food. If you offer him milk he says, 'Let me sleep, leave me alone, I shall loose caste if you give me things, I feel ill, I cannot eat. No more to bother me.' Dr Birch left strict orders that

Bundaro was to eat daily a certain amount, but although the nurses tried to coax him to eat and finally used force to make him swallow, Bundaro's will was the strongest and he became purposely sick rather than eat hospital food. Not even his mother could keep him in order - he would have his own way. After two or three days more struggle however, little Bundaro has become reasonable, and now eats whatever is brought to him. It is the funniest sight to peep round his corner when he least anticipates a visitor, and watch Bundaro sitting up on his bed nursing his stump and singing to it."

One aspect of Empire which later generations have found difficult to view with much sympathy, is the hunting of big game. This was not confined to India of course, African species also suffered severe losses and risk of extinction. In India high ranking dignitaries were taken on shooting expeditions often as the guests of Indian princes, and more often than not the most sought after prize was the tiger, most beautiful and stately of animals. So Sr Lucy's story of the tiger tamer would have appealed to her readers, many of whom would be familiar with the big game trophies proudly exhibited in English country houses, or who might have heard with curiosity about such entertainments as the circus:

"The tiger-tamer is a Mexican by birth, and has been employed by the Chiarini Royal Circus (lately exhibiting in Calcutta and now gone on to Poonah with all their beasts); he came to us on the 11th January [1882] suffering from a tiger's bite. He had been exhibiting tricks in a cage with three tigers when one of them, Brutus, made a spring at him: he gave the beast a blow breaking his staff. Brutus seeing this made another spring and bit the calf of his right leg. He rammed the stump of his stick which he still held into Brutus' ear and stunned him with the blow, going on bravely with the performance with Caesar and Regulus, the other two tigers. Was he not a brave fellow? These three tigers are just seven years old, our Mexican caught them and trained them himself. For months he had tracked them about in a Bengal jungle until he found the den; there he waited patiently until the father and mother had been shot dead. Then he went into the den and took possession of his dear tigers; he loves them as dearly as we do an intelligent dog and was quite downhearted when the Chiarini Circus had to move on, leaving him in hospital. Tigers take nearly two years to train... Brutus had given the leg a good bite with his two fangs, and had scratched deeply with his teeth. The wounds are doing well but they heal so very slowly and his nerve is so much shaken, that he knows he could never return to those tigers, though he means eventually to have the care of a fresh lot!" (Doubtless most latter-day readers would say "well done Brutus"!)

Sr Lucy was not the only Sister to write home to Clewer or to contribute to the *St John Baptist Magazine*. By September 1882 Sr Eleanor Isabel and Sr Sophia were getting to grips with their work in the Medical College Hospital and one of them (it is not clear which), wrote about the work among the non-Christian patients, which had obviously moved her deeply. "You would love [this work] more than any of our other work here, I think it touches the poor outside heathen world so completely. I have nine wards with nothing but Hindoos and a sprinkling of Musselmen [Muslims], and I devote a great deal of my time and thought and spend a lot of the little heart I have upon them. They call me 'Ma' which means mother, and are as happy as possible if I only feel their pulse or turn their pillow or stroke their bare arm or head. Some speak a little English and then the request is generally, 'Ma, you pray to God for me and I be quite well.' Their childish simplicity is very touching. A poor fellow was brought in with both legs broken and became delirious. An old man who speaks English beckoned to me and said, 'Ma, you see that man very ill, he will die, but you pray to God for him and he will be better.' This man knows the Gospel story as well as any Christian, he believes it all, but there is no sense of any *need* of Christ, and so it all remains outside him."

Like Sr Lucy this Sister had a sense of powerlessness regarding the best treatment of the patients and the conflict it caused with their religious observances. "It would take me pages if I were to tell you of all my interesting patients. It is a beautiful work. One seems to feel Our Lord so very near as one passes up and down among these poor benighted suffering ones all so keen about fulfilling the law of their religion, keeping their caste pure and uncontaminated by not touching food excepting that cooked by one of the highest castes, always washing before and after it etc. One poor fellow went without his food all day because it was placed on the bed instead of the floor. He said he could not tell who had laid on that bed before him, and if one was of a lower caste, his food was contaminated. Another with a fearfully smashed foot has scarcely eaten anything excepting the little brought in by his brother, and he weeps all day with hunger because if he eats hospital food he will be an outcast from his people. His father and mother would disown him. He says it would cost him 500 rupees to buy back his caste."

But care of patients and the difficulties surrounding their religious observances were not the only aspects of Indian life to which the Sisters had to adjust. Weather and wildlife accounted for a good deal and might have discouraged any but the toughest. Writing from the Lady Canning Home in an undated letter published in the autumn 1882 edition of the *St John Baptist Magazine*, Sr Lucy wrote graphically: "You shall hear our first experience of a Calcutta thunderstorm which everyone says was nothing, quite nothing to what we shall experience in the hot season. About 5 p.m. heavy storm clouds began to gather, the breeze sprang up and the lightning began. In an hour's time the incessant lightning was all around us on every side with occasional claps of rolling thunder. Two hours later the thunder was over our heads crashing, growling and rolling, never stopping, sometimes near, sometimes at a distance. All nature was perfectly silent, no insects buzzing, no frogs or crickets, no mosquitoes, nor yet the jackals! Only the increasing thunder and lightning... The rain fell gently and for a quarter of an hour the storm lulled, but once more the thunder crashed around us. The rain fell heavily, and for half an hour the two raged against each other, the storm then going on in the distance quite audibly growling away, the lightning continuing a vivid blue with golden streaks of light like a curtain being drawn up and down. At 10 o'clock a hurricane was blowing and then the thunder rolled away a long way off and the jackals ventured into our part of the town with a prolonged howl. There could not have been much for them, the deluges of rain must have washed away all refuse."

"Next day," continued the Sister, "we had a little idea what the heavy rains must be like. If only you could have seen the torrents - bucketsful pouring down. The Asylum which is close by could not be seen through the rain. The natives wearing but one small garment could be seen paddling along in the running water with a native umbrella up to keep off the sharp rain from their shiny skins. The small dyke close to our quarters was quickly filled and the water dashed along in it. The roads were pools of water whilst the sound of the falling rain obliged us to shout instead of to speak. The kites sat still in the trees drawing their wings tightly round them through the whole storm, but all the other birds took refuge in a less exposed spot."

Would anyone complain of the English weather anymore, one wonders? But then there was the wildlife too. "I must reassure you about the jackals," wrote Sr Lucy. "They are dreadful cowards, and if they hear a footstep they fly as fast as they can. They are only to be feared when driven into a corner and cannot escape - then they make an attack. I shall have some stories to tell you about snakes no doubt, but they don't come till the rainy season. At present the mosquitoes are our only tormentors. It is quite an art to get into bed with the mosquito curtains, for if one introduces itself in with you, you will get no sleep the whole night."

As predicted, snakes were a hidden peril and Sr Blanche was given a very nasty fright one night as she was crossing the compound of the Presidency General Hospital. "I was going to one of the wards to read prayers at 7 p.m. As I crossed a bridge over one of the stone ditches I almost trod on what I fancied was a large toad, but as I turned to throw the full light of my lantern on it, I saw something a few inches from me upright in the grass swaying backwards and forwards and felt sure it was a snake. When I returned from the ward I looked for it and found it by the stone coping of the bridge ready to dart at me, its head erect. I turned the light on it, saw it was a cobra and it happily disappeared. Some of the sailors had a hunt for it then and again next morning. It has not been found. It was very providential that I did not tread on it. This shows how needful it is to have a light after dark."

But it was not all peril. There was some recreation too although the extreme heat made it virtually impossible for the Sisters to walk far. So most of their journeys were made by carriage as was this evening excursion described by Sr Lucy: "We first of all drive to post our letters at the General Post Office. This is about two miles and a half from the Canning Home and is an enormous building. A hundred years ago the Black Hole of Calcutta stood close by this very spot. Then we try and make coachman and syce [groom] understand that we wanted to drive back to our quarters by the riverside, but we fail completely; to our great relief a baboo [clerk who speaks English] is passing by - the syce hails him to interpret our wishes. He soon made all clear and we start on our drive. The setting sun was dipping into the sea, a huge fiery red ball, beyond all the masts and shipping. Such glorious tints colouring everything during the very short time before darkness closes in. The river looks so broad and calm and it was beautiful to see a sunset once more. In some places the Hooghly widens to nearly a mile, but I think just about here is one of its narrow spots. The Strand Road runs for its whole length about four miles and a half on the bank of the river, and is a most beautiful drive, broad and tastefully laid out. The Sailor's Home is here. It was built and opened by Government in 1868 and can accommodate about 250 men and 20 officers. The shipping at all the different ghats [jetties] is so fascinating; we know there is scarcely a mast which has not come from England. But we must leave the Strand Road and its fashionables. We pass innumerable native huts, horrid looking places, and at last come into Circular Road and can recognise the drive from Garden Reach the day we landed, December 8th 1881. In a few minutes we are at our lodge entrance and it is not long before we are over at the wards reading prayers and seeing that the work is going on correctly."

What the Sister had described in 1882 was the typical English evening recreation which remained unchanged throughout the years of the British Raj. Fifty years later another English writer[1] described the same activity in similar words: "Few Europeans took their evening recreation on foot - or, indeed, walked anywhere - instead a recognised 'Driving Hour' existed just before twilight, when all Calcutta society would appear on the maidan and drive along the Strand Road by the riverside to draw up, perhaps, by Eden Gardens, to listen to the band playing national airs and hackneyed classical pieces."

Because the Sisters had been invited to India by the government they acquired a kind of semi-official status in the eyes of some of the leading dignitaries. People who back home might have regarded Religious Sisters as a suspiciously High Church faction tended in India to cultivate them. Perhaps it was the sense of all being strangers together in a foreign land. Also of course, it must be remembered that many of the Sisters came from wealthy backgrounds and were perfectly at home in the higher echelons of society even though they had given up all claims to wealth and status. But doubtless the fact that their initial invitation had come from the Lieutenant Governor of Bengal accounted for the very welcome offer made by Lady Ripon, wife of the Viceroy[2], and duly accepted, for Sisters to use the Flagstaff Bungalow in the grounds of the Vice-regal country house at Barrackpore. This offer came at an opportune moment as Sr Eleanor Isabel and Sr Sophia had just arrived (June 2nd 1882) from England after a very unpleasant voyage. They were able to have a break before starting work at the Medical College Hospital. But the offer was extended to the other Sisters too, so that all in turn were refreshed by this break. The next Vicereine, Lady Dufferin, who was very interested in nursing, struck up a friendship with Sr Lucy having met her whilst visiting the hospitals. She made the following entry in her diary[3]: "Wednesday January 4th 1888. On my return [from visiting the Little Sisters of the Poor] Sister Lucy (a Clewer Sister) came to tea with me, and we had a very long gossip indeed upon affairs that interest us both." Alas, Sr Lucy did not record her impressions of Government House, though Lady Dufferin did not mince her words about the discomforts of the place and once described living there as sitting in twenty draughts at once!

In the midst of all the activity and adjustment to their new way of life it could be easy to lose track of the Sisters' spiritual life. In fact this was not so, and the Bishop of Calcutta had assured them before they left England that every effort would be made to provide for their spiritual needs. On Sundays and festivals the Sisters worshipped at the cathedral and following their first Christmas they remarked that the decorations there seemed more like Easter because of the lush flowers. "Poinsettias grow like weeds here, and would be such treasures to you at home." In June 1882 a small oratory was opened for the daily use of the Sisters in the Lady Canning Home. Here they would gather for the recitation of the Divine Office and for the Eucharist. In addition, the Sisters had also begun to forge links with the Oxford Mission whose clergy ministered to them, and also with other local clergy. One such was the Revd A.C. Seal of St Barnabas' Church, Kidderpore. Mr Seal was an Indian by birth who ministered to Indian Christians in a poor part of Kidderpore not far from the docks. The Sisters were very keen to encourage his ministry and his name recurs many times in their letters home.

For an Indian to become a Christian meant the risk of losing everything and the Sisters were greatly impressed by Mr Seal's work and by the people who came to Christ through it. One of Mr Seal's converts had just died when Sr Lucy wrote home early in 1885: "Ten years ago he was baptised and from that time he was regarded as dead, neither wife nor child would speak to him. He had to cook his own food and do everything for himself. When he fell ill they would still do nothing for him and he might have starved but that Mr Seal brought him to the parsonage where they nursed him as well as they could. When he got worse they sent him to the Medical College Hospital where he soon died. When his relations heard he was dying they gathered round and with threats and prayers strove to make him renounce his faith, but he died confessing Christ... We can hardly fancy what it would be to live as the only Christian in his village for 10 years, no one holding intercourse with him except on Sundays when he walked five miles to attend the services at St Barnabas." Stories such as this spurred the Sisters on and made them hope for real mission work. But already their work was expanding, although expansion and setback were for a time destined to walk hand in hand.

Footnotes

1. PEARSON,R. *Eastern Interlude: a social history of the European Community in Calcutta.* Calcutta: Thacker, Spink & Co. 1933 The quotation will be found on p.224.

2. Lord Ripon was Viceroy from 1880-84, and was succeeded by Lord Dufferin and Ava 1884-8.

3. MARCHIONESS OF DUFFERIN AND AVA *Our Viceregal Life in India: selections from my Journal 1884-8.* 2 Vols. John Murray 1889.

The quotation comes from Vol. 2 p.243.

C S J B

I N D I A

-6-
THE WHITE MAN'S BURDEN

The Clewer Sisters had not been in Calcutta very long when a new hospital in the same compound as the Medical College opened. This was the Eden Hospital for Women and Children, also known as the Lying-in Hospital, founded in honour of Sir Ashley Eden by his friends and admirers. The Sisters were asked to organise the nursing there and undertook it in combination with the Medical College. It specialised in obstetrics and gynaecology and soon built up a highly respected reputation. The hospital compound eventually housed a number of institutions - the Eye Hospital had been added through the generosity of a wealthy Indian whose mother was cured by one of the Medical College doctors; and the Ezra Hospital for Jews was added later.

The work of the Clewer Sisters and the improvements they made to general nursing standards became well known and their hospitals began to form part of the official itinerary for visiting dignitaries. Thus Lady Dufferin,[(1)] the Vicereine, made the following note in her diary for Wednesday January 7th 1885[(2)]: "In the afternoon I visited the General Hospital and the Lady Canning Home. The Clewer Sisters live at the Home and train nurses. Most of the women are Eurasians, and they seem to make very good sick nurses when once they have learned by precept and example that it is not beneath them to hand a glass of water to a patient, and that such little offices may be performed without the intervention of a coolie..." Doubtless Sr Lucy had told her some of the problems, and the Sister would have found a very sympathetic ear. Lady Dufferin was extremely interested in all aspects of nursing and during her time in India established the Lady Dufferin Fund for training, and the Dufferin Victoria Hospital for women. The latter, situated not far from the Medical College Hospital, became a government hospital after the British left, and remained in service until the early 1990s.

A few days after her visit to the Presidency General, Lady Dufferin noted in her diary for Tuesday January 13th 1885 [(3)]: "In the afternoon I went to visit two hospitals, one the Medical College, the other the Eden. They are very large and airy, but I don't think it will profit you much for me to describe them. Medical students swathed in sheets with bare heads, stood on the steps to receive me. Sister Lucy and her nurses were there, and native women who have taken nursing diplomas were in attendance, wrapped in silk saris; and in the Eden, which is a lying-in hospital, there were some very tiny brown babies to be seen. In the other [i.e. the Medical College Hospital], all sorts of ills are mixed together, and even the cholera patients are not isolated. I suppose, that being able to have the air rushing in on every side, the danger of contagion is not so great as at home." At this time of course, the cause of cholera was still thought to be air-borne rather than water-borne.

More hospital work came along in 1883 in the form of the Eden Sanatorium at Darjeeling, but such a departure from Calcutta to the foothills of the Himalayas requires a chapter to itself in due course.

Meanwhile, the much sought after expansion to the Sisters' work in the form of education suddenly became a reality in 1882, very soon after the Sisters' arrival. On October 12th 1882 three more Sisters had left England for Calcutta - Sr Blanche (whom we have already met calmly encountering a cobra in the hospital compound), Sr Cuthbert and Sr Mary Agatha. Sr Blanche was destined for hospital work, and the others for a new work undertaken at the invitation of the Bishop of Calcutta - the management of the Pratt Memorial School.

There were many schools in Calcutta of differing standards, varying from the higher colleges such as the Presidency College, the London Missionary Society College, and La Martiniere (Roman Catholic); to higher grade schools teaching up to University entrance such as Loretto (Roman Catholic), the Bethune Institute, and the Calcutta Girl's School; to primary and vernacular language schools, which were often run as part of Christian missions. The oldest of these was the Calcutta Free School founded in 1789.

The Pratt Memorial School was fairly new having been founded in 1876 in memory of Archdeacon Pratt of Calcutta. In the early days it catered primarily for the Anglo-Indian community (still known as Eurasians at that time), but also took European girls, the latter increasingly so. There was a great need for good quality schooling for girls whose parents could not afford to send them to England, or to the more expensive hill-station schools, and the Pratt School sought to cater for these needs. The Sisters were invited to run the school by the Bishop of Calcutta who had been impressed by their hospital work. There were some secular teachers to help the Sisters and the whole undertaking was under the Calcutta Diocesan Board of Education, so a good standard was maintained. About 50-60 English speaking girls (mostly boarders) were being educated at the Pratt School at the time of the Sisters' arrival, in buildings which were far from adequate.

Sr Cuthbert and Sr Mary Agatha began work at the Pratt Memorial School on January 1st 1883 and immediately work was set in hand to improve the buildings. But there was a shortage of money, and so for the time being little could be done. After only four months Sr Cuthbert had to withdraw. The Community *Annals* record the following entry dated April 24th 1883: "Mother heard from Calcutta that Sr Cuthbert was seriously ill in rapid consumption. She was obliged to be removed from the Pratt School of which she had charge."[4] The reins were taken up by Sr Mary Agatha and she brought great energy and enthusiasm to the task. So greatly did Sr Mary Agatha make an impression on the school that later records even go so far as saying that she was sent out to be in charge. It seems she was the driving force even during the short time of Sr Cuthbert's charge.

The success of the Sisters' non-hospital work depended very greatly on the generosity of people in England. A body called the St John Baptist Calcutta Mission Association had been formed in England in 1882 with the object of supporting the Sisters and their work by giving financial and other help, and by spreading the word about it. The honorary secretary was a Miss Arbuthnot who seems to have been Sr Mary Agatha's sister. Writing to the Clewer Associates in the *St John Baptist Magazine* for Easter 1884, Sr Mary Agatha refers to the work of this body, and also gives an insight into the dire needs of the Pratt School at this time: "Our fresh school term has begun brightly with numbers of new pupils. My sister will, I think, have written to you for papers of the S.J.B. Indian Mission Association. She and my aunt all worked so hard and collected nice, useful things for us to sell and give away - frocks, pinafores, chairbacks, dolls, and all kinds of nicknacks which are much appreciated here. Any presents of story books, prayer books, *Hymns Ancient and Modern*, music, part songs for children, children's underclothes, dolls, toys, games of any kind, we should be so grateful for. Many of the children are very poor indeed, and have not sufficient clothing, and as the school also is very poor and has barely sufficient to carry it on, the smallest gift is a boon to us. I am trying to stir up everyone I can think of in England to help us."

The school went from strength to strength, as indeed did all the work undertaken by the Sisters, and by March 1884 their numbers had increased to 11. It is very difficult to keep track of all the comings and goings, to and from Clewer to Calcutta. But on March 7th 1884 Sr Christian arrived to work at the Pratt School having had a good voyage aboard the P. & O. steamer *Khedive*. She wrote home enthusiastically on May 4th 1884 and the letter was reprinted in the autumn issue of the *St John Baptist Magazine:* "I find my scholars bright and intelligent children and very teachable. I like the little brownies. Mine is the lower school, the fourth class in three divisions, and the infants. I have an infant of my own now, her mother is a widow and penniless. She is beginning her training as a nurse so I have undertaken May. She is not quite four; we got her elected [i.e. sponsored] on the foundation and the rest of the money I have to raise. I am making all her clothes. She had next to none when she came in and I have to stitch away hard to get her a change of apparel."

This letter reflects a trait which became very common with the Sisters: the adoption of destitute children whose parents simply could not afford to keep them. Many a child was saved from a life of abject poverty by the kindness of an individual Sister.

The letter continued: "I am going to give an arithmetic class tomorrow in rupees, annas and pice.[5] I like pounds, shillings and pence much better." This must have been a difficult lesson to teach for one so new to India, but doubtless she took it in her stride. Certainly Sr Christian seemed to have fallen in love with India despite the extremes of climate. "We had an awful storm yesterday, it lasted off and on from 12 to 9 p.m. Then it cleared off. When the children were all in bed I took my books and read in the south verandah. It was so lovely, the calm moon overhead and stars, and the trees outside perfectly motionless, and the little insect sounds with an occasional jackal the only sounds. I like India very much, perpetual summer, and the warmth and brilliant colouring, soft breezes and peaceful nights are all delightful, and after two months of a most unusually hot season I have not yet felt the heat too much."

Sr Christian's letter had begun by alluding to Sr Mary Agatha's failing health but at this stage there seemed to be no immediate cause for concern. It was well known that the climates of India and Africa were not good for the English constitution: it was in Kipling's words "the white man's burden" - part of the price of Empire. Thus Sr Mary Agatha made no reference to her health when she wrote to Clewer on May 25th 1884, a letter which was published in the autumn *St John Baptist Magazine*. "I returned to the school on Monday morning for a fresh term, and a very important one, as the Government Examination will take place at the close of it. We have such a nice full school, one full of boarders so that it makes us long more than ever for increased accommodation. However, we mean to *hope* and are sure we shall get what we want in time. Our large hall is just roofed and finished and looks so nice, all clean. We are going early tomorrow to arrange the new desks in it." So it seems as if some improvements had been made to the buildings even if they were not as ambitious as the Sisters would have liked.

Sr Mary Agatha went on to describe a girl who had just left the school - girls' education was still very new and largely unaccepted in India, and the Sisters had a mammoth task if they were to improve the long-term prospects of their pupils. "I started our first girl yesterday for a situation as a nurse," she wrote. "She was entirely homeless and destitute and we have been training her for this since Christmas... She has gone to a kind mistress who gives her clothes and good wages. She went off in great spirits all alone, 14 hours journey by train, but that is considered a short way here! When I speak of our girls going out as nurses I only mean those who have been so neglected that they could never learn enough to be teachers. Most of them ought to have a much better education than industrials,[(6)] and we shall, I hope, raise it by degrees as they get better grounded. We cannot be too thankful for the little improvement we do see in tone and character."

Sr Mary Agatha's health did not improve, and a second letter from Sr Christian (dated June 28th 1884), makes direct reference to it: "We are getting on very happily now. Sr Mary Agatha came down last Monday, much better but not strong yet - she is drinking port wine. Mrs C. and

Mrs N. have sent her some. She is at the Canning Home today and Sunday - it is really my "Sunday out" but we agreed she had better have it this time." It would seem that the decline in Sr Mary Agatha's health was of the type which afflicted many English people in India - nothing specific, just a general reaction to the climatic extremes.

Meanwhile, life at the school went on and standards gradually improved. It was not all work and no play as Sr Christian's letter of June 28th 1884 showed: "On Wednesday we had a grand expedition by way of keeping St John Baptist's day. We took all the children, 48 boarders, 15 day scholars, several old girls, and the teachers, to the number of 72 in 12 gharies [carriages] to the Zoological Gardens. Although the rainy season has begun we could not have had more perfect weather. The gardens are fairly extensive and beautifully laid out, quite throwing the Regent's Park gardens into the shade as regards trees etc. Such lovely groups of palms, fan palms, date palms, cocoa palms, in every graceful arrangement you can fancy, with creepers in every corner. The Baugainvillier [sic] is very common here, it grows like a weed. The animals are less noticeable than the vegetables in this particular Zoological Gardens. The carnivora house contains six melancholy tigers looking, as is natural, as if putting them in cages on their own native soil of Bengal was insult to injury. The monkey house is very good - one monkey has a human nose, really prominent - too hideous! There are ostriches and a few other birds, a giraffe and several rhinoceri, but the whole collection is but recently begun. Mr Buckland gave us leave to have a picnic there; so clothes were spread under a group of palms and the whole party had tea - and a very good one too. Sr L. [Lucy] and Sr S. [Sophia] joined us, and the Archdeacon came and brought Mrs K. and Mr and Mrs M. It was a most successful day."

Sr Christian's letter concluded with a reference to "May" the little four year old girl whom she had virtually adopted and to whom she had already referred in her letter of May 4th: "My 'little May' is much improved. I have, I think, enough money for her as the money they send me from home nearly pays her fees... But any money which friends could send out to the school to help pay for some poor Eurasians would be very much appreciated indeed. Eurasians are very poor as a rule, and they are in a very trying position, looked down upon by both races. There is *so* much work to do. I do long for an orphanage, a mixed one, Bengali, Eurasian and European, all mixed up together like a plum pudding. We want to obliterate race distinctions. We have four native girls in the school now."

The remark about obliterating race distinctions may of course be interpreted in two ways. It could mean an "Anglicising" process - turning the non-English races into pseudo-English (and Anglican) subjects of the Empire. This is what many of the Christian missions set out to do as part of the process of (so-called) civilisation; indigenous customs being regarded as heathen and inferior to those of the conquering race. Thus scantily clad "natives" were dressed up in western clothes, and the Gospel was preached to them as though God were an Englishman who spoke in the language of the *Book of Common Prayer*. The other interpretation is that Sr Christian was nurturing a healthy respect for the customs of her non-English pupils, and that she hoped to give them the best of her own culture and teaching, whilst also preserving the best in theirs. Records of the Pratt Memorial School were left behind after the Sisters' withdrawal from India in 1945, but it seems as though the Sisters attempted to preserve their pupils' indigenous customs whenever possible, whilst giving them the benefits of a good education. Thus a few years later when the Sisters took over a Bengali school, the English language took second place to Bengali, and the children retained their native costume and basic customs. Religious instruction was given at the Pratt Memorial School and regular Confirmations held - it was always a missionary enterprise. But the Sisters seem to have had a growing respect for India and its people which comes across refreshingly in their writings.

In the meantime all was not well with Sr Mary Agatha. The Community *Annals* have the following rather stark entry for September 23rd 1884: "Telegram from Sr Lucy at Calcutta said that Sr Mary Agatha was dangerously ill with fever. A second telegram on the 24th saying that Sr M.A. passed away at 11.00 p.m." Further details were provided in the autumn 1884 issue of the *St John Baptist Magazine*: "A fever which did not at first cause any apprehension gradually turned to typhoid, and after 21 days she sank quietly and peacefully into her Saviour's arms. It is the first death that has thinned our little band of Indian Sisters, but it is not without a real ground of thankfulness that so truly surrendered a life should have thus finished its course and left so blessed a memory as an offering to God in the great work of training up a people for the Lord in that vast heathen land."

The same issue contained a letter from a Sister identified only as Sr S. (probably Sr Sophia), who described the funeral which had to take place the next day because of the heat. "The next afternoon at 5.00. p.m. we were obliged to have the funeral. It is holiday time in Calcutta and the choir of the Cathedral and the organist are away, but Mr Brown[7] of the Oxford Mission kindly brought some of his boys. They were native Christians and all but three, sons of native clergymen. We had the first part of the burial office in our oratory, the coffin covered with our own pall was placed in the middle just opposite the altar. The Sisters knelt on each side and the bishop and clergy were in our stalls. Mrs Kitchin sent a lovely cross and wreath to put on the coffin. Mr Brown brought a wreath and his choirboys nosegays of flowers. Mr Brown said the service and the bishop gave the blessing at the grave. The Archdeacon,... and Mr Seal,... and several more followed her to the grave. The flowers on the altar were all white and we lighted the 6 tall candles. The procession to the grave was headed by the processional cross of the Oxford Mission, then about 10 of the choir, next Mr Brown, then the coffin carried by native Christian bearers, then we Sisters and the rest of the mourners. The cemetery is quite close, and as we got to it the choir sang "*Jerusalem the Golden*." In the next sentence the Sister contradicts herself and says: "It was such a long way I thought we should never get there! After the service was over they sang *Lights abode celestial Salem*, then the bishop gave the blessing and we all returned leaving our dear Sister's body to sleep till the Resurrection morning. The bishop offered to come and Celebrate for us the next morning, which he did."

The bishop had paid tribute to Sr Mary Agatha, describing her as: "a new power which has been brought to bear on the work." He noted that she was: "so cheerful, imparting brightness to all about her." He concluded: "I mean to persevere, believing that help will come to us. Ask all to pray earnestly that we may know God's will concerning this work. I seem to feel that the possession of that grave will be a blessing to us. It contains the first seed sown by the Community and it will bear fruit for India." Sr Mary Agatha's grave in the cemetery at Alipore, not far from the Lady Canning Home, was the first of a number over the years. The burden of India would take other lives from Clewer and break the health of even more.

The bishop's faith in the work was not unfounded. The mantle of Sr Mary Agatha fell onto Sr Christian and the school went from strength to strength. In a letter published in the Easter 1885 issue of the *St John Baptist Magazine* she wrote joyously: "I have just this instant heard that the new house is at last taken on a three years lease to be renewed. Oh I am so thankful! Think, of having an Oratory... and such *lots* of schoolrooms." The new building was near to the old one on the Lower Circular Road and the actual move took place on May 15th and 16th 1885. It was, by all accounts an eventful two days, as the Sister graphically described: "Orders had been given to our Chuprassie [messenger] to procure 20 coolies. Accordingly before daylight on the 15th, 20 black coolies in the scantiest possible attire were sprawling asleep on the grass beneath the pipal trees. It was the day of the Confirmation so we could not begin until 9.o'clock. The order of the day was as follows - I took up my station in the new house with a teacher, the matron remained in the old one, and our outdoor servant scurried about splendidly. It is really wonderful to see huge wardrobes, pianos, heavy school desks, [and] dining room tables going along on the coolies heads. Each article I saw put into its place, and then each coolie received a ticket which would entitle him at the close of the day to 2 pice, little more than a $^1/_2$d."

The Sister then went on to describe the dedication ceremony: "We decorated the... new Chapel with palm branches. Mr A. W.[8] lent us some plants in pots to group about the altar, Mr N. gave us two lovely caladeums and several ladies sent flowers for the altar. It looked really very well. At 5.30 our friends came and we had quite a nice little procession. I caught and trained a boy living near to carry the banner in front. Then followed the children (24 who remain at school during the holidays), in white frocks and the uniform red sashes. Then the Sisters (7 of us), then Mr Brown carrying the processional cross, then 7 or 8 priests including 3 native clergy, then the bishop's chaplain carrying the crozier. Lastly the bishop [followed by] the visitors."

Associates in England with no experience of India might have found Sr Christian's description of the building rather unusual, but it was all due to the hot, humid and often very wet climate which dictated building styles. "The house has no passages at all," she wrote, "nor any front door or hall. This sounds odd, but the portico where carriages drive up runs alongside the verandah into which the lower rooms open, and the stairs are there leading to the upper verandah into which all the upper rooms open. The oratory [chapel] was a large bathroom. One end I have had raised 6 inches to form a sanctuary, and the whole is matted. There are three windows at each side and it is connected by a bamboo and tile covered passage with the house."

The new house soon proved too small for the fast growing school. Writing in the *St John Baptist Magazine* for Autumn 1886 in a letter dated April 4th 1886, Sr Christian noted that: "We are very full - four more than the House will really hold. I want to move the 'little ones' into the old Pratt School, but it will involve additional expense unless the numbers become more overpowering. They will!" So it was a case of turn and turn about with the overflow moving back to the old premises. "The move to the old Pratt School has come to pass, five new children of one family [with] ages from 4 to 16 came yesterday with two bullock carts laden with their almirahs [a type of wardrobe], and their chest of drawers. So I moved ten children and two teachers, engaged a fourth ayah, [nursemaid] and two bheestis, [water-carriers] and saw them safely settled before night. It was all done in one day and that being Easter Even! You may imagine that I was weary when I got to bed!"

The work at the Pratt School continued to prosper and meet a well established need amongst the Anglo-Indian community. But there were other categories of children in need - low caste Indians and European orphans. Now it seemed as though the horizon of the Sisters' work was about to widen still further to embrace these children.

Footnotes

1. Hariot, Marchioness of Dufferin and Ava. Her husband, Frederick was Viceroy from 1883-8. She was a tireless worker for nursing and medical care for Indian women, having initially been asked by Queen Victoria to do something about this. The *National Association for supplying Female Medical Aid to the Women of India* soon became known as the *Countess of Dufferin Fund*. Hospitals and dispensaries were founded in every province by the time she left India. She has been described by Mark Bence-Jones in his book *The Viceroys of India* as the perfect Vicereine, and her departure at the end of her husband's term of office was widely lamented. She had a rare talent for breaking down the snobbery and pseudo-grandeur of Imperial officials, especially the memsahibs, and managed to put all at ease. She outlived her husband and sons, dying in 1936 aged 93.

2. DUFFERIN AND AVA, Marchioness of. *Our Viceregal life in India: Selections from my journal, 1884-8.* 2 vols. John Murray 1889.

This extract from Vol. 1 p.33.

3. ibid. Vol. 1 p.36.

Lady Dufferin was not the only Vicereine to be favourably impressed by the Medical College and Eden Hospitals. On Friday January 29th 1899, Lady Curzon made a similar visit and wrote to her family: "I went to two hospitals and to a Nurses' hostel this morning. Colonel Fenn and Lord Suffolk went with me, and Colonel Harris, the Head of the Medical College, took us all over that Hospital, and Dr Joubert took us over the Eden Hospital, and Miss Taylor took us over the hostel for Nurses who are training for the Dufferin Fund. The streets between Government House and the Medical College Hospital were crowded to see us pass. It was very hot indeed, and the beautiful cool stone-floored wards of the Eden Hospital were wonderfully comfortable." (Quoted from: *Lady Curzon's India: Letters of a Vicereine* ed. John Bradley page 28).

4. Sr Cuthbert. Despite the gloomy entry in the Community *Annals*, Sr Cuthbert does not seem to have died from her illness. The manuscript list of Sisters in India in the Clewer archives records her homeward passage as taking place on April 20th 1886 aboard the P. &. O S.S. Ballarat.

5. In 1882 Indian currency was calculated thus:

1 pie (p) = 1/2 farthing

3 pie = 1 pice (ps) = 1 1/2 farthings

8 pie = 1 penny

12 pie (or 4 pice) = 1 anna (A) = 1 1/2 pence

16 annas = 1 rupee (R) = 2 shillings

16 rupees = 1 gold mohur (G.M.) = £1/12/-.

(Source: *Bengal Directory* 1882.)

6. Industrials were girls trained for domestic work. In England at this time an "industrial girl" would be living in a House of Mercy or orphanage such as those run by the Clewer Sisters and would learn all that was necessary for earning a living in domestic service. In writing of "industrials" Sr Mary Agatha is harking back to her Clewer days, but her readers would know exactly what she meant by using such a term.

7. Mr Brown of the Oxford Mission. Revd Ernest Brown one of the original Oxford Mission brothers who became Superior in 1898 and lived until 1933.

8. Mr A.W. This is possibly the Hon. Alex Wilson, husband of Isabella Wilson, of the Ladies' Committee of the Lady Canning Home.

-7-
FRAIL CHILDREN OF DUST

In June 1885 Community of St John Baptist agreed to take over the European Female Orphanage Asylum in Calcutta. This had been founded in 1815 by Mrs Sherwood, the wife of an army officer and the author of "improving" children's stories in the genre of *Little Henry and his bearer.* The object was to provide a home and education for the orphans of British soldiers of the East India Company. With the demise of the Company orphans of civilians were also taken, or children with one parent living, but preference was still given to army children. It is not absolutely clear whether both parents had to be of European origin, certainly many of the children in an existing photograph appear to be of mixed race. The home was governed from the outset by a Ladies' Committee which was the state of affairs when the Clewer Sisters agreed to take over.

Since 1817 the European Orphanage had been housed in a fine looking building on the Lower Circular Road. When the new Pratt Memorial School was opened these two Community works were conveniently opposite one another. Set in a large walled compound with lawns, flower gardens and a large pond, the orphanage looked very imposing with its wide colonnaded verandah at first floor level giving it a stately appearance. But as already noted in chapter 2, many of these impressive buildings were very badly constructed.

This additional work meant that more Sisters were needed and so on January 11th 1886 Sr Sophie, together with Miss Parsons who was to be governess, sailed from Liverpool aboard the *S.S. Mira* [sic]. After a good voyage without incident, they arrived in Calcutta on February 8th. It was a case of being thrown straight in at the deep end if Sr Sophie's letter to the Clewer Associates is anything to go by: "Till Sr Annie and Sr Honora go to Darjeeling we have Sr Eleanor Isabel here. She is invaluable as we have eight children down with Scarlatina and she is nursing them. When she goes back to the Canning Home I shall have to look to the angels and your re-doubled prayers at home to help me with these delightful, affectionate, unruly children. It is a week today that I arrived and we are gradually getting into shape."

Sr Sophie seems to have settled down very quickly amongst her charges. Writing on April 7th 1886 she says: "We are getting on very happily in this work. The children are very interesting and intelligent. We have 6 candidates for the Confirmation next week. They are very much in earnest. Sr Christian will bring her children over too" [i.e. from the Pratt School]. A gate has been made in our wall just opposite the Pratt School so that we are not much further off from each other than St John's Home is from the House of Mercy" [at Clewer]. In fact eight children were Confirmed from the Pratt School with the orphans.

But it was not all work and no play. On Sundays Sr Sophie was able to visit Sr Christian at the Pratt Memorial School. "Sr Sophie comes over to tea here every Sunday," wrote Sr Christian on April 4th 1886. "Then we sit out on the verandah in the starlight and talk, and then say Compline and Lauds together... As soon as the sun is down we have a hanging lamp hung in the middle of the verandah and we sit out beyond. This is on Sundays; other days we have no time. We have flowers and shrubs all round, palms and scented verbena, and just now two lovely white lilies."

The children had treats too, just as they did in England. "The children have an omnibus belonging to this Home and periodically we are allowed to send for two horses to take eighteen children and two teachers for a drive," wrote Sr Sophie on April 7th 1886. "We have to go in three detachments. These drives took place last week. We went to the Zoological Gardens which are very pretty and with lovely palms; but the animals are very poor, all except the splendid tigers. Next we went along the river and all the ships made me feel very near England."

Occasionally there was an extra special treat such as the one recorded by Sr Sophie in the Easter 1888 number of the *St John Baptist Magazine.* Admiral Sir Frederick Richards had visited the orphanage and had been very impressed. He repaid the Sisters' hospitality with an invitation to visit his ship the *Bacchante.* "The Admiral took us through his own cabins, and the Captain and some of the officers followed his example. Then we had a sumptuous tea, the Admiral and the officers waiting on the children and enjoying it as much as they did... After tea there was a tug-of-war and then we were all photographed by one of the officers. A good band was playing off and on, and dancing became irresistible. Before I could look round, some of the officers, quite old men, were dancing with the little ones. Soon after sunset I gave the signal for departure to the great regret of the dancers. "God save the Queen" was sung, and then a hearty "Thank you, Sir" and we were conducted to our gharies by the Admiral and nearly all the officers... On Saturday the *Bacchante* sailed for Italy, and the day before, the Admiral came to bid us farewell. As he left he gave me an envelope which contained, I afterwards found, 100 rupees to 'give the children a treat'. The elder girls wrote him a letter of thanks ..."

So it would seem that all was well, but there had been rumblings below the surface which had exploded early in 1887. Sr Lucy had concluded the negotiations for the management of the orphanage but had nothing in writing. Everything between herself and the Ladies' Committee had passed in the manner of a gentlewoman's agreement. This was unsatisfactory because her own health was failing, and members of the Committee were likely to come and go. In June 1885 the Community Chapter at Clewer had voted in favour of taking up the work with a majority of 18; 53 Sisters had been present. But they had stipulated that the Sisters were to exercise control over the secular matron and governess, as well as the correction, discipline and religious instruction of the children. In short, the Sisters did not want any interference from the Ladies' Committee. This was totally in keeping with their policy back home: the Community never undertook work without first understanding the terms under which they were invited, *and* they always made their own terms clear. This had been one of the principles upon which Mother Harriet, the foundress, had stood firm. This is not to suggest that the Community had free rein in their work; there was usually some sort of Committee or Council which governed them, and as a rule it consisted of clergy and laymen. Such bodies were not always easy to work with[1] but the Sisters usually managed to effect a working relationship. Ladies' Committees were another matter especially in India where rivalry between the memsahibs was exacerbated by heat, boredom and imperial etiquette.

In a letter dated April 4th 1887 to Mrs Kitchin, a member of the Ladies' Committee, Sr Lucy explained how the difficulty had arisen: "Unfortunately you were not on the Committee at the time when we accepted the charge ... I am sure that the negotiations were all conducted viva voce as far as I was concerned, so that I have no written documents to refer to... I prepared a memo according to my instructions from home, which required that the position and powers of the Sisters should be accurately defined, as they could not be expected to submit to the surveillance which it might be thought right to exercise over an ordinary matron and governess, as well as the correction and religious instruction and discipline of the children, giving rewards and punishments with every other detail I could think of at the time... I mentioned cases in England where we had taken charge, and it was agreed that certain rules should remain in abeyance while in connection with our Community, and suggested something of the kind for the European Female Orphanage Asylum. The page was turned to and I was told that those rules would not re-appear, they were done away with. I was satisfied and thought no more of the matter till a few weeks ago when I was speaking of our position to the Sisters and, turning to the Report to explain it, I found the rules had never been removed, but stood as in the day of the matron..."

Such a grave mistake obviously had to be put right and Sr Lucy continued: "I have felt very troubled about this misunderstanding as I committed our Community to a work under conditions they would never have accepted, against which I was specially cautioned. I am not asking for any change at present, but I wish you to know that I protest against the rules as they stand. I believe the Ladies now in the Committee are our very good friends, but they may go away and a fresh set come in who might be antagonistic and you can see how very disagreeable they might make it, for there is no safeguard as to the election of new members, nor have the Sisters any voice in the matter. I remember among the many questions I was asked at those preliminary negotiations if there would be any means of getting rid of us if it was so desired, so I may as well repeat what I said then, that if at any time the Committee agreed that they would prefer a different management, we should be ready to go on the shortest possible notice."

Mrs Kitchin replied somewhat curtly on April 7th asking Sr Lucy to state in writing exactly which rules she wished the Committee to alter. The Sister replied in a letter dated April 9th, only part of a copy of which has survived. "...I specially object to Rule 2[2] because it gives to the Ladies the superintendence of all that the Sisters should naturally superintend, and such double management is at once inconvenient and impractical. If the Ladies wish to keep in their own hands all that may belong to the general Executive Management then the Sisters are better out of the way. If the Sisters undertake it then it becomes a work of supererogation for the Ladies. I should therefore wish that Rule 2 be omitted, also Rules 7 and 8 which relate to the Visiting Members. I hope no one will think that I wish to discourage the visits of the Ladies. On the contrary, I attach the greatest value to their personal interest in the work and in the individual children, and to their advice and experience. They will be an assistance and support to the Sisters who would turn to them in any emergency. We do want their help and sympathy, but we do not want their permanent regular inspection. We should endeavour, as far as possible, to carry out the work on the old lines which are excellently planned."

All's well that ends well - the Committee having duly met, Mrs Kitchin replied much more warmly in a letter dated April 14th 1887, which began "My dear Sr Lucy," and ended "Yours affectionately." A compromise had been arrived at whereby the offensive rules had been altered though not omitted completely. A note from Sr Lucy concludes the saga: "I did not keep a copy of my answer, but I said I should be quite satisfied with the alterations proposed[3] as that would secure to the Sisters the independence that their position required, that I was sure the Ladies would have no cause to regret having given us this authority as we should endeavour, as far as possible, to carry out their wishes and the intentions of the founders." It may all seem like a storm in a tea cup but important principles were at stake. Sr Lucy had won her corner, even though she still appeared reluctant to keep written copies of business matters.

In spite of the confusion about rules and terms of reference the work seemed to proceed happily enough. Letters home to Clewer written by Sr Sophie and subsequently published in the *St John Baptist Magazine* give a favourable view of life at the orphanage. Inevitably there was an "Englishness" about it all, but at least these were European orphans, and not indigenous Indians whom the Sisters were attempting to Anglicise. This Englishness is particularly obvious in Sr Sophie's description of the prize giving ceremony in a letter dated January 2nd 1887. Thousands of ceremonies such as this were taking place simultaneously throughout the British Empire from Clewer to Calcutta:

"The giving away of the prizes to the children took place yesterday. Lady Rivers Thomson gave the prizes as Lady Dufferin was unable to come. The bishop was present. All went off very well. We had prayers in the chapel first, and hymns, and the children sang well. After the service the whole company went up to the grandly decorated schoolroom where the bishop, Lady Thomson, Archdeacon and Mrs Atlay, and Mr Mitchell [sat] at the table where the prizes were laid. Eva Kennedy got the prize for good conduct (a watch), and Jessie Ross the prize for Scripture lessons. After this part of the programme was ended, Ruby (the baby child) and I led the way to the playroom where two of the kind ladies had prepared a Christmas tree round which the children stood delighted, singing their carols "Noel, Noel" and "Good King Wencleslaus". Then followed a sumptuous tea with pink and white towers of cake. Many of the visitors stayed for it and waited upon the children."

1887 was the year of Queen Victoria's Golden Jubilee, an event which was perhaps more meaningful to the Sisters than to their young charges. Even so it was an excuse for more parties and the Empire celebrated in style. On February 20th Sr Sophie reported that: "There have been grand doings here this last week for the Jubilee of the Empress. They saw more at the Canning Home than we did here. We only saw the illuminations from the top of our house on the Thursday night, and certainly it was more like what one might imagine fairyland to be than anything I ever saw. Last Wednesday was the children's Jubilee Day; about 7,000 children met on the Maidan to greet the arrival of the Viceroy and Lady Dufferin. Our children were invited also... They had been wrongly told that 30,000 children were to sing "God save the Queen" on the Maidan and one remarked quite seriously, 'Oh, then they will hear it in England won't they Sister'."

Trouble with the buildings necessitated a temporary evacuation from the end of January 1887 until the end of March. Fortunately the Pratt School was able to provide accommodation so that too great an upheaval was avoided. "It is rather a squeeze but being the cold season it does not matter much," commented Sr Sophie stoically. There was a good relationship between the school and the orphanage which was further cemented in 1893 when the orphans over eight years of age began attending the Pratt School as day pupils. Children under eight continued to receive their schooling at the orphanage.

Sometimes diplomacy had to be employed in dealing with well-meaning English Associates who wished to support the work but did not always find out the best means of doing so. Thus in the Easter 1888 number of the *St John Baptist Magazine* Sr Sophie tackled the difficult question of clothing (and also gave a pen portrait of how the children dressed): "Now about the children's clothing which it is so difficult to supply with the very small sum we are allowed for it. Cast off things would not do for them for they wear a uniform; dark blue serge frocks and white calico aprons, [with] pinafores for the little ones in the winter (three months out of the twelve); the rest of the year white unbleached calico frocks. They look very nice, fresh and clean. The younger children are obliged to have clean frocks every day, so one piece of calico is soon used up, but it is the cheapest thing we can get. We must make the frocks here to fit the children, but we should be most grateful for undergarments or quite plain pinafores, or aprons with a bib; also of unbleached calico and no trimming of any kind."

The European Orphanage was a work of great necessity and was undertaken by the Sisters as a work of mercy. Doubtless they were strict, and institutional life must have been hard at times. But such records as have survived seem to testify to a well-run Home where the children were well cared for, given a good Christian upbringing and a start in life. An existing photograph shows a group of healthy looking, well groomed young women and girls, as well as small boys.

By 1888 the Sisters' work in Calcutta was thriving, but Sr Lucy's health was giving cause for concern. These two factors prompted the Mother Superior at Clewer (Mother Jane Frances) to make a visit to India. She had always been supportive of the work and when she came to India she fell in love with it. But before we look at her visit which was to alter the whole course of her life in the Community, we must first look at another important branch of the Indian work - Darjeeling.

Footnotes

1. For examples of difficulties encountered by the Sisters in England with Councils see BONHAM, Valerie *A Place in Life* pp. 174, 216, 260.

2. The Rules to which Sr Lucy objected were appended to the correspondence but were written with a thick pen on very thin paper making legibility difficult. Insofar as they can be deciphered they were as follows:

> Number 2. "The Ladies forming this Committee take charge of the superintendence of the Institution comprehending all matters which usually falls under the heads of Education, Religion, Expenditure and [? 1 word] conditions of the children, giving rewards or censures whatever [? 1 word] belong to the general Executive Management."
>
> Number 7. "Four members of the Committee are to be invested as Visiting Members for the Institution in rotation, not however to the prevention of other members for the frequent attendance of the members of the Committee and shall have opportunity [? 1 word] materially contribute to the prosperity of the Institution, but to secure some permanent regular inspection of the establishment."
>
> Number 8. "Such remarks and observations of the Visiting Members as may [? 1 word] the management of the Institution shall be submitted to the monthly meeting and communicated after full discussion through the Committee by the Secretary to the Sisters."

3. The amended Rules were as follows:

> Number 2. "The Ladies forming this Committee take charge of the superintendence of the Institution, but they submit the general internal Executive Management to the Sister Superior of the Community of St John Baptist, Clewer."
>
> Number 7. The rule ends with "prevention of other members."
>
> Number 8. Ends with "the Sister Superior" instead of "the Sisters."

-8-
TO THE HILLS

The British soon discovered that summer in the plains of India was unbearable - the rigours of heat, dust and monsoon, combined with vicious disease-bearing insects claimed many lives before they had outlived their prime. Small wonder then, that between 1815 and 1947 that peculiarly British creation, the hill station came into its own. Over 80 grew up from the foothills of the Himalayas in the north, to the Nilgiri Hills in the south. All were different in detail, yet all were the same in ethos - a little England in India. Mussoorie, Naini Tal, Murree and Simla in the north; Poona and Mahabaleshwar in the west; Ootacamund in the south. But arguably the finest, exceeding even Simla, was Darjeeling with its view straight across to Kanchenjunga, and even (if one is awake early enough and the skies clear enough), a glimpse of Everest.

Built along a spiny ridge 7,000 feet above sea level and about 380 miles from Calcutta, it was an incredibly inaccessible place. The ridge had been ceded from the Maharajah of Sikkim in order to establish a sanatorium [health resort] for servants of the East India Company, the deal being completed on February 1st 1835. From then onwards Darjeeling had developed layer upon layer in a kind of terrace arrangement, always susceptible to landslips. Tea-planting, so synonymous with Darjeeling, was only introduced into the area in 1841, tea plants having been found growing wild in Assam in 1820. The introduction of the plants to the Darjeeling area was to transform the whole countryside as well as establish a thriving industry. Thence the hill station would be the resort not only of weary servants of Company or Raj, but also of planters needing rest and recuperation. But all yearned for home - a sentiment which was reflected in the English sounding house and street names, and the esplanade leading to the town centre complete with its bandstand, public gardens, and buildings such as the Post Office, Library and Club. Above all, the hill stations were green - trees, leaves, grass, all abounded, unlike parched Calcutta which was (at its hottest time), 30 degrees Fahrenheit hotter than Darjeeling. But the greenery was bought at a price: Darjeeling was wetter than most hill stations. Nor had all the nuisances been left behind in Calcutta. A Victorian book on housekeeping(1) complained that the leeches and ticks "are a perfect pest."

Hill stations were not simply the resort of a few individuals who could not stand the heat of the plains. Each hot season the entire government of India embarked on an exodus from Calcutta to Simla 1,170 miles away. It has been said(2) that Hannibal's army crossing the Alps had nothing to compare with the British Raj ascending to its summer retreat! Certainly the logistics of such an exercise were of nightmarish proportions(3). It was Sir John Lawrence[4] who, in 1863, decided on the annual trek and it thence became part of the way of life despite complaints from some quarters, notably those who had to bear the brunt of the actual move. But others enjoyed it. The irrepressible Lady Dufferin declared that once she was in the hills she got into quite a "tally-ho" frame of mind. In 1888 her husband had built the vast Viceregal Lodge at Simla, five storeys high and furnished by Maples of London. Because it was the seat of the government of India from March to October every year, there was a certain air of officialdom about Simla which Darjeeling lacked. Even so, most of the larger hill stations hosted their regional government, Darjeeling being the centre for the Lieutenant Governor of Bengal and his minions for four months each year.

Darjeeling was a singularly inaccessible place and early travellers had to cope with a combination of horseback and bullock cart. In 1861 a cart road from Siliguri to Darjeeling was begun by military engineers and completed in 1869. The idea of a steam tramway was first suggested by Sir Ashley Eden, and work commenced in 1879 following roughly the same course as the cart road. The tramway was opened in March 1880 to coincide with the visit of the Viceroy, Lord Lytton[5]. At that time it reached only as far as Tindharia, but in 1881 it was extended to Darjeeling and henceforth was known as the Darjeeling Himalayan Railway. This was the first mountain railway to be built in India and it still functions. It consists of 82 km of narrow gauge track (0.610 m. or 2 ft wide), and in order to save building tunnels employs a system of loops and zigzags to negotiate the steep gradients. In all there are three loops, one figure eight, and four zigzags. The cart road still exists, crossing and recrossing the railway, and hanging onto the hairpin bends in a precarious way. As late as the 1920s the journey from Calcutta took anything up to two days.

The Darjeeling Himalayan Railway has fascinated all who have ever travelled on it and Lady Dufferin was no exception. She described a journey made on Wednesday March 16th 1887[6]: "I had a special train consisting of a tiny engine, two small carriages, and 2 trollies, or open trucks. We sat in one of these last, so that we could see the view, not only of the magnificent mountains, but also of the front part of our own little train... [The railway] is a 2 ft gauge [and] you climb 8,000 ft right through the mountain, turning and twisting, and running after your own tail; playing hide-and-go-seek, as it were, with different parts of the train; rushing under a bridge, and then sweeping round in a loop and going over it; sometimes stopping suddenly and going backwards on another line, then in a few moments forward again up a higher road, and then looking back from some point at the three lines forming the zigzag you have just accomplished."

On November 18th 1882 the Community Chapter met at Clewer and decided to accept the offer of work at the Eden Sanatorium in Darjeeling: the work was actually begun on April 21st 1883, but the negotiations had been going on since the previous June. The first overture was an informal letter to Sr Lucy from Dr Charles H. Joubert, Secretary to the Hospital Committee, dated June 26th 1882. Dr Joubert explained that he was writing in a private capacity to explore the possibility of the Sisters working at the hospital, and that if Sr Lucy thought there was any chance he would put a formal proposal to the Committee. There would be a resident medical officer, who would probably be an apothecary; the Sister would fill the role of matron and probably provide some nursing, although Dr Joubert thought that as most patients would be convalescent, the need for nursing would not be great. Evidently Sr Lucy's response was positive because she received another letter dated July 1st in which Dr Joubert promised to see the President of the Committee and the Lieutenant Governor with a view to a formal proposal being made.

However there were practical problems which had to be overcome. Firstly, there was the question of finance. The Sisters' passages for the Calcutta hospital work were paid for by the government of India, but passages for extra work such as that in the schools, had to be paid for by the Community at Clewer.(7) It would seem reasonable to expect government funding for the passage of the Sister undertaking this work which was the brainchild of the Lieutenant Governor of Bengal, Sir Ashley Eden. In an undated letter to Sr Lucy (but which "fits" into the sequence of correspondence at the very end of June or the beginning of July), Dr Joubert told her that the Committee seemed: "quite in favour of the proposal, provided that the government is not put to the expense of bringing the Sister out. At present the hospital could hardly afford to advance the amount necessary as we are depending on public subscriptions for the furnishing and equipment of the hospital."

Secondly, there was the question of the philosophy which governed the running of the sanatorium. In England the Sisters ran several hospitals and convalescent homes(8) where the emphasis was on caring for the poor. Some patients were poorer than others, thus many were free cases whose treatment was subsidised, although all patients were given the same quality of care and diet. But it was impossible to compare the Eden Sanatorium, which was intended for tea planters and Raj officials, with the hospitals back home. A brochure which was written by Sir Ashley Eden in 1881 explained the aims and objectives of the new Sanatorium:

"Now that the tramway has been brought into Darjeeling, and that the sanatorium is placed in direct and easy communication with Calcutta and with most of the civil stations of Bengal, and now that tea planters from the unhealthy Dovars and Terai [regions] can reach the station easily and without exposure in a few hours, the question of providing a good, well organised European hospital for the comfortable reception of patients and convalescents from the plains forces itself upon the consideration of government. Representations [have already been] received regarding hospital accommodation for sick persons and convalescents connected with the Eastern Bengal Railway, the Northern Bengal Railway and the Darjeeling Tramway, and it appears that if nothing else be done, some arrangement must at once be made in communication with the managers of those lines for supplying a great and growing need of this sort. But as Darjeeling increases… we shall have to provide hospital accommodation for the permanent residents of the station and district."

Sir Ashley continued: "There are the tea planters and their assistants scattered about all over the district, some of them placed in very unhealthy situations, cases in which young men are brought in suffering from a fever of a severe type. [These cases] are very common. And a difficulty is frequently found in providing them with accommodation during their illness. The hotels and boarding houses are generally full and a sick person is not always a welcome inmate in a public establishment of that sort, and it is found that many useful men have lost their lives in the Dovars and the Terai [regions] who would at once have come up for treatment if a comfortable hospital existed for their reception. Then again, there are many cases of persons residing in outlying plantations who desire attendance during their confinement, who can only obtain it at an enormous expense altogether beyond their means, and who are not within reach of the civil surgeon. [Such] cases are not unknown in which it has been found impossible to procure accommodation… But besides these there are frequent cases in the Mofussil stations [outlying countryside] of persons pulled down after severe sickness or suffering from obstinate disease who are unable to take the change to sea which richer persons could afford, and for whom a change and careful medical attendance are absolutely necessary. There are also persons who could undergo operations in the cool climate of the hills which they could not bear in the heat of the plains. Lastly, there are patients convalescing in the Calcutta hospitals to whom a change to a convalescent ward in Darjeeling would be of the utmost importance… As a European hospital has to be built, we should not only keep in mind the requirements of Darjeeling but also of the province generally."

Sir Ashley was adamant about payment. "I do not wish the hospital to be a charity hospital. It should pay its expenses, the building once having been provided and equipped. I am disposed to give a grant from Provincial Services of 50,000 to 60,000 rupees for the purpose of establishing the hospital, providing such a hospital is erected as shall afford accommodation to invalids from all parts of the Lower Provinces; the fees should be so fixed that they afford a reasonable prospect of the hospital covering its expenses."

This brochure had been sent to Sr Lucy by Dr Joubert and it had definitely whetted her appetite. At the same time (the end of June 1882), a formal offer of the work had been made, though the practicalities were still being worked out, not least obtaining sanction from the Clewer Chapter which met twice a year. Unfortunately, the matter had missed the June Chapter which meant that it had to wait until November. However, there were still two unresolved matters - the Sisters' passages to India, and the question of free cases. Both were addressed rather unsatisfactorily by Dr Joubert in a letter dated July 11th 1882: "I am sure we should be glad to have two Sisters instead of one," he wrote. "The food of the second one would not be a matter of importance and I am sure would be sanctioned by the Committee… If you think there would not be a difficulty about the passage out, I think we may almost count on having some of your Community to work with us." As to free cases he remained immovable: "You speak of free cases. The charge for third class cases has purposely been put low so as to meet the circumstances of poor people. A hospital like this must either be entirely free or entirely paying, but I have no doubt we shall often have patients in the third class ward who are paid for by friends, though apparently to the other inmates of the ward, paying as themselves. We shall certainly get occasional acute cases and operations, though not many."

Meanwhile Bishop Johnson of Calcutta was enthusiastic about the project. In a letter dated July 12th 1882 he wrote: "I do indeed rejoice to hear of the offer made to you from Darjeeling and most heartily approve… I am especially thankful to hear that the Lieutenant Governor welcomes the proposal that the hospital should be placed under your charge." This was confirmed by Dr Joubert in a letter to Sr Lucy dated July 25th 1882: "At a meeting of the hospital Committee held yesterday I laid before [them] my correspondence with you on the subject of a Sister being appointed as 'Lady Superintendent' or 'Sister in Charge' in place of matron, as originally proposed. My proposal was received with great favour and I have been directed by the Committee to ask you to use your best endeavours to secure for the Darjeeling hospital the services of two Sisters. In [that] event… the Committee now also proposes to allot the sum of 1,000 rupees for passage money and expenses from England to India. One of the members of the Committee, Mr Curtis, will write to the principle proprietor of the Star Line, a friend of his, asking him to obtain a special reduction of the passage money so as to bring the expenses of the passage out within the means of the new hospital… What we offer I may sum up as - quarters, board, fuel, lighting and washing for two Sisters, with one salary of 50 rupees per season… We ask you to do your best in endeavouring to carry out the arrangement."

Building problems had prevented the Sanatorium from opening until Monday April 23rd 1883. Dr Joubert had referred to these difficulties several times in his letters. It seems that the roof had not been completed before the rains began and the interior had got very wet - hardly a healthy start for a convalescent hospital. A contemporary photograph shows a large two-storeyed building with wide verandahs at both levels giving the place a rather exotic appearance. This is further enhanced by the tall chimneys and pointed turrets - the latter may be ventilation shafts. The ground appears to fall away leaving the building perched quite precariously on a small hill. The Sanatorium could accommodate 60 patients, all of whom were European. In 1887 a similar institution, known as the Lowis Jubilee Sanatorium, was opened for Indian patients.

The Clewer records are unclear as to which Sisters first went to work at Darjeeling, although they may have been Sr Annie and Sr Sybil who left England aboard the *S.S. Mira* [sic] on February 3rd 1883, and despite a great storm in the Bay of Biscay had arrived safely at Calcutta on March 9th. This had brought the number of Sisters in India to a total of 10. The Sisters were quite thrilled with the journey to Darjeeling just as Lady Dufferin was to be four years later, and they sent an account home which was published in the Autumn 1883 number of the *St John Baptist Magazine*:

"About 8 o'clock on Saturday morning April 21st [1883], we saw our first peep of the hills, so lovely, blue and misty, with the very flat low country between them and the train. About 9.30 we reached Tilligori [sic] and must leave the Bengal railway and travel on the Darjeeling and Himalayan tramway. Our route lay along open fields with a grand view of the hills on either side, then through a jungle of high grass, trees and ferns looking impassable. Now the mountains looked lovely - all wooded, the sun lighting them up, and their crests disappearing into the clouds. Through a big forest we tore along till the train began to go up the mountains. Up and up we steamed in a zigzag fashion, round corners, along the sides of dells, and over the tops of trees. The mountain ranges were rising one on top of the other, round and round the corners we turned, and snakelike, could see the tail of the train rushing round after us. The engineering of the line is quite marvellous - 50 miles, up 8,000 feet of mountains, along precipices shelving down perpendicularly. The mountains were now covered with a dense white fog. It felt chilly and we began to put on our thick wraps and to cover ourselves with knitted shawls. The sun was still shining on the tops of the mountains, which looked like islands standing out of the mist and fog. Suddenly we turned around a corner and the fogs were gone,... merely a thin blue mountain mist through which the landscape could be clearly seen, and there dotted about all over the hill lay Darjeeling. The temperature was 58 degrees Fahrenheit, so different from Calcutta by quite 30 degrees."

The Sisters went on to describe the various races of people in Darjeeling who were quite different from the inhabitants of Bengal. "The *Sepcha* [is] armed with a long knife which serves equally for plough, toothpick and tableknife. [They carry] a bamboo bow and poisoned arrows, [and are] loaded with necklaces of cornelian, amber and torquoise. The *Limboos* [are from] East Nepal. [They are] slender and sinewy, [and] do not plait their hair or wear ornaments. [Then there are] the wild, black uncouth-looking people of Tibet, who, wrapped in loose blanket robes, and wearing silver ear rings set with turquoise and amulets on the neck and arms could be seen on their way to the bazaar. First comes a middle aged man or woman driving a little black yak who grunts under his load of salt, besides pots, pans and kettles, stools, churns and bamboo vessels, keeping up a constant rattle, and amongst all these is a baby sucking a lump of cheese curd. The men and women follow in due order amidst sheep and goats each with its two little bags of salt. Beside these stalks a huge bull headed mastiff loaded like the rest, a bushy tail thrown over his back, a thick collar of scarlet wool around his neck and shoulders."

The Sisters who worked in India soon became accustomed to the presence of other religions all around them which they viewed with a combination of abhorrence and interest: abhorrence at their non-Christian nature, and interest at their often colourful customs which were so unlike anything the Sisters had seen before. So the presence of a Buddhist temple quite close to the Sanatorium provoked the following comments: "The temple at the foot of the Sanatorium hill awakens us at sunrise daily by three bells ringing, conch shells blowing, tambourines and thigh bone trumpets sounding, one against the other, for a quarter of an hour. The head of the lamas lived at Sikkim, but since the large temple has been built at Darjeeling, the head lama and his monks have removed here, and they have built a monastery for the various dependants [and] lay brothers... The dependants carry water and wood and cultivate the land; the lay brothers are good workmen and are sometimes hired out as labourers, house builders and decorators."

The *St John Baptist Magazines* are full of the comings and goings of Sisters to and from India so that it is difficult to keep track of who worked there and for how long. An emergency might mean the temporary withdrawal of a Sister from one place to another, or she might be invalided home. Thus Sr Honora who arrived in Calcutta on February 26th 1885 was despatched to Darjeeling where she worked at the Sanatorium until August 1887 when she was invalided home "by the preremtory orders of the doctors." She left Calcutta aboard the *S.S. Capella* on August 25th and arrived home on October 3rd, her health being greatly restored during the voyage. Nor did it mean that a Sister who was invalided home would not return to India if she recovered sufficiently. Thus in November 1894 Sr Honora returned to India and stayed until March 1900. Others reached the end of their term and went home on furlough, only to return a few months later, rested and ready for another three or five years.

During her time at Darjeeling Sr Honora wrote an account of the work there which, though undated, was published in the *St John Baptist Magazine* of Easter 1888. It gives an insight into prevailing attitudes to other Christian denominations in a pre-ecumenical age, and also shows the problems of being an exclusively European institution: "We think you may like to hear a little of the human beings with whom we come in contact here... men, women and children of all sorts and denominations and *European* nationalities, for one of the strictest rules of the institution is to exclude all natives of India… At the beginning of the season children predominate; then padres all holding different views, Roman Catholics, Protestants, Dissenters, and even Salvation Armyists! For we had a gallant Captain and his wife, a most earnest young couple, who with curious inconsistency found great 'comfort' in saying their prayers in the Sisters' oratory… Then there came S.P.G. and C.M.S. missionaries and some of them took the Wednesday Evensongs which are held in the oratory, and some Celebrated for the Sisters. We were much interested in one native padre belonging to the S.P.G. His wife was allowed to come into the Sanatorium as there was some European blood on her mother's side, but her husband had to seek for lodgings in the station [hill station]. He is a converted Hindoo, of Brahmin the highest caste, and has a touching story. Since all these padres have gone… we have had a relay of zenana teachers(9) and mission school ladies, all very good and earnest in their different ways… Associating with so many who are connected with mission works makes us long all the more for the time when our Community will be able to commence work among the natives of India."

By 1890 Sr Anna Frances and Sr Muriel were working at the Sanatorium, both having been in India for some time. Indeed it was Sr Anna Frances' second visit, as she had been one of the original group from Clewer. They left Calcutta on March 14th for this new phase of their work and it must have felt rather like being thrown in at the deep end: "We found a great deal to do to get the rooms ready for the incoming patients," wrote Sr Muriel to the Clewer Associates. "We had two durzis [tailors] who worked well when we cut out and tacked all for them, but they could not or would not do anything by themselves. We began the season with 16 patients, 7 of these being in the first class. One gentleman was very ill having been severely stung while sitting on the stump of an old tree in which some millions of ants were living, which caused blood poisoning. Pleurisy and pneumonia afterwards set in from a chill, and several times we thought he must die; but he recovered at last, and we hope he may soon go home. We have some very severe cases of illness now but only two deaths have occurred. The first was a tea planter who died very suddenly. He was a Roman Catholic and had been one of the Christian Brothers; but as he died without the last Sacraments the Jesuit fathers refused to bless the body or to allow the friends to take him into their chapel, and almost refused to bury the poor man! The other patient who died was E.C. the Commissioner. He had signed a cheque in the morning for his passage home…"

"We had the influenza in the Sanatorium for many weeks, the servants all had it and many of the patients. The nurse succumbed and was in bed for some days. Our chaplain took it unfortunately on Easter Eve so we had no Celebration on Easter Day… Till lately this hospital has been very full and yet very quiet. Dr O'Brien, the head physician, is very strict about persons who are admitted. He has made a few rules which *must* be kept. He has also had barriers with little doors put across the verandahs to keep the classes from encroaching on each other's quarters, and which also protect us from anyone passing by our rooms."

Children were also admitted to the Sanatorium as Sr Muriel related: "We have some children here left in our charge whose parents have returned to the plains, and a charming little trio in St Patrick's ward - one of 3 [years], another of 2 years old and a baby of 4 months old. Their mother died of heat apoplexy while taking them down to the plains about a month ago. Their great uncle and aunt brought them back here and placed them under our care."

The Sister concluded her letter with a short account of a recurrent problem: "Since the rains set in we have had some very bad landslips. The railway has suffered considerably. In one place a huge boulder fell across the line. They tried to remove it by dynamite blasting but it was such a long process that a new line of rails was laid outside it very near the edge of the khud [hillside]. Passengers coming or going to Calcutta have to be carried in dandies [litters], or walk, sometimes for 6 miles. Traffic is impossible and goods are at famine prices. We can get up neither flour nor coals, so bread is treble what it ought to be."

Nine years later Darjeeling was to suffer a landslip of disastrous proportions, but that will be dealt with in a later chapter. So too will the other great work at Darjeeling undertaken by the Clewer Sisters in 1895 - the Diocesan Girls' High School, later known as St Michael's. Meanwhile the Eden Sanatorium prospered, even though the Sisters always felt constrained by the rules and regulations imposed upon them by others. But now it is time to return to Calcutta and examine the epoch-making visit of Mother Jane Frances.

Footnotes

1. STEEL, Flora Annie & GARDINER, G. *The Complete Indian Housekeeper and Cook* new ed 1898.

2. MOORHOUSE, Geoffrey *India Britannica* Paladin 1984 p.113.

3. MacMILLAN, Margaret *Women of the Raj* Thames & Hudson 1988. See chapter 11 and especially p. 184 which quotes from STEEL & GARDINER op. cit. above.

4. Sir John Lawrence: Viceroy, 1863-9.

5. Lord Lytton: 1st Earl of Lytton, Viceroy, 1876-80.

6. MARCHIONESS OF DUFFERIN AND AVA *Our Viceregal Life in India: selections from my Journal 1884-8*. 2 Vols. John Murray 1889.

The quotation comes from Vol.2 p.130.

7. The financing of the Indian work was always precarious because in the first instance the Sisters were invited by the government with expenses paid, but as the work expanded into schools and missions the Community had to finance these subsequent ventures. Not everyone at Clewer shared the enthusiasm for India, and there were many branch houses at home which needed financial assistance. After Sr Lucy's death, Sr Jane Frances attempted to clarify the situation. A business-like woman, she had, before coming to India, been Mother Superior at Clewer, an office she had resigned in order to take on the Indian work. In a letter preserved at Clewer dated February 27th 1890 and headed *About Indian money matters* Sr Jane Frances attempted to explain the situation to her successor at Clewer, Mother Betha:

"The whole subject of Indian passages seems to need some thinking over now. As the works increased here Sr Lucy explained which passages could, and which could not, be provided from out of the different public funds. After a term of service varying from three (if paid by the Canning Trust) to five years the regular hospital Sisters could ask for theirs backwards and forwards. But certain passages at [? shorter] intervals or for other works must fall upon the Community. For example, the Pratt School never could be counted... The hospital Sisters' passages come out of some government grant which can be applied for through Sir Alex Wilson. Even Sr Mary Virginia [Bursuress] tacitly accepted the fact and acted upon it that certain passages would have to be made up as the one sacrifice in money to the Indian work. The account of these cannot be kept very clearly, the money refunded as we know to our cost, is often months behind the time it is promised from these public funds. Sr Mary Virginia and Sr Lucy had certain disputes on the subject as Sr M.V. imagined that only one or two of the passages had been actually paid for from India. Till before her death Sr Lucy sent a carefully drawn up paper, of which you have either copy or original, showing that up to that time only four passages out of sixteen had been made up or paid by Clewer..."

8. The Clewer Sisters' work amongst the sick poor in England was considerable: St Andrew's Hospital, Clewer; St Andrew's Home, Folkestone; St Lucy's Children's Hospital, Gloucester; St Raphael's Home, Torquay; St Luke's Home, Torquay; and later, St Barnabas' Home, Torquay. For further details of this work see BONHAM, Valerie *A Joyous Service: The Clewer Sisters and their work* 1989.

9. Zenana teachers: women missionaries who went amongst Indian women who were kept in purdah [seclusion].

-9-
A GREAT DEAL OF LOVE TO YOU ALL

Sr Jane Frances had succeeded Mother Ellen as third Mother Superior of the Community of St John Baptist on December 21st 1881. She was born Fanny Jane Callander, and was a grand-daughter of the 2nd Lord Erskine; her sister had married the second son of the 8th Duke of Argyle and in later life Sr Jane Frances maintained a close connection with the Argyles. On March 23rd 1872 she was professed in the Second Order[1] of the Community of St John Baptist and remained thus until January 20th 1874 when she joined the First Order, and was professed as a choir Sister on July 3rd 1875. Tall and somewhat stern looking, she was a very observant woman with an eye for detail and a business like manner. She had seemed the ideal choice for the office of Mother Superior, but was very unhappy in it. Despite the stern visage, she was a person of great warmth, with a wry sense of humour, and she loved to be amongst people. The office of Superior weighed heavily because it took her away from the active work of the Community and immersed her in administration which she did not enjoy.

The first Sisters had sailed to India just one month before Sr Jane Frances became Mother Superior and from the outset she had a close connection with the work via Sr Lucy. It had her wholehearted support, as is evident from the letters written to Sr Lucy, and in later correspondence when she herself was Sister Superior in India. These letters, written in a flowing and somewhat spidery hand, paint vivid pictures of the work and of the people; and her own attractive personality shines through. Clearly Mother Jane Frances was fascinated by India, so when Sr Lucy's health began to fail she decided to visit Calcutta.

Mother Jane Frances, accompanied by Sr Anna Frances, left England on December 31st 1887. Unlike the first Sisters who had made the journey through the Bay of Biscay, she had decided upon the overland route through France, Switzerland and Italy, boarding ship (the *Mongolia*), at Brindisi. It proved to be a tedious journey as related in a letter to Sr Mary Virginia dated January 2nd 1888, and which the latter received at Clewer on January 15th: "We got to Brindisi at 3 a.m. and into our berths at 4 a.m. so had a short night and oh, what a noisy one, and… it felt intensely cold. I don't feel in love with the ship as yet, but am beyond words thankful that we make a fair start as to weather, as a very stormy day on top of the fatigue of the overland journey would have been very trying. The gain in time is certainly a great thing and the Bay of Biscay might have horrors of its own, otherwise I can't think anyone would choose this route for enjoyment. That day through Italy is very tiring and one feels that it is so much more tedious than it need be on account of the dawdling and slow pace of the Italian railway." The letter did not get finished until January 5th, Mother having succumbed to sea sickness: "Now I shall finish up in haste, not being very brilliant after two days collapse of which the less said or remembered the better, the first day especially... From bad weather or illness we missed seeing what we might have seen of the Grecian Archipelago, and now we shall not sight land till Alexandria... In the Red Sea perhaps we may have a quieter time." She finished her letter in good spirits with a greeting to all at Clewer: "A great deal of love to everybody."

A change of ship to the P. & O. liner *S.S. Clyde* saw an improvement in conditions and raised spirits. Writing on January 6th she was even able to laugh at the climate: "All my ideas of climate are turned upside down. If I trusted to my own impressions I should say that Italy was an intensely cold country, that the Mediterranean was a dingy grey with a continuous curtain of clouds, that in Egypt it rained as nowhere else that one had ever seen. As we at last neared Alexandria, rain (tropical rain I suppose), fell in sheets, and continued to do so all the time (some hours), that we lay in harbour waiting for the mail train for Suez." The passage through the Suez Canal and the Red Sea with its glimpse of Sinai was familiar to those Sisters who had made the journey themselves. A fellow passenger, the Revd Dr Jex Blake, sometime Headmaster of Rugby, was travelling to Bombay with his wife and daughter, and they befriended the Sisters who were glad of their company. He conducted Matins and Evensong on board ship which the Sisters much appreciated, and had promised to celebrate the Eucharist on the following Sunday. "I feel this [is] very kind, as from Rugby's traditions one would not have expected him to think of it," wrote Mother Jane Frances.

By this time the weather was warming up: "It gets hotter and hotter and I am conscious of my letter getting more and more stupid as it goes on," she wrote. The familiar conclusion: "A great deal of love to everybody" was followed by a long postscript in answer to letters received from Clewer, and there is a very thinly veiled hint of homesickness: "This is the twelfth day since I left you all. Many thanks to Sr Louisa Dora and Sr Mary Charlotte for their notes. Yes, the short and hasty sight of Milan Cathedral was the one little pleasure in our land journey. As for the Swiss mountains, I am very sorry to say, my dear Sr Mary Charlotte, St Gotthard has left me such a feeling of shivering and general gruesomeness that my enthusiasm for them is at present *chilled*. Just at this moment one is gasping with heat [and] they might come in better, but one can't have everything all at once. This is for Sr Ann Elizabeth and Sr Maria if they will condescend to read such a stupid letter. I meant it to be better but the heat clouds my faculties."

The *S.S. Clyde* arrived at Bombay on January 16th, but when the Sisters endeavoured to assemble their luggage a trunk was missing and could not be found. It was not until the end of January, by which time they had reached Calcutta, that it turned up: "I am very indignant but very pleased to hear that the missing trunk is at the Custom House, Bombay, which proves therefore that it must have been in the *Clyde* all the time stowed away in some corner of the hold. I have therefore requested the P. &. O. Company to forward it here at their own expense. We lay the mistake to the charge of a certain careless young 4th Officer who was responsible for the baggage." Meanwhile the Sisters disembarked with what luggage they could find. Writing on January 16th from St Peter's School, Bombay which was run by the All Saints' Sisters, Mother Jane Frances recounted the otherwise safe landing: "While at breakfast, and before we had finally done up packages, Fr Page(2) most kindly appeared with one of his native boys from their mission, and a little wherry to take us and our goods on shore. We found Sr Gladys, the All Saints' Superior waiting for us with a gharrie [carriage]. This house looks to me charming for its purpose, but with the open verandahs and tropical plants so very pretty. One seems to go through a succession of *dreams*."

From Bombay the Sisters travelled overland to Calcutta via the hill station of Poona where the Community of St Mary the Virgin, Wantage, had work. The Indian countryside took some getting used to after Scotland and England: "The scenery, after an Indian fashion is very fine, but I have not yet got over the sense of weirdness and strangeness in some of the farms and tropical vegetation, rather than *beauty*", she wrote on January 19th. But she was impressed by the work of the Wantage Sisters: "There was much of interest in the Wantage work here especially the two native girls' schools, native church, and Mr Cecil Rivington's work(3) among the native lads... One felt in the thick of heathenism and there are three hideous idol temples, small ones within a stone's throw of the Sisters' school."

On January 22nd 1888 Mother Jane Frances wrote to tell the Sisters at Clewer of their safe arrival in Calcutta: "We have been to the Cathedral for Matins with Sr Lucy. The four Sisters from the Pratt School and the European Orphanage have been to see me, and in their black habits(4) and clean Sunday caps and collar, look very much like themselves at home." She came to love Calcutta but her first impression was unfavourable: "Calcutta does not impress me at all. I am glad to have seen Bombay as a specimen of an Indian city, for it is beautiful in situation, and every turn was striking and picturesque. Considering what a bad traveller I am, I have stood all better than I might have expected by a long way. This cool weather has revived all the Sisters. After the Red Sea, the Indian Ocean, and the heat of southern India, it feels chilly to me."

Mother Jane Frances intended to stay until March 10th so a tremendous amount was packed into the six weeks of her visit. At first, people came to her, but after she had recovered from the arduous journey she visited the various works with much interest. The letters to Sr Mary

Virginia at Clewer are packed with her detailed impressions: "As yet, I have not till today been farther from the Canning Home than to the Cathedral for [the] service, and that is only 10 minutes walk," she wrote on January 27th 1888 from the Medical College Hospital. The Canning Home was still the headquarters of the Sisters' work, though it proved more and more unsatisfactory as the work increased and diversified. "Two afternoons we had to be at home to entertain first the European orphans, and next day the Pratt School. Each set had a big tea in the verandah and amused themselves in a miscellaneous fashion afterwards. Both schools seemed a nice set of children in their way. The Pratt children interested me most just because they were so unlike pure English. Many of the little ones were very bright and engaging. The orphans are thoroughly sturdy Britons, very Teutonic, and although only of the class of St John's Home children, [are] quite conscious that they belong to the dominant race." A post-Imperialist age will cringe at this last statement, but Mother Jane Frances was a woman of her time - a Victorian of the landed class brought up to believe that Imperialism was right, good, improving and civilising. But later she grew to love India and its people and was never happier than when she was with Indians.

But for all her Imperialism, there were some aspects of Empire which Mother Jane Frances met with a combination of amusement and tedium: "Another day the bishop sent for me. Endless *ladies* and some clergy called," was her wry comment. These ladies - the memsahibs - really took some getting used to, and they were so easily offended with their over-bearing manner and self importance. The presence in Calcutta of the Mother Superior of Clewer would be marked on their social calendar as of major importance: Mother Jane Frances with her Scottish baronial connections, would have been quite swamped with their visiting cards. But after the first few days she was able to attend more to the Community works, though she still found Calcutta uncongenial: "I have been over every part of the Canning Home and General Hospital from flat house top to basement," she continued in the letter of January 27th. "We have had a thunderstorm, a mild one I fancy, and a fair amount of rain which has washed the trees a little, but nature never seems to waken in a burst of joy out here. I still think Calcutta very ugly, so perfectly flat, all the buildings have such a heavy look with their flat roofs, and walls weather-stained from heavy rains, though handsome, I suppose, after their fashion. The town looks more Europeanised than the others we have seen."

Completing the letter next day (January 28th) she noted: "I have now seen in a superficial way all the works, and I am going to stay next week a night or two with Sr Sophie which will combine the [European] Orphanage and the Pratt School, and another time with Sr Annie for the other two hospitals. Both house and grounds in the Orphanage are the most attractive of our works. The grounds so spacious, I should have said equal in extent to all that belonging to the House of Mercy [i.e. at

Clewer]. It would make a delightful Community House were it more in our own hands. It looks so much more homelike than this [i.e. the Canning Home]. The weather still keeps quite cool, people out here call it *cold*, but I do not know what season at home to compare it with."

The visit to the Pratt School was successful, Mother pronouncing it to be "in very good working order." But she longed to see some specifically *Indian* work and the opportunity came early in February as she recounted in a letter dated February 6th/7th: "We had an interesting day yesterday visiting two upper class native schools in the native part of the city, and then the Oxford Mission. Their present quarters are what was a rich native's house with its two quadrangles, (the inner being the women's quarters)... Fr Gorek(5) is staying with them. He is quite an elderly man, not so dark as many Hindus. It was quite interesting to have a talk with him and to make acquaintance with one who had had such a strange spiritual history. So to my great delight I felt I had come into contact with Indian life in various aspects for the first time."

Not all aspects of Indian life were found to be so congenial. "I had hardly any sleep last night," she complained in the same letter. "A horrible 'Nautch' [dance] going on at the servant's quarters in one of the neighbouring institutions not a stone's throw from one's open window. The singing team turning jingling of bangles and cymbals sounded unearthly, and the house, as if inspired by the evil one himself, very hideous, and with such a wicked sound in the women's shrill voices. Perhaps being kept awake by drunken men in the London streets is quite a sad [thing] in every way, but heathenism brings a new phase of the kingdom of darkness before one."

The letter concluded with details of an engagement which would have been the envy of many a *memsahib*: "I have been to see my cousins at Government House this week. Lady Dufferin kindly came to fetch me one afternoon, so I went off in state with a mounted native bodyguard in gorgeous uniforms. Saw the children, several of whom are grown up and had a very affectionate welcome from Dufferin whom I had not seen for 20 years nearly. But there I think our intercourse will about cease." Mother was wrong in making the last assumption, for Lady Dufferin came to see her again at the end of February before her return to Clewer.

As the visit progressed, so Mother Jane Frances grew busier and the temperature hotter, but she did not fail to be impressed with all she saw. "I have just come back from a 3 night stay at the Medical College Hospital with Sr Annie and Sr Sophia, she wrote on February 13th. These are such huge institutions, there is a good deal to see in them, though I feel that I visit the schools (of which I have seen a variety), with more intelligent eyes. The Medical College is a rough, unattractive looking place inside, though outside a massive looking building in the classical style. The Eden Hospital, as everyone at home has heard, is very smart and well appointed... The Sisters are always discovering interesting Scotch sailors who I am requested to visit [at the Presidency General Hospital]." The only one of the hospitals which Mother did not visit was the Eden Sanatorium at Darjeeling which had not re-opened after the cold season.

Lent was rapidly approaching, but before that there were some social engagements. "On Shrove Tuesday we are all going to meet for tea and Vespers at the European Orphanage, [but] before going to the Orphanage I am going with Sr Lucy to see Lady Wilson and the jute factory on the river. Sr Lucy thinks it worth seeing, and that I shall get an idea of the Hooghly, otherwise it is not in my line of interest so much." The letter concluded with its usual greeting: "A great deal of love to everybody." The next letter (dated February 16th) gave an account of the excursion: "Lady Wilson took Sr Lucy and myself in their steam launch up the Hooghly to see their jute factory, the chief interest of which was that under the direction of 8 Europeans (Scotchmen from Dundee), 3,000 natives, men, women and children, are employed. Sr Lucy was anxious also that I should get some idea of the Hooghly higher up above Calcutta. It is curious and interesting but all too flat to be really fine. We passed some numbers of temples and some burning ghats i.e. stone porticoes where the dead are taken on the bank of the river, and at one or two [of them] *Cremations*(6) were going on as we could see very plainly, the mourners sitting around. Before quite settling into Lent Lady Wilson also kindly took a whole party of us across to the Botanical Gardens one afternoon. They are on the opposite side of the Hooghly, a long drive round by the bridge but a short way crossing by steam launch. Besides fern and orchids in the houses, (the latter not yet in their fullest flower) there are avenues of palms and a great banyan [tree] with more than 200 secondary stems (more like a wood than a tree). These are the great features of interest."

With the coming of Lent there were extra religious activities in conjunction with the Oxford Mission in which the Sisters joined. "Mr Townsend, Superior of the Oxford Mission(7) wanted to have a 'Quiet Day' for their lady Associates and asked Sr Lucy if it could be held in the chapel here. So between 25 and 30 ladies gave in their names and had breakfast, tiffin [lunch], and a cup of tea in the afternoon, but so many of the native ladies were keeping so strict a fast that little justice was done to the meals provided by Sr Cara(8) and at which she and Sr Anna Frances waited. Sr Lucy and I headed the tables and joined the services. Many of the ladies were of the same set who belong to their Committees, but 6 or 8 were pure natives of high class, very good Christians, and some of them interesting people; it pleased me much to join in spiritual exercises with them. We had a litany of intercession for India at noon. Mr Townsend's three meditations on prayer were really beautiful. I do not think in any of our retreats we often come in for such beautiful or spiritual teaching. Sr Lucy was as much delighted as I was, and thinks very highly of Mr Townsend's spiritual gifts which indeed seem to me of no common order. Though he is one of those shy and reserved, quiet people who do not attract all round, quite the opposite of Fr Black who knows how to meet the world on its own ground and has all the world sitting at his feet."

Back at Clewer Sr Maria had died on February 24th after a fairly short illness and a telegram was sent to Mother Jane Frances. Sr Maria had worked in the Community branch houses at Oxford, Folkestone and Clewer St Stephen until deafness brought her back to the mother house, after which she made altar frontals and banners for mission churches. Mother was saddened by the news and wrote back to Sr Mary Virginia on February 27th: "The telegram about dear Sr Maria reached us on Saturday 25th, the day after her call home, the particulars of which one can only conjecture, i.e. that no long illness can have preceded it since she has been mentioned in the last letters I have had, and one will only get full tidings up to that date on the way home. It is blessed to think of her resting from her labours after her long life of faithful work and waiting. But I grieve to think of one dear old familiar face missing when I return."

The visit was proving increasingly exhausting as the weather became warmer and by the end of February it was taking its toll on Mother Jane Frances: "One or two days last week I was a little upset," she wrote on February 27th. "The shopping expedition in the heat of the day was the finishing touch, but I am alright again now... Sr Lucy has not been so well and has had to keep quieter. We may expect Sr Fanny Gertrude any day now, but the river is so low and tides slack that ships are often delayed a little getting up; the navigation of the lower Hooghly is at best difficult and dangerous on account of the shifting sandbanks." In fact Sr Fanny Gertrude, who was returning to India for her second term, arrived safely next day, February 28th. On the same day Mother Jane Frances noted with concern the worsening condition of Sr Lucy: "Sr Lucy is not up yet. She has had a suffering night, though not more bleeding."

Mother Jane Frances always welcomed an opportunity to meet Indian people and to visit work among them, so she would have enjoyed the last two weeks of her stay with its increasing amount of contact with Indian people. "We had a visit today from Miss Bose the native Headmistress of the Bethune Institute, this high class school which we visited a fortnight ago," she wrote in the letter of February 27th. "She brought one of her teachers who belong to the Brahmasoraj. Miss Bose is a Christian of the second generation, but a strong Presbyterian. Her family, like many of the most intellectual and rising of the native Christians, being the fruits of a certain Dr Duff whom I remember well in Edinburgh when I was a young girl. He did great work by excellent Christian schools, and has left his mark to this day. I hope our Church may have as much to show 20 years hence but doubt it, (except the Oxford Mission which I much believe in)." Her comments about Dr Duff are quite remarkable for her time - these were not ecumenical times and negative comments about 'Dissenters' were more frequent than complimentary ones. As well as this visit from Miss Bose, Mother Jane Frances was also looking forward to: "some zenana visiting with Miss Hoare, both among rich and poor which may be interesting, but with so eccentric a conductor one cannot quite foretell one's experiences." An interesting comment considering the close connection the Clewer Sisters were to have with Miss Hoare in due course.

The Sisters at Clewer had to wait for Mother's letter written on March 2nd (which they did not receive until March 26th when she was halfway home), before hearing about the trip with Miss Hoare: "I have had a day of real heathen visiting with Miss Hoare, whom Sr Louisa Dora will remember. I got a glimpse of a very superior family still *nominal* Hindoo, but very intelligent as to their minds and refined in their manners; of some zenanas of middle class or lower professional people, which were very different, and also visited a hamlet of the poorest people, where a native mission woman works among them and gives them simple religious instruction. A little group of these women were gathered together and I had to give them two impromptu Bible lessons... which Miss Hoare interpreted to them, and I *hope* greatly improved in the process... At a few feet distant was a mud heap and three hideous shabby *idols*, the titulary gods of the village, stuck into it. But it would take too long to give fully my first impressions of those strange people. When we have our recreation [at Clewer] under the poplar trees, there will be more time and many queer things to be told."

The missionary visiting was in stark contrast to the Hindu festival which had just passed and which filled Mother Jane Frances with revulsion: "A very horrid Hindoo festival is just over which was at its height at the last full moon. It is in honour of some of the adventures of Krishna one of the favourite incarnations of Vishnu, one of the Hindoo 'triad'. The people go about with their heads, faces and sometimes bodies smeared with vermillion powder, and the whole institution or *spirit* of the festival is morally bad or degrading. What a difference from our holy seasons, even irreligious people are better for the time by only thinking of Christmas Day or Easter, while the poor Hindoos are really *better* than their religion which in its popular forms at least is truly earthly, sensual and *devillish*."

The Sisters were very supportive of all missionary endeavours amongst the Indian population and longed for closer and more active involvement. As yet most of their work lay with Europeans or Anglo-Indians (Eurasians as they were still called). But whenever there was any special activity aimed at the Indian populace the Sisters were there to support it. Therefore when the foundation stone of a new Bengali church was laid, Mother Jane Frances, Sr Lucy and four other Sisters went along to the ceremony. This took place at 7.30 a.m. on March 2nd

1888, on a piece of ground designated for the new building which adjoined Miss Hoare's mission house. The enterprise was sponsored by the Cathedral as a special project to provide a Bengali-speaking church for the Indian members of the congregation. The bishop was ill so could not officiate at the ceremony which was decidedly English and Anglican despite everything being in Bengali. "The service was of the usual orthodox type," wrote Mother Jane Frances. "*Onward Christian Soldiers* as a processional, Psalm 134, appropriate Collects, versicles and responses, Psalm 120, and *The Churches One Foundation* - all in Bengali. It was touching to hear these familiar hymns to their proper tunes sung in this strange tongue by a goodly array of native choristers..." The widow and family of the Indian priest who had done much to build up the Indian congregation were also present. Mother Jane Frances felt an instinctive rapport with Indian people (though not, as we have seen with Hindu customs), and noted that: "I believe I should get quite a following of singular native Christian friends if I stayed much longer at Calcutta, and I should get very fond of them!"

A final expedition brought much enjoyment before the long voyage home, the only regret being that Sr Lucy's worsening condition prevented her from accompanying Mother Jane Frances on the visit to some of Mr Seal's mission schools. As noted in chapter 5, the Revd A. C. Seal of St Barnabas' Kidderpore, was working very hard to bring the gospel to his own people. He had opened a number of mission schools which greatly interested Sr Lucy. Now it was necessary to move one of them because of the encroachment of Kidderpore docks, so Mother and another Sister went with Mr and Mrs Seal to inspect a site in the rice country south of Calcutta. "The survey of the piece of ground had to be assisted by an audience of quite 30 people, children included," wrote Mother in a letter home on March 5th. "Certain Hindoo teachers belonging to the little hamlet were deeply interested in the transaction and anxious that the little school should be settled there. You would have laughed could you have seen the group we made in this country, each in the middle of swamps and rice fields and clusters of palm trees. Some unripe coconuts from trees, the common property of the village, were then gathered for us and the tops sawn off. In that state the liquid inside is very refreshing and clear as spring water, very cold, just a little sweet. I think the people very engaging." Then a thought for Sr Maria, lately departed brought the letter to a close - "Dear Sr Maria, she would have liked to have heard or read my little glimpses of foreign mission work."

In the event Mother Jane Frances was to have much more than a glimpse of all the Indian work, for within 18 months she was to return to take charge of it. But for now this last letter from her first visit to India was brought to a conclusion with the familiar ending: "A great deal of love to all." On March 12th 1888 Mother Jane Frances accompanied by Sr Sybil sailed from Calcutta on the *City of Cambridge*. The voyage took a month and they arrived safely in England on April 12th. The Community *Annals* record that "They had a *very* good voyage and Mother was a capital sailor."

Mother Jane Frances can only have been encouraged by all she had seen, although Sr Lucy's failing health was the cause of increasing anxiety. The hospitals, schools and orphanage were well established and links were being forged with Indians chiefly through the work of Mr Seal in Kidderpore and Mr Bannerjee at St Mary's Bengali church. These were works especially dear to Sr Lucy and now it is time to take a closer look at them.

Footnotes

1. Second Order: this was founded at Clewer in 1860 for those who felt called to the Religious Life but who were prevented from leaving home by family considerations. These Sisters were admitted for three years at a time, spent part of each year at Clewer where they wore a blue habit, and part of the year at home where they wore ordinary clothes. At Clewer they were addressed as Sister followed by their Christian name and surname. If their circumstances changed they were permitted to join the First Order as choir Sisters after a year long novitiate, provided they had been in the Second Order three years. For further details about the Second Order see BONHAM, Valerie *A Place in Life: the Clewer House of Mercy, 1849-83*. 1992.

2. Fr Page was Superior of the Indian work of the Society of St John the Evangelist (the Cowley Fathers).

3. This probably refers to Father Rivington, who was working at St Peter's Mazagon not far from the All Saints' Sisters.

4. Black habits: The thick black habits worn at Clewer came in time to be modified for India. Whilst still as voluminous as those back home, a lighter weight white material was used.

5. Fr Gorek. This is probably Fr Nehemiah Goreh, sometime novice of the Society of St John the Evangelist, formerly a Brahmin. He had worked at St Peter's Mazagon and was well known amongst the English missionary community. He died on October 29th 1895.

See also: GARDNER, C.E. *Life of Father* Goreh 1900

6. Cremation was not a common mode of disposal of the dead in the West at this time and would have been both alien and un-Christian in the eyes of the Sisters. The first English crematorium was opened at Woking during the 1880s but cremation remained controversial and did not gain favour with the Churches until well into the 20th century.

7. The Revd Charles Townsend became Superior of the Oxford Mission to Calcutta in 1889 but soon afterwards left to join the Roman Catholic Church. This dealt a blow to the Oxford Mission whose critics had accused it of "Romanism". However, the Mission survived. Townsend returned to England and became a Jesuit, and died aged 91 in 1945.

8. Sr Cara. This is probably Sr Carolina who was in Calcutta at the time of Mother Jane Frances' visit, having left England on November 19th 1886; she returned to England at the end of 1889.

-10-
DREAMS AND REALITIES

One of Sr Lucy's most earnest wishes was to work amongst the Indian people because this was regarded as *real* missionary work, but as yet there seemed to be no opening for it. Mother Jane Frances had inspected the work of Miss Hoare with interest, not least because she was a distant cousin of Sr Georgina Mary at Clewer. But it seemed that the most the Sisters could do was to give such support and encouragement as they could to the various Indian priests working in Calcutta, notably Mr Seal at Kidderpore and Mr Bannerjee at the new Bengali church.

As early as Easter 1883 Sr Lucy had written to the Clewer Associates that "Mr Seal wanted me to go with him to the Church [i.e. St Barnabas' Kidderpore] to see if I could suggest anything to improve the altar which is a great trial to him." Mr Seal had also begun a Refuge for Indian women in moral danger and was anxious to extend this work. Sr Lucy was supportive as it was similar to the rescue work carried out by the Sisters in England. But at Clewer, Mother Jane Frances was sceptical about the success of this type of work in India.

The Sisters had not been in India very long before they began to realise the pitfalls of having no real Mother House. They were still living at the Lady Canning Home which was comfortable enough (especially after its extension in 1884), but they had no freedom to adapt the premises for other work. Thus they could not help Mr Seal by establishing the Indian refuge under their roof because it was not their own, but was governed by the Trustees of the Calcutta Hospital Nurses' Institution.

Similarly, the Sisters would have liked to establish an orphanage for Indian children but had no means of doing so. "What we earnestly desire is an orphanage for natives as well as Europeans," wrote Sr Lucy in the Easter 1884 *St John Baptist Magazine*. "Strange to say, there is none belonging to our Church in Calcutta, and so every year numbers of these friendless little ones fall into the hands of the RC's and Dissenters who are very actively carrying on this kind of work. We ought to have a reserve fund ready to enable us to buy any suitable house and compound for it that came into the market. It is very difficult to find a site, for the natives cling to the possession of land and it is only the need of ready money that would tempt them to part with it... Meanwhile you may imagine how painful it is constantly to refuse some poor child because we have no House of our own, and see it carried instead to the RC convent which seems to serve here for a poor house, and receives a subsidy from the government for the work it does." Sr Lucy reckoned that £5,000 would be needed for a large enough house and grounds but acknowledged that: "this is still a dream, but I hope some day it may become a reality."

From 1882 a body known as the St John Baptist Calcutta Mission Association had been in existence, based in London and consisting of clergy and lay people pledged to help the Indian work of the Clewer Sisters. They held meetings and organised fund raising events, and had a large body of Associate members. Their activities were publicised in the *St John Baptist Magazine* which was available to all Clewer Associates, not just the Associates of the Calcutta Mission Association, though there was a good deal of dual membership. Writing to the members of the Calcutta Mission Association on July 4th 1885, Sr Lucy outlined her vision for the Indian work: "I want you to know our hopes and fears and expectations... The time has now come when we seem called to do something for the Christian natives. For some time past there has been great pressure from the Oxford Mission to make us do something towards the education of the native girls. I have resisted this, knowing how impossible it is to get Sisters from Clewer for this fresh work; but as the pressure increases, and the individual appeals from native clergy increase, we are now thinking [whether] we can make a beginning without Sisters. I have only lately taken in the real poverty of the native clergy. There are a few exceptions where the priest may have 150 or 200 rupees a month, but the average salary is 30 rupees, and some are as low as 15 rupees, equivalent to £15 per annum. Of course out of this they cannot pay for education. They do manage something for the boys, for that is essential and remunerative, but nothing for the girls; and our Church does nothing. The Dissenters have large flourishing schools, so have the Roman Catholics; we have none. The native clergy come to me saying, 'We do not want to send our children to Dissenters, they will only fall out of the Church; cannot you help us?' It is very hard to say no."

The response of the Calcutta Mission Association has not been preserved but presumably Sr Lucy was not overwhelmed with donations, nor with offers of practical help, both of which she had appealed for. But there was another problem which she had not foreseen. "The Bengali school is still in embryo, partly because no one quite satisfactory has appeared as its head, and partly because our bishop will not sanction our beginning till we have at least one year's funds in hand," she wrote to the Association in a letter dated December 4th 1885, and which was read at their meeting on February 5th 1886. She continued: "Of course it would be advisable, if possible to buy, but land is so enormously expensive in and near Calcutta. Nothing at all suitable could be found under 60,000 rupees (£5,000). There is a charming compound for sale now, so large and shady, and a good sized house. Just what we want if you know of any millionaire who will *give* it to us! We should get on swimmingly without the drag of house rent. The necessity of counting the cost before we begin, and being sure that we shall be able to carry it out is so pressed upon me by our good bishop that I am doing so very literally."

Sr Lucy had been doing some groundwork which she recounted in the same letter: "I have been visiting some of the Dissenting schools; I wanted to see how they managed them; and I saw beautiful schools for native girls. As far as outward organization and good instruction went, there was nothing left to desire, and at each school I heard the same, that if they had more accommodation they could soon double their number of boarders. And the children are so bright and intelligent that it was pleasant to look at them. The London Missionary was the one I liked best, but as I left I could not but feel sorry and shamed that we have nothing of the kind. The Church Missionary Society has a small boarding school in Calcutta, very nice in its way, and they mean to enlarge it. And that is all our Church can show."

Sadly, few seemed to share Sr Lucy's enthusiasm for the Indian school as a direct work of the Sisters, but by 1888 Mr Seal at St Barnabas' Kidderpore, had begun similar work, and Sr Lucy (despite her failing health), channelled her energy into this. Writing on August 1st 1888 she described a visit to Kidderpore: "The weather has been so hot I have not been able to get about much lately, but I did manage early one morning to pay a visit to the school at Kidderpore. It is just outside the late King of Oude's[1] palace... Mr Seal was most grateful for the £5, and we added the small sum needed to cover the whole expense of the Christian teacher. He is a nice looking young man, a Brahman convert. The bishop has since taken up another school and provided a Christian teacher; and so has Miss Hoare. Mr Seal has generally managed to put a Christian teacher into each school in addition to the Hindoo already in possession, and it has answered very well so far." The editor of the *St John Baptist Magazine* went on to explain that the population of Kidderpore was 67,686 in an area 16 miles long and 3 miles wide; that there were 20 mission schools in the area; and that Mr Seal attempted to provide a Christian teacher to supplement the Hindu teacher in each of them.

These schools would have been familiar to Mother Jane Frances because she had visited some of them just a few months previously and had accompanied Mr and Mrs Seal on a site inspection for a new school. Similarly she would have known Mr Bannerjee who had been ordained priest in St Paul's Cathedral, Calcutta at the end of 1887. He had trained under Fr Whitehead[2] at Bishop's College, Calcutta. Following his ordination Mr Bannerjee was appointed priest-in-charge of the, as yet unbuilt, Bengali church, (St Mary's, Bhowampara)[3] the foundation stone of which had been laid on March 2nd 1888 in the presence of Mother Jane Frances. The missionary work which lay behind this church had been going on for 30 years and was chiefly carried out by an Indian priest called Mr Sandel. From a group of 11 he had built up the present congregation of nearly 300 worshippers, but had died before the new church was begun. Within a year or so of the foundation stone being laid the church was complete. The consecration service took place in the presence of a large congregation of both Indians and Europeans. The service was conducted by the Bishop of Calcutta in English and Bengali, and the petition for consecration was read by one of Mr Sandel's sons.

It is unclear whether Sr Lucy was well enough to attend this service but at least she saw the completion of the church. Writing of it she said: "It is hoped that when the Community have a house of their own for native work, that it will be in this same neighbourhood and in connection with this church and congregation." This cherished hope would become a reality but Sr Lucy was not to live to see it.

Ever since her visit to India early in 1888 Mother Jane Frances had felt that her work lay there rather than at Clewer. Sr Lucy's health was failing rapidly; practically every Indian mail brought worse news. On February 11th 1889 the Community *Annals* record the following entry: "The accounts of Sr Lucy are much worse. She is quite an invalid now and only gets as far as the sofa and is very suffering at times." On March 28th the *Annals* tell us that: "Mother went up to London for a night and after Vespers Sr Mary Virginia read the Warden's letter telling [us] that Mother was going to resign at the end of this year, her second term of office, and would take charge of the work in Calcutta. Sr Lucy is too ill now to carry it on. We have for long felt this blow was coming and it is a great sorrow to us all to think of losing Mother."

Just three weeks later on Maundy Thursday (April 18th) 1889 Mother Jane Frances received a telegram from Calcutta during Evensong which simply said "Sr Lucy died at 5 p.m. today." (Calcutta time was six hours in advance of English time). Within a few hours of her death all the Clewer Sisters throughout the world had been informed: Sr Mary Virginia telegraphed the news to the American Affiliation in New York, and the Sister Secretary wrote by evening mail to all the scattered branch houses in England. But little detail was known until the arrival of the mail from India on May 6th and May 13th. It seems as though the disease had spread to her lungs and by Saturday April 13th death seemed imminent, and the Sisters had been summoned from the outlying works in Calcutta. But, as often happens, she rallied and the doctor thought her life might be prolonged, but she died quite peacefully on Maundy Thursday. She had received her last Communion on Palm Sunday and was buried in the English cemetery at Alipore, just opposite Sr Mary Agatha. Sr Lucy had chosen the plot herself "for the next Sister who died."

The funeral took place on Good Friday at 5.00 p.m., the first part of the service being conducted by Fr Whitehead of the Oxford Mission in the chapel of the Lady Canning Home. The service at the graveside was conducted by the Bishop of Calcutta in the presence of local clergy, members of the Oxford Mission, Sisters, the choir of Bishop's College and many friends. As the coffin was lowered into the grave Sr Lucy's favourite hymn *Forever with the Lord* was sung. She was 68 years old and had been a professed Sister for 20 years. Next day - Easter Eve - the bishop

Celebrated in the Sisters' chapel at the Lady Canning Home and alluded to Sr Lucy and her work for India. The Community *Annals* note the kindness of Bishop Johnson and how he had often visited Sr Lucy during her last illness.

As noted elsewhere, Sisters came and went to and from India with amazing mobility considering the lengthy voyage, so that it is difficult to keep track of exactly who was in India at any given time. However, the Community *Annals* record that at the time of Sr Lucy's death the following Sisters were working in India:

Lady Canning Home and Presidency General Hospital - Sr Annie, Sr Fanny Gertrude, Sr Gertrude Emma;
Eden Hospital - Sr Sophia;
Medical College Hospital - Sr Sybil;
Eden Sanatorium, Darjeeling - Sr Carolina, Sr Anna Frances;
Pratt Memorial School - Sr Sophie, Sr Mary Angela;
European Orphanage Asylum - Sr Muriel, Sr Mary Thekla.

This is by no means a definitive list as Sisters were often moved from one work to another.

Mother Jane Frances' decision to resign and go to India, followed by Sr Lucy's death had dealt a double blow to the Community. Despite her dislike of the Superior's role, she was greatly loved by the Sisters in her care and it was not going to be easy to fill her place. Writing up the Community *Annals* on the Feast of St John Baptist 1889 the Sister Secretary ruefully commented: "A threatening of rain and a few slight showers, but it passed off... though rather cloudy, but a lovely evening - symbolical of the state of mind we are all in just now, as to Community affairs and sorrow at Mother's going... But *what* a privilege for our Community to be called to take part in the evangelisation of India side by side with the Oxford Mission, filling up the *woman's* part of the work untouched as yet by Religious."

On October 11th 1889 the Clewer Chapter met to elect the new Mother Superior. All choir Sisters who had been professed five years or more were entitled to vote, which entailed a postal vote for all Sisters in branch Houses. Thus the Warden had written to all voting Sisters as early as September 17th with names of the two candidates: Sr Betha and Sr Lydia. Sr Betha was elected, and was installed as Mother Superior by the Visitor, Bishop Stubbs, on November 11th 1889. Next day Sr Jane Frances was formally appointed Sister Superior of the Indian work, and on November 13th 1889 she left Clewer for India accompanied by Sr Blanche. There was a massive send-off: the Warden, Canon Carter, met them at Paddington; a number of Sisters from the London branch Houses waved them off from Euston; and two more Sisters travelled to Birkenhead. They sailed on November 14th aboard the *S.S. City of Chios* and had a very difficult voyage. The ship was wretched and Sr Blanche (who was returning to India after only eight months back in England), was ill en route. However, they arrived safely on December 17th 1889 with Sr Blanche much improved. The coming of the new year brought about several changes, with Sr Annie and Sr Sophia returning to England at the end of March, and the arrival in February of Sr Mary Alethea, Sr Mary Christine and Sr Mary Isabel[(4)]. The latter had been professed just six months.

So just over 18 months after her return to England Sr Jane Frances now found herself once more in Calcutta, but this time as Sister Superior. It was to be her life's work and, except for periods of furlough, she was to remain in India until 1919. Sr Lucy had worked long and hard until a month before her death, and Sr Jane Frances found all well and in good order. She shared Sr Lucy's enthusiasm for work amongst the Indian people, but knew that little progress would be made while the Sisters had no House of their own. In a letter to the Secretary of the London Branch of the Calcutta Mission Association which was published in the *St John Baptist Magazine* for Easter 1890, Sr Jane Frances voiced her plans:

"I was in hopes of telling you something definite as to the site of our future House and native work in which I am so anxious to interest our Calcutta Association, but as yet all still hangs in uncertainty, and it is misleading to pass on conjectures and possibilities which may be mistaken for facts and certainties. The first idea was that one might look out for something in the immediate neighbourhood of the Bengali church of which you have heard so much, but one has a limited choice if one keeps to that idea as most of the land there is otherwise occupied. Two small houses with some lots of land adjoining did present themselves to my mind as they did to Sr Lucy's... But the price was large in proportion to the value, and other difficulties have arisen. So now, with the advice of our good friends of the Oxford Mission, I am turning my mind to find something a little nearer their works which would be only ten minutes walk from the Bengali church... The Oxford Mission priests have two distinct centres of work. They have now a mission house, lecture rooms and chapel in the native part of the town near Calcutta University, where they carry on their work among the *non-Christians*, Bengali students chiefly. Then, very near St Mary's Bengali church are their educational works from Bishop's College down to the industrial school for boys of the lowest class. But all these are *Christian* works, and that with the girls would be our starting point too. This time of investigation and preparation is not, I am sure, lost; and I only hope that our friends at home will not tire of us meanwhile, and lose their interest in us."

The one area of Indian work about which Sr Jane Frances remained sceptical was the idea of rescue work. As noted previously, Sr Lucy had been approached regarding work begun by Mr Seal. During the course of 1892 the subject was raised again, and in a letter to Mother Betha dated August 14th Sr Jane Frances attempted to explain the situation: "This present application is a fresh chapter in an old story. Two grand ladies, Mrs Pugh and Mrs Evans (sisters) were much stirred up about 'rescue' work some years ago, and when I was at Clewer paid me anxious visits to talk over the matter. Their own plans were very hazy, and we had more than enough on our hands out here. Sr Lucy and I were quite of one mind. She was very anxious I should show them what sympathy I could in the way of getting advice and finding some kind of worker to help them, but did not wish or expect we should do more. Finally, after various experiences they got a certain Mrs Buchanan, (a Scotchwoman who had worked a great deal as a kind of lady matron at the Albion Hill Penitentiary, Brighton), to come out and work up a kind of Refuge. She has gone in for a great deal of 'rescue' work visiting houses of evil fame, and I do not think her plans for the employment of the inmates have been very successful, and the whole thing shows signs of collapse on account of her health. She is a very stout, florid person [and] must return to England before the next hot season."

Sr Jane Frances continued: "The one Penitentiary in Calcutta, very fairly managed and [in] grand premises is not in distinctive Church management, indeed the grand lady who endowed it was a Dissenter of some kind, though some Church people are on the Committee. Mrs Pugh and Mrs Evans are Church people, but I should imagine Low Church, since this Mrs Buchanan whom they imported, is by nature a Presbyterian, though she attends the Cathedral and takes the girls to any church that becomes convenient. Supposing that we wish to step into Mrs Buchanan's shoes, (which I cannot say I do), we should certainly not take up her special work. And I do not think at the same time that the ordinary traditions of a Clewer penitentiary would help us at all out here. If ever such a work developed, my idea is that it would be a quiet homelike... refuge for 'first falls'. For example, at this moment there are three former European Orphanage girls in this Dissenting Home because there was no other place to send them to. Laundry work... is impossible for them out here[5]. Harder work is very difficult to get so that the emplacement and after disposal of girls is an immense difficulty. Penitentiary work would not touch Hindoos or [reduce?] immorality, nor a particular class of professional bad women, who out here are Germans or German governesses, and make quite a class by themselves."

So the idea of any form of rescue work in India was laid aside and nothing more was heard about it. But in the meantime great developments were taking place in other directions. The Easter 1891 number of the *St John Baptist Magazine* contained the triumphant announcement: "It is with great pleasure and thankfulness that the long wished for native work in India can now be begun by the Sisters, the Bishop of Calcutta having offered the Pupulputty[6] [sic] Mission to our Community by the desire of the foundress, Miss Hoare..." Writing from the Lady Canning Home, Sr Jane Frances took up the theme: "I am glad now to be able to speak freely about our future native work. We shall within a few months have a large field of genuine native work entrusted to us on account of the personal withdrawal of Miss Hoare from what is known as the Pupulputty [sic] Mission House. It is at no distance from this House, on the same side of Calcutta... in a suburb called Ballygung. The property was bought for the purpose some years ago by Miss Hoare from a native Rajah. The compound is large, dry and well drained. There is plenty of space for additional building when required... Going through a little door in the wall on the farthest side you find yourself in the compound of St Mary's Bengali church..."

Sr Lucy's dream had been realised at last - a mission house to serve as the Sisters' headquarters, with real work amongst the Indian people, and situated next door to the Bengali church. But it had not been an easy acquisition. A great deal of hard bargaining had been required and there was still a good deal of prejudice to be overcome. But before examining the process by which the Sisters found themselves entrusted with this important new work, it is necessary to focus upon its foundress - Angelina Hoare.

Footnotes

1. The late King of Oude. There was much ill feeling amongst the British towards the late King of Oude (a title conferred on him by the British in 1819 after the annexation of Oudh), because of the horrors perpetrated in the capital, Lucknow, during the Indian Mutiny.

2. Fr Whitehead. Principal of Bishop's College, Calcutta, the Revd Henry Whitehead was Superior of the Oxford Mission from 1889 (after Charles Townsend left to join the Roman Catholic Church) until 1898. He was consecrated Bishop of Madras in June 1899.

3. St Mary's, Bhowampara. This is also referred to in the Sisters' records as St Mary's, Bhowanipore, and St Mary's Ballygunge which was sometimes spelt Ballygung or Baliganj.

4. Sr Mary Isabel, surnamed Julius, was related to Dr Frederick Guilder Julius of The Hermitage, Clewer Green, who had allowed his name to be used as the chief complainant in a series of legal proceedings against the Rector of Clewer, the Revd T.T. Carter. The allegations were of Carter's increasing "Romish" ritual in the parish church, despite the wide support of his parishioners. Carter and Dr Julius never met during the litigation, though they met later and parted as friends. The Bishop of Oxford appealed to the House of Lords on Carter's behalf and won his case: Carter in turn resigned the living of Clewer but remained Warden of the Community of St John Baptist which he had co-founded with Harriet Monsell. For further details of what came to be known as *The Clewer Case* see:

BONHAM, Valerie *A Complication of Circumstances: Canon Carter and the Clewer Case* in **WINDLESORA** Number 8 1989 pp 15-24.

5. Laundry work was one of the main practical occupations in the penitentiaries run by the Clewer Sisters in England. It provided an income for the House of Mercy, and was part of the girls' training for domestic service. But it was impractical in India because of the climate.

6. Pupulputty. The first reference to Miss Hoare's mission house is spelt in this way, but it was subsequently given as Pipalpati, altogether a difficult word to know how to tackle!

-11-
SARI AND TOP BOOTS

Angelina Mary Hoare was born in London on May 17th 1843, the fourth daughter of Henry Hoare, banker, of Fleet Street and Staplehurst, and his wife Lady Mary, daughter of the 3rd Earl of Romney. There were twelve children in all and they were brought up religiously, both parents being committed Christians. Besides being a member of the well known banking family, Henry Hoare was known for his role in the campaign for the restoration of Convocation[1]. Like most girls from wealthy homes, Angelina and her sisters were educated by governesses whilst the boys were sent to public school, in this case, Eton. Part of the year was spent in London and part at Staplehurst, the country home in Kent. As she grew up Angelina became increasingly interested in Church work, initially in visiting the sick and poor, but increasingly in Sunday School teaching, running Mothers' meetings and supporting foreign missions. In addition Angelina was an active person who enjoyed travelling, holidays and riding, despite a weak heart which was the legacy of a childhood bout of rheumatic fever.

Several of Angelina's brothers became clergymen and it was through one of them (Walter), that she first became interested in India. Walter Hoare served his first curacy at Great Marlow under Robert Milman who in 1867 became Bishop of Calcutta. Robert Milman and his sister Maria (who lived with him), came to know the Hoare family well. In 1874 while on a visit to England, Maria Milman met one of the Hoare sisters and invited her to India to help work amongst Indian women. Bishop Milman had begun a high caste girls' school and was desperate for helpers; also there was a programme of zenana visiting which needed more volunteers. At Miss Milman's suggestion the Revd H.H. Sandel, the Indian missionary priest from the Cathedral (see previous chapter), had begun writing to Angelina Hoare, and in response she had begun collecting money for the upkeep of a number of poor Bengali Christian children.

In response to Miss Milman's plea Angelina decided to work in India rather than British Columbia which had been her original plan, but she was still very uncertain about the work she would do. Despite Miss Milman, Angelina's aunt, Lady Kinnaird, thought Delhi [2] would be more suitable, chiefly because she had missionary friends there. Also, Angelina had decided to wait three years until her youngest sister[3] had turned twenty five. But the work in Calcutta seemed very urgent, especially after the retirement of one of the chief helpers, and early in 1875 Angelina consented to go as soon as she was able. The preparations seem to have taken all year, but on December 11th 1875 at Angelina's own request, she was given an episcopal send-off by her diocesan bishop, the Archbishop of Canterbury (Archibald Campbell Tait). He presided and preached at a Eucharist in the chapel of Addington Palace during which he spoke of the importance of women's work in the Church and, laying his hand on Angelina's head, commissioned her for the work she was undertaking.

Accompanied by several members of her family as far as Egypt, and the rest of the way by her brother Hugh, Angelina finally arrived in Calcutta on Sunday January 30th 1876, and was met by the bishop's chaplain. She stayed at the bishop's palace for two or three weeks after which she moved to a small house in the compound where some of the women helpers lived. An immediate difficulty was language: Angelina had attempted to learn Bengali before leaving England but she soon realised how inadequate her lessons had been. Writing back to England she lamented: "It is a terrible drawback not being able to speak the language… Do you take in that the written language is so different from the spoken one, that if you speak in the written language, they do not understand you!"[4] But by May 1876 she was able to report on a conversation with a Bengali tradesman: "… I did the talking in Bengali nearly entirely. You can imagine that I led the conversation to matters which I could understand, or I should soon have been out of my depth!"

Eventually Angelina mastered Bengali, but those early problems must have seemed daunting. Even so, the sense of vocation which she obviously felt, and her wholehearted embracing of it are clear from a passage written later in 1876: "I count on nothing, except going home under ten years' time, if I am alive, and having one of my sisters out here, if they are alive. I really can't see how I can go home, unless somebody comes to take my place. I am thirty-three tomorrow; am I not old? I can think of nothing I want, except a *house and school in Bhowanipore* and a knowledge of Bengali." Perhaps it was this matter of fact attitude towards life and death, coupled with few needs and even less wants, which made Angelina Hoare seem a strange person to many people.

Very soon after her arrival in Calcutta, Angelina's work suffered a tremendous setback in the sudden death of Bishop Milman. He had been on a lengthy tour of his large diocese but cut it short in order to receive the Prince of Wales in Calcutta just before Christmas 1875. He then resumed the tour at Peshawur (where he had left off), even though it was an unhealthy time of year, and was taken ill with exhaustion at the end of February. He was moved to Rawalpindi, a hill station about 100 miles away, and he died there on March 15th 1876 aged 60. His sister, who had been his constant companion, was still in Calcutta at the time of his death, and she returned to England soon afterwards, where she wrote a biography of her brother and his work[5]. The loss of both the bishop and his sister left Angelina bereft of most of the English people whom she knew in India. But she remained cheerful and resolute: "Of course I am not going to leave Calcutta! I am part of Calcutta, though I am afraid that Calcutta does not know it!" was her comment in April 1876.

Maria Milman was accompanied back to England by Miss Hurford who had previously been head of the high-caste girls' school founded by Bishop Milman and which was later to bear his name. This left just one helper, a Miss Grey, who now assisted Angelina Hoare in the charge of the school along with a number of Indian teachers. The financing of the school now fell largely to Angelina who bore it quite stoically, though there was some help from the Ladies' Association of the Society for the Propagation of the Gospel. The summer of 1876 saw the formation of a Committee which aimed to raise funds to build a new school building bearing Bishop Milman's name, together with an endowment to secure its future. Clearly Angelina saw the future of missionary work as lying in schools rather than in the zenana visiting, for she wrote home: "We hope the Zenana Mission will soon die a natural death, because the ladies will all be educated, and if not, they will not mind coming out to be taught."

Angelina Hoare's large family in England were always supportive of her work and her sisters in particular spent much of their time fund raising by means of tea parties, sales of work and missionary talks. Even so, at first her requests for money took some getting used to, especially the initial demand for £3,000 for a house (the house in the bishop's compound being only a temporary arrangement). The family must have expressed surprise and offered delaying tactics, if her response is anything to go by: "You say there is no hurry for a House Fund. Are we then, while the money is being collected, to live as the barbers do here, under umbrellas by the roadside? There is a great deal of need for hurry."

But there were some encouraging signs too, notably the visit of her sister, Sophia, during the winter of 1876-7, who was then able to go home and report first-hand all the things she had seen, not least the pressing need for a permanent mission house. Also, there was the appointment of Edward Johnson as Bishop of Calcutta and his subsequent arrival in India, accompanied by his sister and niece. The Johnson's were to be very supportive of Angelina and her work. More helpers in the school enabled Angelina to resume work in the zenanas despite her reservations about this type of missionary work. One of the main difficulties of zenana work was that the Hindu husbands of the women objected to Christian teaching - general education was permissible, but as soon as the Bible was introduced, the men would object or present counter arguments. The whole object of zenana work was to win Christian converts so that general education was only the means to the end. Missionaries like Angelina saw zenana work as largely labour in vain.

In 1878 Angelina became aware of the need for work in an area which was to change the face of her mission - the swampy, rice growing district south of Calcutta, known as the Sunderbuns. She first became aware of this need through visiting in the poor Indian quarter near the Cathedral. The people who lived there spoke of their Christian relatives south of the city in a practically inaccessible area stretching about 60 miles. Almost the only method of travel during the eight month long wet season was by flat bottomed boats between the wide, open paddy fields. Above water level on slightly elevated ground there were a number of villages of varying sizes. The people lived in mud huts, thatched with rice straw and eked their existence from the rice crop. Part of the area was dense jungle where tigers (often man-eaters) roamed, so that no one could be certain of living in safety. Despite the romantic qualities of the scenery, it was an unhealthy area being full of malaria-bearing mosquitoes - quite uncongenial for Europeans and certainly no place for a lady. Angelina made up her mind that she must go!

Refreshed by a visit to England, she returned to Calcutta in October 1879 accompanied by her youngest sister (Katherine) and another helper, Miss G. Harte. Having already reconnoitred the Sunderbuns before her holiday in England, she now set about organising the mission work there in collaboration with the clergy of the district. It was not entirely barren ground, for there were already some Christians in the villages, and a few of these were Indian women who had been educated in boarding schools established by English missionary societies. These women were nurtured by Angelina to become teachers in the village schools which she established. At first she only went to villages where there was already an established Christian presence.

Katherine Hoare stayed with Angelina for a year and found the routine quite exhausting. Each tour of the Sunderbuns would last up to twelve days and several villages would be visited each day with constant repetition of lessons. Indian food and eating habits did not come easily to Katherine who described the curry as "greasy and oily," and the practice of eating with one's fingers was uncongenial to her. Clearly Angelina attempted to Anglicise the Indian women in matters of dress, a trap which many missionaries fell into. Thus in the biography[6] there is an account of how: "the poorer women did not take kindly at first to the undergarment she wished them to wear below their saris, because the sari alone does not form a decent dress in public." Clearly the only people to be offended by the sari were the European missionaries. However, the women were induced to wear the undergarments by the gift of sweets. The underwear had been specially made by a working party of earnest ladies in London who doubtless thought that the wearing of pantaloons would somehow help win India to the Gospel!

Not all Angelina Hoare's supporters both at home or abroad, fully agreed with her work in the Sunderbuns, chiefly because they felt it was too great a health risk. To such critics she replied that: "the object is worth more than shooting snipe etc., which men do here knee-deep in water, exposing themselves to dangers of various kinds, and no one abuses *them*." Others felt she was neglecting the work in Calcutta, but she was encouraged by a letter from Maria Milman saying: "Go on quietly with what your hand has found to do." This she did and gradually her critics were won over so that at Christmas 1880 Lady Garth, wife of the Lord Chief Justice, agreed to visit Raghabpur to present the prizes to 280 children. She wrote rather wryly to her family: "Now that Lady Garth has been down, the water country will become quite fashionable." That same Christmas life was made much easier by the gift from her family of a 40 foot long native *shalti* (a flat bottomed boat made from a hollowed out tree trunk).

As well as establishing the work in the rice country, the quest for a suitable house in Calcutta continued unabated until the summer of 1882 when a house was found in Pipalpati Road (later called Lansdowne Road). The same house had been on the market six years previously but had been outside Angelina's budget. It had consequently been purchased by a Maharajah who spent a great deal of money on improvements. In 1882 the house was for sale once more, oddly at the same price as before, and thanks to the fund-raising efforts of her English supporters, Angelina was able to buy it. She wrote enthusiastically to friends in England: "I scarcely know how to write about anything except the £3,000 which you have sent out, for the purchase of the Maharajah's house. It is the house we have wanted all along... The property, you know, is to be vested in the hands of the Bishop and Archdeacon of Calcutta, in trust for the Church of Bengal. It is a grand house, with nine acres of land. We shall be able to have a boarding-school, teachers to train, a larger English staff, - anything you like!"

Bishop Johnson visited Angelina soon after she moved into the house in August 1882: "He came at six," she wrote, "and the first thing he said when he came up the stairs was, 'I congratulate you.' The second, 'Are you frightened?' I replied, 'Very pleased, with of course a certain amount of fear.'" Angelina had evidently thought carefully about the nature of the work once she had moved into the new mission house: "My idea for the future of our mission is, that it should be a sort of Deaconess's Institution, not confined to any particular society or nation, and that it should work anywhere in the Diocese of Calcutta, this being the centre, as Clewer is to the Clewer sisterhood."

The new mission house did not divert Angelina's attention away from the rice country schools, indeed this work grew in numbers and importance. In 1887 Lady Dufferin visited the work in the Sunderbuns and left a record of the day (which she evidently enjoyed greatly), in her diary[7]. "Thursday February 24th 1887. Today I had to breakfast early in order to visit some schools in the 'paddy fields'. I was told that in the way of costume I had better wear an old gown, a sun hat, and as much jewellery as possible;... thus armed for conquest, I started off on my long expedition. Fred [i.e. Lord Dufferin], myself and Lady Wilson drove together for about half an hour, and then we picked up Miss Hoare and proceeded on through some pretty country lanes and palm-shaded villages to a ghât on the canal, where a boat and missionary teachers and a large school awaited me. They had put up little arches, and they read me an address and sang to me, and I thanked them and then got into the boat. It was a real native 'dug-out', made by hollowing out one gigantic tree, and it proved to be a most comfortable conveyance. I sat on the floor, which was cushioned, and leant back on piles of pillows with my feet stretched out before me. Miss Hoare faced me in the same attitude. Fred squatted behind her." Lady Dufferin's sense of humour is apparent as she goes on to describe the eating arrangements in the shalti: "... at either end was a liveried servant, the one presiding over Her Ladyship's luncheon - which, even on this occasion, she was not allowed to have without silver egg-cups, spoons and plates, and great paraphernalia of inconvenient things - and the other [servant] carrying her cloaks and parasols... When we got near our destination we found palanquins[8] awaiting us, and I had my first experience of a ride in one of them."

Evidently this was Lady Dufferin's first visit to the Sunderbuns and she was favourably impressed with all she saw, and clearly admired Angelina's dedication. Her description continued: "The village when I reached it, seemed to me a most delightful place. I was not prepared for such clean and picturesque little houses... The front of the houses is generally open, the roof supported on pillars, making a kind of verandah. Some of the largest open sheds are used as 'clubs' for the men, and the domestic apartments, cooking-place, and rice-husking machines are behind. In many villages the 'club' is used as a schoolroom during the day. Miss Hoare has one of these three-sided rooms for her own residence when she comes down here, and she and her sisters occupy three beds in a row, and dress behind a mat at one end, and have a movable matting screen to hide them from the villagers in front. Miss Angelina Hoare is the ruling spirit of all this work. She lives amongst the natives in the paddy-fields almost as one of themselves, wearing a sari, and tramping up to her knees through the marshy rice-fields. Another sister looks older and more delicate, though Miss Angelina is far from strong, and the third is still young. They are well off, but they give up everything to their missionary work."

Having arrived at their destination, Lady Dufferin proceeded to give out the prizes: "There was simply a great carpet of children before me... Each one of the 900 had something, and although some very big boys got the tiniest of pink flannel jackets, while the infants were presented with more masculine attire, I am in hopes they were all more or less pleased; and all, from the bishop downwards, received at my hands a copper Jubilee medal with a blue tape through it. I was next asked to say 'a few words' which I whispered into the ear of an interpreter who seems to have made a splendid speech out of my murmurings; and then the bishop spoke, and they all cheered for me, Miss Angelina Hoare in her enthusiasm mounting a stool and waving her handkerchief, but as three cheers for her were next given, she had rapidly to descend and retire to a corner." The account ends on a satisfactory note: "I got home at 6 o'clock and really enjoyed my day immensely."

The trip to the Sunderbuns may have been Lady Dufferin's first, but it was not her first meeting with Angelina Hoare. This had taken place two years previously when Lady Dufferin had presented prizes at the Milman School, which she wrongly referred to in her diary as a zenana mission. The whole essence of zenana work was of missionaries going to teach women and girls in purdah in their homes, whereas in schools they were obviously mixing together, albeit within the same caste. Lady Dufferin left an account of the day in her diary[9] which is of interest, not only because she recorded her impressions of AngelinaHoare, but also because of her views on the Anglicising of the Indian people. "Wednesday February 11th 1885. I went to give prizes at a Zenana Mission... managed by Miss Hoare, a very energetic lady, 'with no nonsense about her'. She nearly made me laugh by nodding at me after I had distributed a certain number of dolls and boxes, and saying 'Those are the prizes, now these are the bribes.' The little Hindu girls are most attractive... It was most amusing to see them come up for their prizes, but I grieve to say that symptoms of European costume are to be seen amongst them... Is it not dreadful? - jewels, and green and gold garments wound round with crimson muslin, and then striped cotton stockings and shoes! And I was made a most unwilling accomplice, for I had to give out English cotton jackets, and dolls dressed in the 'height of fashion' and well calculated to spoil the taste of the rising generation. These atrocities are sent out by kind people at home. I wish they would get patterns of Indian garments, and make them both for the children and the dolls!"

The Indian climate was notoriously unkind to English constitutions and Angelina's was no exception. Her weak heart and generally frail health found the heat and humidity of Calcutta and the general unhealthiness of the Sunderbuns very trying. Since her arrival in India Angelina had only re-visited England twice - firstly in 1879, and again in 1883, and both visits involved exhausting rounds of talks to groups about the work in order to raise funds. Arriving back in Calcutta in January 1884 she resolved to remain there four years before taking another furlough, but this was not to be. Within two years (in January 1886) she was invalided home and was not allowed to return to India until the September. Having returned, she accompanied Lady Dufferin on her visit to the Sunderbuns in February 1887 as noted above, but soon afterwards had to return to England yet again.

It was at this time that she began to advocate the idea of an Indian Church, something which she began to feel very strongly about, though few people understood the concept. Writing to Maria Milman on June 10th 1885 she broached the subject: "I hope the feeling for an 'Indian Church' as different to the English Church in India and the Native Church in India, is growing... The present system, I feel convinced, nourishes race distinctions, by having a church and separate ministers for the dark races, and for the whites..." Two years later she wrote (again to Miss Milman), "We must not have an English church separate from a native church. It must be a church for India, consisting of all the peoples of India." This concept was way ahead of its time and it was to be another 60 years before a united Church in India became a reality.

Visits to England on doctor's orders became more frequent, although she usually managed to put them to good use by giving talks about her work. These visits caused no small stir because she habitually wore her sari - even to church and garden parties. Her brother Walter's parishioners at Colkirk in Norfolk had never seen such a sight before, and she soon gained a reputation for eccentricity both in England and in India.[10] Meanwhile, when returning to Calcutta in these last years, she was usually accompanied either by visiting relatives, or by new recruits for the work. Thus in October 1889 she returned to India after four months in England, accompanied by Miss Margaret Robertson, a young niece of her sister-in-law, Mrs Walter Hoare.

It was becoming clear however, that Angelina's health was unequal to the increasing demands of the work and to the rigours of India. So it was that in December 1890 she told Bishop Johnson of her decision to resign. Her biography records her words thus: "I am retiring because it seemed to me, and to those I consulted, that God would have me retire. He has prepared my successor - the Sister Superior of the Clewer Community in Calcutta, who is essentially a woman of love. In December last, I therefore resigned into the Bishop's hands the charge which had become too heavy for me to bear." However, there were strings attached, and as will be seen her intention was not a total resignation from the whole work. The note in the biography belies the complexity of the negotiations which now require a more detailed examination.

Footnotes

1. Restoration of Convocation: The Convocation of Canterbury was prorogued in 1717 and virtually suppressed. After the revival known as the Oxford Movement there was increasing pressure on Parliament to revive Convocation. Chief among the protagonists were Bishop Samuel Wilberforce, and Henry Hoare, the latter being one of the leaders of the "Society for the Revival of Convocation." The Convocation of Canterbury was allowed to function once more in 1852, and that of York in 1861.

2. Delhi. This of course refers to the old city of Delhi.

3. There were four maiden sisters - Caroline, Angelina, Sophia and Katherine. They lived together after the death of their parents (father 1866; mother 1871).

4. *Life of Angelina Margaret Hoare* by her sisters and Mrs Walter M. Hoare. Gardner, Darton & Co. 1897. p.51-52. All the letters quoted in this chapter come from this biography.

5. *Memoir of the Rt Revd Robert Milman, D.D...* by his sister Frances Maria Milman. John Murray 1879.

6. *Life of Angelina Margaret Hoare...* op. cit. p.121.

7. MARCHIONESS OF DUFFERIN AND AVA *Our Viceregal Life in India: selections from my Journal 1884-8* 2 Vols John Murray 1889. Vol 2. p.125.

8. Palanquin: a litter with sliding doors or curtains, carried by four to six men, usually in relays.

9. DUFFERIN op. cit. Vol.1 p.57.

10. Details of Angelina Hoare's death are given in Chapter 13, but the Easter 1892 issue of the *St John Baptist Magazine* remarked on her eccentricity thus: "Into this work she threw herself with characteristic energy, and those who have seen her in her native sari and a pair of top boots plunging through the mud of the ricefields, are not likely to forget the sight."

CSJB

INDIA

-12-
A GREAT WORK IN HER OWN WAY

When Mother Jane Frances visited Calcutta in 1888 she met Angelina Hoare and accompanied her on a prize giving trip which filled her with enthusiasm. Even so, she had felt more than a little trepidation mostly on account of her hostess. As already noted in chapter nine, she had commented in a letter to the Sisters at Clewer that: "with so eccentric a conductor one cannot quite foretell one's experiences." But the two seemed to get on well together, Mother Jane Frances' strength of character and sense of humour complementing the oddities of Angelina's personality. For her part, Angelina recognised a kindred spirit in Mother Jane Frances whom she described at the time of her own resignation as, "essentially a woman of love." Perhaps it was this which more than anything else persuaded Angelina that the charge of the mission would be in good hands now that Jane Frances had returned to India as Sister-in-charge.

"It is with great pleasure and thankfulness that the long wished for native work in India can now be begun by the Sisters, the Bishop of Calcutta having offered the Pupulputty [sic] Mission(1) to our Community by the desire of the foundress, Miss Hoare," was the triumphant announcement in the Easter 1891 issue of the *St John Baptist Magazine*, as already noted in chapter ten. It went on to explain that: "This mission takes on several objects of work - schools for Bengali Christian girls; general mission work among the Bengali natives whether Christians or not; visiting in the zenanas as the need arises; and the supervision of the schools in the villages in the ricefields. But the Bishop desires that this new charge of work is not to weaken or to set aside any work in the hospitals and schools which have now been long under the care of the Sisters."

However, the period of negotiation had not been an easy one and it had dragged on for several months. The announcement came after a period of long and complicated talks. It seems as though Angelina Hoare had directly approached Sr Jane Frances about the possibility of the Sisters taking responsibility for the Calcutta mission house. Taken off guard, Sr Jane Frances consulted Bishop Johnson who replied from Darjeeling in a letter dated June 18th 1890. "Miss Hoare's proposal to you does not surprise me as it may very naturally have surprised you. The fact is that it is an old story... The place which Miss Hoare occupies was bought out of money raised by her, and when it was purchased she made it over to the diocese by formal trust deed which is in my possession. I am trustee and therefore, practically owner of the property, and can deal with it under the terms of the trust deed. Some years ago Miss Hoare was obliged to go home unwell and her family were anxious that she should withdraw from the work. She talked the matter over with me and I told her plainly that whenever she withdrew I should offer the place to your Community. I don't think at the time this was quite according to her ideas, but anyhow she got better, came out again and has remained ever since. Of course as she raised the funds for the purchase of the property I never think of endeavouring to supplant her, and I never mention the subject unless she does. But every now and then she talks as she has done to you. She did so to Sr Lucy, and Sr Lucy went over the house with her and ascertained its capabilities, but I fancy she found that the prospect of Miss Hoare's actually retiring was so uncertain that the best course was to purchase some place independent of her."

Sr Jane Frances' letter to the bishop has not survived[2] but it is easy to discern the contents from his reply which continued: "I always look forward to your Community becoming established on those premises which would, I fancy, be suitable in every way. But I feel strongly, as Sr Lucy did, and as you also seem to do, that it would never do for you either to build in her compound or otherwise connect yourselves with her work as long as she is on the premises. Moreover, it would never do to build where she proposes. You would be having two establishments which could not live together in the same compound, and yet again, if you were in possession you would probably build more in immediate connection with the existing house... Finally, my advice is that you should endeavour to fix Miss Hoare in the assertion that she really means to withdraw in three years (she has stated this to several persons I believe), and then bide your time. If you were sure of possession in three years it would be well worth your while to wait. The premises are very suitable and when you were in them you would judge as you cannot do now what new buildings were required. As far as I am concerned, if I am spared so long, you certainly should have the place when Miss Hoare goes... I should therefore advise you to get Miss Hoare's proposal in a definite shape, and then we would let it be generally understood that this arrangement has been made... It is just possible that if the understanding was publicly announced, Miss Hoare might make up her mind to vacate sooner. She has done a great work in her own way, but the change would be a blessing in many ways. If you can talk matters over again with Miss Hoare before you come up here we should better see our way."

A month later on July 23rd 1890 the bishop wrote again from Darjeeling to Sr Jane Frances: "I have had a letter from Miss Hoare in which she expresses her regret that I have not approved of your building in her compound, but she does not say anything as to what your relations with her would be. I hope that you understood my grounds for objecting..., but I write again to say that if you can arrive at any clear and satisfactory arrangement with Miss Hoare I would gladly consent to your accepting her proposal. I understand that Miss Hoare declares that it is her intention to retire from her work in 1894. But if you now build in her compound I don't see how you are to work together during the four years that have to elapse before you take full possession. Moreover, it seems to me that in view of occupying Miss Hoare's premises eventually, it is not necessary to spend money in building a separate institution..." This last remark related to the Sisters' idea of buying land in order to build their own mission house, the Lady Canning Home being wholly inadequate for their needs.

At almost the same time (July 21st 1890) Sr Jane Frances wrote a letter to Mother Betha at Clewer outlining the work and giving her thoughts on it. "Miss Hoare came out some twelve years ago. Her house and compound are close to St Mary's Church in a suburb this side of Calcutta called Ballygunge, ten minutes drive from the Canning Home. It is a very good roomy house with great capabilities... Her indoor work is at present not at all beyond our grasp as you can imagine when I tell you that her staff consists of herself and a young niece, a Eurasian widow and some odds and ends of matrons and teachers. She has a workroom for native girls and women, and a low caste board school, chiefly gathered out of the rice field districts, all managed in a rough and ready haphazard way which we could much improve upon as regards order and method. The house was originally to be the S.P.G. mission house, but she sunk so much money, either in purchase [of the] building from her own or family resources, that it is virtually her own property, and she has made it over to the Bishop of Calcutta by a Trust Deed with the understanding that it should be passed on to us when her time of work came to an end. But this was supposed to depend on her life or health failing, and she is only 50, if as much, and very vigorous, and her health better than it was a few years ago. From what I can make out both from her and the bishop we should be very free. The S.P.G. gives some yearly grant for the work which, if native schools are continued, I do not doubt would be continued, (the amount I have not heard)."

Continuing with her thoughts on the development of the work one can sense Sr Jane Frances' growing excitement as her thin, spidery writing spreads over the pages and becomes more difficult to decipher! "[The work] might be developed in any direction but the present outlook is (if we could get our better class native school formed), when the time came we should on succeeding to Miss Hoare's home, have two grades which are so much needed and of such missionary value in building up the native Christian family life of the future. Zenana visiting... was at one time a branch of the work but Miss Hoare has dropped it lately and has ceased to believe in its value... What has really been personally her forte, is arranging and setting on foot a number of little mission schools scattered over an area of 30 or 40 miles in the rice districts between Calcutta and the sea. These places have to be visited in boats, they must be a tropical variety of the fen country. This I tell her will be the part of the work that we can hardly cope with. Still, when the time comes a way will be found out of that difficulty, and if only we have a couple of years or so to get our hands into responsibilities of native work, there could be no difficulty at all in compassing the work of Miss Hoare's house."

The problems attaching to the Canning Home serving as the Community house had increased as the Sisters had branched out into other work, and consequently there was no focal point. This was brought out in Sr Jane Frances' comments: "... It would be the Community house, and the Sister Superior would find herself much more in her right place and with a little kingdom to rule over and to bring the spirit of the Community into it. Here we are three units, for Sr Anna Frances has her own 'quarters' and establishment, and the Sister Superior is just on a level with the two others who are much more the *doctor's workers* than *her* Sisters. No Sister Superior or Sister-in-charge at home has such an odd feeling... I feel we should never have a Community centre in Calcutta while the Canning Home has to be Headquarters." Returning to the subject of Angelina Hoare's mission house she concluded: "I have said that the house was grand - so it is better than anything we could hope to buy or build, but at the same time, additions or alterations would be necessary. There is a schoolroom in the compound also used as a chapel, and according to our notions [it] would not do either for one [or] other. But there would be money enough for that if we have not to use it all up meanwhile."

A major problem attaching to the undertaking of Angelina Hoare's work was how to deploy the Sisters so that the existing work did not suffer. The work at the Eden Sanatorium in Darjeeling was fraught with difficulties. Sr Jane Frances regarded it as the weak point and would like to have withdrawn from it, but others, notably the bishop, were equally anxious that the Sisters should continue there. Sr Jane Frances attempted to address the problem in a letter to Mother Betha at Clewer dated August 5th 1890: "With regard to working it [i.e. the Pipalpati mission house], if I see my way to get out of Darjeeling, and our numbers remain the same, we should be alright. Indeed, the work at starting would be so small that if I could arrange to be there a good deal or Sr Sophia were the person, she would do single-handed as far as a Sister was concerned, (Sr Muriel would do if not wanted elsewhere). My *personal* work at the Canning Home I consider very little indeed, a mere fraction of the work of any Sister Superior at home, simply because one has next to nothing and no one working *up to you.* Anyone else might do what I do here, as well or better, and without any burden. Of course one has the supervision and responsibility of the other work and much to plan for and ponder over for the future, but I feel that I should quite be able to divide myself between this and the little embryo work which would need a good deal of hatching... In the future, whoever may live to see it, it seems to me as if it would be [? 1 word] to transfer the 'seat of government' to Miss Hoare's house, that the Sister Superior should live [there] and any trustworthy hospital Sister should head up the Canning Home. Sr Anna Frances would do very well *at present* as a kind of deputy here."

Of course the abilities of the Sisters varied tremendously and had to be taken into account. Thus: "If Sr Fanny Gertrude went home, Sr Blanche if she returns to the Nurses' Quarters is *the* great problem in the future. She is such a senior Sister and yet so very unable to be the head of anything and give the *tone* here. They would be miserable with her I fear. However, ways out of difficulties do open out when the time comes to meet them. If we cannot get out of Darjeeling next year, and you would allow Sr Blanche to be an *extra*, I should like to try to arrange that she should be the one in charge *there*. It might make things easier to settle down here and an advantage to her health if she recovers in some measure... I hope to judge better as to all these pro's and con's when I have been there..." (Sr Blanche had been invalided home to England in the spring of 1889, but had returned to Calcutta at the end of the year with Sr Jane Frances when the latter took up office as Sister Superior).

Sr Jane Frances was still thinking in terms of taking a temporary house until Angelina Hoare finally withdrew. Sr Lucy had left some money(3) to the Community which might be used for obtaining temporary accommodation until the Pipalpati mission was available, but naturally the Community did not want to use it if Angelina Hoare was likely to hand over sooner rather than later. And then on August 12th 1890 Sr Jane Frances was able to report a further development: "At his second visit the Bishop told me he had just had an important conversation with Miss Hoare who was seriously debating whether it would not be well for her to retire finally before next hot season, in which idea the bishop and his sister encouraged her. He could not, according to the terms of the deed, make over the property to us, but proposes when the time comes, to let us occupy it on a lease of some length, renewable after a term of years at a nominal rent. That covers repairs, so that we should feel ourselves secure when the next bishop succeeded. I do not think there would be any fear of our being turned out."

Security of tenure was not the only problem; there was also finance. "As to money matters," Sr Jane Frances continued, "a certain amount of support will go when Miss Hoare goes, but we should have to try to supplement that. The serious question will be whether the S.P.G. Ladies' Association will withdraw their grant which is a considerable one. The Secretary, a Miss Bullock, is a prejudicial person who does not like Sisters, and some years ago had expressed great horror at the idea of the work being passed into our hands by the bishop(4). But it is thought that with the support of the bishop and the Oxford Mission, who now work a good deal for the S.P.G., these difficulties will be overcome when the time comes, and we should have Sr Lucy's and other small capital sums to back us up. The interest would make us a little endowment, but part would have to go in improvements and additions. It need be no strain on our numbers at starting, though it has capacities for being developed into a much larger work."

Despite the growing importance of the Indian work, all decisions regarding it were still subject to approval by the Community Chapter which was held twice a year at Clewer. All Sisters professed more than five years had a vote, those at branches having a postal vote, but the necessity of Chapter approval for the Indian work was complicated by the difficulties of communication. Thus in the letter of August 12th 1890, Sr Jane Frances commented: "I do not know what you will think about the November Chapter. Miss Hoare will not, I believe, finally make her mind up whether or not to retire *now* till her sister comes out. She will not arrive till November so I doubt it being a Community question by that time. I do not fancy there could be any doubt throughout the Community that the offer was an advantageous one to accept and that an effort should be made to meet the call should it come earlier than we expected. Of course this makes me feel all the more desirous for Sr Sophia to come out again, and at the same time I feel hiring a small house must be postponed till one sees what will come of this new turn of matters."

The whole process seemed to fall into abeyance for several months, but on October 7th 1890 Sr Jane Frances wrote again to Mother Betha at Clewer. She wrote resignedly that: "There would be great difficulties in getting rid of Darjeeling Sanatorium at a short notice." Also, it seems as though she was expecting the Pipalpati mission house to be transferred soon after Easter the following year (1891), and was under no illusion as to it being easy. "There will be a great deal to be grappled with, as I expect we should not find the work in what we should consider a very ship shape condition. I feel more and more Sr Sophia would be *the* person to help me at starting... She is not irritated by the peculiar ways of the people of the country, and would be kindly and pleasant with the under-workers of one kind and another whom Miss Hoare will leave behind, and whom it would be to our advantage to utilise."[5].

Sr Jane Frances then expanded on the life at the mission house which was quite different from any of the other work of the Sisters. "Miss Hoare has about 40 boarders, divided between children and bigger girls, young widows etc, who do needlework. The workroom might I think, be developed into a useful department; anything of an initial training, whether for boys or girls, is so specially valuable for the native Christian population for whom fresh lines for earning their living are often necessary... for all are of the simplest kind. They all sleep on the floor in one large room, bathe in the tank[6], eat their rice in the native manner sitting on the ground... Hardly any of them are *paid for* as they are mostly from the very poor agricultural class, from the rice fields." The financial side was still as uncertain as ever: "But," wrote Sr Jane Frances, "whatever charitable funds come would be not for us, but for these poor Indian girls and children. Miss Hoare's private income will of course, go with her, but she has sunk a great deal in the place by which of course, we should benefit."

Angelina Hoare still resolutely clung to the idea of retaining the village work, a plan which well suited the Sisters. "Miss Hoare would like to keep her hand upon the village schools, and hopes to come out on visits to Miss Solomon in future cold seasons. I don't think she cares much for the indoor work [i.e. the Pipalpati mission house], and my feeling is that if she kept the rice country work as we call it,... it would be a very good thing. I do not forsee any clashing. *We* could not do it personally... Both Sr Lucy and I have always shaken our heads over therice country work and told Miss Hoare that though it might sound poor-spirited this style of thing was not in our line."

By November things had begun to move again and on the 25th Sr Jane Frances was able to write rather excitedly: "I was summoned yesterday by the bishop to meet Miss Hoare and her sister. Miss Hoare had finally done the deed and sent in her resignation at six months date. I assured the bishop that you knew as much as I did of the whole course of events, but he was anxious that you should *at once* be informed officially, as it were, from him that now this step, having been taken, his next was to offer the work to our Community out here, asking for sanction and acceptance [by] Chapter at home." The question of the S.P.G. Ladies' Association had to be addressed regarding funds but: "Miss Hoare read us a letter she proposed to send them and the bishop will send a letter too. With his support and that of Mr Whitehead [Oxford Mission], I do not think it could be refused. Miss Hoare told me the names of some of the ladies on the Committee who are thorough Church women, or who would probably like to feel the work was in our management. It is only Miss Bullock, the Lady Secretary, who is personally the difficulty." But a great deal rested on S.P.G. sponsorship: "How we should stand with them is an important matter to secure, as it means in English money £400 a year. An additional grant representing about £120 a year has just been made by the Board of Missions, but one cannot from Miss Hoare's way of keeping accounts, make out what the expenses of the work are (though I have seen her books). But with that secured and other helps and certain resources of our own, I am sure we should do. Many a work at home has floated with less to start it."

Even though Sr Jane Frances did not want to undertake the work in the rice country she wanted to understand it. "The bishop does not care much about that part of the work, and he thought Miss Hoare spent her energies unduly," she wrote in her letter of November 25th. "Still, they exist and I hope to make an expedition one of these days with her, so as to realise better the whole position of things. But that is quite an outlying department. I believe Miss Robertson, Miss Hoare's niece, who wants to stay on and give herself specially to that part of the work, would work very comfortably with us. She is quite young, only 22, hard working and steady going, plodding away at the language at present."

The relatively painless transfer of Angelina Hoare's work to the Community of St John Baptist was really due to the genius of Bishop Johnson who had loyally supported the missionary endeavour of Angelina whilst fore-seeing a more ordered way ahead under the Sisters. Sr Jane Frances tacitly acknowledged this at the conclusion of her letter to Mother Betha on November 25th 1890: "The bishop... will no doubt write to you by and by. I should respectfully suggest... this proposed transfer has been *his plan* much more than Miss Hoare's. Now she is most most cordial over it, but at first, some years back, did not quite like the suggestion."

December 2nd 1890 saw Sr Jane Frances hurriedly writing to Clewer in order to catch the outgoing mail but with a great sense of excitement: "I must begin by telling you that I have promised to do a rather venturesome thing, i.e. go with Miss Hoare right into the rice country, south of Calcutta, and spend two or three days visiting those settlements and village schools. The bishop quite thought I ought to do it so as to understand that outlying part anew, though it would not be worked by us personally; it must remain in connection with the Pipalpati mission house. Miss Hoare said [that] by sleeping two nights down there I could see a good deal, but I am in for rather more than I bargained for as great stress is laid on my spending the Sunday there, getting back early on Monday... I expect my bodily experiences will be very rough and strange, but it is quite healthy just now. Miss Hoare will be examining these little schools as to religious instruction. Mrs Wheeler who came to Commemoration Day visits them as Government Inspector of Schools. I shall be able to help Miss Hoare in a very small, humble way, so shall feel I am doing a little real missionary work. Here my sphere of work is not at all spiritual, as I have told you... It will be very instructive I feel, and quite a necessary thing to do. I hope I shall get on alright..." The planned trip to the rice country duly took place and Sr Jane Frances wrote a full account of it for the Sisters at Clewer. Dated December 12th 1890 it was a letter bursting with enthusiasm: "I have had four such interesting and curious days in the rice country ...," it began. (The full text may be found in Appendix 5).

The question of Chapter arose once more at the end of 1890. The main problem was the length of time taken by the mail between Clewer and Calcutta. Sometimes the mail from India arrived *after* decisions had been made by Chapter and this did not make for a good relationship. Having been Mother Superior, Sr Jane Frances felt acutely aware of the problem, and so in her letter to Mother Betha dated Tuesday December 2nd 1890, she broached the subject once more. "I am going to ask you to think, or to take the mind of the Consultative Council, as to the Indian group of works being recognised as a Province with the right to have a little local Chapter about their own affairs. If we get into Miss Hoare's work I think the time would have come for that. I think it would be a great help out here in doing all together and keeping up a common interest in the various scattered works. It would only mean reviving what exists in the Constitution, but in England it has never come to life, though it was a favourite thought both of the Warden [i.e. Canon Carter] and of Mother Harriet. But here with the Sr Superior over all, it would work and give the Sisters a feeling that there was a way of taking their minds about things affecting ourselves only. For example, about Darjeeling - it would have come in so usefully to have had so recognised a way of discovering the pro's and con's. And it would seem likely with a work more really our own, and a house that would be added to, and develop other sides of work, that such questions may arise."

There had been a suggestion that a Sister in England should represent the Indian work in Chapter, but Sr Jane Frances disagreed with this: "The Sr Superior has the privilege as well as the duty of reporting fully to Headquarters, and the other Sisters writing officially to someone else who was *not* Mother Superior might bring in great discord. On general questions we may have different views and interests, but discord we have none." The suggestion of an Indian Province was not acted upon until 1938, when it was too late. Doubtless it was too radical a suggestion for the 1890s though constitutionally there was a precedent in the American Affiliation.

By late December 1890, having received written assurance from the Warden that the Sisters would not withdraw from Darjeeling, the Bishop of Calcutta sent to Clewer his proposed terms for the Sisters' work at the Pipalpati mission house. At a Chapter held on January 31st 1891, it was agreed that the work should be undertaken: there was only 1 vote against the proposal. The agreed terms had been thoroughly worked out with a view to there being a different bishop a few years hence. Occupation was for a term of 20 years, the agreement to be renewed if both sides so desired it, with a year's notice before the expiry date should either party desire withdrawal. The Sisters were to be responsible for all repairs; and alterations and additions would be permitted subject to approval by the Trustees. At the request of Bishop Johnson, who was also a Lady Canning Home Trustee, the following clause was included: That "the work in connection with this Institution is to be carried on not to the detriment of other work, hospital or educational, now in hand, but this is not to stand in the way of the Community making this Institution their headquarters if it appears desirable."

Writing to Mother Betha before the decisive Chapter meeting, Sr Jane Frances remarked: "It is wonderful how it has now worked round after so many ups and downs." Certainly taking the Pipalpati mission house proved to be a turning point in the work of the Sisters and henceforth they were able to lead much more of a Community life. But they had neither seen nor heard the last of the village schools in the Sunderbuns, for on January 10th 1892, just a few months after her resignation, Angelina Hoare died suddenly.

Footnotes

1. See note 4 of chapter 10 about the spelling of Pupulputty, or Pipalpati. The mission was so named because of the large number of pipal trees (sacred to the Hindu's) in the mission compound.

2. No copies of Sr Jane Frances ' letter to the bishop exist at Clewer.

3. Because of the controversial nature of women's Religious Communities in the 19th century the founders of the Community of St John Baptist thought it wise that Sisters should not resign their personal wealth to the Community when they became professed Sisters. They were free to bequeath it as they thought fit.

4. The S.P.G. Ladies' Association was not the only body which had to be won over to the idea of Sisters assuming the mantle of Angelina Hoare. There was the Hoare family too, and the oraganisation known as the Weald of Kent Association which had been founded to support Angelina's work - see note 5 of chapter 13 for details. Meanwhile, two letters to Mother Betha at Clewer from Sophia Hoare (Angelina's sister), articulate both the reservations and the prejudices which prevailed amongst the wealthy classes concerning Sisters. They were both written before Angelina's death and concern the attendance of Sr Georgina Mary and Sr Annie at the annual fund-raising meeting. The first was dated June 27th 1891: "We saw our cousin Sr Georgy [Sr Georgina Mary] yesterday and had a talk,... Since then, it has occurred to us as possible that the lady at whose house this meeting is to be [held] might be rather afraid of 'Sisters' and my sister wants me to drive over... and see this lady (Lady Hardinge of Hawkhurst), about the Sisters going. I do hope you will understand our position. It is not that we ourselves have *anything* but confidence in you, but you know we must be careful how we move in some direction if we are not to lose any support. I am afraid my letters must seem very lacking in cordiality, but you will observe that it is of others that we have to think... We are anxious that you should stretch your rules if possible, and allow the Sisters to sleep at my house so that they may meet quietly a lady [Miss Edelmann], who is an Associate [of the Weald of Kent Association], for the Chislehurst neighbourhood, but who has not quite your Church views. She is a most good, dear woman and we want her to be won over to like the mission passing into your control..."

The second letter, dated July 19th 1891, was in similar vein. Whilst requesting the presence of a Sister, Miss Hoare seemed wary of the idea: "I do not as yet know that a 'Sister' might not frighten some of our people... My object is to disarm any objection our friends and neighbours may have to our mission being handed over to your body, and with this object we should want you to send us a Sister who could and would speak persuasively and attractively, and win possibly doubtful people over to become firm friends. You must know that this is a critical year with the mission, and we are most anxious that no help hitherto given to my sister [i.e. Angelina] should be wanting to you... I am sure you will understand why I ask for a Sister who shall speak persuasively. Manner with some people goes such a long way, and a bright attractive manner wins people against themselves, does it not?"

5. Sr Sophia had left India in March 1890, and in response to Sr Jane Frances ' urgent plea was allowed to return, arriving in Calcutta on March 7th 1891 with Sr Florence.

6. Tank - a large pond from which all the water for drinking, washing and bathing was collected.

-13-
A LITTLE HANDFUL OF RICE

Amid the exciting prospect of taking possession of the Pipalpati mission house, the Sisters' work in hospitals, schools and orphanage continued. It would be easy to imagine that everything had ground to a halt whilst the negotiations between Clewer, the bishop, Angelina Hoare and Sr Jane Frances were being conducted, but this was far from the truth. The daily round of worship and varied works went on unceasingly. To this end, Sisters were constantly in transit between Calcutta and Clewer - tired Sisters returning home on furlough, fresh Sisters anticipating the work in a new country, experienced Sisters returning for another tour of duty.

As noted in chapter 10, sometimes very inexperienced or newly professed Sisters were sent to India. Thus on January 18th 1890 Sr Mary Isabel, professed just six months, sailed with Sr Mary Alethea from Liverpool in the *S.S. City of Bombay* and arrived in Calcutta on February 20th. A few days later, on January 23rd Sr Mary Christine, accompanied by her own sister (Miss Frost), sailed from London on the P.& O. steamer *Chusan*, and arrived on February 26th after surviving fierce gales. Sr Mary Isabel was destined for the Eden Hospital, and wrote to the Clewer Associates enthusiastically about her arrival: "Our Captain carefully timed our entrance into the Houghly [sic] for the tide so we got up without delay. It is too dangerous a river to navigate by night and it is not always easy to fit in the tide and the daylight. At first we could not see the banks as the river is so broad, but as we got on it was all most interesting. The new vegetation, the difficulty of distinguishing huts from haystacks!, the large factories[1] each with their pier built out into the river, the grand old houses in gardens. Most of the country is quite flat with trees, not dense jungle. One tree without leaves was covered with brilliant red flowers. We have since found out that it was a cotton tree. Another had equally brilliant leaves, the fallen ones making quite a red carpet underneath."

Sr Mary Isabel continued: "Our ship had been telegraphed from Diamond Harbour and several Sisters met us at the jetty bringing two men who rescued our luggage from the chattering coolies. Sr Mary Angela carried off Miss T. to the Pratt School and we two went to the Canning Home. The next day we began our sightseeing by going over the General Hospital. Sr Gertrude Emma showed us her ward. I could not understand so many people being about and asked what was the matter. 'Oh that child has only come because his mother is here'; 'That woman is with her sick child and her mother and sister are too.' Sometimes there are whole families in at once. Afterwards we went to the European

Orphanage, such a nice house in a large garden where all the children were out at play, still in their blue winter frocks, but they are to begin [wearing] their white this week. Then we walked over to the Pratt School but it was too dark to see much of the house. On the way back we saw fireflies, one of the signs of the hot season having begun. My work is to be at the Eden Hospital. It is such a lovely house with its white marble floors so clean and cool."

Sr Mary Alethea had gone up to Darjeeling to work in the Eden Sanatorium and found the whole experience fascinating. Her letter was reproduced for the Clewer Associates in the Autumn 1890 edition of the *St John Baptist Magazine.* "This is such a lovely place... Immediately in front of us is a deep valley and as you look about you can count spur after spur, and each with a valley on either side... The lights and shades are so exquisite. The people are very different from the Bengalis and are a much hardier race, but most of them are short... The women work side by side with men, like navvies. They work on the roads and carry enormous weights on their backs. They act too as porters and bring up great boxes from the station, slung to their backs by a band from the head. You may see children too with great loads. On Monday I saw a little boy staggering up a very steep khud [hillside] with a huge stone on his back, and women and girls do this also. Mothers sometimes go to work with their babies tied on their backs by a shawl, or in a sort of cradle slung from their heads, by which means the hands are free to work or to carry something else in front... From this House you can see where they are making an extension of the railway and women are working at it like navvies... Many men carry great daggers sometimes in a silver sheath with an ivory handle. I believe they are for cutting away jungle, and also for self defence I suppose. They wear ornaments but not to such an extent as the women do... The religion here is nominally Buddhist. Buddha's temple stands a few yards from this Sanatorium and night and morning we hear very pretty toned bells ringing while he is being put up to bed or got up and fed. The people however, laugh at it all. For Christians there is the English church, the Roman Catholic church, the Roman Catholic chapel with a Jesuit establishment, and nuns of the Sacred Heart with their schools for boys and girls. There is a Scotch Mission and a Baptist chapel. I forgot to mention the Mohammedan mosque, so the religions of the world are pretty well represented here. There are also plenty of schools. St Paul's School for boys, which is the diocesan, and the High School for girls, besides one or two other schools."

Sr Sophia had left Calcutta on February 21st 1890, much to Sr Jane Frances' regret. As noted in chapter 12, Sr Jane Frances valued Sr Sophia's gifts of leadership and felt that she was the right person to assist her in taking over the Pipalpati mission house: but she was due for home leave. However, on January 29th 1891 Sr Sophia and Sr Florence sailed from London in the *Rewa* and arrived in Calcutta on March 7th. This released

Sr Sophie (not to be confused with Sr Sophia), for a well earned furlough having been five years in India, and also Sr Fanny Gertrude, one of the original Sisters in India who had served there twice. Both Sisters sailed in the *S.S. Mombasa*, leaving Calcutta on March 30th 1891.

On June 4th 1891 Angelina Hoare set sail for England and Sr Jane Frances and Sr Sophia took possession of the Pipalpati mission house in Lansdowne Road[2] for the Community. Having arrived in England, Angelina Hoare embarked upon a punishing programme of fund-raising events and talks in aid of the work in the Sunderbuns which she intended to resume upon her return to India in the autumn. On July 7th she and one of her sisters attended Commemoration Day at Clewer. The sojourn in England ended on October 22nd when she left for India once more, finally arriving in Calcutta (via Bombay and Poona) on Sunday November 22nd. Just a few days before leaving England she had addressed a meeting organised by the Clewer Sisters at their Convalescent Home in Folkestone. So Angelina Hoare returned to her work in the Sunderbuns little thinking that she would never see England again.

Just a week after Angelina Hoare set off for India, Sr Mary Christine, who had been in charge of the European Orphanage, died suddenly from cholera on October 29th 1891. A telegram was immediately sent to Clewer telling them the sad news, and they replied by return: "Community deeply grieved," but they had to await the mail from India to learn details. This finally arrived on November 21st and the Community *Annals* tell us that "dear Sr Mary Christine had been quite well on October 28th and walked to the Mission House in the evening - half an hour's walk to say goodbye to Sr Sophia who was to go to Darjeeling the next day. She came back, was in good spirits, ate her supper as usual, but was taken ill in the night and when the doctor came he said it was cholera of the worst type. Sr Florence, working at the Pratt School, was with her, besides Sr Jane Frances. She suffered terribly and was unconscious till near the end when she was calm and peaceful. She passed away at 3 p.m. on October 29th. There was a Celebration [of the Eucharist] the next morning at 6 a.m. and the first part of the Burial Service. She was laid to rest in the Sisters corner in the Cemetery."

Sr Mary Christine's sudden death brought about a crisis because, while there was an increasing number of Sisters working in India, none were superfluous. The workload continued to increase, and if one Sister was withdrawn for any reason it meant that the whole personnel had to be reorganised in order to make the best use of everyone's talents. Ordinary comings and goings could be planned for, but serious illness or sudden death caused great difficulty. So it was that despite having only returned to England five months previously after a five year spell, Sr Sophie volunteered to return to Calcutta. She left England on November 22nd 1891, travelled overland through Europe spending 24 hours with her family in Berne, and joined the *S.S. Rewa* at Naples on November 28th.

She arrived in Calcutta on December 28th.

The coming of 1892 was to bring fresh challenges to the Sisters occasioned by the unexpected death of Angelina Hoare. She had wasted no time after arriving back in Calcutta in embarking on a tour of the schools in the Sunderbuns accompanied by Margaret Robertson. This final return to India could not have been easy because, whilst still in charge of the village schools, she no longer controlled the Mission House even though she continued to work from it. Her biography[3] indicates a certain apprehension: "I quite feel that the Sisters are carrying on my work, and not, as it were, starting fresh work on new lines." "The Sisters have done various little things to please me, so that I am as *relieved* as I had hoped to be. The boarding school is much larger already, having come up to 58 names on the roll. The Sisters tell me I may develop a little in the ricefields, so I am looking out for places where new schools may be started."

On December 15th she fainted in the Calcutta University Senate House whilst some of her pupils were taking an examination, and on December 20th, after congestion of the lungs was diagnosed, she finally took to her bed. A few days later a painful foot which was thought to be rheumatic developed into an abcess and she sent a message home: "Tell them it is a perfect blessing to have Sr Sophia in the house, able to move and bandage the rheumatic foot, almost without hurting it. I cannot think what we should have done without her." On January 6th her temperature soared to 104 degrees Fahrenheit and the diagnosis "malignant fever" was pronounced, but after a day or two she rallied, and the doctor said she must go home to England as soon as she was well enough. "When such words are said to anyone, they mean that their work is ended," she told Sr Sophia. Even so, the end did not seem imminent, but during the early hours of January 10th 1892 her life ebbed away. Later accounts tell us that the cause of death was a brain haemorrhage. She was forty eight years old.

The funeral took place next day, January 11th, and many Indian people, both adults and children, were present. At the end of the service Sr Jane Frances invited them to pass by the grave. The grave was later marked by a granite cross sent out from England, and at the west end of Calcutta Cathedral a brass memorial tablet was erected[4]. Angelina Hoare was a larger than life figure who, like so many other pioneers, defied convention and stereotypes in order to make her vision a reality. In her particular case, the vision entailed winning India for Christ; the reality lay in the village schools where she laboured long and hard. "It is my child," is how she had described the work just a few months before her death.

This unexpected turn of events meant more work for the Clewer Sisters. "Our Indian work has entered on a new phase through the resignation and subsequently lamented death of Miss Angelina Hoare... Now the whole work - Calcutta schools and ricefield mission have been transferred to the Sisters," wrote Sr Jane Frances in the Easter 1892 edition of *St John the Baptist Magazine*. Writing to the Honorary Secretary of the St John Baptist Calcutta Mission Association, Sr Jane Frances said: "You will, I daresay realise, that our good friend Miss Hoare's serious illness and unlooked for death, barely a month ago, has thrown a good deal extra upon Sr Sophia and myself."

She went on to remark that Angelina Hoare: "had arrived on her cold weather visit so full of life and vigour... She is a great loss to the missionary cause out here as we have now on our hands the responsibilty of the 30 or more scattered little country schools in the Sunderbuns." Angelina Hoare's death and the consequent extra work imposed upon the Sisters meant yet another re-shuffle. "Sr Sophia is still the only member of the Community at the Mission House, but I have had to be so much backwards and forwards that it has seemed rather like riding on two horses at once! However, the shortly expected arrival of Sr Gertrude Emily will be a great strength to the hospital work, and in time I hope, will set me free from the ordinary business of the Canning Home, so that I shall be able to *live* at the Mission House and make that my *personal* work, while going on with the general superintendance of the Community from there... Deo gratias we are all, I am thankful to say, well. Two Sisters will soon be sailing from India, and three are on their way out to strengthen our hands for this increase of work. All help from home will still be more valuable now that we have so much upon us opening out in so many different directions." This last remark was an allusion to the work of fund raising and general support given by the Association.

The new Sisters duly arrived. On January 15th 1892 Sr Gertrude, Sr Gertrude Emily and Sr Bethia sailed for Calcutta on the *S.S. Manora* and arrived safe and well on February 22nd after a very comfortable voyage with good weather. On March 1st the *Manora* sailed on her return voyage to England, arriving there on April 6th with Sr Gertrude Emma and Sr Mary Angela on board. All the Calcutta Sisters went to the docks to see them off at 6.00 a.m.

The Clewer Associates already had a good idea of the work in the Sunderbuns before the Sisters' inherited it, because of Sr Jane Frances ' well documented visit. But they had less idea about what went on at the Pipalpati mission house. So as soon as the negotiations were completed between the Community, the bishop and Angelina Hoare, Sr Jane Frances had written a letter which appeared in the Easter 1891 number of the *St John Baptist Magazine*. "There are about 40 native Christian girls in the House at present. The elder ones do needlework ... and learn a little dressmaking. The children go through their regular school course. There is a nice school building in the Compound, a little detached from the House. One end screened off, serves as a chapel where Morning and Evening Prayer are said for school and household. The teachers are all native Christians, two of them are young widows. The instruction is purely in Bengali. The teachers seem zealous and some of the children have done well and have gained primary scholarships. I found the children very easy to make friends with, their gentle manner struck one favourably. They are all of the poorer class, many of them of the same standing as those whom I saw in the rice country schools, but from the Hindu point of view, they would not be considered of quite the lowest castes. One of the objects of the school is that it should take in some of the brighter pupils from the village schools who should afterwards return to be teachers in their own village. Their mode of living therefore is very simple and quite after native fashion, which however, can be very orderly on its own lines."

This school was later known as the Lower or Vernacular School, although at the time of the Sisters' takeover it does not seem to have had a name. However, the Sisters also took responsibility for the Milman School and Sr Jane Frances also introduced the Associates to this in the Autumn 1891 issue of *St John Baptist Magazine*: "It is a day school for little Hindu girls of the higher castes - the children of Hindu gentlemen. It is in the same compound with the Mission House though quite separate from it, but it is considered an appendage to the work. The building is the property of the Diocese." This school was the one founded by Bishop Milman in which he had invited Angelina Hoare to assist. After his untimely death it had been continued as a memorial to him and funded by the Ladies' Association of the S.P.G. Since Angelina Hoare's withdrawal from the Mission House, the S.P.G. funding had been withdrawn too, which left the Sisters with a problem.

In their usual indomitable way the Sisters took all these changes in their stride. The advantages of having a mission house which they could call their own far outweighed any problems the extra responsibilities might bring. "It seems [as] Sr Lucy often said, that out here we are always called to enter into the labours of others rather than to break fresh ground for ourselves," wrote Sr Jane Frances. "But," she continued, "a great advantage in this case is that we have such very good premises - a large and pretty compound, a work already begun and a considerable amount of support already to hand, without which it might take many years to get together." One of the greatest sources of support was Margaret Robertson who took upon herself much of the workload in the rice country schools and without whom the Sisters would have been hard-pressed, especially in the early days.

The other type of support was that given by the Associates in England both of Clewer itself, and of the St John Baptist Calcutta Mission Association; and also by members of the Weald of Kent Association(5). As noted before, fund-raising sales and garden parties were held in England for the Indian work, supplemented by working parties of ladies who made useful garments which were dispatched just before Christmas. This was a mixed blessing because quite often the garments were inapproriate, but the English benefactresses *expected* profuse thanks and took offence if the slightest criticism was made. Lady Dufferin's horror at having to hand out such gifts at one of Angelina Hoare's prize giving ceremonies has already been noted, and the problem seems to have worsened rather than improved. Thus in January 1895 Sr Jane Frances wrote a carefully worded letter to Miss Arbuthnot, Secretary of the St John Baptist Calcutta Mission Association:

"All the jackets of various kinds and colours sent by the various donors are very nice and pretty. I would mention that we now have a sufficient store of *flannelette* jackets to go into next year i.e. next cold season. The superfluous jackets are carefully put away with camphor. In the next box a *larger* proportion of print or calico articles would therefore be acceptable. I would explain once more that for about three months, but *not longer*, the air is sufficiently chilly in the morning and evening to make warm jackets and warm wraps at night, and comforters for the men, very precious gifts, *but only* for a short time. After February nothing but washing materials can be worn, so cotton jackets are in request for nine months of the year. I believe our kind helpers rather tire of making so many jackets, but for our Indian children these and plain chemises are the only *made* articles of clothing that we require, for their saris make skirt, mantle and head covering as well. Some blouses do very nicely for the little ones, but even they must have their saris for *Sundays*, so that they may cover their heads reverently in church as we do not go in for hats or bonnets, or indeed any unnecessary European fashion, which would only encourage vanity or expensive habits. I would also mention another little matter, that though the village children, especially the Hindu's who are there in the majority, still delight in scarlet print and very bright colours, our Christian boarders think it vulgar and, like Hindu's and Musselmen, develop very sober tastes, so that the old suggestions no longer hold good in this case."

The concept of famine is something of which English supporters of the Clewer Sisters could have had little idea in the 1890s. Bible stories of Joseph in Egypt would have been familiar, together with memories of the Irish potato famine in the 1840s. Otherwise famine would have been outside the experience of most English people at this time. But in the 1890s there was famine in Bengal due to the failure of the rice crop. In 1891 the early ending of the monsoon and absence of the cold season rains caused much damage to the winter rice. 1895 saw a very poor rice harvest followed by early rainfall in 1896 and no rain after early September. So great was the distress that relief work was undertaken to alleviate the increasing hardship in the winter of 1896/7.

The Autumn 1893 number of the *St John Baptist Magazine* contains an account by Sr Jane Frances of the famine and the Sisters' efforts at relief. "Towards the end of Lent, Sr Sophia and I paid a visit to one of our larger centres where there is actually a brick and stucco church, and scattered about among the neighbouring villages, a considerable number of Christians. The Bishop of Calcutta held a Confirmation there and next morning we gathered the children of 16 of our little schools, making a total of between 400 and 500 for a collective prizegiving... Besides the prizes, ... dry refreshments had to be distributed to the whole company in the shape of a handful of rice fried with a little treacle. Even then we had thunderstorms and violent rain all night and found we could cross the fields in the little 'shalties' or narrow flat boats, instead of on foot as is usual at that season. However, the tremendous rain accompanying the cyclone in Whitsun week was the crowning disaster, as it hindered the planting out of the year's crop."

Sr Jane Frances then went on to explain to her English readers about the rice crop: "Rice is not sown broadcast in fields like wheat, but first very thickly in small plots. Then, when the rains begin, the plants are set out, each plant apart like garden seedlings, and the young rice keeps pace in its growth with the rise of the waters. This year the country was all flooded by these violent rains in May, the seedling rice, ready for planting out was washed away in many places. And as the fields have remained deeply under water ever since, what remained could not be planted. We heard such lamentable accounts from our people of the condition of the country that in order to see the state of things with our own eyes Sr Sophia and I in July, made two rounds of a few days each, and visited the larger part of the flooded district. The country looked very strange; one is familiar now with the ricelands under various aspects, but this was quite a new experience. Instead of the bright green of the young rice growing out of the shallow water as far as the eye could see, nothing was visible but stretches of water thickly grown with an ugly kind of rush... This state of things meant a complete failure of the rice for this year. Not merely a poor harvest, but none to be looked for till December 1894 - and for these rice cultivators their rice crop is their all."

Of course there were no organised relief agencies at this time, but as the Sister went on to explain, some of the Churches were attempting relief as best as they could. "No doubt the pressure of want will become greater by and by, but already the different religious bodies are organising systems of relief for these poor Christians, and when the distress becomes more severe it is hoped that some general assistance in the shape of relief works will be forthcoming from the Government. But the Government does not profess to move in the matter till starvation point is actually reached. The Oxford Mission, who have the spiritual charge of all this district, have already taken up the cases of greatest distress among the Christians of our Communion. Our own responsibility is chiefly with regard to all the little village schools which, without some extra assistance, would simply wither away during this time of distress. Indeed one cannot expect the children to come to school in a completely famished condition.

So something on the principle of Board School free or ha'penny dinners, we have begun this month, making doles of rice, a small measure to each child on the list of the 'distressed' three times a week; but the roll of distressed takes in over 800 children, distributed over 30 schools, and though individually as small an assistance as could be given collectively, it mounts up to a considerable outlay each month beyond the usual working expenses of the mission. We have had to make a venture of faith trusting that this year some extra help may be vouchsafed to us. In spite of adverse circumstances, some of the little schools are really making a good start, and even a little handful of rice in these hard times is an encouragement to regular attendance."

The little handful of rice which the Sisters were able to give might have meant the difference between life and death to the 800 children who received it. Margaret Robertson took up the same theme in a letter to the Clewer Associates written a few months later, and published in the Easter 1894 number of the *St John Baptist Magazine*: "This year we have had all the horrors of a famine in the rice country to contend with… It is difficult for anyone in England to realise to what a state of utter destitution this reduces the people, for having practically no money, except what they make by the sale of surplus rice, they are absolutely unable to buy food, and live for the most part on roots of water plants etc. To relieve this as much as [it is] in our power we are giving doles of rice to the children who attend school regularly. And although we have had special collections for the purpose, our funds are terribly low."

But the people of the Sunderbuns were never well fed, as Miss Robertson went on to explain: "I myself never realised what starvation meant till three years ago when I went with Miss Hoare on the last journey she ever made to a place called Boddipur, 60 miles from Calcutta and only accessible at certain seasons of the year by boat. This is our farthest school and in a very wild, desolate part of the country - at the very edge of the jungle, so much so that a week before our arrival, a villager was carried off by a tiger, not a mile from his home and in the daytime! In this country the rice is very coarse and scanty so that people are almost always in a state of semi-starvation. We were holding a religious examination in the school and my attention was attracted by one of the children who seemed almost incapable of answering. I thought she must be ill; she was so wan and thin with none of the brightness of her age, which cannot have been more than 10 or 11. However, one of her companions volunteered the information that she *never* had enough to eat, and further enquiry elicited the fact that she had had no food for over 36 hours, but thought *perhaps* her mother might cook a little rice that evening." The same number of the *St John Baptist Magazine* carried an Appeal by Sr Mary Grace, the Assistant Superior at Clewer, asking Associates to help the Indian work by sending money ("last year only £60 were sent to Sr Jane Frances "), besides their regular fund-raising and sending of garments.

In addition to the tragedy of the famine and all the suffering which accompanied it, together with the stretching of their resources in giving relief, the Sisters received another blow to their morale by the death of Sr Sophia who had been such an able assistant to Sr Jane Frances. Rather oddly there was no mention of her death in the *St John Baptist Magazine* - such occurrences were usually recorded. However, the Community *Annals* note that on February 5th 1894, a telegram was received at Clewer from Sr Jane Frances saying that Sr Sophia was very ill and suffering from typhoid fever. On February 8th another telegram arrived at Clewer at 3.30. p.m. saying that Sr Sophia had died that day.

Further details came with the Indian mail: "She was ill between two and three weeks. At first it was thought to be only the ordinary fever of the country and not at all serious, so that she went on one of the expeditions to the rice fields to visit the native schools. She became worse while there and after her return symptoms appeared which pointed to typhoid fever ... On the evening of Ash Wednesday worse symptoms appeared. All Thursday she was quietly dying, but the restlessness and more distressing symptoms had passed. She died about 5.00.p.m. and was buried at the same hour the following day... She was laid at Sr Lucy's feet just opposite Sr Mary Christine who had been professed with her... Sr Gertrude Emily was to have gone to Poona for rest, but gave it up so as to set Sr Mary Isabel free for the nursing, and so [she] lost her rest altogether as she felt the weather was too hot later on to make such a long journey." Sr Sybil, who was to have sailed for England the day before Sr Sophia's death, delayed her departure, but was able to leave Calcutta later in the month and finally arrived in England on March 22nd, "very much broken down."

It is a sad irony that Sr Sophia, who had helped alleviate the sufferings of the famine victims should herself succumb to a fever while the famine was still wreaking havoc. As noted earlier, the famine went on for several seasons, and towards the end of it the situation was worsened by a general outbreak of fever. An unidentified Sister writing in the Easter 1896 number of *St John Baptist Magazine*, mentioned the outbreak. She had accompanied Sr Jane Frances to the Sunderbuns and having described the visit concluded: "We reached Calcutta soon after six, rather tired but very much refreshed in mind and body. Since then there has been a terrible outbreak of fever in this district, and the last time Sr Jane Frances was down there she found that hundreds of the people had been carried off by it, some of the schools being very much thinned. How the people managed to get their crops gathered in at all was a marvel, for in some cases whole families were stricken. And this fever leaves them so terribly weak afterwards that it makes any labour at all a burden and life somewhat of a problem."

In the same account, the Sister had described Sr Jane Frances with a mixture of humour and admiration. The portrait which emerges is of someone totally immersed in her surroundings and at one with the people there. "The Sister Superior in a fit of absence sat down on the box instead of a chair (much to Shonashi's disapproval), so he gave but a divided attention to the net which I was helping him to put up, in consequence of which three mosquitoes flew in during the night and enjoyed themselves immensely at my expense. I settled in and having done that, sat down on the least rickety of the chairs and listened to the even flow of conversation that was going on between several people squatting on the floor and the Superior. They seemed to have a great deal to say for themselves, and she listened with much interest and infinite patience to them all, and then gave her opinion on the matter which seemed to satisfy them entirely. They departed apparently very well pleased with themselves and one another; and I made a mental resolution on the spot that I would study my Bengali step by step to better account, the very next opportunity I had."

Footnotes

1. Factories i.e. warehouses.

2. Lansdowne Road is now Sarat Bose Road.

3. *Life of Angelina Margaret Hoare* by her sisters and Mrs Walter M. Hoare. 1897 p.220.

4. During my visit to Calcutta in February 1995 I did not find the Sisters' graves, nor that of Angelina Hoare. But as will be noted in the final chapter of this book, there was considerable confusion about the location of the Sisters' graves, and this has only been clarified since my return. I now believe Angelina Hoare may have been buried in the English Cemetery at Alipore which is where the early Sisters were buried. However, I found the memorial in Calcutta Cathedral; it is in good condition and bears the following inscription:

+

TO THE GLORY OF GOD
AND IN LOVING MEMORY OF
ANGELINA MARGARET HOARE
OF STAPLEHURST, KENT
Born May 17th, 1843.
+ + +
She came to Calcutta in January 1876, in response to a call
from Bishop Milman, and during 16 years of unceasing
work she founded the Diocesan Mission House
in Bhowanipore, and established many
schools in the Sunderbunds.
SHE FELL ASLEEP
January 10th, 1892, aged 48,
Among those for whom she had lovingly laboured in the spirit
of her life's motto, "Rejoice evermore."

5. In addition to the St John Baptist Calcutta Mission Association there was also the Weald of Kent Association. Founded in August 1883 at a meeting in Cranbrook, Kent, the Weald of Kent Association existed to support the work of Angelina Hoare and was largely run by her family. There was also a strong Norfolk branch centred on the Revd Walter Hoare's parish at Colkirk. After Angelina Hoare's death the Association gave its support to the Indian work of the Clewer Sisters but remained distinct from the St John Baptist Calcutta Mission Association, (and, it has to be said, gave rise to the same type of problems).

-14-
TRAVELLER'S TALES

Amid the Sisters' busy lives there was time for rest and travel. As well as periodical furloughs in England, there were also shorter spells when Sisters would either go up to Darjeeling, or elsewhere if they had relatives in India. Thus Sr Honora was able to spend some time with her cousins at Lucknow: "to see if 'up country air' would do me good." She wrote an account of her visit which was reproduced in the autumn 1892[1] issue of *St John Baptist Magazine.* "The journey to Lucknow from Calcutta takes two nights and one day, leaving Calcutta by the night mail at 9 o'clock[2]. Railway travelling in India is made as easy as possible, but nothing mitigates the heat which seemed ever to increase as we got further away from Calcutta. The rains have not begun in the North West Province [and] the difference between [it] and Bengal is very marked. There is an entire absence of that jungle and luxuriant undergrowth which goes to make up part of the natural beauty of Bengal. But also, the whole land was as barren and scorched as a desert, only the trees retained their greenness and showed more vividly the sandy desert around them... We arrived at Cawnpore soon after midnight and had to wait an hour for the train to Lucknow. It was odd to find the station as bustling and busy as if it had been midday..."

Sr Honora was fascinated by all she saw, especially with seeing, real India: "Lucknow is a charming place and so much more one's idea of an Oriental town than this Europeanised Calcutta. The houses of the Europeans are built in bungalow style on one floor. I believe this is on account of the hot winds which prevail there in the dry season, and which would be unbearable in high houses with large open verandahs such as they build in Calcutta. Lucknow is like one large park full of gardens and grand old buildings. The palaces of the disinherited Kings of Oude are splendid buildings... They look very imposing with their domes and minarets and enormous gateways... Some of the palaces are used as public buildings, some are in ruins... The 'city' of Lucknow where the natives live lies three miles away from the European part of the place - we were not allowed to go there as the cholera was bad at the time."

Still vivid in the English memory was the Indian mutiny which had centred tragically on Lucknow and nearby Cawnpore [3]. So inevitably, Sr Honora's account of her visit would include a patriotic description of the Residency. "But the place of the greatest interest of all in Lucknow is the ruined' Residency'[4]. It stands on an elevation with the church and all the houses around it now in ruins, but still in its own lovely grounds, all cared for and preserved by the Government with most reverent care as befits such an honoured place. The cemetery where Sir Henry Lawrence and all those who fell in the seige are buried, forms part of the grounds. The Banqueting Hall, which was turned into a hospital for the sick and wounded, is preserved; many in it were shot in their beds by the guns of the mutineers outside the walls. Every house carries the marks of shot and shell still, and each house has the name written on it now, according to its use then." It seems as though souvenir hunters are not a modern phenomenon, nor are nuns always immune to temptation! "I brought away some bits of the bricks", confessed the Sister, "but I fear I shall not be as fortunate as the American padre who took some with him to America and sold them for a dollar each!"

But above all it was Indian life which fascinated Sr Honora. "One came across all sorts of curious pictures of Indian life as we drove about Lucknow; elephants carrying a native and solemnly stalking along the roads; camels with their supercilious faces, some of which I used for the journeys into the country; a flock of goats, or a herd of those melancholy looking buffalo-oxen, all driven by natives whose very colouring and dress were a picture in themselves. We often went past a Hindoo temple near the river - there the sacred monkeys caper about and no man dare touch them. One day we met a fakir with a sacred bull which was covered with conch shells and went how and where it pleased. The natives drive about in echa 'carts,' little square carts with a covering. I saw several which had a straw thatch over them and the woodwork inlaid with brass; horses are used in these carts as much as bullocks. The carts have no seats and the people sit on the floor." These images of Indian life still ring true a century later.

If Sr Honora's journey to Lucknow seemed long and arduous, then that of Sr Mary Thekla was even more so. She had a brother who was a tea planter in Assam and the description of her visit there appeared in the autumn 1892 issue of the *St John Baptist Magazine*, along with Sr Honora's letter from Lucknow. It was written partly during her visit to Assam and partly on her return to Calcutta. "I have had a delightful quiet rest with my brother who is manager of this garden," she wrote. "I left Calcutta on the 28th December, a seven hours journey by a jolting railway, and the rest by mail steamer, took us six days from the time of starting from Goalcundo[5]. There were seven passengers aboard the steamer. For the first three days there was little of interest - a large expanse of water with high sandbanks on either side. On the third day we arrived at the river Brahmapootra[6], the mail station Dhubri[7], and we took the Assam mail on board. Dhubri is the frontier station of Assam, very hot, but healthy; it is very picturesque. At Goalpara the river bank is alive with buyers and sellers of seeds of all kinds; a very busy scene. The next station of importance is Gowhatly[8], formerly the seat of government of Assam... There is a very pretty island called Peacock Island, where is the house of the high priest of the Hindu's in these parts." In fact the Umananda Temple on Peacock Island is a very important one, and during the monsoon the priests become marooned on the island due to the swollen waters of the Brahmaputra.

The Sister continued: "Our next important station was Jeyber, the home of the pioneer of the tea industry in Assam[9]. The snowy range of the Himalaya was clearly seen from here, a very refreshing sight. We passed many alligators basking in the sun on the sandbanks, looking like so much driftwood till the near approach of a steamer ... made them move off. Porpoises also enlivened the scene. Soon after leaving Jeyber the steamer ran aground on a sandbank, a great crash and a great heave told us we were hard aground. It was like an earthquake experience - I could not stand but was luckily tossed into a chair. Fortunately the 'down' mail steamer appeared and pulled us off, so we were saved a waiting of 24 hours till the next 'up' steamer could come to help us. After lots of whistling on the steamer's part, a native ran from a vast sandbank on which was a fly bringing Her Majesty's mailbag containing one letter, and let us go again."

The Brahmaputra has 120 tributaries, so it is hardly surprising that once she left the main river the rest of Sr Mary Thekla's trip is difficult to follow on a map. "I arrived at 8.00 a.m. at Dhunsire Mukh where my brother met me," she wrote. "We were glad to get away in a big country boat as far as the mouth of the Dhunsire river when [an] alligator vacated his position and allowed us to land. A change here to my brother's boat was an improvement - it looked very inviting with its white awning. A boat met us with provisions, so after a kind of picnic on a sandbank we journeyed on till dusk when we reached our destination, Remgagora. Crowds of natives came down to see me arrive; asking my brother who I was, whence I came, and what I came here for. So for a week or two I was a nine days wonder, natives thronging the hedges of the garden trying to get a glimpse of me."

If the Sister was of interest to the local people, then they were certainly of interest to her, being quite different by race and tradition from the people of Bengal. "There are several tribes: Assamis, Miris, Nagas, and Racharis. The Miris are a very simple, independent tribe. Great numbers are fishermen and they often bring us presents of fish and game and fruit. The chief and his sons are very handsome men dressed in turbans of silk of all colours, and their other garments to correspond."

"The country [around] is flat and the view limited by the forest, but we can see on either side of the valley the snowy peaks of the Himalaya to the north, and the Naga Hills to the south. My brother's bungalow stands in a large compound. It is built of wood, three feet from the ground, having three very large rooms opening out on a verandah - very quaint and with a wood fire always burning. All his servants are Bengalis. The coolies who work in the gardens come from all parts of India, and there are government depots where the planters hire them. They sign an agreement stating for how long they wish to work, and from time to time Government Inspectors come to see if [they] are well cared for and have any complaint. Their houses are of brick, built in lines, and they keep them very clean."

"There is a Hindu mosque [sic] in my brother's garden standing in a grove of sacred trees where one of their 'holy men' is buried, and they place rice and fruit and vegetables there for him to eat. A white elephant pays visits to this mosque [sic] and feasts on these things. The natives believe he is the the holy man's 'spirit'. I was very anxious to see this white elephant but he did not appear while I was there, I only saw his footmarks." She may not have seen the white elephant, but the Sister was more fortunate in seeing other wildlife. "Bears are very plentiful, and leopards and snakes. One day I saw a large shaggy bear walking in the garden. He looked harmless, however I kept well out of his sight! My brother tried to have him caught, but he escaped. As soon as it gets dark the natives light fires all about the gardens to keep off the wild beasts. The birds here are very beautiful and great numbers are always in the gardens - parrots, houphoos, jays, kingfishers, white cranes, Java sparrows. Nearly all the English flowers flourish in Assam, and a great many wild ones."

The Indian climate was always very trying to the English, so perhaps Sr Mary Thekla's next remark is a measure of how well she had learned to cope with it: "The climate is much cooler than in Calcutta, with the thermometer seldom above 89 or 90 degrees, and lovely weather from October to June. I wish it were nearer Calcutta so that other Sisters might enjoy a change there." All good things must end however, and it was with a tinge of regret that the Sister wrote: "My very pleasant and quiet visit ends this week I am sorry to say. A ride on an elephant to the steamer station has been in contemplation for me instead of going by the boat, but my brother [thought] the motion would be too much for me." Completing her account back in Calcutta, Sr Mary Thekla concluded: "The chief of the Miris and his sons met us in the river and the chief gave me a pure white fowl as a present to bring to Calcutta. Shoals of the tribe followed the boat for about a quarter of a mile. Six days on the steamer brought me again to Goalcundo, and nine hours by rail to the European Orphanage here." We shall never know what happened to the fowl!

Such an exhausting journey was (and is) quite normal in India, but Assam is now almost inaccessible to visitors due to political unrest. In theory it is possible to obtain permits, but in practice it is very difficult to do so. The account left by Sr Mary Thekla is therefore a valuable record by an English traveller, of a visit to what is now virtually forbidden territory. On the other hand, Darjeeling was much more familiar to the Sisters, but it was no less difficult to reach as the following account in the *St John Baptist Magazine* of autumn 1895, will show. Though un-named, it could well be written by Sr Jane Frances. "Here I am after a most trying journey," she wrote. "I left Calcutta on the 18th. Three miles from

Barrackpore we came to a standstill, and after a long wait and expecting the next train to run into us, we went on a few yards and, with many jolts, bumps, hard knocks and an explosion, stopped again. First the engine had broken down (it was a new one), and when that was repaired, the couplings broke between the first and intermediate carriages, leaving all the front vans, third and interclasses, attached to the engine, and the first, second and back third, apart from it. At last an engine came from Kaucharapara and we got to Barrackpore at 7.10.[p.m.][10] On we went slowly, had a cup of tea at Bogoola and reached the steamer at 12.45.[a.m.] There had been a cyclone on the river and the decks were so wet that my skirts got damp nearly to my knees. We rolled a good deal. Most people dined, but I was past food."

In terms of mileage the journey had only just begun and it turned into a real nightmare. "We settled into the night train at 3.20 a.m., no tea to be had till we reached Jalpaiguri at 2.10 p.m., and then I could not drink it. We got to Siliguri at 4.10 [p.m.] and had a cup of coffee. The hill train left at 4.40 [p.m.] and we went at a terrific speed passing the down mail at Rangtong siding; on again to Tindharia and, as it was then getting dark, a torch was fastened to the engine and away we went. The effect of the torch was weird but grand, and the waterfalls were lovely. We got to Kurseong a little before 9.00 [p.m.] and I was too tired and too ill to move to get any food; then at 9.15 we started with a pilot engine as something went wrong with the torch. We reached Ghoom at 11.36 [p.m.] and began slowly descending when, at about two miles from Darjeeling, our pilot screeched out and we stood still. There was a bad landslip of earth through which we could not pass, and water was rushing over the road, so some gentlemen walked on, some went to sleep for the rest of the night, and the guard went on to send dandies[11] for the ladies. The bearers from the school came for me, and we got a coolie for my bedding. When just over the slip the iron of the dandy handle broke, and there I was in the mud and rain. The men went for another, and I walked, very soon being wet through as was my bedding. I got into the dandy as soon as we met it, and at last walked into this room at 2.40 a.m. to Sr Margaret's great delight. I had a cup of soup and went to bed. My things are only just dry and I am only just feeling a little rested after it all. I was very much astonished that the hill train started so late, and more so that it was allowed to go on from Kurseong."

The journey had taken well over thirty hours - no wonder the Sister was exhausted. But there was always the view to look forward to: "Friday was misty, Saturday morning lovely, and then it clouded over. Yesterday we had a good deal of mist with bright bits between and glimpses of the snows, and in the afternoon I sat outside with a lovely view - clouds in the valleys and the hills and snows standing out of them, and there were such glorious lights at sunset.!"

The Sisters would have had no contact with non-Christian religions before coming to India, and so the religious observances of Muslims and Hindus would have been totally alien to them. But once in India they were surrounded by other faiths, the presence of which, especially at festivals, could not be ignored because they often involved public processions. These were usually extremely noisy but also colourful and rather fascinating. Sr Mary Isabel writing from the Eden Hospital in the Autumn 1891 number of *St John Baptist Magazine*, described a procession she had witnessed on the last day of Moharram, a Muslim festival: "High cages made of the most brilliant tinsel and tissue paper containing a paper coffin which is deposited in a tank in the Mohammedan burial ground. It is a sad and dreadful festival to keep, in memory of Hassin and Hossin, two sons of Mahomet who fought till they killed each other. The men sing a doleful tune as they walk and beat their breasts till they bleed, or appear to do so - for one standing by said they carry chillies to rub onto themselves to make them look red. We are told it is a much grander spectacle up the country where so many of the great Rajahs are Mohamedans." This provoked a shocked reaction from at least one Sister at Clewer, who wrote in pencil in her copy of the *St John Baptist Magazine*: "A heathen, hideous festival which no Christian should attend in body, but spend more life and time on their knees before the true God."

Despite this angry reaction from the Sister back home, it is possible to discern a growing sense of respect by the Sisters for devout followers of other faiths, even though the Sisters were in a missionary role and hoped to win souls for Christ. Thus a Sister (probably Sr Jane Frances) wrote movingly of her visit to Benares in a letter published in the Easter 1896 issue of the *St John Baptist Magazine*. "Benares is *the* most sacred city from the Hindu point of belief. The real city stands… on the north side of the most sacred Ganges river. It is built on an elevation, and the view of it from the river is really beautiful; wonderful stone carved temples and grand old houses belonging to the Rajas all built close down to the water's edge. Pile upon pile, these buildings rise and extend for about three miles east and west along the sacred river's banks. The bathing ghats are the most favoured spots, where an endless multitude of devout Hindus, many of them pilgrims, are to be found from early morning, bathing from the broad steps of the ghats in the healing waters of the Ganges; they stand in the water, drinking it, diving in it, and all the while saying their prayers with an eager, restless look upon their poor earnest faces."

The Sister continued: "Yesterday morning we went on the river to see it all, and it is a wonderful sight. There are old grey headed men, and women and children making their devotions in and out of the river, whose waters to them are sacred - hundreds of them all along the stream. The high caste Hindus are allowed to bathe on platforms built out onto the river, and shaded from the sun by large plaited bamboo umbrellas. There were those who were living ascetic lives, sitting in a kind of doorway built on the riverside, some of them *covered* with a white dust, their hair long and matted, prayer beads hanging round their necks and their books of prayers on the ground before them. And there they remained always by the side of the Ganges river, eating little I believe. It seemed to me they looked almost possessed, so stern and painful is their expression of face."

People not only wash and pray in the sacred waters at Benares - they also scatter the ashes of their dead in it. There were cremation ghats alongside the Hooghly at Calcutta which the Sister had seen, and so she seems to have taken this unusual sight in her stride: "We passed the burning ghat too, where all faithful Hindus desire to be burnt after death. The funeral pyres were smoking and there were five or six dead bodies waiting for their turn, laid in the waters of the river in a row till there was room for them also. It was a terrible sight in the midst of all the busy moving scene around. There is one man of the lowest caste of Hindu who supplies the fire which is used on these occasions, and he is said to be fabulously rich; one Rajah gave him as much as 1,000 rupees to obtain the fire for a relative. The Hindus believe that anyone who dies in Benares is *sure* of salvation whatever his sins may have been."

She also visited a Hindu temple: "We went one day to the temple dedicated to Durga,[12] where the monkeys abound; they let us in without removing our shoes. I did not care about the monkeys, but the people who followed me in with sweetmeats and rice fed them and kept them quiet. They wanted us to buy food and give them, but as it is considered an act of devotion to feed these sacred monkeys, I refused to buy. The priests were decking the image of Durga with garlands of flowers, a hideous image in a dark recess."

One important contribution to Indian life made by the British was the network of railways, which provided reasonably fast transport in a country accustomed to taking several days to make a journey. "The river Ganges is very pretty here, a broad, beautiful, bending river. It is very low now but must be over a mile wide at its height. The railway from Calcutta crosses the river by a bridge built in Lord Dufferin's time and called after him. The Hindus believed the Ganges would never consent to be crossed by a bridge; no doubt they sacrificed goats and kids after the deed was complete. Before the bridge, there was no rail to the city itself. Now the pilgrims crowd by it to their devotions in the city, and at the eclipses of the moon I believe special trains are run. We are 476 miles from Calcutta in the North West Provinces, and it takes 15 hours to get here - a short journey as Indian journeys go!"

So the Sisters had some opportunity to visit parts of India where they did not work and these experiences must have added to their understanding of both the country and people. They certainly seemed to have a much broader view of, and respect for, Indian life and culture, than many of the British in India. But such visits were only occasional breaks from the regular routine. The Sisters' lives centred around their Community Rule, regulated by worship and prayer, and lived in the context of hospitals, schools and mission house, both in Calcutta and Darjeeling. Always ready to respond to the call to new work, they had only recently taken over the Pipalpati mission house together with the village schools in the Sunderbuns, when another call was heard. This time it came from the hills - the Diocesan Girls' High School Darjeeling needed someone to run it. Who better than the Clewer Sisters?

Footnotes

1. Sr Honora must have been writing retrospectively, unless her account in the autumn 1892 issue of *St John Baptist Magazine* was held over, because she had by this time returned to England. Her first term in India was from 24th January 1885 (left England) until 3rd October 1887 when she was invalided home; having sufficiently recovered, she returned for a second term from 30th November 1894 until 15th March 1900. (See chapter 8).

2. This was probably the famous Howrah Mail from Calcutta to the Punjab.

3. For details of the massacre at Cawnpore and the seige of Lucknow see chapter 1. For a very good fictionalised account of the Indian mutiny see *The Seige of Krishnapur* by J. G. Farrell.

4. The Residency at Lucknow is still a preserved ruin.

5. Since Independence many Indian placenames have been slightly altered. Thus, Goalcundo = Goalundo.

6. Brahmapootra = Brahmaputra.

7. Dhubri = Dhuburi.

8. Gowhatly = Gauhati or Guwahati.

9. Jeyber. This might be Jorhat which is still the main town of the tea plantation district in Assam.

10. The Sister does not say what time she left Calcutta, except that there was a long wait three miles from Barrackpore. This must have been extremely frustrating because Barrackpore was only 25km north of Calcutta, so the journey had hardly begun.

11. Dandies - a type of hammock on poles carried by bearers.

12. The goddess Durga, destroyer of evil is one of the many forms of the goddess Devi portrayed as riding on a tiger. She is also Kali, and Parvati daughter of the Himalayas, the wife of Shiva (the third god of the Hindu pantheon), and is the mother-goddess.

C S J B

I N D I A

-15-
UP COUNTRY AGAIN

The Eden Sanatorium, Darjeeling, was firmly established as part of the Clewer Sisters' work by the 1890s. But it was not an easy project because of the irksome rules governing its organisation. Sr Jane Frances had already seriously considered withdrawing in 1890 when negotiations were being held regarding the Pipalpati mission. At that time it had been made very clear to her that any such withdrawal would displease the bishop, and so she had deferred. Even so, she regarded Darjeeling as less of a priority than the other Community work. In a postscript to a letter to Mother Betha at Clewer dated September 18th 1890, Sr Jane Frances concluded: "I am sure that you and the Warden and all who have any interest in Indian work, would consider that if in the course of 1891 Miss Hoare carries out her present intention and withdraws finally, it would be out of the question for us to hang back from what we have been waiting for, for so long, and for what all are expecting for us, i.e. to step into her shoes... But if you could not enable me to do this or sanction this without withdrawing from Darjeeling, I should have no alternative. I told both the bishop and Dr O'Brien that the decision by no means rested with me, [and] that I was under the orders of home authorities. The Calcutta works must come first, and if at any time numbers now could not be kept up, Darjeeling would be the work of less account. As a *work* it certainly is..."

When Angelina Hoare's work eventually passed into the hands of the Sisters, they managed to cope without withdrawing from Darjeeling. But in 1894 the offer of still more work was suddenly made to the Community. An extract from an undated letter from Sr Jane Frances to Mother Betha explained the situation: "In the middle of my letter I was sent for to speak to the bishop... It is a subject very likely new to you, but to me a very old one that has again come on the table. There is a somewhat important girls' school at Darjeeling [which] rates higher, and perhaps [has] pupils of a higher class, than the Pratt School... Years ago in Sr Lucy's time, overtures were made as to our taking it. I have still some of Sr Lucy's old letters.(1) But negotiations were only feelers. There was then a change in management, another headmistress was appointed and the whole matter therefore dropped. Now there is another crisis. The headmistress and her teachers had come to such collisions that things could not go on and she has resigned. The school is nominally and by constitution a *Church* school, but latterly has much drifted out of Church influence, and the bishop and clergy are naturally very anxious to seize this opportunity of getting it back into good lines."

She continued: "The first overture however, was by telegram from

Sir Alfred Croft, the head of the Educational Department. Mrs Bamford, the Government Inspector, followed suit, and just before the bishop sent for me I had a letter from the Archdeacon, so I [felt] pretty sure as to what the bishop wanted to speak to me about. It seemed too important a matter, pressed from so many quarters, to negative hastily, merely on my own responsibility. I fancy [that] the bishop may write to the Warden, a kind of prelude by this mail. But till a letter from Sir Alfred Croft giving full particulars as to *conditions* of the offer follows his telegram, the matter can hardly be laid before the proper authorities in a very complete shape."

Sr Florence was in charge of the Pratt Memorial School and had an ear to the grapevine as Sr Jane Frances related: "Sr Florence of course, through various school channels had heard of the Darjeeling fracas just about the time of my first communication received on the subject... Sr Florence, having heard of what was going on privately about the same time as I did *officially*, I did not consider it a breach of confidence to air a few ideas with her as she knows the headmistress [and] various of the teachers."

Meanwhile, Bishop Johnson of Calcutta wrote officially to the Warden, Canon Carter, at Clewer in October 1894: "The Mother will be hearing by this mail from our Sister Superior concerning a proposal which we have long been looking forward to, and which circumstances have now definitely brought before her, namely that she should take charge of our Girls' High School at Darjeeling. I and everybody concerned desire earnestly that the Mother may see her way to accepting this proposal. It would make the position of the Community complete... With the hospitals in Calcutta in your hands and the Sanatorium at Darjeeling in connection with them, together with the Pratt School, and this Darjeeling High School embracing all our Church of England(2) high education, and the mission work, you would really be covering the whole field, and I am very anxious that you should have it all, that is that no other Sisterhood(3) should have to be invited which would create confusion. I may say that our educational authorities... are quite anxious to see the same work done in Darjeeling as they find to have been so splendidly accomplished by Sr Florence at the Pratt School; and Sr Florence feels that the two schools might greatly help each other. The influence of [the Sisters'] presence at the Sanatorium is untold, people from all parts resorting there and carrying home ideas and impressions which I can trace wherever I go. And if the school was also in your hands, I should have nothing more to desire, and everybody interested would be thankful." Canon Carter must have felt very proud to receive such a glowing testimony to the work of the Sisters. It is ironical that in England Religious Communities were still struggling to gain acceptance and episcopal sanction, but overseas there was a greater affirmation.

On November 6th 1894, Sr Jane Frances wrote to Mother Betha: "Since my last letter I have had no further interview with the bishop but have had letters both from him and Sir Alfred Croft. The present headmistress resigns at Xmas, but at Darjeeling, as is the custom in hill schools, there are holidays till March, so any new arrangement would take place then, and one of the present staff is prepared to take charge of the empty house till the new appointment is made. Sir Alfred Croft comes down from Darjeeling this week so I should probably have an interview with him before long... The bishop has greatly set his heart upon it and says he cannot bring himself to face the possibility of rejection. Of course on the climate side, it would not be such a venture as Calcutta, as the object of the hill schools is to meet the necessities of European constitutions for those who cannot afford to send their children to England."

On March 1st 1895 the Community Chapter met at Clewer to consider a number of important issues including the Diocesan Girls' School at Darjeeling and work in Sydney, Australia. It was a long meeting, not concluding until 4.45 p.m.: the work in Darjeeling was accepted; the work in Australia was not.

The summer 1895 edition of the *St John Baptist Magazine* contained details of this new work which was to become increasingly important in the life of the Community: "The Sisters now take the place of the Lady Superintendent and have entire management of the school under the bishop and Committee. The fees are 40 rupees a month (within the means of the Government servants). There are now 61 pupils in the house, of varied ages, and 9 day scholars. The chaplain of Darjeeling is school visitor and hopes now to be allowed to fulfil his duties towards the pupils, which was not possible before."

Darjeeling was the home of a number of prestigious schools as the *St John Baptist Magazine* went on to explain: "There is a very good Diocesan school for boys... Mr Carter, the Head Master is considered one of the best in Bengal. The Roman Catholics (Jesuits) are very active and strong in Darjeeling. The Convent School and St Joseph's College outnumber the Diocesan schools. The former was opened more than 50 years ago, the latter is a splendid building after the style of an old monastery near Bruges. The boys' school was removed there about 4 years ago. They also have two large buildings at Kurseong, about halfway up the hill to Darjeeling. One [is] a theological college for priests for the whole of India, I believe. The other [is] a convent school for upper class girls." Of these schools, the Diocesan school for boys was Anglican: this was St Paul's School, founded in Calcutta in 1845, and which moved to Darjeeling in 1864. It soon acquired an exemplary reputation which it still retains. The Convent School was the Loretto College for girls founded in 1847, and which still flourishes. Similarly, St Joseph's College, founded in 1888 and removed to its present site at North Point in 1892, retains a considerable reputation.

It was amongst such first class schools as these that the Clewer Community accepted the headship of the rather run-down Diocesan Girls' High School. Within a few years it would rank alongside them in importance. One aspect which comes across very strongly in the *St John*

Baptist Magazine account is the great rivalry between the Christian denominations: ecumenism was not on anyone's agenda at this time[4]. Thus the Sister wrote: "The opposition of the Roman authorities in this place is great. If a R.C. parent sends her children to one of our schools the priest will refuse to Baptise her babies or to admit her to any Church privileges."

Sr Florence, previously in charge of the Pratt Memorial School, was sent from Calcutta to open the Darjeeling school. She was a very business-like and capable person and set up a great deal of the administration beforehand. Thus we are told: "Before leaving Calcutta, Sr Florence had engaged all her staff, having borrowed Miss Cox, the second governess of the Pratt School, temporarily to act as general manager, [and] Miss Hicks as Head Teacher. She sifted and adjusted every department - food, accounts, lessons, charges, marks etc, and now we *hope* all may go on smoothly till two Sisters are able to be permanently established there."

The difficulty of the journey to Darjeeling has been noted several times before, and it must have been incredibly trying to know that one was faced with a 24 hour journey after every sojourn in Calcutta. If, as often happened, there was a landslip or some other hold up, then the journey could take much longer. But this never seemed to worry the Sisters, or if it did, they made light of it. At least the journey only had to be undertaken once a year because the school year lasted from March until November, with a long winter holiday. Even so, having arrived at Darjeeling on the narrow gauge railway, the school was still a considerable distance away: "From the railway station to the school is a good half hour's walk. A herd of coolie women are penned up at the station vociferating and making a fearful noise, who are let through one at a time, and carry all the luggage up to its destination on their backs. No size or weight deters them. Those passengers who cannot walk must go in a dandy which is carried on the shoulders of three or four men."

Within two years, the Diocesan Girls' High School was beginning to acquire a reputation for excellence. The Easter 1897 issue of the *St John Baptist Magazine*, carried a lengthy article about the school which had excited much interest amongst the English Associates. The following passage shows how much attitudes towards race, culture and society have changed, but it also provides a commentary on Anglo-Indian education in the heyday of the Raj: "The school in Darjeeling has a higher rate of fees than the one in Calcutta [i.e. the Pratt], partly because the expenses in the hills are greater, and partly because the school is intended for a superior class of girls. At present there is a mixture of Eurasian and English, as is the case in all Indian schools, but in time the latter will probably predominate as the school improves in tone and scholarship." A photograph taken in 1898 shows a motley collection of girls and small boys together with teachers and Sisters (Sr Susanna and Sr Edith Clara), whilst another taken in 1923 shows serried ranks of scholars wearing gym-tunics, who could have been at public school anywhere in England.

Associates in England were anxious to learn about the school, its situation and facilities, and their curiosity would have been well satisfied by the Easter 1897 article: "The school buildings stand on the side of one of the mountains on a wide terrace, and there is a steep decline at once to another platform below, where there is a large playground and servants' houses. The buildings face north and [are] immediately opposite the great snowy mountain range which is crowned by Kanchenjunga [at] 28,000 ft. In the foreground there is first a deep valley, and then ranges of green and wooded mountains rising tier above tier, forming the boundary line of Bhutan, Sikkim and Nepal. The varied cloud effects and the indescribable majesty of the mountains with their perpetual snow cannot be imagined, and are an ever renewed wonder and delight. There are however, weeks almost months, when everything is shrouded in thick mist or drenching rain, and when one almost despairs of there being a 'beyond' at all. This last year the rains were so violent that over a hundred small landslips occurred in one night, and all the roads were blocked for some hours."

The Sister then described the school buildings and the facilities they afforded: "The school consists of six buildings all more or less connected, and stretching for about 320 yards along an unlevel platform. There is the cottage which the Sisters occupy and which includes a small oratory. Next come two nice classrooms used for the infants, and a painting studio, and over these there is a large schoolroom for the middle sized children. There is very little masonry about these buildings; they are nearly all of painted wood and glass with corrugated iron roofs, and are neither very warm nor weatherproof. Next to these classrooms, and joined by a passage, is the dining hall where we can seat just 80, and above these are the hospital and matron's room. The kitchens stand behind the dining hall. After this is another detached building - the large schoolroom, which is given up to the senior pupils in lesson time, and is the general room at other times for recreation or dancing. Then there is a flight of steps down to the old original house known as 'The Grange.' This is the part we hope to dismantle next year as at present we can use so little of it, and rats abound. It is proposed to add another floor and to re-arrange the basement so as to secure a school chapel of which we are greatly in need. The expense of these improvements, together with a new recreation hall will be about 20,000 rupees of which we hope the Government will give half and the rest will probably be advanced by the Diocesan Board of Education... which the school will have to pay back. There is still another block of buildings consisting of four large dormitories and dressing rooms, which will hold 20-25 beds, [with] teachers rooms at each end. Our household at the present time numbers some seventy boarders, eleven teachers and two Sisters. The school is under Government inspection and at present depends on the annual grant and pupil's fees for its support."

During the winter months the school was closed and left in the charge of servants as the Sister recounted: "The servants belong to the hill tribes and have a very strong Mongolian look about them. They are most cheerful and hard working, and the larger number have been at the school for years and throw themselves warmly into all its interests and affairs. They are nominally Buddhists, which means almost nothing with them. The only manifestations of religion among the working classes are a few coloured rags mounted on poles round about their houses, which represent prayers, and a terrible noise of tomtoms and horns at a death... Perhaps as time goes on and we become better acquainted with the language, we shall be able to teach and help them in a more effective way than we can at present."

All in all, the Diocesan Girls' High School at Darjeeling seemed well appointed and in a good position, though some major building improvements were needed. As events turned out, the whole school had to be rebuilt following the disastrous cyclone and landslip which destroyed much of it in 1899 - but more of that later.

Meantime the work in Calcutta had not been at a standstill, indeed between the taking of the Pipalpati mission house and the school at Darjeeling the work both in hospitals and schools had gone from strength to strength. So now it is time to examine these advances before looking at the series of natural disasters which afflicted Calcutta and Darjeeling in the closing years of the century.

Footnotes

1. "Sr Lucy's old letters." Presumably these were written to Sr Jane Frances when she was Mother Superior at Clewer, but there is no sign of them in the Indian material at Clewer. As intimated in the correspondence between Sr Jane Frances and Mother Betha, the school had inauspicious beginnings. Two English ladies had founded a private boarding school for girls in 1883. After a few years these ladies returned to England and the school became a diocesan establishment headed by another lady and governed by a local Committee. When the situation arose which led to the Clewer Community taking over, the school came directly under the Diocesan Board of Education and became subject to Government Inspection.

2. Church of England. At this time the Anglican presence in India was officially still part of the Church of England. In 1930 it became the Church of India, Burma and Ceylon and achieved autonomous status. The Church of South India was formed in 1947, bringing together Anglicans, Methodists, Presbyterians, Congregationalists and other Reformed traditions. In 1970 the Church of North India was formed on similar lines. For further details see chapter 30.

3. "No other Sisterhood..." There was considerable rivalry between Anglican Religious Communities at this time (and between Missionary Societies too, especially where the latter reflected a particular brand of churchmanship). Whilst the Clewer Community seem to have had a good relationship with other Sisterhoods working in India, notably Wantage and All Saints, the Bishop of Calcutta here shows his own particular bias towards Clewer.

4. Relations between the Church of England and the Roman Catholic Church were bitter in the period under review following the secession to Rome of leading Anglicans such as Newman and Manning. The publication by Leo XIII of the Papal Bull *Apostolicae Curae* in 1896 which condemned Anglican Orders as "absolutely null and utterly void" resulted in further adverse effects.

-16-
LARGER AND FAIRER PROSPECTS

The Pratt Memorial School had been improving and growing steadily under the wise guidance of Sr Florence, (latterly, helping establish the new school at Darjeeling), and of other Sisters before her. In 1885, within a few months of moving into new buildings, the school had outgrown them and was using the old buildings as an annexe. By 1892 the situation had necessitated a move to yet more buildings on Lower Circular Road next to St James' Church, which are still occupied by the school. Sr Florence wrote to Mother Betha on February 26th 1893 describing the buildings and the opening ceremonies: "We moved into the new buildings last October but... the benediction of the school had to be deferred until our prizegiving day in December... You enter by gates in the Lower Circular Road, into a rather large compound bought in 1889 for the school in which already stood an old house too small for its intended purpose. The new building, consisting of a very long schoolroom and two dormitories of the same size above, is attached to the old house on one side and runs down the length of the compound to the road. It has its own entrance and staircase, and though joined on to the old house is practically a separate building."(1)

The building was blessed by the bishop on December 20th 1892, followed by a prizegiving ceremony and tea party, which all sounds very English! Sr Florence then continued her account to Mother Betha with some plans for co-operation with the Oxford Mission who were running St James' Church nearby: "We are about to amalgamate the infants and lowest standards of the Pratt Memorial School with those of St James' Boys' School [for Eurasians]. Living as we do side by side, it becomes more economical to join forces, whilst the junior standards in each school will be strengthened. The parents are pleased that the little brothers and sisters will be taught together, though the play hours will still be kept distinct."(2) The Sister concluded her letter with an anxious note about finance, but with long term hope: "With the starting of our large new building, great expenses are necessarily connected and our boarders' fees are only £15 p.a., or 240 rupees; the day scholars pay about £4 p.a. The school has only the fees to depend upon, and the yearly government grant which is about £154 p.a. The new house is capable of housing about 90 or 100 boarders, so that all our hopes for financial success rests on our having a full number. We have an excellent staff of eight resident teachers and two assistants, and quite mean to do great things some day; meanwhile, we are content to go on slowly and to live rather a hand to mouth life, looking forward to larger and fairer prospects in the future."

Mother Ellen had died at Clewer in 1892, having resigned as Mother

Superior in 1881. Although she had never visited India she had always been interested in it, especially the smaller village schools, and she sent a yearly donation. Sr Lucy, the first Sister Superior, had probably inspired Mother Ellen's interest, and she had certainly inspired Sr Jane Frances in her enthusiasm for "real" Indian work. St Mary's Church, Bhowampara, next to the Pipalpati mission house, led by Mr Bannerjee, and St Barnabas' Church, Kidderpore, led by Mr Seal, always had the support of both Sr Lucy and Sr Jane Frances. And the latter regarded these small struggling churches and their dependent schools as being just as important as the large girls' schools in Calcutta and Darjeeling.

So it was that Sr Jane Frances wrote to Mother Betha on July 8th 1893 regarding this part of the work: "As I hear now that Mother Ellen is no more," she wrote, "the money she used to collect for what was called Mother Ellen's School is rather uncertain of continuance. I want to explain what it really went to help. Long before the large native work in Ballygung and the rice country came to our charge, Sr Lucy and some of the first Sisters took much interest in a humble kind of mission work in one of the suburbs under the charge of Mr Seal, one of the native priests. St Barnabas' Kidderpore(3) is a small Bengali church, and the regular congregation are quite poor native Christians. But is also the starting point for much work among the non Christians, chiefly in the shape of little mission schools scattered over an area of a good many miles. Since Sr Lucy's time one little school has always been maintained out of what the Sisters' could save and is called St John Baptist's School. One may reckon the cost at from £5 to £6 a year... What Mother Ellen sent kept another little school going which was called after her. Mr Seal is such a good, hardworking priest, and has so few to take an interest in his work or to help him in any way, that though we are now rather weighted with little village schools, I feel that... we must still keep faithful to our *St John Baptist School*."

The Sister continued: "It has gone through a good many vicissitudes. When I first saw it on my visit to Calcutta during Sr Lucy's lifetime, it was at a comparatively short distance from here and in a very pretty situation among palm trees, and near a large tank [pond]. But that neighbourhood was all broken into by the construction of large new docks, and most of the inhabitants were dislodged, so the school was transferred nearly four miles off quite towards the limit of the mission district, and could only be reached by a very bad country road full of ruts and holes. This move did not turn out very successfully, but now it has found a permanent resting place a good deal nearer, and after immense delays, the little plot of ground on which it stands has been secured and registered. The situation is really rather pretty, some ricelands about and groves of palms, chiefly in the background. A fairly tidy little mud house has been built for the Christian teacher and his family, but the school building itself is only a very indifferent shed which must be replaced by a better one, as it hardly affords the little scholars any protection from the weather."

"Mr Seal has for years been ambitious of making a place large enough to hold little mission services in; also that he or one of the catechists could sleep there occasionally, so that the school should be a little mission station for the outlying part of the district. All this only means a mud hut with thatched verandah and walls, but about twice as large as the actual school would require. I have seen a plan and estimate of this splendid building which would come to £10 or thereabouts. It is only the realisation of what Sr Lucy had planned with Mr Seal when the school had first to be transplanted to a more distant site, so I am anxious somehow to help Mr Seal to carry out this plan. I thought it would be well therefore, if any contribution comes this year representing what used to be Mother Ellen's, to concentrate all efforts on improving and developing the already existing St John Baptist's School. The Christian teacher is a very poor man, but rather well educated for his class [caste]. The neighbourhood is entirely Hindoo and only boys attend at present; but he has got a good school together and they are getting on well. They have simple religious instruction every day, and what they have learned they know very well."

"These Hindoo's are still too backward to care about having the girls taught, but we might, as time goes on, get a girls' school together. That would entail more expense, as the boys and girls would have to be taught and fetched separately. We have the teacher's eldest girl as a free pupil at the Ballygung school [i.e. at the Pipalpati mission house]. She is a bright child and very pretty, not perhaps one of our pattern girls for goodness, but not the reverse and rather a favourite of mine… Anything in Mr Seal's district has to be maintained quite separately from the Ballygung or rice country work, and yet I should be very sorry if we had to desert our oldest friends."

The last decade of the century was indeed a time of larger and fairer prospects, but not simply in terms of school work. The Pipalpati mission house had also been extended, and the Christmas 1894 issue of *St John Baptist Magazine* carried a description of the opening ceremony and of the new wing itself: "Our day in India begins somewhat earlier than it does at home so that between the hours of 5.00 a.m. and the hour fixed for the service [4.30 p.m.], there was ample time for all preparations to be made. The new wing is a two-storied building connected with the old house by a covered bridge. There is a chapel and two classrooms on the ground floor, and a large dormitory and two bedrooms with bathrooms attached on the upper floor. A wide verandah runs around the south, east and west sides of the house keeping the rooms both cool and shady. The whole is well built with plenty of windows opening down to the ground on either side causing a pleasant current of air through the rooms."

The dedication service was conducted by the bishop in the presence of the choir from Bishop's College, many local clergy, the Oxford Mission priests, and the Sisters. Mr Bannerjee, from St Mary's Church Bhowampara, translated the sermon into Bengali. Afterwards there was a tea party in which the school children joined, and an entertainment in which they performed. The weather had been very heavy all day and in the early evening the storm broke, as Sr Jane Frances related: "The storm which had been brewing all the afternoon was just breaking. The lurid and threatening sky sent forth vivid sheets of lightning disclosing stray groups of little creatures standing together in their weird attire." (This refers to the children in their fancy dress, especially from the Milman School). "The bright light was flashing in and out amongst the gold and silver jewelry, the ear rings and nose rings, the bangles on ankles and wrists, that kept up a perpetual jingle, the very sound adding to the strange beauty of the scene. They appeared to be utterly regardless of the storm and showed no signs of fear. The rain did not fall until about an hour later, so that there was no chance of the precious garments being spoilt."

The storm sounded horrific, but doubtless the Sister was used to such phenomena after several years in India. Her account continued: "The storm was a fascinating and beautiful sight to watch, for the whole heavens seemed to be on fire, and once a shower of brilliant sparks fell quivering into the ground close to our feet, but nobody seemed to mind; wonder and admiration left no place for fear. We were safe in our own quarters before the rain came down in torrents. A cold fresh wind rushed through the house from top to bottom, banging the doors and windows, and knocking down everything that came in its way, but doing no particular damage. Next morning we awoke to a fresh green world with rows of stately lilies, crimson and pink and white, lifting their beautiful heads in the early morning sunshine."

One aspect of the Sisters' work which was not well documented for this period was that of the Calcutta Hospitals - the Presidency General, the Medical College and the Eden. It is safe to assume however, that all had been going well, because nursing standards had greatly improved under the Sisters' supervision. The hospital Sisters were still based at the Lady Canning Home near the Presidency General Hospital, but those working at the Medical College stayed at the nurses' quarters there, because the two hospitals were separated by a 35 minute drive through a very densely populated area. In 1891 the nurses' accommodation at the Presidency General was further extended to accommodate 32 (i.e. secular nurses and Clewer Sisters), but this was still deemed inadequate. The secular nurses were mostly Anglo-Indian [Eurasian], though a few were European. The Sisters noted that the general calibre of trainee nurses was higher than before - a sign of growing awareness of nursing as a profession. Even so, the Sisters felt there was room for improvement, as they related in the *St John Baptist Magazine* of Easter 1897: "The system of training is still insufficient and we are much behind the times in this respect. Still, progress is being made, and the old stamp of the nurse who considered her only duty was to take temperatures and to give medicines, leaving all else to the ward coolies, is happily fast vanishing away. The above was the actual response made by a senior nurse only two years ago. At the same time, it is pleasant to record that some of the senior nurses will rank with any in India in their care of, and devotion to, the sick under their charge."

The Medical College Hospital had been gaining in importance. Just a few years previously in 1883, Sir Robert Koch had begun research at the hospital into the treatment of cholera, a disease which had begun near Calcutta earlier in the century, and had swept in waves across the world. Koch's research resulted in the identification of the cholera bacillus in polluted water - a major breakthrough. The Sister may have been alluding to this as she continued her account: "The European doctors are all men 'up to date' carrying out as far as lies in their power, and circumstances permit, the latest scientific discoveries of the day, and they look for the assistance of duly trained and intelligent nurses. The latter on their part are commencing to realise this and it acts as an incentive to them to seek for further instruction in their profession which is becoming an increasingly good opening for Eurasian women..." The Sisters realised the importance of their task in training these nurses - and also that the training went beyond nursing skills and was about affirming the Eurasian women as people: "They are warm hearted and impulsive and respond readily to sympathy shown in their family joys and sorrows... On every side there is much work to be done and many difficulties to encounter. There are the light and dark sides to Indian hospital life, but nevertheless it is an intensely interesting one, full of hopefulness, though like everything else it needs courage, patience and perseverance."

The English ladies who supported the Sisters through the St John Baptist Calcutta Mission Association were still being difficult over the question of garments made at their working parties. At a time when parts of Bengal were still in the grip of famine, during which the Sisters had been at their wit's end to know how best to relieve their suffering, one can sense the frustration felt by Sr Jane Frances as she endeavoured yet again to explain to Miss Arbuthnot the needs of the village children. "I am sorry that the Associates get so bored by the jackets. If they could see the joy and pride on so many little smiling brown faces and see how the same bright coloured jacket appears from years end to years end (whenever a jacket is worn), I think they would not grudge their trouble. Probably most of our good friends do not realise that *made up clothing* in most shapes is of very little use to people who dress chiefly in *draperies.* Plain cotton chemises would be the only other *made* article of general use. The Christian grown up girls and women like a chemise to wear under their sari, especially when they go to church, but unbleached cotton chemises are bulky, tedious to make, and can be made here with sewing machines very cheaply. I should have thought jackets would be more entertaining to the makers as well as more valuable to the receivers. Coloured prints here are rather dear to buy, so from all points of view the jackets from England are such a help to us that I hope our yearly gratitude may be accepted by them, and encourage some of them at least to persevere..."

This letter, which was dated February 12th 1897, ended with a cameo of the famine situation which had eased slightly in the local area, though other parts were still suffering. "We are so grateful for all our poor Christians to be out of the famine region here. In lower Bengal [i.e. the Sunderbuns] the rains last year were over the average, and the *local* rice crops good. Prices are high on account of the general scarcity, for a terrible state of things prevails about 15 hours west by rail, and onwards. Calcutta is healthy just now but the plague might reach us any day; some doctors think it will be a miracle if it does not. One has always some great visitation before one's mind out here in India."

Sr Jane Frances ' last sentence was prophetic, for during 1897 there was a serious fire at the Pipalpati mission house and a major earthquake in Calcutta, followed two years later by a catastrophic landslip at Darjeeling. All these disasters seriously affected the work of the Sisters, and it is to these events that we must now turn.

Footnotes

1. Except for the "old house" which may not have survived, this description of the entrance to the Pratt Memorial School is exactly how one first sees it today. There are many 20th century buildings, but the new building of 1892 with its long schoolroom and dormitories overhead, is still there and fully functional.

2. The Oxford Mission withdrew from St James' Church in 1897 when the bishop appointed a married priest in charge (who of course could not join the Brotherhood).

3. St Barnabas' Church, Kidderpore is still in use - a rather sad looking little building in a very run down and predominantly Muslim area. The miracle is that it has survived at all.

C S J B

I N D I A

-17-
SOME GREAT VISITATION

1897 was not an encouraging year for the Sisters working in Calcutta. Their problems began in May at the Pipalpati mission house where a fire swept through one of the older buildings, fortunately leaving the new wing unscathed. Even so, the loss of the schoolroom was keenly felt, for it had held 80 children quite comfortably. "It was," wrote Sr Jane Frances, "a very special feature in the mission as it had been planned by Miss Hoare and part of it was used as a chapel until the new wing was built." The sides of the building were open in order to achieve maximum ventilation, and no doubt this helped fan the flames which quickly consumed the thatched roof. Fortunately, the children had broken up for the school holidays the day before, so there were only 20 or 30 there. These were evacuated to the new wing, out of harm's way. The cause of the fire was unknown: "there is no saying how [it] began," wrote the Sister. "Fire engines were fetched and worked hard for two or three hours but nothing could save it. The wind caught pieces of the lighted thatch and blew them towards the House [i.e. the mission house], so that there was great fear for that also, but the splendid old fruit trees which stand between the school and the House caught the firebrands and the House was saved."

A new building of stuccoed brick was begun at once on the site of the old one, costing between 4,000 and 5,000 rupees (£450). But as if the fire were not a great enough visitation, a month later there came an even greater one which affected the whole of Calcutta and beyond - the great earthquake. "The old Mission House, which the fruit trees saved from the fire, has been seriously damaged and a new building will be necessary," wrote Sr Jane Frances. In a letter dated June 13th 1897, the day after the earthquake, Sr Jane Frances graphically described the events: "No local papers being out yet, I have not heard the direction or extent of the earthwave, but it seems at least to have gone all along the course of the Hooghly and Ganges. The whole of Calcutta was shaken and a great many houses cracked and otherwise seriously damaged. It took place on Saturday afternoon June 12th soon after 5.00 p.m. The Hospital buildings which are old and not at all in good condition, indeed but for the famine were to have been rebuilt this year, have been much damaged. The upper part of the Cathedral spire has fallen down. The Canning Home and nurses' quarters, being newer and so very solidly built, are quite uninjured, but I am told, rocked greatly; and the great banyan tree in the compound, which has 12 separate stems, was seen to sway backwards and forwards like a punkah [swinging fan]. Of course everything great and small was swaying along with the so-called solid earth."

"We had had first Vespers for Trinity Sunday and I had gone to the Mission House to settle some things as to the re-opening of the school on Monday. Sr Katherine Maud [(1)] and I were out on the site of the burnt schoolroom discussing the plan of the new building. We heard a rumbling sound and felt a trembling under our feet. We were standing on what had been the cemented floor of the school which has been rather cracked and damaged by the fire. One said to the other, 'What an odd feeling this floor has, as if it were moving under our feet.' We thought the steamroller or some heavy carts must be passing on the road outside. Then this curious trembling motion got stronger… Looking casually towards the House we saw the parapet from the roof falling,… the large fruit trees swaying, and all the crows rising in the air cawing loudly. Besides the rumbling sound there was a general booming of gongs from all the little Hindu temples in the neighbourhood. This is always done in eclipses or earthquakes to drive away the powers of evil. All these simultaneous sights and sounds at last brought to our minds the conviction that an earthquake was going on, but without any sense of how serious a one it was, or any kind of fear. The House was empty, the children out in the garden, so there was no anxiety. I said, 'They never last long, it will stop in a minute.' This one however continued from five to seven minutes we are told… We wanted to go down into the garden from the raised level of the floor and found that we had to steady ourselves by holding on to the brickwork. It gave one a very giddy sensation. Two Sisters were in the new building; the rumbling noise at first made them think the children had gone on the roof and were running backwards and forwards. The new wing is quite uninjured, the old part very much cracked and will need much patching up."

The hospital Sisters also had a lucky escape: "The Sisters were all in different parts of the Canning Home, one in Chapel, one on the verandah etc, it being the one time that, as a rule, they are not in the wards. But they went out to the compound and they found all the patients who could move, outside; and the rest were being carried out to be out of reach of falling plaster or even bricks. All three blocks have suffered, the private ward and female ward most severely. Some of the rooms in each (the end ones), have been condemned."

The courage of the Sisters in the face of such a frightening experience is quite amazing. Obviously the full impact of the disaster was not immediately apparent, but even so it would have been easy to have given way to panic. Continuing her letter next day, June 14th, Sr Jane Frances sounds a thankful note: "One only realises by degrees what a tremendous force has been at work when one hears of the condition of Calcutta, and the small number of lives lost, or even of injuries in proportion to the damage done to houses, is very wonderful and merciful. Evensong at the Cathedral yesterday evening had more relation to the earthquake… than to Trinity Sunday, but I would say that, 'O God our help in ages past,' seemed most appropriate after one had realised by sense and sight the complete instability of all that seems most solid and lasting. Most of our friends' houses have suffered severely."

The aftershock from the earthquake brought cyclonic storms which made life even more difficult, especially with all the structural damage to buildings. Writing from the mission house, Sr Muriel mentioned the difficult conditions: "This House is in a very precarious state. It seems almost as if it might collapse in one of the cyclonic storms... Repairs and patchings have run away with 200 rupees, and then the new school is still in progress, and demands for advances are being continually made by the builder." And there were other problems too: "Rice is 50 rupees a load dearer than this time last year, and we consume a load in less than three weeks. We are now paying 108 rupees a load."

The European Orphanage was also badly damaged, as one of the Sisters recounted: "Fortunately it was visiting day and all the children had left their dormitories, otherwise it would have been serious, as those rooms suffered so much and the children would have been frightened. I was expecting a new teacher to come with the secretary, and had gone downstairs to the lower verandah. At first I thought the train was passing, but not seeing it in sight I knew at once what it was, and called all the children to follow me and took them out of reach of the house. Every second I thought the house would fall, it was swaying to and fro. I found the head teacher was still indoors so I rushed in to find her, knowing she was very nervous. It was an awful time. One heard crash, crash on all sides, and one did not dare stop and see where it came from. I had time to run to the top of the house and out again before the earthquake stopped. It must have lasted from five to seven minutes. The house has suffered terribly but it is safe, though every room is damaged. We are thankful it is no worse - many have suffered much more."

Newspaper reports confirm the Sisters' accounts of the severity of the earthquake and the widespread damage done by it. *The Friend of India* for Monday June 15th 1897, contained a lengthy account of the disaster: "Within the memory of the oldest inhabitant, no such quake of the earth has been felt in Calcutta as that which shook the city to its foundations on Saturday. The hour - a few minutes after five - was indicated by the stoppage of most of the clocks in the city. The first vibration was very severe... and the first impulse was to seek safety in the open. But once there the aspect of rocking buildings... did not inspire much confidence. The only hope was that, as on former occasions, the shocks would end in a few seconds; but the earth kept rocking violently, the motion being accompanied by a rumbling sound. As the trees shook,... the birds, especially the crows, seemed very disturbed, and expressed their distress in loud cawings. Horses, where stabled, became restive and almost unmanageable. Among the natural phenomena accompanying the quake, was an almost inconceivably beautiful sunset... During the earthquake the [mullahs] of the many Mahomedan mosques in the city ascended the minarets, and called the Faithful to prayers, Hindoo priests sounded their conch-shells with a quite new energy, and, particularly in the poorer respectable Eurasian quarter of the town, women and children rushed out into the streets and knelt in prayer. The effect of the earthquake was felt with as much severity on the river as on shore. The waters became so disturbed that, ignorant that it was a seismic shock, boatmen afloat thought a 'bore' had suddenly come in, and as the little country shallops were dashed violently against their moorings, the air resounded with cries of 'Allah! Allah!' from the numerous Mahomedan crews. It was a moment of panic."

The newspaper report then proceeded to give details of the major damage sustained in various parts of the city: "When the shocks began, the sisters in charge of the Military Orphanage Asylum(2) hurried their charges out into the open playground, and waited in prayerful silence [for] the collapse of the building which, it is pleasant to report, has only suffered from a few bad cracks and a considerable displacement of plaster." The catalogue of damage included the Indian Museum in Chowringhee; the large iron cross which surmounted the Cathedral spire had crashed through the roof of the south transept, though the spire itself was intact; the Town Hall was seriously damaged; and similarly the High Court nearby; the steeple of St Andrew's Kirk was badly damaged and the building cracked in several places; the Campbell Hospital in Lower Circular Road sustained cracks, but the Pratt Memorial School and neighbouring St James' Church are not mentioned. The report goes on to state that there was not much damage in College Street, so it may be assumed that the Medical College Hospital remained intact; neither does the report mention the Presidency General Hospital.

Clearly this was a major earthquake - there were shocks from north to south and from east to west, the latter being the severest. Amazingly, there were very few fatalities or injuries. *The Friend of India* report tells us that: "a woman and a man were killed in Amherst Street by a falling wall, and that one or two others met a similar fate in Bentinck Street." Also in Amherst Street: "a part of a house came down and, falling on a hut house buried three persons under the debris." Many people had lucky escapes from falling plaster or blocked up doorways, but many were able to return to their homes later. Some however, camped on the Maidan (the great open space in the centre of Calcutta) their homes being either unsafe or destroyed. There were also several cases of panic: "A lady threw herself from an upper window of a house [in Waterloo Street] and was much hurt... In Meredith's Lane the occupants of the various houses ran out into the lane as soon as the first shock was felt. A ludicrous incident occurred at the hackney carriage stables in this lane. A syce, [groom] evidently alarmed by the number of people congregated in the lane, and seeing the buildings swaying to and fro, loudly called out for a parawallah, as though the police had the power to stop the earthquake, and it was some time before he could be convinced that the shocks could not be stopped, even by Mr James himself. In many instances, ladies half dressed rushed out of their houses, some of them with babes in their arms and other children following them in a state of terror, and at times praying." Whenever disaster strikes there is always someone waiting to cash in on other peoples' misfortune. Thus we are told: "landladies are alive to the monetary value of an earthquake. A gentleman, whose rooms were in a very shaky condition, went to the manageress of a certain boarding-house and asked if there was a room he could occupy for that night only. He was told that he could have a room on payment of 50 rupees. It is needless to say that he did not take the room."

The earthquake was not confined to the area around Calcutta. Darjeeling was also seriously affected, and it must have been a very anxious time for the Sisters in Calcutta as they awaited news. Thus in her letter dated June 14th Sr Jane Frances wrote: "We can have no letters from Darjeeling as railway bridges are broken and communications stopped except by telegraph. From the telegrams we are at least assured that, though the violent shock was even felt up there severely, no lives were lost, and no mention is made of either the Sanatorium or School among the houses injured." Sr Muriel had a little more information but it was hardly comforting: "The shock of the earthquake was very severely felt at Darjeeling, and a great part of the railway and bridges destroyed. We are told it will be two years before all can be completely repaired. The Sanatorium being a solid structure, escaped without injury, and our school suffered very little beyond a few cracks in the walls, though the Sisters' cottage swayed to and fro over the mountainside in a most perilous fashion. The Sister says she ran first to the Hospital [i.e. school infirmary], a large room upstairs where there was one little sick child. She found the matron with the child in her arms wrapped in blankets, and the nurse holding on to the kerosene stove which was in immediate danger of upsetting and igniting, while the medicine bottles and crockery were rolling about the floor, and a stream of brandy flowed down the middle of the room."

"Terrific shock at Darjeeling" was the headline of the fairly short report in *The Friend of India* of June 15th 1897. The earthquake was: "the severest ever known here. The shock lasted three minutes, and has done incalculable damage. Nearly every house has been more or less affected... For fifteen minutes after the earthquake there was a distinct rumbling sound and a peculiar stillness and oppressiveness of the atmosphere, which seemed to forebode evil, and, as we expected, there were no less than four shocks from eleven to four last night [June 12], another at nine o'clock this morning [June 13], another at noon, and another at five this evening. Fortunately they were slight shocks which have apparently caused no further damage. It has been raining off and on since noon

[June 13], and the general opinion is that we are not safe yet... Through traffic to Calcutta is suspended in consequence of some bridges beyond Siligoree [sic] having collapsed."

Darjeeling, queen of the hill stations, perched precariously on its ridge under the Himalayas, was never a safe place because, at the best of times, the ground was unstable and would slip downhill with no respect for whatever was built upon it. So the dak bungalows and planters' cottages with pretty English names like Sunnyside, the Shrubbery, Castleton, the Hermitage and Rosebank, were all casualties to a greater or smaller extent when the ground shook so violently in June 1897. The Diocesan Girls' High School was not listed amongst the casualties, although Sr Muriel's account shows how dangerous the situation was. But the school's good fortune was not to last much longer. No sooner had the residents of Darjeeling recovered from the earthquake and either repaired or rebuilt their properties, than a far worse disaster overwhelmed them. On Sunday September 24th 1899 Darjeeling suffered the worst landslips hitherto recorded: there was catastrophic damage and widespread loss of life. There was also much heroism and many acts of courage, not least on the part of the Sisters. Now it is time to take a closer look.

Footnotes

1. There is a mix-up here! Sr Katherine Maud was still a novice at Clewer in 1897 and did not travel to India until 1902, when she left England on January 17th on board the P. & O. liner *S.S. Sunda*, together with Sr Mary Pauline who was going for the second time, and Sr Helena Maria, going for the first time. Sr Katherine Maud made five visits altogether - three as a serving Sister, and two short visits whilst Mother Superior. It was while returning home from the last visit (1935), that she was taken ill and died before returning to Clewer (see chapter 27). Sr Jane Frances' statement that Sr Katherine Maud was with her on the day of the earthquake is more likely to be a printing error - her erratic and spidery handwriting has already been remarked upon. The Sister who was with her might have been Sr Kate Mary, who was in India from early 1893 until February 1899.

2. This is probably a reference to the European Orphanage, which was founded originally for the children of soldiers, although there was another institution called the Military Orphan House, but this was not run by Sisters - see chapter 23.

C S J B

I N D I A

-18-
STORMY WEATHER!

The *St John Baptist Magazine* for Autumn 1899 contained an account of the disaster which struck Darjeeling during the night of Sunday September 24th: "So far as we can glean from the scanty information as yet received, what happened was as follows," wrote Sr Jane Frances from Calcutta. "There had been an unusually dry season and the rain was anxiously expected. On Saturday September 23rd at 3.00 p.m. it came in torrents and continued all through Sunday. On Sunday night the landslips began… Late on Sunday night the Sisters brought the children into the only part of the building which seemed at all safe. There are a few little boys in their charge from seven to nine years old. These slept in a room above the dining hall which was considered safe, and were allowed to remain in their beds under the care of two ladies. Between 12 [midnight] and 1.00 a.m. they heard the rumble of the earth slipping above the house and in a moment the whole side of the girls' dormitory was torn off and carried away. The children were naturally terrified and would have run out, but the teachers stopped them and they all dressed quickly and went into another part of the house. Here they stayed together till about half past one when a large slip, together with huge boulders, stones and falling trees, struck the building with such force that the lower walls immediately collapsed. The boys' dormitory was thrown forward and fell with a crash into the compound burying the fourteen little boys and the teachers in charge of them in the ruins."

"The Sisters and governesses went out quickly to their rescue, and with the help of one of the native servants, succeeded in extricating all of them from under the debris of the splintered wood, beams and shattered glass. This was no easy matter, as they had no implements to help them, and the rain was pouring in torrents, the earth slipping, and the lamps giving only a flickering light. But the boys behaved with great courage and instead of being terrified by what they heard around them, as soon as they were themselves rescued, began to help in finding and aiding the others who were still in need of it. One of the little boys, Ray Symons, made an heroic attempt all by himself, to raise a beam which had fallen on another boy, Gal Gregory, who lay helpless, blinded by slime and mud under the weight of it. When at last Gal was discovered by a governess repeatedly calling his name, he was heard answering piteously, 'I am here, but I am blind.' With the help of Ray Symons, she was able to lift the beam, and he was afterwards taken to the Sanatorium where he soon recovered."

Not all the boys suffered like Gal Gregory, although all had lucky escapes, as the Sister recounted: "Two little boys were asleep when they were taken out of their beds, and one little lad of five years old awoke smiling quite happily, wondering what was happening around him. But their escape was most merciful, for the house stood very near the edge of a precipice, and the floor on which their beds were standing slid bodily down till it overhung the edge, and there by the mercy of God it was stayed."

"The girls meanwhile were assembled in the new part of the school buildings which have only been erected this year, and owing to the good workmanship of the builder, Mr Moriarty, it suffered much less than the other portions of the school, the roof remaining unbroken by the weight of the trees, stones, etc that fell upon it, so that when it fell the children were all safely rescued from it, creeping out one by one from under the gables amid the ruins of chairs, tables, cupboards etc. In the course of the night, Mr Timme and his rescue party called twice at the school, and the second time Mr Timme, finding the road washed away, slid pluckily down the landslip to where the children were. Mr Moriarty also came, and the next day gave them most valuable assistance."

"The miseries of the night were increased by water which poured in and filled the floor knee deep where the children were, while rats and other drowned animals floated around. About 4.00 a.m. the Archdeacon and others came to see what could be done, but our children being in tolerable safety, they went on to where help was more [seriously] needed. About 6.00 a.m. kind Lady Woodburn[(1)] sent for them all, and soldiers to carry the little ones to the Durbar Hall. Both Lady and Miss Woodburn have since busied themselves doing everything in their power for the comfort and convenience of the school. The girls had their mattresses on the raised dais round the Hall and the governesses occupy the small rooms adjoining. The Sisters have now recovered some of the school books and have begun a temporary school in these novel surroundings. The day scholars, who were invited to join them if they pleased, quickly responded, and the large number of 105 daily assemble, the girls much enjoying their new condition of school life and looking on it all as a kind of large picnic..."

"No part of the school remains intact but the Sisters' cottage and the chapel at the far end, though the new part of the building erected only this year suffered less than the older portions which were entirely destroyed, with all the kitchen apparatus, crockery etc. The children have since recovered much of their buried clothing. It was much damaged, and a gang of 30 men under the superintendence of Mr Greer (a former, most able and energetic Chief Commissioner), were hard at work trying to recover as much of the school property as was possible."

The irrepressible good spirits of the girls doubtless turned the disaster into an adventure which they would always remember: an experience to tell grandchildren, and one which would take its place in the history of the school. Indeed, in later years Gal Gregory's daughter, Emmeline, became a pupil at the school. But despite the novelty of lessons in the Durbar Hall, and the brave attempt at "business as usual", the whole episode was a major catastrophe for the life of the school, although eventually a much larger and better school replaced it. It is only when resorting to the daily newspapers that the full scale of the disaster can be appreciated.

The first reports in *The Friend of India* appeared on September 28th having been telegraphed through to Calcutta on September 26th. "Never has Darjeeling been visited by such a lamentable disaster," ran the report. "The Diocesan Girls' School is ruined. No one however, was killed. There were many miraculous escapes. The school has moved to the Durbar Hall." But it is in the issue of October 5th that the full story of the school is recounted under the headline: "The Diocesan Girls' School a complete wreck." The report continued: "...It is doubtful whether the site can be rebuilt upon or not, as many large rocks, hundreds of tons in weight have moved and are menacing the place. At midnight on Sunday the girls were awakened and ordered to congregate in the only building which was not severely damaged by the landslips. The boys, whose dormitory is on the second floor above the dining hall, were allowed to remain in their dormitory in [the] charge of the Misses Stewart, Cowper, and Lefranc. At 1.00 a.m. a large slip, accompanied by the rolling of large boulders and the falling of trees, struck the building with irresistible force, and caused the lower walls to collapse. The dormitory was hurled forward, and fell with a terrific crash into the school compound. How all escaped with their lives is marvellous."

The report goes on to tell of the heroism of the teachers and Sisters: "Miss Stewart was the first to extricate herself from the ruins, and she ran to the building occupied by the terrified girls, for assistance. Sisters Florence and Grace Ancilla[2] were immediately in attendance and commenced operations, extricating those who were buried. The little boys behaved with exceptional courage, and Ray Sims [3], a boy of eight who had released himself by his own exertions, immediately and without any regard for his personal safety, commenced to assist..." His help in rescuing Gal Gregory who was trapped under a beam and located by Miss Middleton's repeated calling of Gal's name, is then recounted and corroborates Sr Jane Frances ' account. "Great credit is due to Sisters Florence and Grace Ancilla and the teachers for their energy in keeping the children calm. It is extraordinary how they have escaped pneumonia. Many of the teachers have lost all their clothing and effects, and are practically destitute. Gal Gregory, whose eyes were injured through the fall of the beam and mud, is progressing very favourably, and will soon be discharged from the Sanatorium. Dr Lewtas is working early and late, devoting himself with commendable zeal and energy to the patients in the Sanatorium."

Further detail is given to the plight of the Diocesan School in *The*

Friend of India for October 12th. Because of the difficulties in reaching Darjeeling - road and rail links were severed - news reports took several days to reach Calcutta. Thus the issue of October 12th carries a report dated October 2nd which fills in a few more details, and gives an accolade to the Sisters, who seem to have kept remarkably calm throughout. But first there is a note of criticism about the position of the school - it seems it had been built in a particularly vulnerable spot, although nowhere in Darjeeling would have been safe on that fateful night: "The location of the Diocesan Girls' High School is to the north of Observatory Hill. The hill above it is precipitous, and the huge boulders inbedded in loose gravel and broken clay, have always been a standing menace to the buildings of the school. Mr G.F.Bartlett, late P.W.D. Engineer [Public Works Dept] in Darjeeling, whose extensive experience of the soils and geological formation of the hills in the district was excelled by none, was consistently adverse to the opening of a school in this dangerous position. He was not alone in his opinion, but was supported by every engineer of experience." However, the Sisters had not built the school; they had merely taken up responsibility for running it, but no doubt such expert opinions were taken into account when the time came for rebuilding.

"The report continued: "...On Sunday night the school maintained its creditable reputation by the heroic behaviour of the teachers and the girls when a panic, which would have resulted in many deaths, was inevitable. To Sr Florence and Sr Grace Ancilla, the parents who have children in the school cannot be sufficiently grateful, as it was the efforts of these two courageous ladies who, sacrificing all thought of personal safety, exposed themselves to unknown perils in their attempts to safeguard the interests of their pupils and save life." Having explained that increased numbers had resulted in the construction of a new building, the report continued: "This new structure issued from Sunday night's disaster all but unscathed; and it was in the teachers' rooms above the recreation hall that the whole school, mistresses and girls, took refuge while all the other buildings were either entirely swept away, or so severely destroyed as to render rehabilitation hazardous. It was at midnight on Sunday 24th, that the senior girls who had instinctively recognised the dangers of the raging storm, and who were unable to sleep in consequence, were afforded tangible proof of their fears by hearing the dull concussion of a slip above them on the Mall, and by seeing the whole side of their dormitory torn off and carried away. The girls, as was to be expected, sprang from their beds and manifested their intention of running out, but fortunately at this juncture one of the senior teachers entered and ordered all the girls to immediately dress and move into the teachers' rooms. Sisters Florence and Grace Ancilla, who occupied a small cottage [in] the grounds, were summoned and responded immediately. Throwing towels over their heads they hastened to the girls and, although drenched by the torrents of rain, busied themselves in the task of cheering and infusing courage into their distracted pupils."

Having calmed the girls, the Sisters and teachers settled themselves for the night. As previously noted, everyone was confident that the small boys would be safe in their own dormitory and the Misses Cowper, Stewart and Lefranc opted to stay with them. In fact the three governesses had a very lucky escape for next morning their usual quarters were found crushed under great boulders and large trees. All seemed well until about 1.00 a.m. when "the girls... were startled by a terrific crash which was succeeded a minute or so after by a fearful yell. A large slip of Observatory Hill had struck the walls of the dining hall. The walls collapsed and the dormitory above was hurled forward and smashed into fragments. Beams were splintered, rafters broken into matchwood, corrugated iron twisted and bent into fantastic shapes, and beds, floor-boards, glasses, broken windows, and splintered doors strewed the compound in one wild chaotic heap. Under this pile of debris were entombed more than a score of young lives; but regardless of the fury of the elements, regardless of the rolling rocks and shifting earth, regardless of the falling trees and the flood of water rushing in a mad turmoil down the hill, Sisters Florence and Grace Ancilla ran out to encounter a task from which men would have recoiled in consternation, but which to these two heroic ladies presented no dangers so long as their youthful charges were in deadly peril of being suffocated. The rain beat fiercely against their faces, the wind was howling, and the lantern flame flared and cast only a precarious glimmer to guide their footsteps; the earth was trembling under the repeated concussion of falling slips, there was the roar and thunder of warning elements in their ears, and the impenetrable blackness of night around them, and the uncertainty of not knowing where they may have trod and been killed by the fall of the impenetrable hill side."

Here the account of the school stopped and moved on to other places in Darjeeling. However, the rest of the story is well known - of the frantic attempt to free the boys, how none were killed, and only Gal Gregory sustained injuries from which he later recovered. But the nightmare of the situation and the heroism of all who were involved comes across vividly in the newspaper account. The immense scale of the disaster is shown by the fact that on October 5th 1899 *The Friend of India* devoted six entire pages to it, as well as extensive coverage on September 28th and October 12th; similarly, *The Times of India* gave detailed coverage on October 7th.

As with all natural disasters, meteorological and geological experts later made detailed analyses, and concluded that the landslips had been caused by an unprecedented amount of rainfall followed by a cyclone. Up to June 24th, there had been 17 inches of rain over the average - followed by the cyclone. A total of 28 inches fell in the 38 hours between the Saturday afternoon and Monday evening. The full effects of the cyclone were felt over a fairly restricted area, the highest rainfall being recorded on the Tiger Hill tea estate (29.42 inches), closely followed by 27.20 inches on the Happy Valley tea estate. At Kurseong a few miles south, a rainfall of 19.85 inches was recorded, and only nine lives lost in the surrounding administrative area. But 219 lives were lost in the administrative area surrounding Darjeeling, all of whom were non-European. Deaths in Darjeeling itself amounted to 62 non-Europeans and 10 Europeans. So great was the effect of the various landslips that many people thought they were experiencing an earthquake, but although the heavy slips may have caused local earth tremors, there were no recordable seismic shocks. Even so, it was conceded that the great earthquake of 1897 could have sufficiently weakened the top soil which, combined with the excessive rain, caused landslips in places which otherwise would have been more stable. Some of the worst slips took place in the vicinity of Observatory Hill, starting from the top and taking everything in their path, including the Diocesan Girls' School. The Eden Sanatorium escaped lightly because it was not directly in the path of slips from Observatory Hill even though it was quite near.

But the school was by no means the only casualty, nor was it the worst; elsewhere, there was much devastation and loss of life. The first report in *The Friend of India* of September 28th told briefly of several children killed at the Arcadia School and neighbouring Ida Villa; three Europeans and several non-Europeans drowned crossing the Tieesta river when their boat was swamped; the children of the Revd D. H. Lee were killed when their house, Mall Villa, was buried; several Indian bazaars were swept away; and extensive damage was done to the tea gardens. Communications with Darjeeling (except for the electric telegraph), had been virtually cut off: the Darjeeling-Himalayan Railway was breached in several places, and the line was washed away in more than one spot. The cart road, which ran parallel with the railway was also severely damaged. For several days the only way of reaching Darjeeling from Siliguri many miles to the south, was by pony. But some places escaped virtually unscathed: St Paul's School was unharmed, so too was the Loreto Convent, and St Joseph's College at North Point.

The Friend of India for October 5th contained extensive details and not a few horror stories. For instance, the fate of the Arcadia School and neighbouring Ida Villa where several people were killed. Fearing for the safety of the children at Arcadia School, the Principal took them to Ida Villa close by. The children and teachers had settled down for the night, when a large landslip fell on the house, demolishing two walls which fell on several people including some of the children. Four were killed and others trapped. Having done what they could to rescue the casualties some of the teachers went to fetch help - at great personal risk. *The Friend of India* implied that the children panicked and that this was partly why the decision was made to evacuate to Ida Villa. However, no one could blame anyone for panicking under such terrifying conditions, especially young children. The school Principal and the governesses certainly seem to have done their best to keep order and calm under apocalyptic conditions.

The four victims of the Arcadia School were not the only young lives to be lost that night. All six children of the Revd and Mrs D. H. Lee died when their home in Mall Villas next to Arcadia School, was swept away. Mr and Mrs Lee were American Methodist missionaries who had returned home due to Mr Lee's health, but his wife had subsequently returned to India, and now ran a school for Indian girls in Calcutta. Their children were in Darjeeling in the care of their eldest daughter, Veda, aged 17. The household was sleeping when the landslip crashed onto the house and all were swept away. The body of one of the girls was recovered, but the search for the others was abandoned after several days. The sole survivor, Wilbur Lee, was very badly injured and was taken to the Eden Sanatorium where he was nursed by Sr Sybil, but he died of tetanus on October 3rd. His parents were with him.

There were many acts of heroism, not least the boys from St Joseph's College who risked life and limb to rescue some trapped villagers. The College football team was accustomed to a morning run, and finding their buildings largely unscathed, went out as usual. They soon discovered how extensive the devastation was when they came to the village of Singamari, most of which had been washed away. Approaching for a closer look, they found many people buried and crying out for help. The boys were shocked to find that a number of village men were unharmed but were doing nothing to rescue the other people. The boys did what they could but had no spades or implements, and the village men were unhelpful. Most of the people were dead by the time the boys could help, but they were able to free two women, one of whom was holding two small children, both dead. The boys managed to get a charpoy [a wooden framed bed with webbing], and having laid the woman on it, carried it with difficulty to the Indian hospital. The village men refused to carry the charpoy, and it was with great difficulty that the boys waded through the mud, which was sometimes waist high, in order to reach the hospital.

Three English men were drowned while crossing the Tieesta river by ferry. Two of them were officials of the Bengal-Dooars Railway, and the third was Superintendant of a tea estate near Jalpaiguri. The ferry boat was attempting to cross the river for inspection purposes at the point where the Assam-Dooars Railway crosses it. Suddenly a heavy wave broke over the boat and swamped it; the three European passengers and seven Indian crewmen were washed away, although one of the crew was later picked up alive 14 miles downstream.

The tea estates sustained major damage as related by *The Times of India* for October 7th: "The Hope Tea Estate has lost 100 acres of tea land, and the factory has been entirely destroyed. The coolie lines have been buried with great loss of life. The Cedars, one of the oldest gardens in the district, has had its factory completely washed away, falling bodily down a precipice. In the Kaley Valley the Dooriah Tea Estate has had its factory partially destroyed... The Lingell Tea Estate has experienced several severe slips. The new turbine pipes have been badly damaged. The Avon Grove Tea Estate has lost 30 acres of tea land, with 4,000 bushes. The coolie lines have been swept away and many coolies have been killed... The factory has been destroyed." Similarly, the Happy Valley Tea Estate was badly damaged with great loss of ground and serious damage to the factory.

The number of Indian casualties was much higher than that of the Europeans because of the greater concentration of people living in the bazaar areas. Thus *The Friend of India* reported that: "Phool Bazaar is completely covered and destroyed, and 200 inhabitants have been killed. 21 bodies were recovered at Tamsong bustee, but another 20 people are believed to have been killed there." Despite all the rain there was very little drinking water due to burst pipes. Also there was no electricity as the dynamo of the "electric light plant" had been swept away. Darkness, and water shortages were inconvenient in themselves, but the lack of communications and damage to the native bazaars meant food shortages too. Food prices soared and became comparable with prices in times of famine.

Prompt action was taken by the government to clear the wreckage and find trapped and injured victims and the bodies of the dead, by sending engineers and rescue workers including men from the Royal Munster Fusiliers. Those soldiers greatly assisted in what had become a community operation - men and women had all worked slavishly to clear the roads and alleviate the suffering. The British Raj had never seen such an undertaking before or since - those immensely respectable ladies and gentlemen, who temporarily cast aside protocol, and frantically clawed and dug at mud and rocks and trees, often standing waist deep in it themselves, in order to rescue their neighbours from a gruesome death. It is gratifying to know that in the midst of it all there were the Sisters and that they won universal acclaim for their heroism on that apocalyptic night. Kipling's words: "If you can keep your head when all about you are losing theirs", comes to mind. Just a few weeks from the dawning of a new century, much of the Sisters' work at Darjeeling had literally fallen apart, but the new century would see something greater arise out of the ruins.

Footnotes

1. Lady Woodburn was the wife of the Lieutenant Governor of Bengal. The Durbar Hall was a large building used for balls and receptions by the Lieutenant Governor in the Darjeeling "season."

2. Sr Grace Ancilla. The report in *The Friend of India* erroneously gives the Sister's name as Sr Grace. Her correct name was Sr Grace Ancilla and she was in India from February 1899 until January 1904: she later left the Community. In view of the fact that there was another Clewer Sister called Sr Grace (in Community later), I have corrected the report in *The Friend of India*, for the sake of accuracy, and to avoid confusion amongst readers who might remember this second, later Sister.

3. Ray Symons/Ray Sims. Sr Jane Frances ' account gives the boy's name as Ray Symons, and the newspaper as Ray Sims. There is no way of knowing which is correct, though one suspects the Sister's account is the more accurate of the two.

CSJB

INDIA

-19-
CROSSING THE RUBICON

In passing from one century to another the British Raj crossed the rubicon, for the new century marked the dawn of a new age. Within a year, Victoria, Queen and Empress had died, and with her died many old perceptions. The reign of the new King and Emperor, Edward VII, was relatively short, and it ushered in an age which was equally short-lived, dying as it did on the battlefields of the Great War. In India itself the tide of nationalism, which had already begun to flow, especially in Bengal, would swell within the next generation. It was a tide which finally saw the end of British rule. But for the moment all seemed well - there was a new Viceroy, Lord Curzon, and during his tenure of office British rule reached its zenith. It was Curzon's idea to build the Victoria Memorial in the heart of Calcutta, as a mausoleum to commemorate the great Empress. And there it remains on the edge of the Maidan, having taken until 1921 to complete. But it was time itself which dealt the final blow, for by the time the Victoria Memorial was finished, the seat of government had moved to New Delhi. Thus passed the glory of Calcutta.

But the winds of change were hardly perceptible at first, and to return to more immediate things, the old century passed in Calcutta and Darjeeling with a mass of clearing up and rebuilding after all the destructive forces which had been unleashed upon them had done their worst. Amongst the buildings which stood in need of repair was St Paul's Cathedral, Calcutta - the Empire's oldest Cathedral. The cross which surmounted the spire had crashed through the roof in the 1897 earthquake. After restoration, spire and cross continued pointing towards heaven until the 1934 earthquake, after which a tower based on Canterbury's Bell Harry was erected instead.

Despite being totally destroyed, the Diocesan Girls' School in Darjeeling managed to function fairly effectively. Writing in later years,[1] Sr Georgina, recalled that: "after a month in the Durbar Hall the children dispersed for their holidays, and the question had to be faced, 'Where is the school to go next?' The long winter vacation of three months gave us time to find and adapt two rented houses on the Birch Hill Road, far removed from the point of danger and to put up temporary dormitories, class rooms, and a dining room of corrugated iron in the available space. Here all met again in March 1900, and a crowded but happy four years passed while the large school began to rise up on a cleared piece of forest land immediately below. On a sunny morning in 1900 the foundation stone of the new buildings was laid with much solemnity. The girls in their new white Chapel veils walked in procession singing hymns, headed by the Thurifer and Processional Cross. The site was a gift from the

Lieutenant-Governor and lay between two good roads in the north part of Darjeeling..."

It was to be another four years before the new school was completed, but in the meantime the Eden Sanatorium was expanding. As already noted, the Eden had escaped serious damage from the landslips, and played an important role in providing medical aid for the injured. In the same issue of the *St John Baptist Magazine* which reported the landslips (Autumn 1899), there was a report about the proposed extension. "The Darjeeling Planter's Association in the course of the year, urged the necessity for providing hospital accommodation for Europeans at Darjeeling, and requested that one half of the Sanatorium building might be converted into a hospital and kept open throughout the year. The Lieutenant Governor, after consulting the Inspector General of Civil Hospitals [in] Bengal, and after a personal inspection of the building, decided that a new block containing an operating room, four bedrooms for patients, and quarters for two nurses, should be constructed from Provincial funds at an estimated cost of 10,000 rupees, subject to the conditions that sick persons be admitted at all times of the year, that patients who are unable to pay the usual charges be admitted and treated free of cost, and that the Committee bear the cost of equipping the new block. These conditions have been accepted by the Managing Committee. When the new section is completed it will remove a long felt want and [will] add materially to the usefulness of the institution."

As the century turned, so it took in its stride a problem which had been rife for several years: bubonic plague. Most parts of India were susceptible to it, but it was worse in the Punjab and Bombay, although Calcutta was also badly affected. More than ten million people died between 1895 and 1902, and it was comparable in mortality to the devastating famines of the nineteenth century. It also bore overtones of the great plagues which had swept Europe in previous centuries. Medical science had not yet discovered that fleas carried by rats were responsible for spreading the disease, but thought it to be a product of the slums.

Whatever the cause of the plague, it fell to the lot of people like the Clewer Sisters to alleviate the suffering. The summer 1900 issue of the *St John Baptist Magazine*, contained the following account of a poor Muslim boy who came under the Sisters' care: "One day in June last year (1899), when that strange disease the Plague was beginning to die out in Calcutta, there was brought into the 'plague ward' of the Medical College Hospital a little Mohammedan lad of about nine years. He had been found lying on the road by the police who carried him at once into the hospital. He was unconscious and convulsed, and so ill that we feared he would not recover. Poor little lad! He was so dirty and dusty, and it took some hours to get him clean, as he was too ill at first to bear all the necessary washing required. His hair was thick and matted too, and we had to shave his head, and then an icebag was applied and kept day and night on the little head, which would not lie in the same position for long. As he became more and more restless and delirious (as the plague patients invariably do), his hands and feet had to be tied down to the sides of the bed. Of course we did not know his name nor anything about him, and it was partly his apparently desolate helplessness that made us feel so much interested in him. He had been there for a day when a man appeared who claimed him for his son, and told us his name was Abdool. The poor father was greatly distressed to find his boy so ill, and he remained on the ground day and night by the little fellow's bed till he recovered."

The Sister continued: "The father was an operative in some manufactory, I think. He said that Abdool had often run away from him since the mother's death... I well remember the morning when the father called me with such great joy to come and see that Abdool had recovered consciousness and was able to recognise him. He was altogether a month in the plague ward. The Government rule in the hospital was that all the clothes of the patients attacked with plague were to be burned, but the natives were allowed a new supply of clothes at Government expense, so the order was given for new clothes for Abdool. These clothes were really only four or five yards of thick white muslin, such as the Bengali's wear round and round and caught up in a graceful fashion."

Thus Abdool recovered and went home after obviously winning the Sister's affection. But there was a sequel: "For a time Abdool and his father passed out of our sight until one day at the end of last August a Mohammedan man was brought into one of the native medical wards of the Medical College Hospital, and the nurse told me that he was Abdool's father. The poor man was very ill with inflammation of both lungs. His little son came several times to see him looking very dirty and neglected. The father's only anxiety was the boy's future, and he told the nurses how much he wished to give the boy into the Sisters' care. The man died [after] five days, on Sunday September 1st, but before his death he bequeathed his little son to me to be brought up as a Christian. The boy was not there at the time of his father's death, but some friends brought him to us the next day - a very miserable little fellow and half starved, and with a finger in his mouth. We cleaned him up and kept him at the nurses' quarters for a day or two, and he made himself very happy and comfortable, and thought himself very useful too as he went around the rooms flicking the chairs with a duster. We had to set him up in clothes again, but the Government did not pay for them that time."

The boy could not stay there permanently but the Sister found a solution: "We took him to the Oxford Mission industrial school and left him there under the charge of the excellent Bengali priest[2] who is Headmaster of the school. When I told him that I feared Abdool was rather a naughty boy he laughed and said that he liked naughty boys if they were honest! Abdool was baptised on Christmas Eve and named David, and I saw him soon afterwards - a well cared for, happy little boy.

1. *Ship passing through Suez Canal.*

2. The River Hooghly from Hastings' Bridge showing the spot on which the Sisters landed, December 8th 1881.

3. Sr Lucy, first Sister Superior in India, 1881-9.

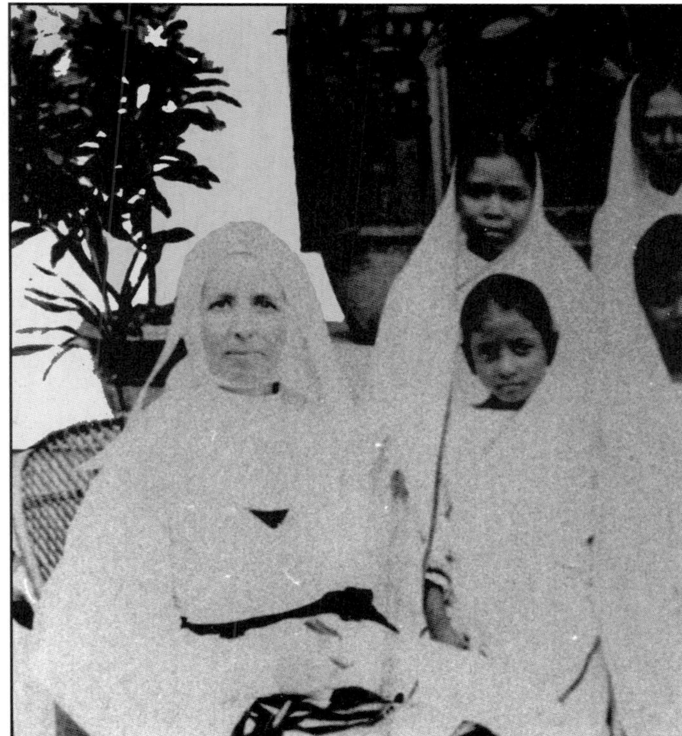

4. Sr Jane Frances, Sister Superior in India, 1889-1919.

5. Lady Canning Home, Calcutta.

6. Eden Hospital, Calcutta.

7. *Presidency General Hospital, Calcutta.*

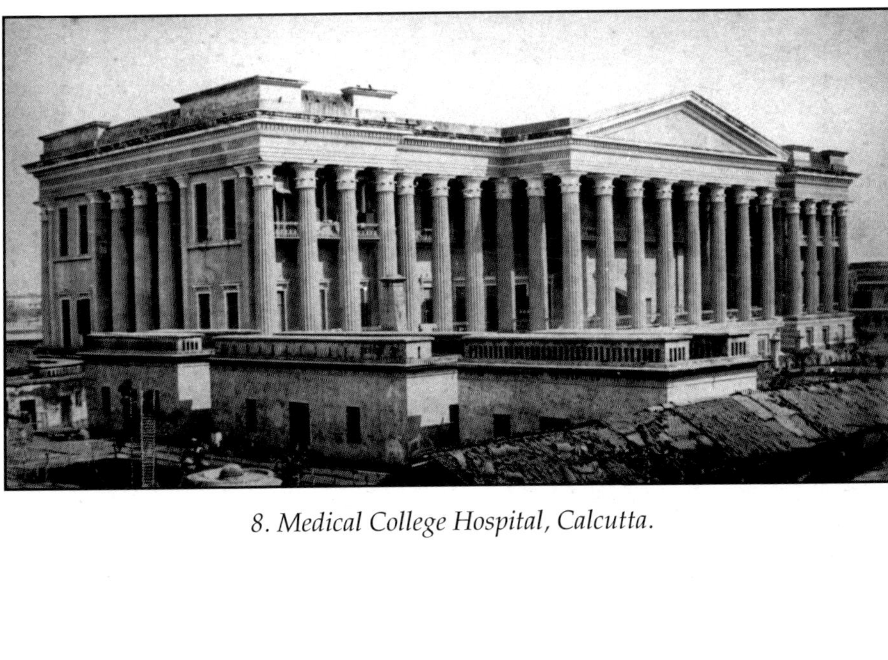

8. *Medical College Hospital, Calcutta.*

9. Doctors, nurses and Clewer Sisters outside Presidency General Hospital, c.1912. The Sisters are: Sr Emily Barbara, Sr Katherine Maud, Sr Jane Frances, Sr Mary Frances, Sr Helena Maria, Sr Constance Ruth.

10. *Sisters' graves, Bhowanipore Cemetery, 1920s.*

11. *European Orphanage, Calcutta.*

12. *Children at the European Orphanage.*

13. *Kidderpore House - later, St Thomas' School.*

14. *Pratt Memorial School.*

15. Sr Florence, heroine of the Darjeeling landslip.

16. Edward Johnson, Bishop of Calcutta, 1876-98.

17. *Angelina Hoare.*

18. *Margaret Robertson.*

19. Sunderbuns village of Jalashi - rest house showing heaps of newly cut rice. 4 Sisters in the background and children from the village school.

20. *Cookhouse at the Lower or Vernacular School at the Diocesan mission house, Calcutta.*

21. Darjeeling-Himalayan Railway. The loop below Tindharia, c.1890. It looks exactly the same today.

22. *Eden Sanatorium, Darjeeling.*

23. *Diocesan Girls' High School Darjeeling, after the landslip 1899.*

24. *Darjeeling landslip 1899 - railway line suspended in mid-air.*

25. *Darjeeling landslip 1899 - a house completely destroyed.*

26. Diocesan Girls' High School Darjeeling - rebuilt 1904 after the landslip, and known after 1929 as St Michael's.

27. Head servant and his family, Diocesan Girls' High School, Darjeeling.

28. Diocesan College, Calcutta. Now part of St John's Diocesan Girls' Higher Secondary School.

29. Pipalpati mission house - now part of St John's Diocesan Girls' H. S. School.

30. Pipalpati mission house, 1922 extension - now part of St John's Diocesan Girls' H.S. School.

31. *Diocesan Collegiate School - now part of St John's Diocesan Girls' H. S. School.*

32. *St Paul's Cathedral Calcutta, before removal of spire following 1934 earthquake.*

33. *Sr Georgina and former students of the Diocesan College Calcutta, 1895-1922, taken in 1922.*

34. Sr Hilda Frances and students, Diocesan College Calcutta, 1934.

35. St Mary's Bhowampara, or Bhowanipore.

He is a nice looking lad with large brown eyes. He has been adopted by a parish guild in Lancashire which is paying the cost of his education."[3]

No sooner had the plague abated than another problem arose to afflict the people of Calcutta and the surrounding area - floods, and in their wake cholera. Writing home to Clewer from the Pipalpati mission house in a letter which published in the spring 1901 *St John Baptist Magazine*, one of the Sisters commented: "Since posting my letter on Tuesday we have had three days of continuous rain with the result that most of the city has been flooded. All the back part of our compound was like a lake, and the road beyond, like a river. Some people started boats, and some went on wooden bedsteads turned upside down. Nearly all the poor peoples' settlements have a pond in the middle, and these overflowed swamping the little mud houses. All the empty houses have been taken for temporary shelter for the homeless, and a large new general hospital which was just ready for use is housing numbers of people and their animals. Of course it has been impossible for the officials to carry on sanitary arrangements as the Government carts have been unable to get about, and refuse of all sorts has been poisoning the water. Yesterday morning two of our younger children were taken ill. We got a native doctor to come round and he said at once, what we had thought - that it was cholera."

The suffering of the people must have been dreadful and the way the Sisters quite calmly coped with it is remarkable. Continuing her narrative, the Sister gave further details about the two sick children: "One child who had no constitution and was full of malaria, died after about seven hours. The other is still living and seems likely to pull through. We hear that a boy has died this morning at Bishop's College. He was taken ill last night. I think he had been playing about in dirty water. And they have a case at the industrial boys' school. We had the [girl's] funeral this morning. Mercifully the rain had stopped, but we had to stand a little way off the grave for the service, and Sister Superior [Jane Frances], walked across on planks to throw in some flowers. It was a very plain little white coffin and no one was there but Sister Superior, myself, Mr Bannerjee, and the undertaker. Her father and mother were in the country and I suppose it was too flooded for them to get up in time. The old grandmother is a servant here. The moment she saw the child was dying she set up the most awful wail and flung herself about on the ground. We got her into the next room because she was frightening the other child, and she threw herself down there. She went all round howling wildly for sometime and then she kept up a gentler wail all the rest of the day, and I seemed to hear her at night too. I suppose they cannot easily give up the old customs, but one trusts that as Christians, in time they will do so."

The situation worsened over the next few days, as the Sister recounted: "At this moment [24th], we have no patients here as Sister took our child to the General Hospital this morning. They think she will make a good recovery. We have another child there who has the disease in a milder form. The industrial boy has died. I think they have two more ill now and have sent off all the rest to the Oxford Mission House. One of the Bishop's College students has died, and another boy is ill. It is so difficult to keep them out of the dirty water. I have to tell the children here that if anyone bathes in the pond they will be caned. The rain has begun again today, but we keep hoping it will stop. The dead donkeys are lying about unremoved because the carts can't get about. Food prices are of course very high. So far we have not wanted, but the children don't eat meat and the fish isn't safe, so they have to have rice and sugar, or rice and vegetable curry when we can get it."

Poor Sister, one can sense the increasing feeling of helplessness as the cholera took its toll and conditions worsened. Thus she continued next day: "25th. Such a night last night, four more girls taken ill and two more sent to hospital this morning. The rain *pouring* all night; today is fine. Sister is sending me to the Canning Home today as they want as few people as possible here while the house is disinfected. It is pretty hard work to have to leave Sr M. [Sr Muriel or Sr Margaret] and the rest of the children. I only hope they will let me help the hospital Sisters, the cholera wards are crammed."

Clearly the Sisters became fond of the children in their care, and of their families too, but the Sister's next instalment written from the Lady Canning Home, highlights the cultural difficulties encountered by Indians converting from Hinduism to Christianity. "27th. I think I left off writing on Tuesday when I came here. That night Sr M. brought another child to hospital, but it is a very slight case, making our ninth from the school, omitting those who have had it since they left us, in their own homes. We had a second death yesterday, a dear little child of about four years old. When I saw her in the morning she was tossing about unconscious, but before she went she became quite conscious and said such pretty things, asking pardon for all she had done wrong, and also for wearing such a dirty frock. She was always getting punished at school for making her frocks muddy, but she was a dear baby. The mother is a [servant] at the Eden Hospital, and the old father is chapel bearer at the College. The mother is a Hindu convert, and poor dear, it was difficult to restrain her wailing and putting mud on her forehead. She has still another child who is ill, but the little one was the pet. Sister Superior and I went with her and the old father to the funeral. Mr Bannerjee read the service in Bengali. I took the mother this morning to put flowers on the grave. Poor thing, she has been with the two children for some days and is quite worn out. I am quite glad to be here as I go two or three times a day to have a look at our sick children... Four of ours have been very slight and may go back tomorrow. We have two rather bad still. The roads by the mission house and the compound are dreadful, such smells now the water is drying up. Sr M. is there with about ten children and all the servants. She writes today that the dhobi [laundryman] across the way died, his child [died] today, and now the woman is ill; there was wailing all night and day. One of our children's sisters has died - a hospital nurse."

But the problems were not confined to Calcutta as the Sister's letter related: "The distress in the country is awful - rice crops ruined, people living in boats and without food for days. One of the Hospital Sisters has collected some money for feeding the people whose houses were swamped near here, and who were given refuge in the new General Hospital. I went to help her today. I should think we had about 300 people, very rough and poor looking. The men kept them barricaded on the stairs and let them down a few at a time while we measured the dry rice and dal into their cloths. There was a leper amongst them and several blind people. One baby looked nothing but bones. Here in the hospital grounds they had been in a sort of oasis. I suppose the drainage arrangements are extra good, but for the next three weeks or so there is great fear of malaria all round, as the water dries up. The young chaplain at the Cathedral lost his wife on Tuesday. They had only been married a short while, and there is a baby not three weeks old. The priests at the College [Bishop's College] had hours of work at a stretch. I believe they could get no nurse for a case they knew must die soon. They had several cases at the boys' industrial school, two deaths, and now four ill of those taken in at the Oxford Mission."

By the beginning of October 1901 things seemed to be improving albeit very slowly: "Oct 1st. Have just taken back our four convalescent children to the Mission House, leaving only two patients here. The four who went back got a nice spoiling by the one nurse in charge of their ward, and they had custard puddings and chicken curries to fatten them the last few days! Yesterday they all pulled up their frocks to show me they had on English undergarments! It is a great favour their being taken into the European hospital. The Mission House is all being whitewashed and sanitary arrangements improved, so we shall be in a better position to beat an illness of this sort. I hope to be back there in a day or two. We hear of fewer cases all round."

"Oct 3rd. We had the rice country teachers at the Mission House yesterday for their monthly pay day - poor things, they have had, and are still having, a terrible time with the floods. Their houses and animals and things all swamped, and many of them, Hindus and Christians, taking refuge in the church (where there happened to be one), and awaiting their last hour, as they thought. Now they are so wonderfully patient about their losses and only thankful their lives are spared. Relief is being started, as not only is there this year's store of rice lost, but next year's crop, which was unusually promising, is likely to be almost if not entirely, lost. We have had some fine, sunny days varied only by thunderstorms, so we hope the rainy season is almost over. We have had no fresh cholera cases, so trust the storm has spent itself."

It was at this time that medical breakthroughs were being made at both the Medical College Hospital and the Presidency General. As noted in chapter 16, 20 years previously Robert Koch, working at the Medical College Hospital, had identified the cholera bacillus. This work was continued there from 1906-20 by Sir Leonard Rogers who developed a saline treatment. Now it was the turn of the Presidency General to take its place in the annals of medicine. Rebuilt after the earthquake of 1897, the main block of the hospital now consisted of an imposing pink-washed building with a vast frontage of 550 feet. Here it was that from 1898 onwards, Surgeon-Major Ronald Ross worked on malaria and discovered that it is caused by mosquitoes. This discovery won him the 1902 Nobel Prize for medicine. His servant, Mahomed Bux, was less fortunate: he had to collect the mosquitoes, and having done so collected malaria too, from the resultant bites. However, this important discovery was not made in that grand building, but in a small hut which passed for a laboratory and which stood in the grounds.(4) Ross composed a poem to commemorate his victory:

This relenting God
Hath placed within my hand
A wondrous thing; and God
Be praised, at his command.
Seeking his secret deeds
With tears and toiling breath,
I find thy cunning seeds
O million-murdering death.
I know this little thing
A myriad men will save.
O death where is thy sting
And Victory, O grave?

The early years of the twentieth century formed a period of transition for the various school departments located in the compound of the Pipalpati mission house, beginning with the rebuilding after the fire and earthquake. The Edwardian years saw the schools going from strength to strength: "There has been a great development in the Upper School in the Mission House," wrote Sr Jane Frances in the autumn 1904 issue of *St John Baptist Magazine*. "This is intended for the daughters of Indian Christian gentlemen, and thus acts upon a higher class in Indian society than the Lower School... The expansion and development of the High School and Upper School department is the great feature of growth. It may not sound so 'missionary' or exciting as actual pioneer work, but nothing can be more important for the recently Christanised families of a better class than a solid Christian education for their children, girls as well as boys. It helps the growing Christian community to take the lead and to become something of a power in their own country, and the advance in that direction in the last 30 years has been remarkable. My own personal delight is still in the elementary village schools."

This period of transition coincided with an improvement in standards at the various schools, so that they began to evolve as separate units whilst remaining under the Sisters' supervision, and sharing the same compound. The Lower or Vernacular School was for low caste Bengali Christian girls who mostly came from the Sunderbuns, and who would return there to teach in the village schools. All school work was done in Bengali with English being taught as a second language. There was no attempt to "Anglicise" the pupils - Bengali dress, food and eating habits were followed by all. This school later became known as St Elizabeth's Middle English School.

The greatest advances were made in the upper school departments. The Diocesan Mission High School had counted its beginnings from the opening of the new buildings at the Pipalpati mission house in 1894, and had survived both fire and earthquake. In 1900 the school gained government recognition as a high school for Bengali Christian girls. The fees were kept as low as possible, and the lessons were given in Bengali to the age of 13, and in English thereafter. Former pupils taught in the lower standards, but English teachers taught the upper standards. This school achieved a good level of education, and in 1909 became affiliated to Calcutta University and changed its name to the Diocesan Collegiate School. At the same time, the Diocesan College began its life, and like the Collegiate School, was affiliated to the University.

In addition to the schools in the mission house compound, there was also the Milman Memorial School[5] catering for higher caste Hindu girls, mostly the daughters of Indian professional men. Its importance lay in the effort to provide education for Indian girls. The difficulty lay in the fact that the girls left at 13, and indeed most of them had been married off at 10 or 11, so it was difficult to provide a very high standard of education.

In Darjeeling the Diocesan Girls' School was ready for use in the spring of 1904. But conditions were still rather spartan as the following letter, written in April, explains: "We came into the new school when the girls all came up, though it was by no means completed, not even the block we wanted to occupy, but we managed somehow to put up 76 girls and 20 people in authority. For some time we had to suffer four pianos in one room, and three in a corridor which had to be used as a classroom for three classes, and also a piano and classes in the dining room which opens out of the corridor. We now have the classes moved into their own rooms which are beautiful. The pianos have been scattered over the building. The 40 children who have hitherto been sleeping in the theatre have gone into their proper dormitories. The teachers are gradually being made more comfortable, and we are feeling quite grand with the front door on. Minor considerations such as locks, handles, fasteners for doors and windows, shelves and cupboards, are still in the future, and unfortunately we have not much money for furnishing, and it is no light thing to furnish this enormous building. We have almost none, as during the last four years we have had hired furniture, and as little of that as we could do with as we were so crowded."

The extent of the discomfort was further elaborated in the summer 1905 issue of *St John Baptist Magazine*: "...The corridors and many of the rooms were workshops, and wherever we went we found ourselves in the company of Chinamen, Punjabi's, Bengali's and hillmen, all carrying on their different avocations, [with] dirty little coolie boys and girls running to and fro, carrying mortar or stones wherever they were wanted. Tiny babies in baskets occupied corners everywhere, while their mothers worked, or waited on the men. The noise was deafening and the most ordinary conveniences not to be had for two or three months. But thanks to the ever resourcefulness and willingness of our hill servants, and the determination of our household as a whole, to make the best of the situation, we gradually got into shape, and each month found us in fuller possession and the workmen at a greater and more respectful distance."

However, the new school started with a huge financial burden. "A heavy debt of £12,500 rests on the school buildings, yet the chapel is free through the gifts of benefactors. The large sum expended on the buildings has been lent from Diocesan funds. On this the school has to find 4% interest. Both the site and buildings have far exceeded our hopes and expectations, and the large sunny classrooms and dormitories are a daily pleasure and very conducive to health. 100 pupils and a large staff can be most comfortably accommodated. The recreation hall and corridors are so large that the girls can use them for wheel skating, and this, in a climate where we have four or five months of continuous fog and rain, is an untold boon. The Sisters' house is charming - wedged in between the school and chapel... Our object is to make it look as home-like and Clewer-like as possible."

This was written after the dedication of the school which took place on September 28th 1904, almost five years to the day from the destruction of the old buildings. The chapel of the school was dedicated to St Michael and All Angels, but it was not until March 1929 that the school officially changed its name to St Michael's. *The Friend of India* for October 6th 1904 contained a report of the ceremony held a week previously: "The Lord Bishop of Calcutta ... dedicated and blessed the new Buildings and the Chapel of the Diocesan Girls' High School... The school authorities selected a new site beyond the cemetery, where for the last two years the present buildings have been in [the] course of construction. The late Sir John Woodburn helped considerably with Government grants, and the public also came forward liberally with donations. The foundation stone was laid just as Sir John fell ill, so he was deprived of the pleasure of seeing the work started, but the P. W. D., which had undertaken to construct the buildings, pushed on the work with the greatest expedition... The school now consists of two three-storied buildings and a chapel. Stretching northwards is a long narrow building, on the ground floor of which are several spacious classrooms; on the second floor are dormitories for the girls, and on the top storey are the teachers' rooms, with dormitories for boys under twelve. In the main building there are also a few classrooms for the senior departments, besides the dining hall. On the second floor are dormitories on one side and a spacious recreation hall on the other, some more teachers rooms being on the third storey, including the quarters of the Sisters who preside over the school. The chapel is to the south... There is a spacious playground to the north of the grounds."

Next followed a description of the dedication ceremony: "The Bishop, attended by his Chaplain the Revd H. T. Ottley,... and several other clergymen, and followed by a choir of girls and teachers, went from room to room reading and singing a special order of service. This lasted half-an-hour from 3.45 to 4.15. A service was then held in the chapel, which the Lieutenant Governor and Lady Fraser attended. The Bishop, in his address, dealt with the hard work that had been put in by Sr Florence and her colleagues of the Community of St John Baptist, Clewer. After the service, tea was served in the dining hall to which His Honor [sic] and most of the guests stayed. On the 5th and 6th of October the school will give a dramatic entertainment, *The Merchant of Venice* in aid of the school building fund."

In her short history of St Michael's Sr Georgina fondly described the chapel of the new school: "...The sanctuary was very simple and dignified. Two figures of angels carved in cedar wood with wings outspread over an 'Agnus Dei' formed the front of the altar, and two other angels holding censers stood on the reredos on either side of a picture of the Good Shepherd. It was replaced in 1931 by a beautiful carved figure of St Michael,... the gift of Mrs Stone, the widow of a former Archdeacon of Calcutta... It was carved in the Cotswolds at Chipping Campden. The seven sanctuary lamps were sent to us from our Community House in Oxford(6)." She then proceeded to recall the other buildings: "The Sisters' small house was charming, wedged in between the school building and the chapel. Eventually the terraced garden was full of English flowers, and clematis and ampylopsis was sent to us from England, and a beautiful wisteria was trained up the wall near the school entrance. Later we had to have half of it cut down as a very obnoxious wild animal called a civit cat climbed up and appeared one night in the elder girls' dormitory to their horror! We had a large bed of arum lilies and they were always our decoration for the chapel at Easter, and our lovely blue hydrangeas were always ready for the Feast of St John Baptist."

Sr Georgina included some personal memories of former pupils, one or two of whom recalled the earliest days of the new school. Thus Kitty Davies (nee Wernicke) wrote: "I can still remember Rivers Hill in 1902 when I was still in the Kindergarten. Folding coloured paper squares, and the sound of Sister's keys jingling, are my two most outstanding memories. The new Diocesan Girls' High School 1905-6, was wonderfully spacious after Rivers Hill. I recall Sr Florence reading aloud on Sunday evenings, and evening prayers in the Long Corridor. 'Lighten our darkness' still brings it all back vividly at every Evensong. There are other memories: the dash for veils; the St John Baptist Day's Dance; the sound of tommies going down the Cart Road singing 'Goodbye Dolly I must leave you.' Most important of all: the teaching of the Catholic Faith. This came back to me 30 years later as I sat at the feet of a C.R. [Community of the Resurrection, Mirfield] Father while in Retreat. Suddenly, I realised that it was Sr Beatrice Mary's teaching which had sunk in unconsciously and had been woven into our lives for good."

Another former pupil from those early years, Minna Shaw, recalled some of the secular teachers: "Miss Cooper came to the school as Art Mistress, soon after the death of Miss Creighton who... was teaching there in 1905-8. Miss Cooper introduced the Royal Drawing Society Exams. She was an excellent teacher. Miss Harper taught gym and dancing at the same time; she and Miss Cooper produced some enjoyable shows which were full of colour, song and graceful movement. They gave pleasure to the children, parents and many Darjeeling friends." Winnie Gregory, a former Head Girl, also recalled those concerts and especially "The Shoe of Rodolphis" an Egyptian play which was staged at the Town Hall. "Sr Marian Edith, a trained artist, was at the school for a year and wrote to the British Museum for a description of the Egyptian pillars, so that the scenery should be absolutely correct. During the performance, one of the scenery shifters was nearly electrocuted. Luckily Dr Bentley was in the audience and was called for to give medical aid. He was introduced to Rodolphis (Miss Harper). A romance began, an engagement followed, and they were married the next year... Mrs Bentley to the end of her life took an affectionate interest in the school." (Alas we are not told what happened to the scenery shifter!)

And so the first few years of the new century saw the Indian work of the Clewer Sisters going from strength to strength. But the world was changing and within a few years the holocaust of the Great War would end an era. At home the Community had been in existence for more than 50 years, and most of the older Sisters who remembered the early days had died. Canon Carter, the first Warden and Co-Founder of the Community had died in 1901, the same year as Queen Victoria. His death had been a crossing of the rubicon for the Community. 1911 would see the optimum year in Community growth(7): after that time numbers would begin to fall, imperceptibly at first, but escalating as the social changes following the Great War began to affect all strata of society[8]. In 1907, midway through the Edwardian years there was another change at Clewer. Mother Betha who had guided the Community as Mother Superior since 1889 was not re-elected. In her place the Community elected Sr Evelyn: professed in 1885, she had been Novice Mistress since 1889. She was to hold office for the next 21 years and proved to be a wise and enthusiastic Mother Superior. Like Mother Jane Frances before her, Mother Evelyn had an instinctive feeling for the Indian work and resolved to visit Calcutta. She did so early in 1910, and as will be seen, she was enthralled by her visit. But Mother Evelyn was not the only visitor to India of note at this time. As we shall now see, the reign of Edward VII was a period of royal tours and durbars - and a very special decoration for one of the Clewer Sisters.

Footnotes

1. Sr Georgina CSJB *Past History of S. Michael's School, Darjeeling* undated typescript.

Sr Georgina was the last Sister to be in charge of the school.

2. The priest was the Revd M. L. Ghose. See *A Hundred Years in Bengal: a history of the Oxford Mission 1880-1980* Delhi 1979. pp 23-4.

3. The Oxford Mission still works in Calcutta, caring for and educating street boys like Abdool, although the Brotherhood itself has virtually come to an end. Secular priests will carry on the work until such time as the Brotherhood can be revived. The work of the Mission relies on support from parishes and individuals, mostly in the U. K.

4. According to Geoffrey Moorhouse in his book *Calcutta* (1971) the hut is still in the grounds of the Presidency General Hospital - at least it was when he was writing his book. But I did not see it when I visited the P.G. in February 1995, although I may well have missed it, because the compound was very crowded. Nor did I notice whether Ross's poem is still on the gates - I was being driven by car.

5. The Sisters inherited the care of the Milman Memorial School from Angelina Hoare. I have not been able to trace its exact location, but have the impression that it was not in the Pipalpati mission compound, but about ten minutes walk away, (although Sr Jane Frances implied to the Clewer Associates that it was in the same compound - see Chapter 13). It was closed before the Sisters' final withdrawal from India, and before Sr Eudora's arrival there early in 1934. Sr Eudora did not recall the location of the school - so perhaps it was not in the mission house compound.

6. The Manor House, Holywell, Oxford.

7. In 1911 the Community of St John Baptist, Clewer, numbered 205 professed choir Sisters; 21 choir novices; 61 professed lay Sisters; 12 lay novices; and 3 Second Order Sisters; making a total of 302. Plus 39 in America. Separate numbers were not kept for India because unlike America, the Indian work did not constitute a separate Province or Affiliation. At its peak there were 20-30 Sisters in India at any given time, although the personnel was ever changing.

8. The reasons for the decline in numbers after the Great War are examined in the general history of the Clewer Community - BONHAM, Valerie *A Joyous Service: the Clewer Sisters and their work* (1989) Ch. 7.

-20-
AN IMPERIAL THEME

When Albert Edward was finally crowned Edward VII on Saturday August 9th 1902, he also became Emperor of India. It had been an anxious time at home, for the euphoria which greeted the end of the South African War in June was soon replaced by vigils of prayer for the uncrowned King. On June 23rd, just three days before the Coronation, the King was taken ill with appendicitis - a life threatening condition. The Clewer Community *Annals* record that on June 24th (the Feast of the Nativity of St John Baptist): "disquieting news came in the afternoon about the King's health; then that he had had an operation and was sleeping. A false report was spread in Windsor in the evening that he was sinking. We went into chapel and the Warden read the Litany for the Dying. The report was contradicted later on... Intercession was kept up for the King through the night, the Sisters taking half hours in turn." Throughout the Empire the festivities were hastily laid aside; instead, prayers were offered and solemn vigils kept, and the King slowly recovered. He was well enough for the Coronation to go ahead six weeks later, although many official engagements were cancelled due to his still frail health.

In India, the Viceroy, Lord Curzon of Kedleston, planned a great Durbar(1) to celebrate the Coronation. When Victoria had been proclaimed Empress of India in 1877, a Durbar had been held to mark the occasion, with the Viceroy (Lord Lytton), attending the ceremonies in her place. Now in 1902, the new King-Emperor, being too weakened by his recent illness to attend, sent in his place his brother H.R.H. the Duke of Connaught. Unlike his mother, Edward had been to India: in November 1875 he had arrived in Bombay on a tour which lasted until the following March, and which took him to Ceylon, Madras, Calcutta, Benares, Delhi, Lahore, and Kashmir, before returning home from Bombay.

The 1902 Coronation Durbar was planned by Curzon to be the most spectacular event of its kind - and it was. Delhi, the old capital of India, was chosen as the venue, and for 12 days beginning on December 29th, a vast site was transformed into an arena dedicated to celebrating the splendour of India. The site was so vast that a special railway was built, five miles in length, to enable people to travel around it. And the people came in droves - a conservative estimate numbered 173,000 of them. There was all the pageantry of the official receptions, but also pavilions and encampments for the various players in this great extravaganza, as well as a multiplicity of Indian arts, crafts and culture. There were sporting events, displays of expertise by the various regiments, and concerts performed by several military bands. However, it was not just a grand show of the English abroad, there was plenty of Indian pageantry too, with around 50 Indian princes and other rulers providing a colourful and much bejewelled spectacle, together with their retainers, bodyguards, camels, decorated elephants and much else. There was a military review when all the troops paraded before the Viceroy, and a similar one for the Indian rulers from the Princely States[2]. There was a state ball and also an investiture at which loyal servants of the Raj, both British and Indian, were decorated.

All this was taking place in Delhi so that most of it was lost on the people of Calcutta, but towards the end of 1905 the Prince and Princess of Wales (later to be King George V and Queen Mary), included the capital in their tour of India. Before that however, in May 1905, Sr Jane Frances had taken a much deserved furlough in England - the first for many years. Writing from England in a letter which was published in the August 1905 issue of *Pipalpati* (the newly established journal of the Clewer Sisters in India), she described her cross country journey to Bombay and her visit to the All Saints Sisters: "Crossing India by the Delhi -Nagpur Line was new to me. The first day we passed through very pretty wild country: stretches of forest land with little streams and ranges of low picturesque hills in the background, on the tops of which thunder clouds were resting. We had something of a storm after sunset, but not a severe one. It gave us a very cool night, and that was our last experience of rain or indeed of any atmospheric disturbance till we sighted the shores of Europe."

"Sr Jane Frances continued: "Two days of quiet at Bombay with the All Saints Community were very welcome after two days and two nights in the train. We could not be taken in at Mazagon, [because] the house was all upset on account of a Plague scare. The day before, there had been found near the cookhouse of the native school a large number of dead rats, which on examination were pronounced to be distinctly Plague-infected. One girl who had been taking 'kitchen duty' was attacked with high fever and other suspicious symptoms and sent to Hospital, and the Orphanage was to be moved to temporary quarters at Bessein by the sea, and the house disinfected. Happily the child was already better before we left, so her attack (if it were Plague), must have been of a mild nature." All this of course was part of Indian life, and Sr Jane Frances took it all very stoically - at least it was in somebody else's school and orphanage! And both she and Sr Mary Victoria were very comfortably accommodated elsewhere. "We were very well lodged with the Sisters at the Cathedral High School. As it is a large day school only, out of school times it is very quiet. The Sisters' rooms are on the third story, right at the top of the house where it is delightfully cool and airy. The pleasant sea breeze lightens and freshens the air much better than our punkahs [swinging fans] at Calcutta, though one is told that a few weeks later when this breeze dies away, Bombay too becomes very oppressive."

"My last visit [to Bombay] was 11 years ago, and in the works of the All Saints Community, many things had changed or developed. The building where we were staying was a new one and the situation a little different from the former Cathedral High School. I spent most of Friday April 28th at the Mazagon House with the Mother Superior. The native school had all but broken up, but there still was a good deal to be seen, specially in the Industrial department, i.e. large workrooms for the employment of poor native Christians out of one of the Mission Districts... The English Boarding School called 'All Saints School' was moved to Khandala on the Ghauts a few years ago when the Plague was so bad at Mazagon. So now this large school building is given up to the Native Orphanage above, and various workrooms below. One part is also a hostel for native Christian young women. The Mother Superior took me to see the new Church of Holy Cross for the Mahratta congregation, which has replaced the little Mission Chapel at Umerkhadi, which I remember formerly. Though simple in design it is very effective and fairly spacious. We also had a drive round Malabar Hill, and I visited the Sisters at Jamsetjee Hospital. As when I first saw Bombay 19 years ago, I was again struck by the lively appearance of the streets after those of Calcutta - so much more variety to be seen. The Parsi ladies in their graceful silk draperies, each made of a single colour only, but always of some beautiful shade, make a picturesque element which we are entirely without in Bengal."

"We embarked in the *Scindia* (Anchor Line) on the evening of April 29th. This was my 6th voyage across these seas, and I never before had such a continuous stretch of fine settled weather... We were only reminded of other phases of life in our peaceful, but very monotonous existence by a fleet of six British torpedo boats passing us in the Red Sea at a good speed - on what errand we knew not."[3] The Sisters arrived at Dover on Thursday May 18th 1905 and were met at Charing Cross by Sisters from Clewer.

The furlough in England passed quickly and at the end of October Sr Jane Frances and Sr Mary Victoria boarded the *Scindia* for the return voyage. They arrived back in Calcutta on November 29th 1905 - just three weeks after the arrival in Bombay of the Prince and Princess of Wales, and in time for the Royal visit to Calcutta. Meanwhile, their Royal Highnesses had landed at Bombay on November 9th and were received by the Viceroy and Vicereine (Lord and Lady Curzon). During their week in Bombay they fulfilled official engagements and received many of the Indian princes. They then visited cities of the Princely States including Indore, Udaipur, Jaipur and Bikaner before continuing on to Lahore, the north west frontier, Rawalpindi, Amritsar, Agra, and Gwalior where they spent Christmas 1905 as the guests of the Maharajah. They arrived in Calcutta soon after Christmas and from there sailed to Burma where they visited Rangoon and Mandalay. The royal party then returned to India - to Madras, Mysore, and Hyderabad before turning north again to Benares. The planned visit to Nepal (for hunting) was cancelled due to an outbreak of cholera there, so the party returned to Gwalior before going on to Karachi and from thence home.

Just as school children in England are taken from their lessons to wave at visiting heads of state, so too the children from the Diocesan High School and the Lower School were taken to see the Prince and Princess of Wales as they passed by on their way to Government House, Calcutta. Writing in the January 1906 issue of *Pipalpati*, one of the Sisters wrote: "Cards had been sent to the Mission House some days before, for admission to a stand on the Red Road to see the procession on the day of arrival, December 29th, and 50 rupees had also been received for the expenses of a treat [for] the children on another day. The Red Road is a broad thoroughfare leading from Prinseps Ghat, where the Royal party were to land, to Government House through the Maidan... Accordingly on the day, those who were considered old enough and strong enough were marshalled together. All looked very nice, the High School with their teachers and day scholars, the in pink jackets and new saris, all eager to see the Rajkumar, or Prince, though whether they quite understood what they were likely to see is a little doubtful."

The Sister continued: "The High School were well provided with their omnibus as a conveyance... and the Lower School had resigned themselves to walking, although at 1.00 p.m. the sun would be rather overpowering, had not the idea struck Sr Kate Mary of journeying thither in bullock-carts. These arrived at our door punctually. We had been told they would have awnings over them, but we saw with dismay only arched cane on them so we quickly brought out red and striped purdahs or curtains to throw over the cane, and when the children were duly arranged in them the effect was very oriental, quaint and picturesque, and they called forth much attention on the way. The white bullocks were adorned with chains and their bells jingled as they trotted along quite quickly, a small boy in a tinsel muslin spangled coat assisted in driving them by pulling their tails."

"At the stand we descended, and took our places on nicely raised benches at the side of the road about 2.00 p.m. and prepared ourselves to wait till 4.00 p.m., the time of the Royal arrival at Prinseps Ghat. The road looked pretty with its Venetian masts at intervals, and troops of children from various schools and institutions already rapidly taking their places on each side. The time passed quickly as the ever changing crowd thronged the way in front of us, sometimes it would be Chinamen arrayed in their best clothes...; then officers would ride [beside] the carriages whose occupants were going to take their places at Prinseps Ghat; then native Rajahs would come in the opposite direction on their way to Government House to await the arrival there. At 3.00 p.m. the crowds were cleared by the Police and the Volunteers took up their position lining the road on each side... At 3.20 p.m. the guns were heard which told us of the arrival at Howrah Station [from] whence the Royal Party was to be taken in a launch to Prinseps Ghat where they were to land and be received by Rajahs and Government officials,... [and then] the Procession was to make its way by the Red Road to Government House. All this was soon over, the Prince making a short speech in reply to the address, so our time of waiting passed more quickly than we expected."

As with all grand occasions such as this, the crowd waits patiently for hours and then suddenly it is all over, and often there is a great sense of anti-climax. The Sister's account conveys this impression: "We were made aware of the arrival by officers riding down to see if the road was clear, then Artillery thundered past, followed by a regiment of Hussars and the Calcutta Light Horse, and then the Imperial Cadet Corps lately formed of the sons of Rajahs... The carriage of the Prince and Princess followed at rather a quick pace, the Princess bowing to the lines of astonished children who received them more quietly than English children would have done. We missed the hip-hurrahs of an English crowd... A few carriages followed with officers of the escort and then all was over. I think perhaps our children were a little disappointed not to see something more imposing. In this country Rajahs make more elaborate show in processions... It did not take us long to find our brightly covered conveyances and join the stream of vehicles as they quickly passed down the shady avenue. On crossing Chowringhee Road the stream of great people was hurrying home towards Hastings House which had been lent for the occasion. In one carriage was the Chinese Ambassador...; in another the little Rajkumar of Sikkim... We were all safely back again by 6.00 p.m., none the worse for this unusual episode in the Christmas holidays."

As noted in chapter 19, a new Mother Superior had been elected at Clewer in November 1907. Mother Evelyn was a far sighted and wise leader, and she wished to get to know all aspects of the Community's work. In 1910 she visited India, and in 1913 she was the first Mother Superior from Clewer to visit the Community in America. At home one of her early actions was to abolish the *St John Baptist Magazine* which had been struggling for several years. She replaced it at the end of 1908 with a quarterly *Associates' Newsletter*. The Sisters in India however, by now had their own journal - *Pipalpati* - which related news about the work at the Pipalpati mission house.(4)

Shortly before Mother Evelyn's visit to India, the Bishop of Calcutta(5) had visited Clewer and, "he spoke most favourably of the work of the Sisters in the hospitals and amongst the nurses, and also in the ricefield mission... It is a cause of deep thankfulness that our work in these distant countries should be so greatly blessed," wrote Mother Evelyn to the Associates in January 1909.

On December 3rd 1909 Mother Evelyn, accompanied by Sr Florence, embarked at Marseilles for Bombay, on board the *Arabia*. Sr Florence, the heroine of the Darjeeling landslip, was a veteran, this being her fourth voyage out to India. Like Sr Jane Frances on her first voyage in 1888, Mother Evelyn was captivated by all she saw - camels, Arabs and bazaars, followed by the tedious (and rolling) stretch across the Indian Ocean until they reached Bombay. "At 4.00 a.m. on Friday December 17th, after a wakeful night and noisy dawn, we found ourselves anchored outside Bombay and the passengers already making for the shore," wrote Mother Evelyn in the *Associates' Newsletter* for March 1910. "We landed by 8.45. [a.m.], and after a tedious wait for our luggage, drove off to the All Saints Sisters ' bungalow at Mazagon, and much valued the warm welcome they gave us." There was no fear of plague this time, unlike during Sr Jane Frances ' visit in 1905, and so Mother Evelyn was able to see all the Sisters' work. "Among their many works, the Sisters have a large one for the seed and bead industry, and we saw about 50 men, women and children sorting, polishing, boring and stringing the seeds and beads on gold and silver wire for satures and chains and various pretty contrivances. These people are all Christians and receive daily teaching from the Sisters while earning enough to keep up their little homes."

Then they were taken sightseeing! "The afternoon was spent in driving about Bombay. First to the Cathedral and the beautiful church of the Holy Cross; both have a very reverent and catholic appearance, and in both the Blessed Sacrament is reserved for the sick. We drove next to the spacious fruit market in the centre of the town. The orange season being at its height, the stalls were piled high with golden fruit, while lemons, grapes, plantains, pomegranates, melons, guavas, and even a few premature mangoes were pressed on us by excited salesmen."

Next day Mother Evelyn continued her journey as far as Poona: "taking with us the Reverend Mother of the All Saints Community who was visiting the Sisters in Khandala, a pretty little hill station reached about two hours before Poona. The line from Bombay to Poona is one of the most varied and beautiful in India. The ground rises gently throughout the journey and the weird Western Ghauts, [with] their castellated summits seem to start up and accompany you almost all the way, the winding course of the [railway] line bringing them first on one side, then on the other. A wide river bearing little boats with brown and white sails was a lovely feature in the earlier part of the journey, and later we were in the midst of beautiful forest land, and hills with herds of cows and buffaloes grazing quietly or being driven home for the night in a leisurely fashion. At one point a new narrow gauge railway was under construction winding round the slopes of the hills. Crowds of patient donkeys were carrying sand away, while their owners bivouacked in groups, and seemed to care little about either the work or the donkeys. The light grew more and more golden as the sun went down, and we watched the lovely subtle colours of the short twilight till the darkness closed in, and we were suddenly reminded that Poona was close at hand."

"The Wantage Sisters had most kindly come to the station [at Poona] to meet us and we were carried off in different directions to the convent and school, glad indeed to leave the train behind and drive through the soft evening air. The Convent garden was lovely with flowering hibiscus, poinsettias, roses, palms, and other tropical plants. Poona, at one time the centre of the great Mahratta kingdom, is still a city of temples and shrines, and a stronghold of Hinduism. As we drove through the narrow streets and lanes we seemed every few yards to pass a shrine with its hideous vermillion painted image. The Mahratta's themselves are attractive, and one could not but be struck by their air of independence and their fearless and open expression."

Their brief sojourn at Poona concluded with a visit to the district called Panch Howd where the Wantage Sisters and the Cowley Fathers jointly ran a mission. Within the compound, gathered around the church of the Holy Name, were schools, hostels and workshops for both boys and girls. Mother Evelyn was very impressed with this calling it, "a wonderful beehive of missionary work."

December 23rd saw the Sisters' arrival in Calcutta after what had been a very long journey with all the diversions, interesting though they may have been. "The Christmas Festival this year has been gladdened by the presence of our Mother Superior among us, on her first visit to India," wrote Sr Jane Frances in the February 1910 issue of *Pipalpati.* "She arrived in Calcutta just two days before Christmas… and was in time to come to the Mission House with the Sister Superior and other Sisters from the Canning Home for the usual present distribution on Christmas Eve." The distribution of presents was a major event in the lives of the children, many of whom had no homes to go to and had to stay in school over the holidays. It also seems to have been the occasion for Baptising converts. Thus the Sister continued: "Besides the holiday children in each School, who were between 40 and 50 in number, our godchildren living in the neighbourhood had been invited, about 20 in number. Every year on Christmas Eve, several new godchildren are added to the already long rolls, and till within half an hour of the time fixed for [the] Baptism… we are engaged in choosing names and fitting out the babies in hood, shoes, dress and warm underclothing fitting for the Sacrament. Sometimes their mothers are old girls who come from long distances, and bring relations with them whose babies also are Baptised. We are asked to choose an English name, and the parents choose a Bengali name… Our Christmas party grows like a snowball, and we have to keep a store of presents for uninvited guests, who, though they now live at long distances from us, remember Christmas times of old and return on the score of a former invitation." The Sister went on to say that four babies were Baptised this year, but sadly one of them, Mary Sorojeni, died on December 27th, the Eve of the Holy Innocents.

The presents which were given to the children had been sent out from England and consisted of dolls, books and items of clothing. The donors were members of the St John Baptist Calcutta Mission Association, the Weald of Kent Association, individual Associates who held sewing parties, Church groups who did the same sort of thing, and other branch houses run by the Clewer Sisters in England. As noted previously, sometimes these well meaning people sent the wrong type of gifts - garments which were too thick, or the wrong colour, or even too English, and at times it posed great problems for Sr Jane Frances. And woe betide her if the name of any donor (plus a note of what had been sent), was omitted from *Pipalpati*. But despite these difficulties, the mission house needed the gifts from England: they were awaited with great anticipation, and gave much pleasure to the recipients.

Mother Evelyn's visit to India coincided with the bestowal of a great honour upon Sr Jane Frances. On January 1st 1910 she was awarded the silver Kaiser-i-Hind medal by the Lieutenant Governor of Bengal, Sir Edward Baker, in recognition of her 20 years work in India: "I trust that the honourable distinction which His Excellency, the Viceroy, has been pleased to confer upon you will serve to indicate in a lasting manner the gratitude which we all feel towards yourself personally, and towards the Sisterhood of which you have been the local head." Oddly, the bestowal of this honour, which Sr Jane Frances had received on behalf of her Community, was not reported to the Clewer Associates until four years later! But it was recorded in the private *Annals* of the Community.

Mother Evelyn may not have shared this particular piece of news with the Associates, but she did write at length about the various works which she had visited in Calcutta, and which gave the Clewer Associates the latest news about the hospitals and schools, which they would have known by name very well. The recently rebuilt Presidency General Hospital impressed Mother Evelyn though she expressed certain reservations: "It is now considered to be the finest in India. Not that it is a handsome structure, I believe there was no money for architectural embellishments, but the interior was most carefully designed for the comfort and convenience of patients, and furnished with every appliance." Of course the architecture of the Presidency General was not at all like the grand gothic revival building opposite the House of Mercy, which Henry Woodyer had designed to serve as St Andrew's Convalescent Hospital. The Presidency General was nothing like that - but there it stood (and there it stands), and there was a solidity and a starkness about its 550 foot frontage which could not fail to impress, (and it still does).

Mother Evelyn was pleased with the Pratt Memorial School and wrote that: "There are 83 boarders and 120-30 day scholars. The buildings have again become quite inadequate both for the growth of the school and for the present requirements of the Education Department. I am thankful to hear that the Church Education League in Calcutta is devoting its energy to the expansion and improvement of these school buildings." Just across the road from the Pratt Memorial School was the European Orphanage which Mother Evelyn also visited, and observed that: "the children attend the Pratt as day scholars and so have the advantage of a good education, and out of school hours they are carefully trained in needlework. Many of them become nurses to English children in India."

Mother Evelyn also visited the confusing array of schools in the Pipalpati mission house compound. She visited the Lower School which had 120-130 on the roll, plus 30 free places for scholars from the Sunderbuns. But the pride of place went to the former High School, known since 1909 as the Diocesan Collegiate School. "It is a rapidly developing work... There are now 60-70 boarders, all Christians, and a much larger and rapidly increasing number of day scholars who come from all parts of Calcutta, and who are Christians of all denominations, as well as Hindus, Brahmos, and occasionally Buddhists, Parsees and Mohamedans. The ages range from 5-25. Until they are 13 instruction is given in Bengali with a lesson in English daily; after that age the system is reversed. In the lower classes all the teachers are former pupils. In the upper classes the teachers are English, except for the Brahman pundit who teaches Sanskrit, and a Mohamedan. From 13-16 they work for the Matriculation of the Calcutta University. If they pass and are not going to be married, they then study for the B.A. and are promoted to the College classes. The higher classes require teachers from England. The girls are few - about 18 at present, and the fees never cover the expenditure." At the Milman Memorial School with its 140 higher caste Hindu girls, Mother Evelyn was touched by the, "specially bright salaams they gave me as I entered the classrooms."

All in all, Mother Evelyn was justifiably impressed with the schools and the educational standards maintained in them. But she was not likely to escape a visit to the village schools in the Sunderbuns, as this work was the particular joy of Sr Jane Frances. Anyone staying for an extended visit was taken on a similar trip to that which Sr Jane Frances herself had enjoyed back in 1890[6]. Fortunately, Mother Evelyn also enjoyed the experience: "I spent two very interesting days in the Sunderbuns to attend prize givings in some of the larger schools," she wrote. "I was greatly impressed by all I saw of the simple family life of the people. It was very enjoyable, I thought, to be punted along one of the water highways in a flat bottomed boat with a little thatched roof to protect one from the sun. Altogether the expedition made most pleasant impressions on me."

Unfortunately, Mother Evelyn did not write anything about sight-seeing around Calcutta, although she summed up her thoughts about the second city of the Empire in less than flattering terms: "Calcutta as a city did not impress me. It covers a vast space of ground but, in contrast with Bombay, it is not picturesque. All is so flat, and the houses in the European quarter are large and somewhat ponderous in appearance. The native part of the town is full of narrow, crowded streets and lacks the colouring and variety of Bombay. One great advantage which Calcutta has however, is the Maidan, a very large open space of grass with several large ponds (or tanks as they are called), and beautiful flowering trees."

Mother Evelyn's visit was however, not just a sightseeing trip. There was a more serious reason: she had come to help resolve a dispute which was brewing with the British Raj concerning the terms under which the Sisters would work at the Presidency General and Medical College Hospitals. The Sisters had originally been invited to India by the government in order to organise the nursing arrangements at these hospitals, and as already noted, great care had been taken in negotiating the terms under which they would work. Now it seems that the government was re-organising the nursing at the hospitals, and this would directly affect the Sisters. A special Committee had been appointed, which had presented its report on December 22nd 1908, the recommendations of which were contained in *Government Resolution Number 266 Medical*, and dated February 5th 1909. Because the recommendations so drastically affected the Sisters, the Lieutenant Governor of Bengal (Sir Edward Baker), insisted that their views should be sought. This may well have motivated Mother Evelyn's decision to visit Calcutta at this particular time. A letter to Mother Evelyn at the Lady Canning Home dated December 28th 1909 from H. Wheeler, Secretary to the Government of Bengal, concluded by saying: "The question has accordingly been held in abeyance pending your arrival in India." A meeting was arranged between Mother Evelyn, Mr Wheeler and Colonel Macrae, the Inspector General of Civil Hospitals, Bengal, which took place on January 10th 1910.

The recommendations embodied in *Government Resolution Number 266 Medical* which most affected the Sisters were the following:

Number 3: "That lay Superintendents should be substituted for the Clewer Sisters at the Medical College and connected hospitals, or if this be impracticable, that five Clewer Sisters be provided instead of only two as at present. In the event of the supervision of the Clewer Sisters being withdrawn, the original recruitment of nurses should rest with the Lady Superintendent."

Number 5: "That the Sister Superior should not exercise any power of control over the nursing arrangements in the Presidency General."

Number 6: "That an additional Sister should be provided for the Presidency General Hospital. This could be arranged if the Sisters were withdrawn from the Medical College Hospital."

These recommendations seem to put the clock back to how things were before the Sisters took over almost 30 years previously, with the mention of lay Superintendents. The recommendations formed the agenda of the meeting on January 10th, the outcome of which was summarised in a letter to Mother Evelyn from Mr Wheeler two days later: "After having inspected the work of these institutions," he wrote, "you expressed the opinion that it had outgrown the capacity of your Community. It was admitted that the duties to be performed at the Medical College Calcutta required the attendance of more than two Sisters, and that the number of five, which had been suggested, was in no way excessive. At the same time, you expressed the opinion that it would be impossible for the Sisterhood to find the additional Sisters required, and to undertake that they should always be provided in future. You were therefore of [the] opinion that however much it was to be regretted, the only alternative open to the Sisterhood was to withdraw from the supervision of the nursing arrangements at the Medical College. In that event, an additional Sister could be posted to the Presidency General Hospital. It was stated that your Community would be glad to meet the convenience of the Government by continuing at the Medical College until other arrangements could be made..."

This rather cold letter from a government official who probably did not know the Sisters, concluded on a slightly warmer note: "The Lieutenant Governor has learnt your decision with extreme regret, although he fully appreciates the difficulties surrounding the question. The work done by the Sisterhood in the past at the Medical College Calcutta, as well as at the Presidency General Hospital, has been of the utmost value, and has been characterised by efficiency and devotion to duty. The withdrawal of the Sisters from that institution will be felt as a distinct loss, and Sir Edward Baker joins with you in regretting that it has been found to be inevitable."

Presumably Mother Evelyn's decision would have needed the consent of the Clewer Chapter when she arrived home, but the matter may well have been discussed in principle before she left England. She would hardly have made what appears to have been a binding decision without some authority from her Community. It seems as if the government was not prepared to make any concessions to the Sisters. Mother Evelyn was leaving India at the end of February 1910, and had asked the government to let her know before she left how long the Sisters would be needed at the Medical College. Not only did they refuse to be drawn on the matter, but also took exception to her request to send one of the Medical College Sisters to work in Darjeeling, saying "it will be extremely inconvenient." It was not until September 1910 that official notice of the Sisters' withdrawal from the Medical College Hospital was sent out to all the Clewer branch houses in England and elsewhere. An entry in the Community *Annals* stated that: "With the arrival of the Lady Superintendent and the Ward Sister on November 11th [1910] from the London Hospital, our responsibility came to an end." However, the Sisters remained at the Presidency General Hospital until 1928.

Mother Evelyn's visit to what she later described as, "that land of wonder and fascination," ended on February 25th 1910 when she sailed from Bombay, accompanied by Sr Kathleen Honora. They arrived safely in England on March 13th. The excitement engendered by Mother Evelyn's visit must have been dampened by the decision to withdraw from the Medical College Hospital, but if the decision had been deferred until after her return, it would have drawn the process out, and would have been further complicated by problems of communication.

Imperial matters dominated everyone's thoughts throughout 1910. On May 5th news broke of King Edward VII's failing health, plunging all at home into a state of shock. Anxious crowds gathered outside Buckingham Palace, and they remained there throughout the day and night until the King's death at 11.45 p.m. on May 6th. On May 10th George V was proclaimed King, and so for the second time within a decade, England mourned the death of its monarch and prepared to crown his successor: and India prepared for a new Emperor.

The Coronation of King George V and Queen Mary took place on June 22nd 1911 amidst great rejoicing throughout the Empire. Just a few years previously he had visited India as Prince of Wales: now he made the momentous decision to be crowned Emperor of India in Delhi. There was also a hidden agenda underlying the visit. During his time as Viceroy (1899-1905), Lord Curzon had unwittingly sowed the seeds of rebellion in Bengal by proposing to partition the province.[7] Curzon's successor Lord Minto, aided by John Morley at the India Office, attempted to assuage some of the bitterness. The so-called Morley-Minto reforms came into effect in 1909 in a revised Indian Councils Act, which attempted to give Indians a greater voice in government. It was, in fact, the first step towards Indian self-government In 1910 Minto was succeeded by Lord Hardinge who fully supported Minto's reforms. Furthermore, the reforms had the support of the new King-Emperor, George V. His previous visit had coincided with Curzon's partition and he had sensed the unrest it had caused. Therefore, he decided to visit India for his Coronation Durbar, and to reunite Bengal as a goodwill gesture.

On November 15th 1911 the new King and Queen sailed for India on board the *S.S. Medina*. They reached Bombay on December 2nd and the Coronation Durbar was held at Delhi on December 12th. From Delhi, the King went tiger shooting in Nepal, while the Queen proceeded to Agra and Rajputana. Calcutta was the next major destination, and there was a proclamation parade and a military review. As with the Royal visit a few years previously, the children from the Pipalpati mission schools were taken to see the grand spectacle of "George Raja" as they called him.

But the chief focus of the Royal visit was the Coronation Durbar in Delhi on December 12th. The splendour and vastness of the occasion even surpassed Curzon's great Durbar of 1902. No reigning British monarch had ever visited India before, nor would one ever visit again during British rule. The vast open sided pavilion was raised up so that the crowd of 100,000 could see the great spectacle of the Emperor and

Empress, wearing their Imperial crowns and seated on thrones of solid silver on carpets of cloth of gold. 50,000 Imperial troops were present, and countless Indian princes and rulers. But the King-Emperor had a greater surprise in store than simply the reuniting of Bengal. In addition to this, the King announced the shifting of the seat of government from Calcutta to the old Indian capital, Delhi, as from April 1st 1912.

It was a master stroke. The jubilation in Delhi was matched with crushing disappointment from the British in Calcutta, where the news was received at a local Durbar on the Maidan. Loss of status, fear of losing business, and a general wave of anger, hit the British community. But the Indians rejoiced. Perhaps they could perceive what the British feared to admit - that this was the first distant drum beating the Imperial retreat.

Footnotes

1. The word Durbar is Persian in origin. The Mughal rulers would mark a new reign with a grand ceremony to underline the Raja's sovereignty over his people. The British thought this was rather a good idea and adapted it to their own ends.

2. British rule by no means extended over the whole of India. There were vast areas such as Hyderabad and Rajputana which were ruled by Indian princes who paid varying degrees of taxes to the British Raj in exchange for their independence. Even so, many of these states were governed in a feudal manner.

3. Torpedoes had been developed in the 1860s but were only now coming into their own as part of the weaponry of the future. Sr Jane Frances ' observation of the torpedo boats was almost prophetic. The race between Britain and Germany to build up a strong naval force was already under way - time was running out for peace.

4. The *Pipalpati* Magazine gave excellent coverage of the activities of the schools in the Pipalpati mission compound, but very little about the other work of the Community, although later issues widened their scope. The newly founded *Associates' Newsletters* issued from Clewer from 1908 onwards, had very little to say about India because of the existence of *Pipalpati*.

5. The Bishop of Calcutta at this time was Reginald Stephen Copleston (1902-13).

6. See Appendix 5.

7. The partition of Bengal - a line would run down the middle of Bengal; all to the east of it, plus Assam, would constitute Eastern Bengal, and all to the west of it, plus Bihar, Chota Nagpur and Orissa, would comprise Western Bengal. As a result, Eastern Bengal would consist mostly of Muslims, and Western Bengal mostly Hindu's. This was perceived by many Indians as an attempt to "divide and rule," and the result was bitter unrest and a growing tide of nationalism. By the time the partition was due to take effect (October 1905), the nationalist leaders such as S. N. Banerjee, B. C. Pal, B. G. Tilak, and the poet Tagore, were inciting people to boycott British goods. The Indian National Congress, founded in 1885, now began to come into its own, although the partition of Bengal proved a divisive factor, some members supporting violence and others rejecting it. Even so, there was a great deal of terrorism by indiscriminate bomb throwing at this time, especially in Calcutta. Another result of Curzon's action was the founding in 1906, of the All-India Muslim League to counter mounting Hindu political pressure.

-21-
PIPAL LEAVES

The new magazine *Pipalpati*, came into being at the beginning of 1904 and painted a vivid picture of life in the various schools of the Diocesan mission (as the Pipalpati mission house was now frequently called), and in the villages in the Sunderbuns. Although the early issues omit news of the rest of the Sisters' work, they contain a wealth of material about the schools in the care of the mission, and how the Sisters attempted to live alongside those to whom they ministered. So it may be well to leaf through the pages of *Pipalpati* during the Edwardian period.

All schools set great store on prize giving, and these schools were no exception. Many issues of *Pipalpati* contain accounts of prize giving ceremonies both in the mission compound and in the villages. An early issue from 1904 gave an account of the ceremony for the mission house schools and the Milman Memorial School. "We have the distribution outside in the compound now, having quite outgrown even our largest room indoors," wrote the Sister. "There are many things to be considered, but above all, the position of the sun; we cannot commence before 4.40 [p.m.], and then one portion is still very sunny. Until the [prize giving] day comes we anxiously study the weather, for though we do not have the constant showers of England, yet in the early months of the year we do sometimes get very violent, short thunder storms - however none arrived, and we had a glorious day."

The Sister then went on to describe how the children were dressed, and was clearly mindful that her English readers would either be unacquainted with Indian customs, or indeed might have very firm views in favour of Anglicising the children - views which the Sisters did not support. "The children are all grouped in a horse-shoe in front of the visitors: the Lower School are on the left, the little ones sit on the ground, and the big ones and the teachers on forms at the back. They all looked very pretty, for on that occasion all down to the smallest, wear saris. The little ones wear frocks as a rule - they find such difficulty in keeping the sari on and frocks are tidier, but we all look forward to the time when they can wear the sari in comfort and neatness. I expect you will exclaim 'Do the Hindu and Muhammadan little ones wear frocks then?' No, but except on state occasions children of that class do not wear anything, or at best, a sari knotted firmly round the waist leaving the rest bare; it is no uncommon occurrence in a Hindu day school for a little one to come carrying her sari, or if she has got wet on the way, to hang it up to dry on her arrival and sit down quite unconcerned to her lessons. But a Christian mother thinks it a disgrace to let her little ones go about without a garment."

"The Milman Hindu Day School sit in front of the visitors - there are about 130 of them, and they are children of the higher castes and many have rich parents. They come resplendent in many coloured silks and satins, gold bangles, anklets, necklaces, and hair ornaments... Many of them are beautiful children with refined serious faces, utterly unconcerned at the notice they attract - they bear the stamp of thousands of years of a refined civilization, different perhaps from our Western ideas, but none the less refined and real.[1] On the right sit the High School, all dressed in white with pale blue ribbons.[2]"

The prizegiving ceremony was accompanied by an entertainment in which the children participated with displays of dance, drill and singing of varying quality. Chicken-pox had claimed a number of the performers just a few days previously. The worst of these cases had been taken to the Presidency General Hospital, others had been sent home, and the remainder had been quarantined, but were able to view proceedings from the dormitory roof. Mr Bannerjee, priest-in-charge of neighbouring St Mary's church and chaplain to the school, read the progress report before the prizes were given. The bishop had been detained but arrived in time for tea and spoke to all the prize winners. Then the Sister concluded: "By 7 o'clock all had gone and we were left to restore things to their right place, very thankful that it had passed off so well, and that it was not going to happen again for another year." Those small flashes of humour combined with great sensitivity towards India and its people, indicate that the un-named author of this article was Sr Jane Frances.

Quinquagesima Sunday 1904 had seen the consecration of the tower, pulpit and painted windows at St Mary's, Bhowampara (or Bhowanipore), next to the Diocesan mission compound. But all had been chaos according to the account written by Sr Jane Frances: "For ten days previous to this the Church was in a state of inexpressible confusion: the work had to be left until after Christmas was over, and that left very little time and Indians cannot hurry; also they very much dislike working after time. They were promised food and bakshish [extra pay] if they would stay, but they ate the food and then tried to get away. The choir boys however, were quite equal to the occasion, and locked the gates and kept guard [so] that they did not climb over the walls, so the work was finished in time." The consecration had taken place during the Choral Communion at 8.00 a.m., the Bishop of Calcutta officiating. The Sister obviously approved of the work which had been done: "The church is much improved, the aisles have been made wider, and the vestry has been placed under the tower and the old vestry thrown into the church; the tank for baptism by immersion, has been placed right at the north end of the church. Now the aisles are wide enough for the choir to go in procession right round the church."

Although the Sisters did not try to Anglicise the Indian children, they did of course hope that the Christian teaching given in the schools would attract converts - and there were a good many. The close connection with St Mary's church was very helpful, for many of the converts were baptised there. The pages of *Pipalpati* have frequent accounts of girls who were baptised - such as Kiroda and Monoharini on Easter Eve 1904. "Kiroda was baptised by the name of Lucy Kiroda. She is a Hindu widow of 22, sister of Biraj Mohini, now married, who came to us as a convert 10 years ago; and both sisters lived in one of our Sunderbun villages, and were taught in the first instance by the Baptist Mission Bible Women. Kiroda is a very sensible girl, and is a diligent needle woman in the workroom, and a most useful housemaid... Monoharini is a nice gentle girl of the Upper Class, and is in the Upper School; she is a sister of Dorothy Kusum Komola, now married, who was also in the Upper School. Both sisters were attending a Hindu Day School till the age of 13 when they came to us. Monoharini was baptised by the name of Constance Monoharini."

Life for an Indian convert was sometimes very difficult as Kiroda was to find, but the Sisters helped her to make her way in life. "Early in January we are sending Kiroda our convert of two years standing to join Priscilla in St Stephen's Hospital, Delhi ," wrote one of the Sisters in the January 1906 issue of *Pipalpati*. "Kiroda is very anxious to go, and thinks less of the difficulties of the distance and long separation from her friends than would most Bengali girls. Although she has a married sister living in Calcutta who has become a Christian to whom she is much attached, she has a sad experience of what it means to become a Christian, for her mother will not allow her to come home, and if she goes to see her in the country, Kiroda must stay with the Bible Woman who was the means of her conversion, and only visit her from time to time." A few months later Kiroda wrote to Sr Kate Mary from Delhi: "The hospital work suits me; I have day and night duty alternately; lady doctors here like me very much. I hope that by the Mercy of God you are in good bodily health. How long will it be before you see again this unhappy one?... I am very happy here, what shall I say? I thought I should not be able to do Hospital work, but now I like it very much... Now I understand that God has shown me much mercy and I thank him for it... What you have done for me you have done well." Sr Kate Mary continued to keep in touch with Kiroda and visited the girl in 1907 when she was on her way back to Calcutta from England.

Many of the children were married from the school, the marriages being arranged by their families. But sometimes, as in the case of Probamoni, the Sisters themselves had to make the arrangements. Probamoni's wedding took place shortly after Easter 1904, and was described in the July issue of *Pipalpati*. "Probamoni and Pooshpobati her sister, have now been with us three years. They were brought to us by the Tamil Catechist of St Saviour's parish when [they were] about 12 or 13 years of age, as a means of rescuing them from the evil home of a wretched father who was earning enough as an omnibus driver to support them, but who soon proved that he had little or no affection for them by refusing to do anything for them. They came to school dressed in red and green silk saris with fair promises of fees to be paid regularly, but we soon found that not only [the] fees were a myth but also the necessary clothing, and that the school must provide all, even a husband in time! They have both been more or less of an anxiety to the Mission,... and as they were of Hindustani birth and not Bengali, the difficulties were increased. They knew no language to read or write in. The Hindustani character is very different to the Bengali and they do not assimilate well together. Probamoni has, however, been trained into a useful housemaid,... but her knowledge of any language is most elementary... She has however, been found a good husband in Government employ who earns a good salary and who undertakes to go on with her education."

The wedding itself went well as the account continued: "The wedding ceremony was a very nice one, being fully choral, and the girls are able to sing the wedding psalm as well, with a little help from two or three choir boys. The bride was dressed in a white silk sari with rosebud pattern silk ribbon border, and she wore the usual wreath and veil. Her husband had given her a collarette of gold on black velvet and long gold ear-rings and bracelets, and as she is a nice looking girl she really looked very handsome. Some of the relatives exclaimed on seeing her for the first time 'what a beautiful bau!' [daughter-in-law]. This relationship is more prominent in India where the young married members of the family usually live with their father and mother, and the mother-in-law is the ruling member of the family. After the wedding, the bride and bridegroom came back to the schoolroom which had been decorated with palms and branches of scarlet poinsiana, and sat at a table covered with a many coloured patch work cloth in the centre of the room. The Sister Superior and the chief guests [sat] in a semi-circle on each side. It is the usual custom for the bride to return from Church at a most funereal pace and then to seat herself half turned from her husband looking the picture of misery, and she is with great difficulty persuaded to take a few of the sweets offered to her and her husband by the next aspirant to marriage. But in this case Probamoni was pronounced to behave well and not to be 'too shy,' and she took an evident delight in the chains of red and white flowers which the children hung round her neck and the bridegroom's, and those of the principal guests. The musical band to which her husband and his friends belong, added greatly to the cheerfulness of the wedding... The bridegroom followed with much pleasure the marriage songs sung in his honour... We were all presented with copies of the songs which had bright illuminated borders."

All was well until the final ceremony: "After several songs had been sung, sweets and iced water were handed round, and Probamoni rose to make her adieux. The children were all drawn up in line to have her parting kiss, but Pooshpobati, her wayward little sister, was nowhere to be found; she had put on her oldest sari instead of the new sari that her brother-in-law had given her, and had run away and hid. When found at the last moment she only uttered a loud wail by way of farewell to her sister, whose marriage she was really proud of, but thought it right to protest in this way. Probamoni lives near us, and often finds her way to the school when her mother-in-law allows it."

The August 1905 issue of *Pipalpati* carried the sequel to this story, together with a typical story of Indian time-keeping: "A few days after the beginning of the holidays, Pooshpobati was married to a young man by the name of John Jacob, who works in the Electric Tram office... Both the girls have given us many a day's trouble, but... Pooshpo (as she is called), wayward as the wind itself, has found a very gentle and good tempered husband whom she will feel it difficult to tease and provoke as she loved to do [with] her companions. Punctually for once! at 4 o'clock we took our bride to Church looking very good and nice in a white silk sari trimmed with a rose-bud silk ribbon which at last was found pretty enough to please the wearer. At 4.15 the bridegroom and bridal party arrived, but still we sat on and waited, for there was no Padre! Time went on - 4.45, and still no Padre, and as the clouds were gathering up for a violent thunderstorm we sent messages asking the reason for the delay. Then it transpired that the bridegroom had fixed the hour for 5 o'clock. Further enquiries elicited that he had forgotten to bring the ring. The time taken in fetching it delayed another half hour, and by the time the Padre and ring were forthcoming a great deluge of thunder and rain had set in, and we had some difficulty in conveying the poor little bride back to the Mission House, for the congratulations and sweets that are the usual finale to the ceremony."

Not all brides lived happily ever after. Some died in childbirth or soon after, as was sadly noted in the May 1909 issue of *Pipalpati*: "Amodini had married happily at Geont-hali near her own home, but succumbed on the birth of her first child, probably from want of proper care and skilled nursing, which the elder members of a family do not consider necessary when they are at hand to help.

Many children in the schools were orphans or had no one to whom they could turn. These "orphaned and friendless children" were the subject of appeals in every issue of *Pipalpati*, because the Sisters needed the financial and material help of the English Associates in order to subsidise the children's upkeep. Thus in the November 1905 issue of *Pipalpati* there was the following appeal: "If anyone would like to adopt a child, that is, to pay a small sum quarterly or annually towards its clothing, maintenance and education, the following children are still awaiting a benefactor or benefactress. £6 is sufficient for maintenance of a child in the Upper School, and £4 in the Lower School" By 1912 the sum required had risen to £10 for what was now the High School, but the Lower School sum remained the same. Sadly, the same children's names appear repeatedly indicating a slow response. In 1905 some of the children listed were: Shubodebala aged 10, from a poor family of the servant class; Katie 9, Esther 7, and Mary 5 - Tamil sisters from a family of nine, the mother having died of plague; Hemangini 8, child of a widow who earns her living selling milk. In 1910 there were appeals for: Nonibala 10, child of a Christian servant; another Hemangini, the child of poor parents, herself half blind; Rajubala 8, mother dead, father a carpenter. The first issue of *Pipalpati* in 1912 devoted a whole page to the children, together with a photograph showing an attractive, albeit serious looking, little group of girls in white saris edged in blue. Among these was Charubala 10, whose late mother had been one of Miss Hoare's pupils; Nolini 5, the child of an old pupil from one of the villages; Kalyani 9 and Esther 8, - father dead, mother living and receiving help from her brother who was employed by the Church Missionary Society.

Even though some of these children were not quickly adopted there was generally a good response from England and the pages of *Pipalpati* contain many acknowledgements of contributions for the upkeep of particular children. Thus in 1905 the Hon. Emily Onslow(3) sent £10.15.6d for Frances and Promela; a Sister(4) sent £4 for Niroda; another Sister sent £5 for Mary Tara. These contributions were kept up regularly(5) and were sometimes increased. Some of the maintenance was done on a collective basis by other branch houses run by the Sisters in England. Thus in 1910 the girls from the House of Mercy at Great Maplestead sent £5 for the Diocesan High School (known since 1909 as the Collegiate School), and in the same year pupils from St John Baptist High School in Newport sent £5 for Shunoyanee. Also in 1910, the girls from St Margaret's House at St Stephen's High School, Clewer, sent £1 for Jagotbashinie, whilst girls at the nearby St Stephen's College sent a Christmas present of bead necklaces for Nolini.

An important element in the support of these children were the gift boxes sent from England in time for Christmas, and for the annual prize giving ceremonies. As previously noted, these were a mixed blessing insofar as the contents were not always appropriate; also great offence was caused if the hard pressed Sisters inadvertently omitted the name of any donor from the long list of acknowledgements. But despite all the pitfalls, the "Christmas boxes " as they were called, were greatly needed and even more gratefully appreciated. They were also a valuable means of enabling people in England to help the work of the Sisters. Even after the useless items had been weeded out, there was always enough to go round.

In order to help the people back home, the Sisters in India published a list of items needed. Thus towards the end of 1911, the *Pipalpati* magazine included the following in its list of requirements: woollen scarves, 2 yards long; books for the teachers' library; coloured wool;

frocks, pinafores and tea cloths for sale; women's flannelette petticoats and chemises; babies' cotton Christening frocks; warm jackets of both small and extra large sizes; Christmas cards; babies' vests and hoods; 2 dozen white jackets for Confirmation, large size and *not* feather-stitched with red; dolls of all sizes - "the Milman School alone needs 100, as each child must have one as a reward for coming to school."

The boxes usually began to arrive in November starting with the consignment from Clewer; if a Sister was travelling out to India they would form part of her luggage. Thus in 1911 Sr Georgina, who was arriving for the first time, came laden with the Clewer boxes, which were very well received: "We were most grateful for the jackets and dolls and especially for the pink flannelette jackets all made in the same pattern. On the day of the State Entry [i.e. of King George V & Queen Mary]... the girls wore these jackets with new saris and looked very nice indeed." The next box came from the St John Baptist Calcutta Mission Association: "Here we had two splendid boxes full of jackets, comforters and presents of all kinds. These presents are so very welcome. We have a large household of English lady teachers, matrons and helpers, and High School girls, all of whom must have some little remembrance at Christmas time: this year we had all we wanted and did not have to buy anything." Finally came the contribution from the Weald of Kent Association: "Those too surpassed our expectations. More jackets, more dolls, and more of everything than usual."

The box from Clewer contained 282 jackets, 22 scarves and 68 dolls, amongst much else from the House of Mercy. It also included 12 dolls from St Lucy's Home, Gloucester; 58 jackets made by Mrs Norris' working party at St Bartholomew's, Reading; 20 jackets and an assortment of other items from All Saints Home, Hawley; and various contributions from individual Associates. The other boxes contained similar assortments of goods.

It is not easy from a distance of almost a century to assess the standard of education given in the schools at this time. However, it may be safe to assume that there was constant improvement as government regulations became increasingly stringent. The Sisters had to cope with the custom of girls being married at a very early age, as well as the traditional idea that Indian girls' education was unimportant, and it often virtually ceased after marriage.(6) This meant of course that the educational work undertaken by the Sisters had a pioneering element in it(7).

It is clear from the *Pipalpati* magazines that work in the schools was an uphill struggle. The Sisters and other teachers from England were working in a foreign language, so it is small wonder if things went awry sometimes. In 1904 a new Inspector, an English woman called Miss Brock, visited the school, and generally found things satisfactory. "I visited the Ballygunge High School," she wrote, "and I inspected the work of Standard IV in Object Lessons and found the teacher doing very good work except in her choice of the first lesson of the course, which should have come at the end... I looked through the teacher's scheme of work and thought it distinctly good. I amended it in certain respects after going through it with her. The grammar work of Standard I is very disappointing. The children are merely learning rules by rote... The Geography of Standard II is very fair. The School appears to be in very good order and the response of the children to the teachers is good."

The following year (1905), some of the High School pupils were entered in the University examinations and there was moderate success. "Mabel Singh has passed the B.A. with Honours; and two out of the three who went up for the F.A. [i.e. First Arts] passed in the Second Division - Rosalie Singh and Benai Dass. Our third candidate failed. This is very encouraging as this is the first time we have sent in any candidates for the F.A. In the Entrance Examination we have nothing but failures to recount. All three who entered failed. Two intend reading again... this looks like determination and augurs well for success next time." In fact the next year, three out of four passed First Arts (second division), and two out of three passed the Entrance Exam (matriculation). The Sister went on to put these successes (and failures) into context: "The Matriculation candidates have as usual failed in great numbers - only 8 girls passed in Calcutta out of 26. About 5,000 boys passed and about 20 girls; these figures give the relative proportion of education. I believe in Bengal, one of the most advanced provinces, only 5 in every 100 girls can read."

Despite all the odds being seemingly against the education of Indian girls, the Sisters soldiered on and there was always a streak of optimism amidst the grim reality. So the November 1909 issue of *Pipalpati* presents a hopeful report: "This is the last time our readers will see this title (High School) to our article, for during this last month we have grown into the Diocesan Collegiate School. This is because our affiliation to the Calcutta University is a completed fact, and we could not send up candidates for the higher examination without changing our name. So far we only intend sending up students for the Arts Course, but we hope in the future to be allowed the Preliminary B.Sc., as that would serve as good ground work for students entering on the medical course. Women doctors are much needed in India, very few get through to the M.B. degree, [but] with a better grounding perhaps this would be more possible."

Schoolwork was not all academic: music had begun to feature in the curriculum. "The latter part of the term the pianos have become very much in evidence: we have 14 pupils entering for the Trinity College Music Examination, and our youngest candidate is a little girl of 7... This year [1909] we are hoping to be able to start a string orchestra - we must have 10 pupils to begin, and so far only 6 have entered. There is an exceptional opportunity for this: a Conservatoire has been opened just near us by a French family of musicians. Their terms are very low and their music very good - they are enthusiasts. The Indians love the violin because it lends itself to both English and Indian music."

Sr Jane Frances had been writing for the November 1909 *Pipalpati* from Darjeeling and she could not help comparing the Diocesan Collegiate School in Calcutta with the recently rebuilt Diocesan High School in Darjeeling. One of the drawbacks to the new status of the Collegiate School was that there was yet another authority to which it would be answerable: "The school is more overcrowded than ever, but we have little or no chance of enlargement for 2-3 years. The Government are now much more particular about granting money for buildings; plans must be submitted and approved of long before the actual building has commenced; now we have to reckon not only with the Educational Department but with the University also. It will take at least two years to get plans through both these departments, and now we are responsible to both." So she looked rather wistfully at the splendid new school in Darjeeling, which seemed so free from many of the problems of Calcutta. "I wish very much we could transplant one wing of this school down to Calcutta. It is a most magnificent building with big class rooms, roomy corridors, and every arrangement for comfort and study. This is quite the most magnificent of all our houses both in England and India. Just now they are in full swing of work, with a full school and every prospect of a most successful year. I expect most of our readers know that the school is for European girls, many are the children of domiciled English, and some Eurasians. They look so refreshing with their bright complexions and robust appearance, after the pale and delicate looking English children of the plains."

Back in Calcutta, the Diocesan Collegiate School was progressing by leaps and bounds, so that the report in the February 1911 *Pipalpati* contained news of continuing progress: "The College Department is the most recent addition; this is the second year of our affiliation, so that we are only in our beginnings. There are 14 girls here, the majority in the first and second year classes. This year we are taking Sanskrit and Botany, in addition to our subjects of last year. The girls are doing steady work. We hope to send in five or six for the First Arts, and two for the B.A. degree in March..." Distinction was now being made between the College department and the Collegiate School, and within a short time the former would evolve into a separate body. One of the requirements of the University was that a governing body should be set up for both the College and the Diocesan Collegiate School, and this had met for the first time in October 1911. Membership included the Bishop of Calcutta, the Maharajah of Burdwan, Canon Brown of the Oxford Mission, Sr Jane Frances and Sr Mary Victoria.

Work had already begun on a new building for the College: "There will be three stories [sic]; the building will provide accommodation for the College girls and staff... The College girls will be separated from the

School girls, their class rooms being on the ground floor and their dormitory on the top floor. Towards this building we have nearly £2,000; we still want another £1,000. It is the only Christian girls' College in Bengal; until we started, all the girls had to go to a boys' college or a non-Christian college. This new building was opened on January 25th (the Conversion of St Paul) 1912[8] by the Bishop of Calcutta in the presence of the Vicereine, Lady Hardinge.

In the midst of all these changes and improvements in the Diocesan mission, it would be easy to overlook that other very important aspect of the work - the village schools in the Sunderbuns. In fact there was little chance of doing so, because out of all the work, this remained closest to Sr Jane Frances ' heart. So every issue of *Pipalpati* had an article about them, usually contributed by Miss Margaret Robertson, who made frequent visits to the 30 or more village schools, either accompanying visitors and school inspectors, or going out to conduct examinations or present prizes. These small schools, like the larger ones in the Diocesan mission compound, were subject to government inspection, and regular examinations were held. They also had a share in the gifts sent from England referred to earlier. Miss Robertson's efforts were tireless and she was sometimes involved in quite odd situations. Thus in 1906, she found herself petitioning the local magistrate to allow the use of guns by the villagers in a locality where there was much fear of a man-eating tiger. She seemed quite oblivious to the considerable physical discomforts involved in her trips to the villages, indeed she seemed to view the discomfiture of her guests with genteel amusement. Thus in the January 1904 issue of *Pipalpati* she took two visitors to a far flung corner of the Sunderbuns, but on this trip even her patience was tested:

"Last week I made a most out of the way expedition by an entirely new route to Baddipur, our most distant school in the real Sunderbuns on the verge of the jungle. We started by river steamer to Geonkhali, our only school on the other bank of the river… We got up at 5 a.m., but with all our best endeavours it was past 6 a.m. before we were fairly under weigh, although we postponed chota hazri [breakfast] until we were on the boat… I had our School Inspector, Gunjor Babu, and one of the women teachers. She had never been in any boat larger than a dug-out before, and although he asserted that he was quite used to sailing even in storms, his extreme nervousness whenever the boat heeled, ever so slightly to the breeze, betrayed him. He was quite indignant over it, and implored me to order the boatman to 'keep the boat straight', while the teacher thought her last hour was come whenever we got into the wash of any of the big steamers that so constantly pass up and down the Hooghly. Our hopes as regards timing ourselves with the tide were sadly frustrated, and 10 o'clock, which should have seen us almost at our destination, found us firmly stuck on a mud bank, about three quarters of a mile off the canal mouth we were trying to reach, though most tantalisingly in full sight of it. And there we had to remain in the blazing sun until the in-coming tide lifted us off, at nearly two in the afternoon."

Things went from bad to worse: "I was very sorry for the boatmen, as they had neither food nor water with them and would not touch anything of ours, but had to remain fasting until we reached Dugra and then go and purchase food. We remained at the dak bungalow until the great heat was over, and at about 4 o'clock started on what Gunjor called a five mile walk... I can only say it was the longest five miles I ever walked, and took me exactly two hours and forty minutes... The school at Baddipur consists entirely of Christian children, and at present there are 20 on the rolls, which number I hope will have increased by the time I go there again... The village is a largish one with a considerable, but very fluctuating, Christian population, as many of the people also have new clearings right down in the jungle, at which they spend about half the year, and this is of course a great hindrance to school work amongst the children... However, I am glad to say that the school results this year shewed a very marked improvement."

Sr Jane Frances often accompanied Miss Robertson on her trips to the Sunderbuns such as on this occasion in 1905: "We started at 8 a.m. for the ghat, or landing stage... We took our places on [the boat] one behind the other, and with the boatmen and our various belongings the boat was quite filled, and there was no room to move about in it. It was an intensely hot September day and I took my veil off to keep cool. Miss Robertson had her topi [sun hat] on when we passed some small boys in a boat. One exclaimed, 'There are the men!' but the other said, 'One is a man and the other is a woman!'... The banks of the river are pretty... Bamboo cluster on each side, and as you get further into the country, rice fields stretch out on each side with their little watch houses in the middle of them... In the distance are plantations or clumps of cocoanut palms... Our boat steers into the rice itself which is coming up through the water. Sometimes we come to patches of water where sheets of water lilies [are growing] with their lovely white or pale pink blossoms just beginning to show. About 1.00 p.m. we clambered out of the boat and walked up a steep bank... and entered a village schools. The school master is rather old and not very efficient, so we have come to see what his children can do. We are not therefore surprised to find they cannot perform the little tasks they are set to do, and are also rather disorderly. He has been told reluctantly that he must give up his post, and we have already looked out for a young teacher who will do his work more efficiently."

The journey continued with one or two more stops until they reached their destination for the night: "We made up our beds in the verandah of a little clean, empty house. Nearby are farm buildings with cows standing outside and dogs prowling about... We retired to bed early, and would have had an ideal night in the cool verandah, with a glorious moon shining over the water, if I had not been awakened (or fancied myself awakened), by a dog pulling at my sheet. When fully awake the dog had disappeared [but] as there are so many,… I think it may not have been altogether fancy. Next morning as we ate our chota hazri [breakfast] in the verandah, the children came bringing us great bunches of water lilies… Then we went down to a little collection of bustis [huts] to watch the rice being husked." Sr Jane Frances even had a try herself and declared that: "after some difficulty succeeded fairly well." Perils were not confined to night predators as the Sister soon discovered: "On going back to our little house I met a huge snake in the verandah. I went back immediately to call somebody to kill it, but when we had returned, it was fast disappearing down a hole close to the water."

On the way back into Calcutta they passed Kalighat, the great Hindu shrine to the goddess Kali, whence Calcutta is named. "Numbers of men and women were bathing and preparing to keep a festival. The idols outside the temple were covered with gaudy garlands of red and yellow flowers, and we saw a black kid being bathed in preparation for sacrifice. Many of the people were standing in groups on the steps of the ghat chattering noisily, and others were bathing or saying their prayers in the water, with some bright blossoms of flowers scattered in it." The tranquility of the rice country, in spite of water snakes and marauding dogs, came as a great contrast to the heat and dust of Calcutta, and the pressures of life at the Diocesan mission. No doubt this is why it appealed so much to Sr Jane Frances. This was *real* India and life went on unchanged from day to day no matter who occupied the seat of government.

Life for the Sisters was a constant struggle against poverty, dirt and disease. While earthquakes and cyclones such as those experienced in 1897 and 1899 were rare, life in India was always difficult. This is conveyed in the pages of *Pipalpati* with reports of illness in the schools and famine in the Sunderbuns and elsewhere. Thus towards the end of 1905, Margaret Robertson wrote of the, "terrible storm lasting about 36 hours, and at the end of that time, the whole country was one waste of water. All the new rice was completely submerged and either washed away or rotted, and in most places the water was too deep for any attempt to be made at replanting, even if the people had seedlings to sow or money to meet the expense… It must be a terrible trial of faith to see what promised to be a prosperous year turned to scarcity,… one more [trial] added to a long succession of bad harvests, and the poor people are deeply in debt." In the same letter she wrote also of the, "epidemic of malarial fever, so bad that in whole households there was none left well enough to tend the sick, and a good many have died." One of the village schools teachers, a young woman with three children, had died in this epidemic.

Diseases such as cholera, malaria, and consumption, (the latter had increased at an alarming rate), all had to be coped with in primitive conditions and without the benefit of modern remedies. But also, those common enemies of childhood, measles and chicken-pox, were just as rife in India as they were in England, and often they were fatal. There was little the Sisters could do: "The rains, though so eagerly looked for as a necessary relief from the long drought are, as far as health is concerned, a great anxiety", wrote Sr Jane Frances in 1909. "Fevers, internal complaints, and dispositions to cholera, may appear at any moment, so we lay in our stock of medicines likely to be needed, and hold ourselves ready." Thus the Sisters ever ready, went about their work in the last years of peace.

Footnotes

1. This statement shows how open-minded the Sisters were, and it might not have been met favourably by all the English readers of *Pipalpati*, many of whom would not have held Indian culture in high regard.

2. The present day uniform of St John's Diocesan Higher Secondary School consists of white dresses and pale blue ribbons.

3. The Hon. Emily Onslow was the sister of Sr Katherine Elisabeth (formerly the Hon Katherine Onslow) who was professed at Clewer in 1889, but did not work in India.

4. Bishop Wilberforce, the first Episcopal Visitor to the Clewer Sisters, strongly objected to them making vows. Therefore the Sisters (many of whom came from wealthy families), were not required to make the vow of poverty. They were free to dispose of their finances in whatever way they wished and were not compelled to give it to the Community. However, some did so either by endowing branch houses or by sponsoring children such as those under the Sisters' care in Calcutta. See also chapter 12, footnote 3.

5. This idea of adopting an orphan is now very common with Aid agencies.

6. It is also necessary to be mindful of educational standards at home at this time. State elementary education had only been compulsory in England for a generation, and it was not free until 1891. In 1899 the school leaving age in England was raised to 12, and it was not until 1918 that it was raised to 14. Despite the improvements made by the 1902 Education Act, especially in the field of secondary education, the higher education of girls was still not taken seriously. The belief that it was the primary vocation of women to marry and bear children cut across all social classes, although as the nineteenth century progressed, a growing number of private schools for the daughters of gentlemen blazed a trail which would eventually lead to women gaining university entrance. One of the first was Cheltenham Ladies' College, founded in 1853, and others such as the North London Collegiate, soon followed. These were secular foundations, but Religious Communities (such as the Clewer Sisters), also founded high quality schools for young ladies - St Stephen's College, Clewer; St Stephen's High School, Clewer; St John's Hamilton Terrace, north London; and St John Baptist's High School, Newport, South Wales. Despite these advances, it was not until 1920 that women could take Oxford degrees (although they had previously been able to attend lectures), and Cambridge refused to confer degrees until 1947.

Further details of the Clewer Sisters' educational work in England may be found in BONHAM, Valerie *A Joyous Service* 1989

7. It still does have a pioneering aspect. In 1995 the 3 schools in Calcutta, once run by the Clewer Sisters (Pratt Memorial: St John's Diocesan Higher Secondary: St Thomas' Kidderpore) were educating 7,500 girls between them.

8. For further details, see chapter 22.

-22-
FROM PAX BRITANNICA TO ARMAGEDDON

1912 began on a high note for the Sisters in Calcutta. On January 25th (the Conversion of St Paul), the new Diocesan College buildings were blessed by the Bishop of Calcutta in the presence of the Vicereine, Lady Hardinge. It was a simple, yet impressive service, the Bishop, staff, students, Sisters and congregation meeting on the verandah and then making their way through the building pausing for prayers on each floor. During the procession the hymn *The Church's one foundation*(1) was sung, and the service concluded with *Blessed city, heavenly Salem*. According to the order of service, the procession made its way through the buildings in the following order: "Cross bearer, Thurifer, Bishop's Chaplain, the Lord Bishop, Priests vested, H. E. Lady Hardinge, the Sisters, the Staff, the Students." Pupils from the Diocesan Collegiate School lined the verandahs. Afterwards there was a programme of music and recitation followed by the annual prize giving. Lady Hardinge presented the prizes, followed by an address by the Bishop, and a speech by the Maharajah of Burdwan, one of the governors.

There was a short report about the College in the Clewer *Associates' Newsletter* dated April 6th 1912: "[The building] is admirably planned, long and narrow, of three storeys, situated on the north side of the compound, and very shortly it will be connected with the Collegiate School block by a covered way. It contains six lecture halls, a library, two sitting rooms, quarters for the resident staff, and a dormitory running the whole length of the building to accommodate all the students. The roof provides a delightful recreation ground."

The ethos of the Diocesan College was discussed in the April 1912 issue of *Pipalpati*. "There is a very limited demand for Colleges for women. In Bengal we have had one College for women; it is here in Calcutta at the extreme north end of the town; we are at the extreme south end. It was endowed years ago by one of the Chief Justices of Bengal and is called after him, the 'Bethune' College. The Government has taken up this foundation and subsidises it generously; it now forms the Government College for the women of the Province. It is staffed by Bengali Lady Graduates and Bengali Pandits... It is entirely non-Christian... I do not know of any other College in India for women. It was imperatively necessary to supply some place for our girls where they would be surrounded by Christian influence... We wanted also that our girls should be taught by ladies, a man cannot train up a woman, and the girls need something more than only literary and scientific lectures.(2) If there had been some College where the Lady Superintendent had been Christian, and where there was a Christian influence throughout, we should have probably kept our girls with us as boarders and sent them as day students."

The decision to open the Diocesan College had not been made lightly as the Sister explained: "It is the outcome of five years consideration, and of enquiry from all religious bodies round as to what their plans were for the future, and what could be provided for our Christian girls... The College girls come from our own school, from the Church Missionary Society and Nonconformist Schools, and also from the Roman Catholic Schools. We stand now for the *Christian* College and all recognize that it is preferable that their girls should be amongst Christians."(3)

Membership of the College was not restricted to Christians: "We do not intend to exclude all non-Christians. They can be admitted, provided they attend all the religious classes and conform to the general rules, and that their admission never precludes the admission of a Christian student... The Christians will always have the preference. As regards fees also, if *necessary* they are reduced for the Christians, but not for the non-Christians. The Bethune College fees are far less than ours - they can always go there." This all sounds very strict and forbidding, but the Sister continued in a more placatory tone: "It would be bringing up our girls in a hothouse atmosphere if we separated them from all the cultured non-Christian classes; these non-Christian girls are not heathens and idol-worshippers, they worship our God, and they reverence our Lord. They do not yet grasp His Divinity, but they are getting nearer, and one hopes that in the future... they will choose for themselves... We do not take girls who are really anti-Christian, or if they come they do not stay [as] they feel out of their milieu and go elsewhere."

But as always, money was a major problem: "So far we have had no help from Government, but there is now a possibility of getting a yearly grant which may pay our salaries and enable us to have a fuller staff... One very kind friend has helped us with the College Building Fund, and has promised, if necessary, she will help us further. We hardly know what we should have done without this help. We still want about £1,000, even if the University does give us the probable sum of 10,000 rupees."

Sisters came and went between England and India; some stayed in India for several years and after a short furlough in England, returned for a further term of three or five years. There often seemed to be Sisters in transit, something which was to become a problem in wartime. It was usual for several Sisters to travel together. Thus the Clewer *Associates' Newsletter* of December 1912 asked for prayers for: "Sr Edith Emily, Sr Edith Alice, Sr Celia and Sr Edith Helen, who hope to sail for Calcutta... on January 11th or 12th." In fact they sailed a day later, on board the *City of Benares*.. The same Newsletter added: "You will like to know that we heard of the safe arrival of Sr Olive who, two days after reaching Calcutta, went up to Darjeeling to work in the Diocesan Girls' High School." Sometimes a Sister travelled alone, thus the *Associates' Newsletter* for

December 1913, recorded the safe arrival home of Sr Emily Barbara on November 16th, after a particularly good voyage. January 9th 1914 saw Sr Blanche Annie, Sr Mary Editha, Sr Helena Maria, and Sr Dorothy Frances [(4)] sail from Liverpool on board the *S.S. City of London*; and the spring of 1914 saw Sr Mary Pauline and Sr Mary Frances starting separately on their homeward journeys.

Early in 1913 Miss Katherine Hoare, sister of Angelina Hoare, visited Calcutta for the first time in almost thirty years. "It has evidently been a great pleasure to her to see the development of the work which she knew so well in its small beginnings," wrote Mother Evelyn in the *Associates' Newsletter* of March 1913. Miss Hoare was able to attend the prize giving at the Collegiate School, which was also attended by the Bishop of Calcutta (who was about to retire), and Lady Carmichael, wife of the Lieutenant Governor of Bengal. Upon her return to England, Miss Hoare attended the anniversary service and annual meeting of the St John Baptist Calcutta Mission Association at St Barnabas' Pimlico, and gave "a most interesting and stirring address," which made all present, "wish we could go out there at once."

The development of the Diocesan College was not the only advance in the Sisters' educational work at this time. The Pratt Memorial School was undergoing marked improvements too. It had last been extended in 1892, but by the time of Mother Evelyn's visit in 1910, it was again suffering from overcrowding and further extensions were being envisaged. Now, in 1913, those new buildings were in use. The March 1913 issue of the Clewer *Associates' Newsletter*, recalled that early in 1912 part of the old house had been demolished to make way for the new wing: "The difficulty of carrying on the work of the school in the midst of all the noise and dust of the building operations, can only be imagined by anyone who knows what the Indian workman is capable of in these particulars," wrote the Sister. The funds had run out before the second storey could be completed, but on December 4th 1912 the Bishop of Calcutta had blessed the new building. This ceremony was followed by the annual prize giving which was presided over by Lady Carmichael. More work was done during 1913, so that by the December issue of the *Associates' Newsletter*, the Sisters were able to report that: "Instead of the old insanitary quarters, each class now has its own airy room. The Kindergarten which numbers 82 has always overflowed its former rooms, and has now the use of the large recreation hall. There is a chapel of convenient size which will, we trust, by degrees be made beautiful, and already we have to thank kind friends in England for providing the marble steps and floor for the sanctuary." If the numbers of pupils are a guide, then the school appeared to be flourishing with a total of 221 on the roll, of whom 107 were boarders, and 30 of whom were small boys. These boys lived in a separate house nearby, until the top storey could be added to the new wing. In the senior scholarship the Pratt Memorial

School had taken the first place in Bengal, and the second place in the junior list. One former pupil had recently taken her M.A. at Calcutta University, and two others had gone to the Diocesan College from whence one had passed her Intermediate Arts and the other her B.A.

Indian weather surpassed all the vagaries of its English counterpart, and the Sisters must have often thought of home when the monsoon lashed down. So much depended on the rains coming at the right time and in the right amount - it was a life versus death matter. The last twelve months before the outbreak of the Great War saw unutterable hardship due to the merciless Indian climate. Writing in the August 1913 issue of *Pipalpati* Sr Jane Frances commented: "We had as great heat in April as we generally look for in May, and in that month so many thunderstorms, cyclonic disturbances, all accompanied by heavy rain, that it was impossible to determine when the Monsoon really began. We had made up the amount of a good average rainfall for the year in June, at the usual date for the rains to begin. Now on the verge of September we have a total of over 70 inches, in comparison with between 30 and 40 inches at the same date last year. In consequence of this, the outlook in the rice lands is very bad indeed, no crops to be looked for in the lower stretches... There have been severe floods too in the Native State of Burdwan on the other side of the Hooghly. The price of rice has already nearly doubled, and in our compound there are many dilapidations from the heavy rain, [with] boundary walls and small, but most necessary, outbuildings to be rebuilt. Meanwhile, the accommodation in the old part of the house which is inhabited by the Lower School, has been stretched to its utmost limits."

A few months later, Sr Jane Frances wrote a letter to Mother Evelyn at Clewer which was published in the *Associates' Newsletter* of March 31st 1914. In it she graphically described the appalling suffering which the previous year's excessive rains had inflicted on the people in the rice country. "My earliest visit was in July during the course of the rains when one saw dimly, through drifting rain and mist, teams of eight oxen drawing the curious Indian ploughs in water nearly up to their shoulders. This was to prepare for a third attempt at planting out seed rice when the water abated, and on that side of the country [it] was at least partially successful. The part that had an entire failure of crops lies nearer Calcutta; it extends in length over 20 miles, and covers altogether a large area very densely populated. We have 14 schools scattered over this area."

Sr Jane Frances continued: "My second expedition at the close of the rains, was to see for myself which of these 14 villages were likely to be worse off. Travelling by boat was easy and pleasant; one could make a beeline from place to place. The effect of the sheets of fresh water like a succession of shallow lakes under the bright blue sky... was very pretty, but meant a lamentable prospect as to rice crops in December. Now at the end of January, these flooded stretches of water have dried up partially into marshy swamps, repulsive to look at... We stayed for three nights at our best 'rest house' right in the centre of the district. Generally at this season all the industries connected with the rice harvest are in full swing, and everybody busy or cheerful. Our landlord is a cultivator on a larger scale, but this year literally not even a tuft of straw has been raised on his land. Nothing was going on and many of the people [were] away in search of work at a distance. We can attempt no *general* relief of distress but... we concentrate our efforts at keeping the schools together; for the worst times for these 14 villages are still to come."

News of this type of privation would not have been common in England with no mass media to show the scale of the suffering, so a first hand account such as this was valuable. And the Clewer Associates duly responded as Sr Jane Frances recounted: "Our Mother Superior [Mother Evelyn] with the help of kind friends at home has just sent out a small sum which I reckon may cover two months of a 'famine price' to start with. The Indian peasantry are so poor that very little assistance is received thankfully, and they are so devoted to their children that what is given for them will not be diverted to other purposes."

Margaret Robertson added her own contribution to that of Sr Jane Frances which reiterated the tale of need. "We begin the year 1914 with rather sad hearts, for we are once more face to face with serious distress, not to say famine, in the north part of the district, a state of affairs which we had begun to hope was a thing of the past since the new government drainage scheme has begun to take effect. Let me say that the money spent by the government was not wasted - the southern part of the district has had no really bad harvest since the large Diamond Harbour sluices were finished, but unluckily they are too far distant and the land is too low lying for it to affect the more northern part known as Bara Bada." Miss Robertson went on to explain the effects of the early, heavy rainfall of 1913: "[There is] a waste of water where there should have been ripe rice, and in the future distress will be great - no rice for food, no seed rice for this year, no surplus rice to sell to obtain money for clothes and curry stuff, vegetables and oil. Worse still, no money for the rent of the rice land which must still be paid... Just now the villages look deserted; all the able bodied men have gone off to gather in other peoples' harvests in districts more fortunate than their own, but when the money they get for this is exhausted, what then? There will be no general rice crop till next December... We are beginning this month to give a little general relief in our Bara Bada schools, though it seems pitifully little. We give 4 annas (4d) in the upper standards of the school; 2 annas in the infant classes, and that not [for] a week but a month. And for that amount of help the children flock to school from all sides, so that we have to be firm and say that before receiving relief it is necessary to have attended school for a certain length of time - poor children! It shows the reality of their need."

If the dawning of 1914 brought sad hearts to those trying to bring relief to the victims of the rice country famine, it certainly ended with many more sad hearts, due to the outbreak of war. A war in Europe might have seemed rather remote to people living in Bengal were it not for the fact that Calcutta was the second city of the British Empire, and the involvement of Britain in war was a threat to that Empire's very existence. So it was that Kitchener's call to arms extended to citizens of the Empire too, and altogether more than 1,200,000 Indians took up arms in defence of King and Empire. From the trenches in Flanders and France, to Palestine, Mesopotamia and Gallipoli, Indian soldiers loyally took their place in the battle lines.

During that long, hot summer of 1914 which ended so abruptly on August 4th with the outbreak of hostilities between Britain and Germany, Sr Jane Frances was in England taking her first furlough in nine years. Travelling aboard the *S.S. Scindia* with Sr Mary Victoria, she had arrived in England on May 11th after a fairly good voyage. Sr Jane Frances has left no record of how she spent her furlough or how she reacted to the outbreak of the war. Like many of her contemporaries in Community she had lost a number of relatives over the years, but to the end of her life she maintained contact with the Duke of Argyll, to whom she was related through marriage[5]. During her later years, the Duke's name was held by the Community as her next of kin.

Sr Jane Frances must have absorbed the general feeling of the nation towards the coming of war, and it must have seemed in stark contrast with the problems she had temporarily left in India - the financial burdens borne by the schools under Community care, and the sufferings of the starving people of the rice country. On the day that war broke out Mother Evelyn had gone to London to visit a sick Sister (Sr Kathleen), and upon returning to Clewer had reported that crowds of Londoners had been awake all night singing *Rule Brittania* and *God save the King*. Ironically, just at the time that Lord Grey was declaring that the lamps were going out all over Europe, the Sisters at Clewer were basking in the completion of the first stage of the installation of electric lighting! But the reality of war came home within a day or two when the two horses belonging to the Community were requisitioned - and were quickly returned having been deemed unsuitable for service! But after this wry entry, the Community *Annals* take on a sombre note with details of the Sisters' prayerful contribution to the war effort in the form of days of intercession and vigils of prayer.

Meanwhile in India, Sr Florence who was temporarily in charge of the Diocesan mission, wrote in the September 1914 issue of the *Pipalpati* magazine about the outbreak of war: "Probably Bengal is less in the 'run' of things than almost any country at the moment and our Banks, Post Offices and Firms are working as usual. Traffic is not in any way disturbed and buildings are not requisitioned for troops or hospitals." But she went on to say that a day of solemn intercession had been held throughout

India, "and every mosque and temple took part in it according to their lights." This must have been a rare and early example of "interfaith" prayer and co-operation. Also, the chaplain at the Cathedral had begun a daily Eucharist "for all engaged in the war, and for the peace of Europe." But whilst daily routine went on in much the same way as before, life was not entirely unaffected as Sr Florence recounted: "Troops, both English and Indian, were quickly mobilized and sent to the seat of war, while Volunteers were requisitioned from all sides and are being put through a severe course of drill in the early hours of the morning. While Factories and Mills are only doing half work and reducing the number of their employees, the newspaper editors are having a great time. One paper issues five or six editions a day..."

Sr Florence then proceeded to describe an incident which would become all too common in the next four years. "Commerce, which has been somewhat thrown back, was just making a fresh start when the impertinent little German cruiser Emden sank five merchant vessels in the Bay of Bengal and has just succeeded in sinking a sixth; besides feebly bombarding Madras and setting some oil tanks ablaze. The Commander has been a Captain on one of the Hansa Line ships and knows the Bay of Bengal thoroughly. He appears to be a most courteous, kindly man, and has treated his prisoners with greatest consideration, sending the greater number back to Calcutta on an American ship and landing others at Rangoon. The Emden is assisted by two other smaller ships which act as scouts, and it is impossible to approach her without being observed. The Captain says he is 'going to play the war-game to the end,' and the only thing he fears is a British warship, and that if he comes into contact with that 'his game is up,' but he will sink his ship rather than let her be taken..."

"Another effect of the war," wrote Sr Florence, "is the recall of all members of the Indian Civil Service who were at home on leave, so that at this moment... it is difficult to find billets for the different officers... Social events in Calcutta have more or less given way to ambulance classes and relief parties - lectures, concerts, entertainments are all 'for the war', and most effectual aid in money and hospital apparatus and comfort is being sent to the front... So far the financial stress has not been keenly felt in the mission. As time goes on, subscriptions will probably slacken... The poor village folk are expecting a good rice harvest, as we have had a most favourable monsoon... There have been no floods this side of India." That at least was good news.

On November 13th 1914 Sr Jane Frances was re-appointed Sister Superior of the work in India and, her furlough having come to an end, she sailed from Tilbury on November 23rd aboard the P. & O. *S.S. Caledonia*, accompanied by Sr Kate Mary going for the fourth time, and Sr Norah going for the first time. They arrived safely at Bombay in mid-December, thus avoiding the wily Emden lurking in the Bay of Bengal.

This would be Sr Jane Frances ' last term of duty in India. The Clewer *Associates' Newsletter* for March 1915 recounted several arrivals and departures amidst the heightened dangers of wartime: "We have much cause for thankfulness that in this time of unrest and danger both on land and sea, our Sisters have so far had prosperous voyages. Sr Mary Victoria and Sr Honor, who were to sail from England on January 9th [1915], reached Bombay in very good time; and on March 8th we had the great pleasure of welcoming home Sr Florence and Sr Mary Thekla." Sr Florence, veteran of the Pratt Memorial School and the Diocesan High School, Darjeeling, was now returning to England permanently. From the same issue of the Newsletter, we also learn that another veteran, Sr Constance Ruth, had been invalided home at the beginning of March, although she returned to India at the end of the war. Her place at the Presidency General Hospital was taken by Sr Katherine Maud (6), who left England for this her third term in India, on February 27th 1915 aboard the P.& O. *S.S. Arabia*. "Our state of warfare was speedily brought home to her and all the passengers, by strict orders being given regarding lights, and by their being shown where to assemble in case the ship had to be abandoned, and warned to have on warm clothing."

So the Sisters went about their business in a world which had gone to war, and it took time before it had any major effects on their work. In England the people thought it would all be over by Christmas: but Christmas 1914 came and went, and the shells continued to rain down. And so 1915 dawned and the Sisters congratulated themselves on getting to and from India in safety. But the most perilous voyages still lay ahead. And great challenges too as old workers became unavailable and exciting new work presented itself. These last years of Sr Jane Frances ' charge were to see Britain emerge from the conflict into a world whose youth and idealism had died in the carnage. Into that world would be born a new India which would seek to govern itself. The death knell which heralded the Great War tolled also for the British Empire.

Footnotes

1. *The Church's One Foundation* was written by the Revd S. J. Stone, sometime curate of Windsor. For further details of this prolific parson and his famous hymn, see:

BONHAM, Valerie *S. J. Stone: the hymn writer of Spital* in *WINDLESORA* No.7 1988.

2. This rather odd comment does not attempt to explain itself but presumably it alludes to turning girls into ladies!

3. This is a remarkable statement in a pre-ecumenical age when denominational rivalry was still extremely common.

4. Sr Blanche Annie was born in 1862, the 7th of the 14 children of the Revd John Kitcat, vicar of Swallowfield (1855-75), and curate of Clewer St Stephen (1875-81). She was professed in 1893, and in 1894 was sent to University College Hospital to be trained in nursing. She sailed for India for the first time on January 1st 1897, and served five terms, (not consecutively), finally returning to England in 1934. In the 1923 New Year Honours, she received the Kaiser-i-Hind medal for services to nursing in the Presidency General Hospital. She died on November 19th 1951.

Sr Dorothy Frances was a future Sister Superior of the Indian work (1931-39) and resigned from office when she was elected Mother Superior at Clewer, an office she was to occupy from 1939-1958. It was she who finally succeeded in obtaining Provincial status for the Indian work.

5. Sr Jane Frances ' sister had married the second son of the 8th Duke of Argyll.

6. Sr Katherine Maud, like Sr Dorothy Frances, was a future Mother Superior of Clewer, serving as such from 1928 until her death in office in 1935. She served three terms in India at the Presidency General Hospital, and made two visits as Mother Superior.

-23-
A LESS PROPITIOUS TIME

On her return to Calcutta just before Christmas 1914, Sr Jane Frances found all well with the Community work there. Within a few months however, the Community was to sustain a major loss by the withdrawal of Miss Margaret Robertson from the rice country schools. This was indeed a blow, for she had been the mainstay since the death of Angelina Hoare[(1)]. Whilst Sr Jane Frances had always cherished the work in the rice country because it was what she called "real Indian work", the day to day running of it was done by Miss Robertson.

Sr Jane Frances wrote about Miss Robertson's contribution in the May 1915 issue of *Pipalpati*: "No one knows so much of its value as myself, for no one now at the Mission House can remember all the first beginnings, 25 years ago, when as quite a young girl she came out with her aunt and became her companion on her venturesome expeditions in the water country. I happened the other day to light upon an old letter of Miss Hoare's of about 1890, in which she offered her young relation, then little more than 20, to my special care, as a volunteer to train up for the village work in which she already showed much interest and a certain aptitude; but all the *drudgery* of careful superintendence of these scattered very elementary village schools had yet to be learnt. Soon after that, in July 1892, came Miss Hoare's unlooked for and much lamented death. Miss Robertson then went to England for two years furlough. She was somewhat out of health, and the death of her aunt had been a great shock to her... But since her return in 1894 she has been a most constant worker and no one can testify better than I can to the value of her steady work during all these years."

Perhaps more than anything else, the impending departure of Margaret Robertson brought the passing years home to Sr Jane Frances - and her own increasing frailty: "In the early years of her work with us, Miss Robertson and I did many journeys together and shared many odd adventures for which I should no longer be equal, but which remain very happily and vividly in my memory. As the years went on, I was able to pass on a great deal of responsibility to her, yet always felt absolutely in touch with all the places and people which I could no longer visit so frequently; and by her carefully kept records, the progress and personality of all the children... in the 34 schools is familiar ground as before... Our scattered native Christians in that curious water country are still quite in the minority... But Miss Hoare always made her first aim, by means of these very simple village schools, to cherish the Christian life of these scattered flocks; and this purpose her young relative and our faithful helper had thoroughly grasped, and at the cost of much personal self sacrifice, strove earnestly to carry on." News of Miss Robertson's departure from India was also reported in the Clewer *Associates' Newsletter* of July 1915 together with the footnote that: "after some weeks of rest [Miss Robertson] hopes to go and minister to our brave soldiers at the Front."[2]

Back in England, Sr Sophie[3], who had worked at the European Orphanage, met with a tragic accident. According to the Community *Annals* she was knocked down by a motorbus in London late in the evening of October 10th 1915: "Some soldiers passing by carried her carefully into St Barnabas' Mission Room[4] and gave her First Aid. She was then taken to St George's Hospital where she died about 11.30 p.m., never having regained consciousness. She had had a very busy, happy Sunday - amongst other things having conducted a service in Robert Street, no priest being available. She then took home from Evensong an old woman fearing she might be knocked down by the traffic, little thinking how she was to meet with an accident."

Returning home from India did not always imply "light duties" - in November 1915 Sr Florence, who had recently returned to England, took up major work as Sister Superior at Newport[5] in South Wales. She replaced Sr Selina who had returned to Clewer after nearly 40 years. Newport was a busy and flourishing work, and Sr Florence was to remain in charge until 1926. Even so, she found time to write an account of the Diocesan Girls' High School, Darjeeling, which she had supervised for 18 years. Sr Florence's account of the school appeared in the October 1915 issue of the *Associates' Newsletter*, and after a retrospective view of the school's beginnings, brings the reader up to date. An early problem, recorded by Sr Florence (but not by Sr Georgina in her school history written much later[6]), was that when the Sisters took over the school in 1895, they were unable to run it personally for the first year, and a secular teacher was put in charge temporarily. One of the Sisters stayed a month to see her established and then returned to Calcutta. "During that year," wrote Sr Florence, "the Sister Superior and other Sisters visited the school and all seemed [to be] going on happily and well. However, after it was closed in November it became gradually apparent that the parents and children were rather 'shy' of Sisters (to them a quite unknown quantity), and preferred throwing in their lot with the temporary headmistress whom they knew and liked, and who shortly opened a school on her own account a few miles distant. When the school opened again in February 1896 with the Sisters in charge, only 26 of the old pupils remained, 50 had gone elsewhere. This was somewhat discouraging, but new girls gradually arrived and a very happy, though uphill time began lasting for four years."[7]

At the end of that four years, and just after the school buildings had been extended and improved, there came the cyclone which destroyed it, and which Sr Florence only mentioned in passing because the story was already so familiar to her readers. So too was the tale of the rebuilding on a different and safer site, the land for which was given by Sir John Woodburn, the then Lieutenant Governor of Bengal. "But," she continued, "all the expense of the building which had been preceeded by four years of heavy rent on the hired temporary houses fell very heavily on the school and crippled the finances terribly for about eight years. A munificent gift and gigantic efforts which were met by government aid, eventually cleared off the debt and left the school unencumbered - but with no reserve funds whatever." At the time of writing (1915), the school was free from debt but the dividing line was always very slim because the Sisters tried to run the school as cheaply as possible, whilst maintaining a high standard. "The fees are surprisingly small, £25-£27 per annum provides the pupils with board, tuition, laundry, doctor and ordinary medicine. Accomplishments and a small charge for use of books and stationery are the only extras. Yet even so the Sisters are constantly asked to reduce the terms as the Roman Catholic convents and Non-Conformist schools are on a lower scale. It is therefore clear that the financial success of these schools depends on numbers as well as on efficiency. This year, the twentieth of our tenure, we are able to record for the first time overflowing numbers and an increasingly high standard of scholarship... An extension is needed and will shortly be put in hand. There are already 130 boarders and others waiting to come."

The new school which was opened in 1904 looked very impressive, but its shortcomings soon became apparent: "the new buildings are both large and picturesque - more picturesque than convenient, as the gabled roof seems incapable of being made waterproof." But apart from the roof, the rest seemed well appointed. "...The chapel was paid for by gifts from home, as was the greater portion of the Sisters' house, which not only provides for the Sisters who are in charge, but also receives those working in Calcutta who need rest and change. The classrooms are large and airy and are supplemented by an excellent art studio, laboratory, gymnasium hall and infirmary. There are two playgrounds and the afternoons are largely given to games."

As noted when discussing the Calcutta schools, it is difficult to assess educational standards, but by 1915 the girls at the Darjeeling school were mostly English, though some were Anglo-Indian. Their parents would be looking for something comparable with an English girls' public school, but without the inconvenience (and expense) of sending their daughters to England. This is what the Sisters set out to create at Darjeeling. Thus Sr Florence wrote: "The staff is drawn partly from England, graduates being essential in the higher classes, and partly from English training schools in India. The pupils follow the ordinary secondary high school curriculum and are prepared for the Cambridge Local, Junior, Senior, and Higher Local, as accepted by the Education Department in India. The school is government aided and is annually examined and inspected by government officials." In conclusion Sr Florence added: "The Darjeeling Diocesan High School has weathered attacks from within and from without; it has been subject to evil report and good report; it has been submerged, and again has emerged with ever increasing vitality and purpose and is today a standing witness to the protecting care and love of God for the children of his Church in India."

The war was beginning to make travelling very difficult for the Sisters. The Clewer *Associates' Newsletter* for December 1915 contained a letter from the Warden, the Revd Arthur East: "As this letter reaches you two of our Sisters, Sr Alexandrina and Sr Dorothea will be on their way to India in the P. & O. *S.S. Caledonia*. Two more, Sr Mary Frances and Sr Kathleen Prisca will sail in the *S.S. Kaiser-i-Hind* on January 1st. I commend them to your prayers: the prayer 'for those in peril on the sea' has a new and terrifying significance." The *Associates' Newsletter* for April 1916, and the Community *Annals*, between them brought news of the safe arrival home of four Sisters - Sr Frances Anne, Sr Mabel Theresa and Sr Mary Evelyn on February 1st, and Sr Beatrice Mary, who unusually was travelling alone, on March 29th. All had perilous voyages. On the earlier voyage: "From Port Said to Marseilles all the passengers were requested to take their life belts with them wherever they went. Boats were lowered and rafts prepared in readiness for whatever might happen, and for a long distance [they] took a very zig-zag course which proved to be a most trying experience and of course lengthened the voyage." But at least they reached home safely as did Sr Beatrice Mary, whose experience was similar. Her ship, "crept along the Channel preceeded by minesweepers, and followed by a number of smaller boats anxious to share in the safety thus afforded."

A closer shave was experienced by Sr Katharine Hope and Sr Georgina who arrived in England on December 17th 1916. Readers of the *Associates' Newsletter* were merely told that these Sisters were, "welcomed home with special joy and thankfulness on account of the very great dangers of the voyage." In fact the Sisters had been shipwrecked! The Community *Annals* record that: "their boat struck a mine about $1^1/_2$ hours from Marseilles. It reached Marseilles but all the passengers were put into little boats. Our Sisters were picked up by a destroyer and brought to Marseilles. Two of the crew lost their lives, but all the passengers were saved. P. & O. particularly asked that the accident should not be publicly spoken of in an effort to keep the news from the Germans." No doubt this accounts for the lack of detail in the *Associates' Newsletter*. It was this type of danger which, early in 1917, made the British government refuse to allow women to travel by sea. Thus the Sisters in India were stranded, as were those on furlough in England. Sr Katharine Hope and Sr Georgina were unable to return to India until the end of the war.

Amidst all this difficulty, the offer of new work in Calcutta was made to the Sisters in the summer of 1915. "I have been asked by the Governors of the Free School to approach you on the subject of the new departure... which is shortly to be made at Kidderpore, and to find out whether there would be any likelihood of your Community undertaking the management of the new school," wrote the Bishop of Calcutta(8) to Sr Jane Frances in a letter dated July 29th 1915. The Calcutta Free School was begun in 1789 as a charity school for European orphan boys (later girls were included too), but the name "Free School" was not used until 1800. The Bishop of Calcutta was numbered among the governors and from 1814 onwards began to take an active role in the administration of the school. In 1882 the school came under Government inspection and was ranked at higher elementary level. By the time the Clewer Sisters were invited to help, the school numbered 233 boys of whom 156 were free cases, and 181 girls of whom 126 were free cases. In 1915 the government of India made over to the Free School a large mansion called Kidderpore House, and the school authorities decided to transfer the kindergarten and junior pupils, numbering about 124. It was this aspect of the work which the Sisters were being invited to take over.

Kidderpore House dated from the 18th century and was an elegant mansion on an estate once owned by Warren Hastings. At this time the Kidderpore/Alipore district was a select suburb of Calcutta and many of the wealthy East India Company officials had built residences there. Warren Hastings was one of the most prolific, and he bought a large estate with several houses on it. Amongst these was The Belvedere, sold in 1780 to Colonel Tolly, and later much altered and enlarged (and now serving as the National Library). Another was Hastings House, built and lived in by him until he left India in 1785; it was subsequently bought by Lord Curzon for the use of visiting Indian princes and other distinguished guests, and is now a school. Kidderpore House is less documented(9). However, it seems to have been one of several properties on Hastings' estate and is probably that which subsequently belonged to Richard Barwell, and which in 1790 became the Military Orphan House for children of British Officers (a similar institution for the children of private soldiers was at Howrah on the opposite side of the River Hooghly). A coloured etching by William Baillie shows the Military Orphan House alias Kidderpore House in 1794 looking very much as it did in 1915 when it was handed over by the government to the Calcutta Free School.(10)

Despite Sr Jane Frances ' repeated requests, the Indian work of the Clewer Sisters was not a separate Province, and therefore this offer had to be considered by the Clewer Chapter. Thus Sr Jane Frances ' immediate reaction was to send the bishop's letter of July 29th 1915 straight to Mother Evelyn. However, her accompanying letter (dated August 5th 1915), revealed her reluctance to undertake this new work, and also gave an insight into her relationships with the bishop and others. "I have already warned [the bishop] very plainly that there could not be a less propitious time for entertaining plans for any fresh departure than the present," wrote Sr Jane Frances, "but that from many points of view the offer was so generous and opened out such great possibilities that I felt it right that you should know about it at once. You will understand that in this the bishop is only the mouthpiece and figurehead of the governing body. The real mover is Colonel Harrison, an elderly military man whom we have known for *years* in connexion with the European Orphanage, as he is one of the Trustees. He has always been *very much* our good friend, an excellent, sensible, solid man, and a very good Churchman, and of late has been on a good many of the Committees for Church Institutions and carries weight."

Colonel Harrison had access to the Calcutta grapevine, and so Sr Jane Frances had heard about the school's proposed move to Kidderpore before receiving the bishop's letter: [Colonel Harrison] "came to see me a few weeks ago on private matters connected with the future of the European Orphanage, and then told me a little about the proposed transference of the Free School to Kidderpore which has been a Calcutta subject of discussion for some *years* I should say, but it was never suggested that it would come our way. I was rather astonished when, having finished the Orphanage business, he gave me to understand that by lifting a finger of encouragement the Trustees of the Free School would be thankful if we could undertake its management in these new superior quarters. However, I lifted no finger of encouragement, and these overtures from the bishop came quite separately and unexpectedly..."

Unfortunately there is a page missing from this manuscript letter, but the narrative resumed on a philosophical note: "I think however, though I shall not see it, that Kidderpore House and Park may turn up again. One door shuts and another opens in India as elsewhere... I think that the bishop will be prepared for a negative answer... I warned both him and Colonel Harrison that there could not be a more unfavourable time or year than the present for proposing any extensions of work." Indeed this may not have been the most favourable time or year, but it was not the end of the story. In a letter to Mother Evelyn dated September 24th 1915, it is clear that Sr Jane Frances was beginning to warm to the idea, and had even visited the school. It is also clear that her reluctance stemmed partly from the knowledge that her time in India was drawing to a close. "I have not been giving [Kidderpore House] much thought as it did not seem to me likely to take any practical shape in my day," she wrote. After explaining that both the bishop and Colonel Harrison were absent from Calcutta the Sister continued: "The person who is most in touch with [Colonel Harrison] through educational matters is Sr Beatrice Mary, as she has the gift of reticence. I took her with me when I went to see the house under the guidance of Colonel Harrison." Clearly her enthusiasm was growing as she continued to write: "During the course of this next week I shall gather up whatever further information I can. All old Indian Sisters now in England will bear the look and situation of

Kidderpore House well, and Sr Margaret could give you any amount of information about the Free School. I suppose the children would in class be considered somewhat below the Pratt School. In early days all our most respectable nurses had been educated there. They went there for a good plain middle school education, i.e. to 7th Standard, and there was an excellent European matron who brought up the girls very well. Though called the Free School and an endowed charity school, I think there are grades as to payment." Then she closed on a personal note: "I ought to have gone, and meant to have gone, to Darjeeling in September, but am so tied this year. I have to end this disjointed letter, heavy rain and early darkness has stopped me. We are all well in Calcutta just now, D.G."

Sr Jane Frances had enclosed the bishop's letter with her own to Mother Evelyn on August 5th, but it had not been returned and this became increasingly inconvenient. So on October 14th 1915 she wrote to Mother Evelyn once more. "I shall be very glad when you are able to return the Bishop of Calcutta's letter, for without having it to refer to I cannot feel sure how much he said, and how much he left out as to particulars (or conditions) of the proposed offer, for I remember he ended up by saying that till he knew whether the matter would be even seriously considered by the authorities at Clewer, it was not worthwhile going into many details. I posted it to you the first mail out in August... I am trying to get in touch with and gather some particulars, from one or two of the officials connected with the Free School... By what I have heard it seems likely that the move to Kidderpore House will not come off nearly as soon as had been first planned, so that as long as the School remains in its present premises no important changes would take place. The two things hang together - the transfer of the School to Kidderpore House and change of management."

Referring to the Community custom of writing to all Sisters at outlying Branch Houses with reference to Chapter business,[11] Sr Jane Frances continued: "I think you will find abundant leisure to call any member of Chapter, and what is of more importance, to weigh all the various points of view, which according to my way of thinking would be an immense gain." But clearly Sr Jane Frances was still very sceptical about taking on this large extra work at a time when communication with England was becoming increasingly difficult. So she concluded cautiously: "When I agreed, as indeed I could not well do otherwise, to send on the bishop's letter to you (at first he spoke as if he were going to write directly), I told him... that I could not imagine any year or time so unpropitious for thinking of fresh undertakings on our part, and shall be deeply thankful myself if the matter could be shelved for the present."

Four days later on St Luke's Day, Sr Jane Frances wrote to Mother Evelyn once more. She wrote of two "official interviews," but the last part of the letter is missing, and so the details of the second interview are unavailable. The first had been with the Revd H. O. Penley, Honorary

Secretary to the Free School who also served as Chaplain, and who had recently been appointed to St Thomas' Church, Kidderpore. Fortunately for him, Sr Jane Frances considered him to be: "a nice sort of man, [and] something of a personality." Being a considerable personality herself the Sister appreciated similar people, and remarked that Mr Penley was quite unlike the: "very mediocre government Chaplains that fill up Calcutta charges [i.e. parishes] at present." It seems as though Sr Jane Frances had laid down the ground rules for both interviews at the very beginning: "The line I took [was that] if [we were] pressed or even expected to take up the charge very soon the subject might be considered *closed*. I knew it to be impossible, and from my side should do nothing to farther it. But if they could make some temporary arrangement (i.e. till the cold weather of 1916), I gathered you would be at least willing to give the whole matter careful consideration, but meanwhile wished for some more information." And now the matter of the bishop's letter came up again: "I had none to give beyond the bishop's letter which was still in your hands at Clewer and proposed not to go into details at the present stage."

As a result of the interview with Mr Penley, Sr Jane Frances had ascertained more about the proposals for running the school - and she was not pleased with them. Moves were afoot to permanently secure the services of two Eurasian school mistresses who were at present sharing the running of the junior department between them. While Sr Jane Frances always respected and affirmed Indian people, she seems to have been staunchly opposed to these two Eurasian women. Perhaps it was because of their mixed race (Indians also shared reservations about Eurasians), or maybe it was simply an objection to working *under* anyone else. Whatever the reason, her objection rang forth loud and clear: "I pointed out that we could not take up charge of the junior part in any way subordinate to these Eurasian mistresses who are no doubt *not at all* suitable for a responsible charge, but was assured that *nothing* was further from the minds of the governors... I feel more strongly that a year's delay would be a gain all round." Then there is an insight into Sr Jane Frances ' relationship with the bishop: "I would very strongly urge you to write just a note at least, to the bishop. We would commit you to *nothing* at present. If I were on the same friendly terms as I was with Bishop Johnson first of all, and later with Bishop Copleston, it would really not matter so much. As things are, it would strengthen my hands, whichever way it all works out..." [the rest of the letter is missing].

Communications with England were becoming increasingly difficult because of the number of ships (many of them carrying mail), which were wrecked by U-boats. So on November 11th 1915 Sr Jane Frances was still pleading for the return of the bishop's letter: "I must ask for an interview with the bishop... as soon as I can. I still hope that perhaps by next mail I may have his letter returned to me, as I must start from that basis. I would now copy it myself without delay and return to you either a copy or an original.[12] I cannot reckon whether by this time you have received mine in which I gave a full account of all that I gathered from Mr Penley… I would ask you *not* to pay much attention to Mr Parker. We all know him and that he is a talker and busybody and carries little weight, only I believe he will at least for the present, have Kidderpore church which the children would attend. I make little doubt that the governing body would be ready to wait a year, but *not* without some definite promise being given that eventually we would take the work."

Clearly Sr Jane Frances was feeling pressurised by Mother Evelyn who had drawn a parallel between the beginnings of the Sisters' work at the Darjeeling school and the present situation (see note 7). But Sr Jane Frances insisted that Kidderpore was quite different: "Chapter had first unanimously, or nearly so, accepted the [Darjeeling] offer… Many of the circumstances in this case are quite different. I should certainly in 1916 have no one ready… I could not undertake now to shove off a new venture this next year, and think that if there is to be an interim the governing body had better be asked to find their own lady-in-charge… But connected with that there are questions which I must lay before the mission. I feel this is not a matter to be *rushed*. A good deal needs thinking over and adjusting and understanding." Also, the difficulty of all Indian business having to pass through the Clewer Chapter, possibly involving two meetings because of the necessity of consulting Sisters in outlying Branches, was a major obstacle. "Ten or twelve years ago," wrote Sr Jane Frances by way of concluding, "two Chapters were not necessary for the acceptance of a work, but I believe that whatever passed the first would pass the second, only of course [now] it is a longer process."

On December 11th 1915, Sr Jane Frances at last had her interview with the bishop, and on the 15th she wrote to Mother Evelyn. "One matter is quite settled," she began. "The Governor's do *not* expect us to take up any charge for another year even should the work be accepted by the Community sooner." That must have been a great relief, and had been the chief stumbling block. The other problem relating to the Eurasians also seemed to have been resolved: "Meanwhile the two rather "low grade" Eurasian sisters, the Misses de Cruze have resigned, and the Governors have engaged a much superior, trained English woman who was in Calcutta in some special educational employment for a year." She was a Miss Fautell whom the Sister described as, "a good Churchwoman." Her brother had been in the Indian Civil Service - the Resident[13)] in the diocese of Lahore, and had resigned in order to be ordained. All seemed well.

On December 31st 1915 the Bishop of Calcutta wrote to Mother Evelyn expressing his pleasure that the Community hoped to take up Kidderpore House; she had written to him on November 25th. "I have every reason to hope that [the governors] will send you a formal offer and cordial invitation." However, this letter was followed by a quite different one dated January 14th 1916. The bishop had just seen the official letter which the governors were sending to Clewer, and he was clearly alarmed. The mail was about to be collected for dispatch to England, but the bishop managed to quickly write a letter to Mother Evelyn. "Only a very few minutes are available to me for writing by this mail, but I am anxious to send a word as I am rather afraid that your Community may be put off by the terms... The proposals of the Governors are a good deal less cordial than I should have hoped..."

Apparently some of the governors objected to the dismissal of the Eurasian school mistresses and wished to retain the right of appointment of staff. There was also an anti-Sisterhood faction. The bishop explained: "Two or three of the Governors are country born and bred, they belong to the community from which the present mistresses are drawn (i.e. Eurasian), and I believe, they do not in their hearts like the idea of these being displaced, and perhaps would not be sorry if negotiations with you fell through. Several of the other Governors are elderly laymen of a more or less conservative frame of mind, who are less keen on the change than I should like... But the Archdeacon, who carries a good deal of weight on the Board and has for long been a warm supporter of your Community's work here, and the Honorary Secretary [Mr Penley], most heartily desire your help, and as you know, I do myself. You may rely on wholehearted backing from all of us..." The bishop was clearly anxious that Mother Evelyn should not discontinue negotiations: "I sincerely hope you will not simply break off negotiations, but write and explain if possible trying to suggest some path that may not be too difficult for the Governors to accept."

The terms offered to the Sisters by the governors in a letter from Mr Penley, dated January 13th 1916 were as follows:

"1. The Governors are prepared to pay the outward passage of 2 Sisters, and also to provide a passage home and back for each of the Sisters employed when they proceed for their usual furlough;
2. The Governors will provide free board and quarters for the Sisters working at Kidderpore House;
3. The Governors will be glad to know if there are any further expenses which they will be asked to meet;
4. The Governors understand that the Sister-in-charge will be directly responsible to them in all matters connected with the working and management of the school;
5. The Governors will retain in their hands the appointment and dismissal of the teaching staff;
6. The Governors propose that any arrangement arrived at may be terminated by either side at not less than 1 year's notice."

Having warned Mother Evelyn about the governors' terms, the bishop now hastened to visit Sr Jane Frances, during which he shared the contents of his letter to Clewer. She clearly appreciated his visit and wrote to Mother

Evelyn about it. "The *hitch* with certain members of the Governing body has rather taken him by surprise," she wrote on January 18th 1916, "though I know and had been warned that there was a section who were against the charge being offered to our Community. I did not imagine, and do not think now that their opposition would carry any lasting weight. They represent quite a lower stratum of society, [and] also have all along been the upholders of the outgoing Eurasian mistresses..." Regarding clause number 5, she wrote that: "all school Sisters out here would, I am sure, be strongly opposed to such an arrangement, and it was quite against the mind of the bishop, archdeacon and Mr Penley." She continued: "I felt that there would be a good deal to adjust if we took up the *internal management* of such an old institution which has a history and traditions of its own of 150 years nearly. As to the title deeds and holding of property, these questions do not touch us. Out here we are *occupiers* not owners of anything, anywhere that we work, but we must have our hands free as to internal management. I do not doubt that with the leading clergy at our backs, that if we *politely but firmly* refuse to undertake the charge on a different footing to what we work at the Pratt School or Darjeeling High School, that Mr McGluskey and his party will climb down."

Meanwhile Mother Evelyn received the letter from Mr Penley (and presumably the bishop's too), and she replied to the former on February 17th 1916. Taking each clause in turn, all was acceptable until clause 5: "I am afraid it would not be possible for us to accept the conditions mentioned in this clause; judging from all our past experience of educational work, I am quite sure it would be impossible to work the school smoothly and satisfactorily if the Sister-in-charge were not free to engage and dismiss the teaching staff. Therefore I fear I must ask at once that we may have the same freedom in this important matter at Kidderpore House as we have always had in all the schools placed under our care in England, Calcutta and Darjeeling." She concluded on a conciliatory note by saying what, "very real interest" the work would be to the Community and how greatly they would value it.

Mr Penley replied on behalf of the governors on March 24th 1916. They had met and clearly wished to accommodate the Sisters' terms within the framework of the European Schools Code which laid down certain regulations for aided schools. Thus a compromise resolution was passed and presented to Clewer as follows: "That the selection, appointment and dismissal of the teaching staff shall rest with the Sister-in-charge subject to the confirmation of the Governors, and that the Honorary Secretary be instructed to write to the Mother Superior of the Clewer Community that the Governors have no intention of interfering with the teaching arrangements at Kidderpore House, but that they cannot legally divest themselves of the power of dismissal under the European Schools Code, and therefore would retain power on appeal to determine the conditions of any such dismissal."

Mother Evelyn replied on April 27th 1916: "as the Governors of the Free School have so generously reconsidered the conditions mentioned in clause 5... I am now quite willing to bring the whole matter before the Sisters for their careful consideration. Owing to the size of our Community and its very widespread houses I am afraid it will not be possible now to arrive at a *final* decision before September, but I think I can promise to *cable* to you the final result not later than September 10th." The first Chapter was held on June 3rd and five days later Mother wrote to Mr Penley indicating that the, "Community are favourably inclined" towards the work but also telling him that a resolution had been passed requesting that the Sisters, "should not be obliged to undertake the work until the cold weather of 1917." On September 7th 1916 the Chapter met once more and formally accepted the work at Kidderpore House. Mother Evelyn cabled the news to Mr Penley on September 12th. After such tortuous progress the outcome seemed satisfactory, although there are no surviving letters which record how Sr Jane Frances felt about it. The bishop wrote: "It is splendid and relieves me of a great anxiety."

In the midst of all these negotiations it might have been easy to forget that the Empire was at war. "The end of the War seems so very uncertain," wrote Mr Penley to Mother Evelyn on July 5th 1917. As already noted, the reality of the war was being experienced in perilous voyages, delayed mail, and from 1917, government restrictions on women travellers. Thus the new work had to be held over indefinitely. Writing to the Clewer Associates in September 1917 Mother Evelyn explained: "We cannot move Sisters to and from India in safety. No one who is not already on the staff may go out there. This means that the work at Kidderpore House ... must stand over till happier times."

Footnotes

1. As noted in chapter 11, Margaret Robertson was the niece of Mrs Walter Hoare, Angelina Hoare's sister-in-law. Like the rest of the family, Miss Robertson always referred to Angelina as "Aunt Ina."

2. Sr Jane Frances mentioned that Margaret Robertson kept careful records, but these did not find their way back to Clewer. Margaret Robertson died towards the end of 1922 following a "long and painful illness nobly and cheerfully borne". Her death was reported in the January 1923 issue of *Pipalpati*. She was in her early 50's.

3. Sr Sophie served twice in India - she left England on January 11th 1886 and arrived back on May 30th 1891; and she left England for her second term on November 22nd 1891 and arrived back on January 19th 1897.

4. St Barnabas Mission Room. The Clewer Community began work in the parish of St Barnabas, Pimlico in 1860 and continued there until 1933. For further details see: BONHAM, Valerie *A Joyous Service: The Clewer Sisters and their work* 1989.

5. St John Baptist Mission, Newport led to the building of St John Baptist Church. Also, under the care of the Sisters was an orphanage and a girls' high school. It was a major centre of CSJB work, and Sr Selina was the guiding influence from 1877. She died on December 16th 1916 and is commemorated in a stained glass window in St John Baptist Church.

6. Sr Georgina CSJB *Past History of St Michael's School,Darjeeling* undated typescript.

7. Sr Florence's recollections of Darjeeling differ in some details from those in Sr Georgina's school history. However, Sr Florence's story of the temporary headmistress who spirited a large number of pupils away, is substantiated by Sr Jane Frances. During the negotiations about Kidderpore House, Sr Jane Frances made the following digression in a letter to Mother Evelyn dated November 11th 1915: "You mentioned the care of the Darjeeling School. Chapter had first unanimously, or nearly so, accepted the offer, and as it was out of my power to send a Sister and to take personal charge till the next season, i.e. 12 months later, the temporary arrangements were entirely my own responsibility. Sr Florence was already *the* person chosen by me, which choice delighted the authorities, as she was quite the person for the place. So they were ready to wait for her. Our joint choice for her [1 word unreadable] was her headmistress at the Pratt, but I can't say it was wholly a success. Miss Cox, the said mistress, was rather *too* capable, had many ambitions and made use of the time to gather up a school for herself which she started in Darjeeling which we took up permanently - the Diocesan High School, and had years of worry in consequence."

8. George Alfred Lefroy.

9. Lord Curzon (Viceroy 1899-1905), did extensive research into the houses owned by Warren Hastings in Calcutta. He devoted a chapter to the subject in his major work *British Government in India*, published in 2 volumes in 1925. On page 141 he mentions Kidderpore House when referring to a well known duel involving Warren Hastings: "Hastings… still retained the greater part of his property, with more than one house on it, and it was upon a spot on this estate between Belvedere and Kidderpore House … that he fought the famous duel on 17th August 1780…"

10. BAILLIE, William *Views of Calcutta - 11.* This is shown in LOSTY, J.P. *Calcutta - City of Palaces* 1990 p.68

11. It had always been part of Community policy to allow Sisters absent from Clewer at branches to express their opinion by letter. In 1874 it was decided that if the number of letters proved sufficient to turn a decision, a second Chapter must be held. After 1886 only Choir Sisters professed five years or more, had a vote in Chapter. By the end of the century there were so many Sisters at branches that major decisions required a second Chapter.

12. "Either a copy or an original." The letter which I examined at Clewer was a MS copy.

13. The Resident - an Indian Civil Service term denoting European chiefs of districts; also the official British representative at an Indian princely court. See also, chapter 1 note 2.

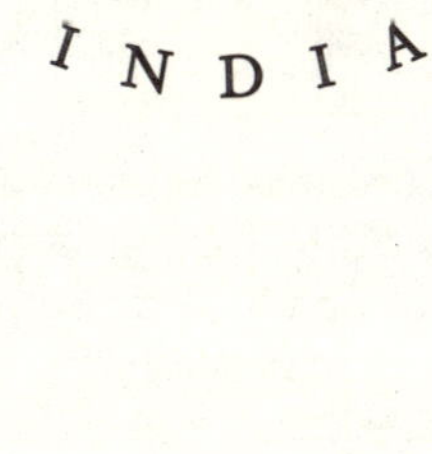

-24-
A GLIMPSE OF THE INEVITABLE

In 1916 the Bishop of Madras[1] delivered a lecture called *India and the War*, which was printed in *Pipalpati*. In some ways it was prophetic because the bishop rightly predicted the war would have far reaching effects on India: "After the war India will enter a new stage of her history. Up to this time India has never played any great part in the politics of the world. Foreign races have invaded her and strongly influenced her social, political and religious life; but India herself has not, until now, reacted upon the outside world... During the last 50 years the barrier of isolation has gradually been breaking down and India has been coming more and more into contact with the western world; but now this war has suddenly brought India right into the full stream of the world's political life... The day on which the Indian troops landed at Marseilles, therefore, was a great day for India. It marked the rise of a new relation of the peoples of India towards the nations of Europe." But the bishop was not so prophetic when predicting how the war would effect India. An Englishman himself, he was dismissive of any idea of self-government: "The British Government is now, and must be for many years to come, the only possible means for securing peace and order in the continent of India... The ideal to which many Indians look forward in the distant future is national self-government; but no sane or reasonable person could imagine for a moment that India is ripe for it for many years."

The bishop was right in predicting that the war would put India on the world map in a new way; he was right too in his assumption that Indians would look for self-government. He had glimpsed the inevitable, but like many other Englishmen he had drawn the wrong conclusions. He had not taken into account the growing force of Indian Nationalism, nor the increasing power of that small, enigmatic Hindu, Mahatma Gandhi. Nor had the bishop understood that after seeing British soldiers dying in the trenches of Flanders, stranded on the beaches at Gallipoli, and starved into submission in Mesopotamia, the Indians who had fought alongside them no longer saw them as the indestructible masters of Empire, but as mortal men with feet of clay. The mud, mustard gas and chaos of the Great War into which India had been drawn as part of the Empire, helped set the sub-continent on the road to Independence. August 1917 saw the Secretary of State for India promise the same kind of government as that given to the white dominions, a radical step indeed, but only one step on the long march away from Imperial rule.

For the time being, Britannia still ruled the waves, but even Britannia was increasingly hard pressed by U-boats as the war progressed. In 1917 a total of 1,222 British ships were sunk by mine or torpedo, of which 773 were larger passenger vessels of over 1,600 tons. A further 617 ships were unsuccessfully attacked by submarines. As 1918 dawned, the situation grew worse with 31 large vessels sunk in January and 31 unsuccessfully attacked; 49 were sunk in February and 35 unsuccessfully attacked; and 45 sunk in March with 41 unsuccessfully attacked. In the first fortnight of April, 15 large ships were sunk and 23 unsuccessfully attacked.

During the early part of 1918 special permission was given for three Sisters to sail home from India. On April 26th 1918 Sr Alexandrina, Sr Marian Edith and Sr Edith Helen arrived at Clewer after what was described in the Community *Annals* as, "an adventurous voyage." Sr Alexandrina had been invalided home and the other Sisters were sent to look after her on the voyage. The account in the *Annals* continued: "They were torpedoed in the Mediterranean and spent about two hours in open boats on a rough sea. They were picked up by a British sloop-of-war and landed at Bizerta where they remained for four days. They were then taken on board a French mail boat carrying troops and were safely landed at Marseilles after a very uncomfortable voyage. From there they travelled to Paris and so on to Le Havre and Southampton." The April 1918 issue of the *Associates' Newsletter* gives a little more detail. "Along the banks of the Suez Canal they saw many traces of recent fighting in Egypt, deserted trenches and dugouts, and in one place a camp of considerable size... Port Said was reached on Easter morning. After waiting four days [there] the steamer joined a large convoy of vessels bound for England protected by several destroyers and sloops. All went well during the first six days, then at 7 a.m. on a date I am not allowed to mention, the ship was struck by a torpedo. Mercifully no one was seriously injured, the bomb having passed through the bows exploding on the other side. Fearing another attack the Captain immediately transferred all the passengers to the boats." The sloop which rescued them took them to Bizerta in Tunisia (the site of Carthage), and four days later the mail boat from Tunis took them safely to Marseilles. The Sisters do not seem to have suffered any long term ill effects from their ordeal, and despite being invalided home, Sr Alexandrina lived until 1938.[2] The manuscript list of Sisters serving in India, which was kept at Clewer by the Sister Secretary, records that the Sisters were travelling on board the *Warwickshire* which belonged to the Biby Line, and that it was struck by the torpedo on April 10th.

Despite such dramatic inconveniences the Sisters' work in India went on in its daily routine. By April 1918 the roll of the Diocesan Collegiate School had increased by 50 to 220, and the Sister-in-charge reported that they had to rely on a number of absentees each day as there were insufficient desks! By this time the Diocesan College numbered 76 which was stretching the capacity to the limit. Four students had taken their B.A., all of whom had passed; eight out of nine had passed the Intermediate Arts; five had gained University scholarships; seven had taken the teacher training examination and had passed, and several of them were already headmistresses of village schools. The Lower School was also full and the girls were doing well with 100 boarders, 29 of whom were free cases. The Milman Memorial School for high caste Hindu girls had a roll of 240, and the pupils had been very successful in the annual examinations.

As well as running the village schools in the rice country, Miss Margaret Robertson had also founded a Hindu day school for poor girls in Calcutta. Upon her retirement this school had passed to the Clewer Sisters and it proved to be a struggle to maintain it. At the beginning of 1918 it was holding its own, and the Sisters hoped that after the war they would be able to put it on a firmer footing. However, further problems regarding the lease forced the closure of the school in December 1918 and the transference of the pupils to the Milman School nearby.

The European Orphanage just off the Lower Circular Road, was still in the Sisters' care at this time, and was still catering, as the name suggests, for children of Europeans, but also children of mixed race. By 1918 there were about 50 orphans and the Committee had plans to increase the number to take in children whose fathers had been killed in the war. Since 1893 the children had been educated across the road at the Pratt Memorial School; under eights were educated in the orphanage kindergarten. The older girls stayed at the Pratt School until reaching 16, after which they proceeded to the orphanage workroom where all the clothing was made, as well as taking external sewing and embroidery commissions. At 18 the girls would leave for employment as nursery governesses, children's nurses, or employment in shops and offices.

1918, the year of the Armistice, saw the decoration of Sr Mary Victoria with the Kaiser-i-Hind medal for services to India, in the King's birthday honours. Sr Mary Victoria had been Sister-in-charge of the Diocesan College for many years[3], but ill health was soon to force her back to England. She was the second Clewer Sister to receive this award, Sr Jane Frances having been similarly rewarded on two occasions.

But it was not all honours. In November 1918 the Sisters were shocked when Sr Dorothea suddenly left the Community, leaving a note for Sr Jane Frances saying she was going to visit relatives up country. Family concerns had weighed heavily upon her and she felt unable to remain with the Community, a timely reminder perhaps that the trials of war and climate were not the only pressures on the Sisters. Even so, it must have proved to be an added burden for Sr Jane Frances to carry in these last months before she resigned as Sister Superior.

As November 1918 dawned, the India Office gave notice to the Community that three Sisters would be able to travel by the Mediterranean route within fourteen days. In reality, plans took slightly longer, but on December 4th Sr Margaret, Sr Constance Ruth and Sr Ursula sailed for India on board the P.& O ship *Nagoya,* and arrived on January 2nd 1919. Soon afterwards, on January 6th 1919, Sr Georgina and Sr Margaret Monica sailed on board the *City of Marseilles*, and on January 30th, Sr Helen Kathleen, Sr Frances Clare, and Sr Katharine Hope sailed on board the *City of Cairo*. Sr Georgina and Sr Katharine Hope had been stranded in England after that fateful voyage home in December 1916 during which they had been shipwrecked. Their return voyage to India was described as, "safe but rather unpleasant."

Sr Margaret's arrival on January 2nd 1919 signalled the start of a new era, because she was to be the new Sister Superior in succession to Sr Jane Frances who was returning to England after nearly 30 years. So it was that Sr Margaret rather than Sr Jane Frances, on behalf of the Community, took over the charge of Kidderpore House on January 30th 1919, the new influx of Sisters having enabled this at last. Sr Jane Frances stayed on for several months as it was some years since Sr Margaret had worked in India. Clothed in 1885 and professed in June 1887, Sr Margaret became Novice Mistress at Clewer in 1889. She had served in India twice before - from 1894 until 1900, and returning at the end of 1900 until 1905. Sr Margaret was to remain Superior of the Indian work until 1931, and after living to a great age, died in 1954.

Surprisingly little was written in the Clewer *Associates' Newsletter* about the departure of Sr Jane Frances. But the *Calcutta Diocesan Record* paid fitting tribute in its October 1919 issue: "On June 2nd there sailed from Calcutta one who had given long and devoted service to India... Sr Jane Frances had been Mother Superior of the Community for two periods of office before she came to India, and for nearly 30 years she presided over and guided the numerous works to which the Community has set their hands in this country. She watched these works grow and increase... The burden of increasing years was unable to daunt her, and she continued to pay her visits to the villages almost to the end. She had learnt Bengali and Sunday by Sunday conducted a Bible class in that language. During her latter years in India she had to struggle against attacks of bronchitis and asthma, but however bad her night had been she was anxious to tackle the work of the day. Such a life as hers, with its special devotion to the Bengali people, is a witness to the enduring vitality of our Church... She has left an example which will long endure in Bengal of consecrated womanhood, endowed with fine natural gifts and a position [in] a great and famous family all surrendered to the service of Our Lord. Government twice decorated her during her long career and she received the decorations as a recognition of the services of her Community. The gratitude of the Diocese will be with her in the evening of her life, and many will be the good wishes of her friends in India, that something of her strength and health may be restored."

Similar tribute was paid in the first *Pipalpati* magazine of 1919, but a more realistic portrayal was rendered by Sr Olive at the time of Sr Jane Frances' death in 1924: "I can only speak of what I know of the last years (1915-19), when to have been associated with Sr Jane Frances in the rice country work, has been one of my greatest privileges. She had a wonderful love for the Indians, especially the poor, and used often to say, 'My *friends* are the Indian poor; that is where my heart is.' Her attitude towards them, even the very poorest, was never one of superiority or patronage, but always of unfailing, dignified courtesy, real love, - and they all knew it, - but not a trace of familiarity… She had a great respect for personality, and one day I said to her, 'There is a woman waiting to speak to you, Sister." She turned on me almost fiercely and said, 'A *woman* indeed! She is a human being, a *person*. A *person* is waiting to speak to me.' The people loved her and liked to look at her fine face. 'You must never mind being stared at,' she said to me once. 'It gives them pleasure.' On one occasion I heard some women say to each other, 'It is good to look at her face. She loves God so much.'"

Sr Olive's account continued: "The Village School Prize givings in the simple mud sheds were dignified and stately proceedings… No detail was too small for her attention, and she would give generously of her time and sympathy to every tale of woe, even a child's. She had an intimate and wide knowledge of all the Rice Country families with whom she had ever come in contact… and often acted as a mediator in family quarrels… In her work in the schools she laid stress on the evangelistic and missionary side of the work, and left the scholastic side mainly to her second worker. In the diaries(4) that she kept of all the Rice Country expeditions, detailed mention is made of the children's progress in Catechism [etc], and general mention only of progress in the three Rs. There were long uninterrupted talks in the boat when she used to tell of the early history of the Mission… and of Miss Angelina Hoare of whom she used to speak with great affection… She loved the freedom and lack of conventionality(5) in the Rice Country; we always used tin mugs and plates and she would rather scorn such amenities as a clean cloth for the table or a plate for the loaf. She enjoyed the rough unhusked rice and the peoples' cooking of various curries for her. A fish's head was generally procured as a special luxury, and the old boat-man-cook Shahadeb, would stand over her pointing out the special delicacies he had put on her plate. Not that she cared in the least what she ate, but 'food' is one of the paths to the heart of a Bengali."

Recalling those expeditions Sr Olive ruefully remarked: "We got up by the sun, had our mid-day meal when the morning's work was done, went to bed when it was dark, always saying Compline together by the light of a small hurricane lamp. One day in the boat when I was a novice at the work I rashly said, 'Shall we have tea at four?' 'We don't go by *watches* in the Rice Country,' was the characteristic remark. 'We shall have tea before we get to the next place," which left me as wise as before. Her quiet time after *chota hazri* [breakfast] was never omitted. 'Tell them we are going to do *jog*,' [meditation] she would say. She was seldom irritated or annoyed by mishaps, but always saw the humorous side of things. I remember her laughing heartily one day when we (she at 76!), were squeezed into a tiny and very narrow boat, on which we sat on some straw at the bottom, and had a sleigh ride over the slippery mud for about a mile, drawn by ropes by our faithful boatmen, Abraham and Jacob."

"The last two years during which she went down to the country, she was stiff and almost crippled at times with rheumatism, but her physical efforts were heroic. It would take her almost five minutes to get out of the boat, first kneeling on the boat bottom, and then being gradually helped out by the boatman and others on the bank. She had a wonderful knowledge of Bengali, learnt late in life. She had read several classics of the language, and she spoke fluently the colloquial speech of the poor people."

And so Sr Jane Frances came home to England, though home for her most truly was India. She sailed aboard the *S.S. Thongwa* on June 2nd 1919 accompanied by Sr Celia, and arrived in England on July 3rd 1919. The wrench must have been considerable, but she left behind a thriving work and hearts which loved her. The last years had been difficult owing to the war and increasing infirmity. Times were changing: the old Victorian and Edwardian world - her world - had died defending King and Empire. Everything stood on the brink of change, because the new political and social order which emerged from the battlefields of the Great War and the negotiations at Versailles, bore within it not only the seeds of an even more destructive war, but also the end of Empire. Inevitably the Sisters, who had come to India at the invitation of the British Raj, would be profoundly affected by this.

But these glimpses of the inevitable demise of the Empire were still relatively fleeting. The Sisters were preoccupied with the daily struggle to run all their works against what sometimes seemed to be insurmountable odds. And indeed it *was* a struggle, for just as one school overcame its problems and all seemed set fair for success, so another crisis would develop elsewhere. The dawn of a new decade brought a new crisis in the diocesan mission compound, which was reported to members of the St John Baptist Calcutta Mission Association at its annual meeting, an account of which appears in the Clewer *Associates' Newsletter* of July 1920. "The Diocesan Mission House which formed part of the property purchased by Miss Hoare in 1881 is an old house and now very much out of repair. We are obliged to face the alternative of either rebuilding it or incurring a large outlay on very extensive repairs... The house was carefully examined in June 1919, and the surveyors then reported that the roof beams and woodwork of doors and windows were in a very bad state. Their initial estimate for immediate necessary repairs was 13,000 rupees with a recurring expenditure of about 8,000 rupees every five years during a period of 20 years, the estimated limit of time that the house could be expected to last. Since [then] there has been another rainy season which will have increased the damaged condition, judging by our experience last year of leaks and falling plaster! We do not welcome the prospect... to say nothing of a possible shock of earthquake as has been experienced before. The alternative to extensive and very expensive repairs is to rebuild, and we have had plans and estimates drawn up for a new mission house which contain as at present, dormitories, workrooms for a mission boarding school for poor Christian girls, and better accommodation for the staff. It would at the same time give more accommodation for the Sisters and enable the Community to establish its centre at the Diocesan Mission."

There was another aspect which also needed attention: "We must also enlarge the Collegiate School building which at present is very overcrowded. Classes have to be held on the verandahs, which is bad for their work and contrary to government regulations. We hope eventually to obtain a new chapel for the use of the Sisters and all the schools in the compound... The plans for this part of the work have not yet been drawn up. The estimates for the Mission House amount to 110,000 rupees (£11,000). Towards this we have applied for a grant from government... The serious condition of the present house makes immediate action urgently necessary..."

The meeting was also addressed by Fr Hubback of the Oxford Mission which was closely associated with the Sisters[6]. He described the work of the Vernacular School (formerly called the Lower School), the Collegiate School and the Diocesan College, and then went on to add his own plea for the rebuilding: "I know how difficult financial matters are at home just now; but as I visit churches up and down the country I cannot help thinking that though it is good to adorn them with costly offerings for the altars and with memorials to our heroic dead, yet that the higher form of worship and devotion is to bring souls to Christ. Souls brought to his feet are of infinitely greater worth than jewels on the chalice or the glories of stained glass or costly vestments. How splendid it would be if, within the next year or two, the Sisters' project... could be carried out as a thank offering for our deliverance from the awful peril of invasion, and as a continual and abiding memorial of those who have died in and for the faith."

The Bishop of Calcutta[7] was visiting England, and he firmly endorsed the Sisters' appeal, and addressed a special meeting of the Association held at Lady Cable's house in Grosvenor Square in July 1920. He strongly advised against repairing the old buildings and favoured rebuilding: "I think it is not a business proposition to contemplate spending money in that way, and then after a time having to scrap what you have been trying to save and start building up a new place entirely. It seems to me that the right, business-like way is to build now,... and then you will get a good building suitable for the purpose you want, and one in which you are not ashamed for the Sisters to live... If you spend £11,000 in keeping that place in repair, at the end of 20 years you will have to scrap it..."

The bishop was unequivocal in his recommendation for rebuilding and also in his support for the Sisters: "The Sisters are working hard to secure the money necessary, and I am sure that you will do your very best to help them because you know something of what their work is here in England, and I can only say that their work in India is not one whit behind the work here, either in devotion or efficiency... One of the Oxford Mission Brothers said lately that he believed the most potent Christian influence in India today was the example and pattern of the Religious Life and I, who am not a Religious, absolutely endorse the truth of that..."

The Sisters endeavoured by all possible means to raise funds for the rebuilding, and many friends and Associates both in England and Calcutta organised sales of work. The Bishop of Calcutta gave a generous donation of 1,200 rupees, the Anglo Catholic Congress movement gave £500, and the Community at Clewer gave £1,000. By the early part of 1921 the situation began to look encouraging, but then there came a major setback. In May the Sisters heard that the new Indian government was unable to give any large building grants for two or three years, but were prepared to consider a rebuilding grant. Thus the Sisters reluctantly decided to accept it because the building was getting more dangerous. The funds collected were used for some extension work, as they were specifically earmarked for building and not for repairs. This renovation work was completed by the summer of 1922 and cost 17,000 rupees. The rebuilding fund was used for a new refectory for the Sisters and a visitor's room, with two bedrooms above and wide verandahs on both floors. This was blessed by the Bishop of Calcutta on November 8th 1922.

By the early 1920s there were 23 Sisters in India, and while it is normally difficult to keep track of who was working where, the April 1921 issue of *Pipalpati* provides a list:

Sr Margaret - Sister Superior of all the Indian work:

Diocesan Mission Boarding School (Vernacular school) - Sr Olive (in charge), Sr Celia (in charge of Work Room), Sr Frances Clare (Village schools):

Diocesan College - Sr Mary Victoria (in charge) March 1921;

Diocesan Collegiate School - Sr Georgina, Sr Edith Alice;

Presidency General Hospital - Sr Constance Ruth (in charge), Sr Blanche Annie, Sr Edith Emily[8], Sr Mary Evelyn, Sr Norah, Sr Helen Kathleen, Sr Ursula, Sr Isabel Jean;

Pratt Memorial School - Sr Beatrice Mary (in charge), Sr Katharine Hope;

European Orphanage - Sr Mary Frances (in charge);

Kidderpore House - Sr Margaret Monica (in charge), Sr Kathleen Prisca (in charge of school);

Eden Sanatorium, Darjeeling - Sr Mabel Theresa (in charge);
Diocesan Girls' High School, Darjeeling - Sr Mary Editha (in charge), Sr Helen Muriel.

In April 1919 the integrity of the Raj became indelibly stained by an act of aggression by the British which Indians would never forget: the massacre at Amritsar. Gandhi had led a nationwide protest about British rule by means of a one day hartal, or strike. In the Punjab, rioting had broken out in several places, and contrary to Gandhi's ideas on non-violence, five Englishmen had been killed and an English woman missionary assaulted in the capital, Amritsar. Public assemblies were forbidden, but in spite of this, several hundred people gathered in the Jallianwala Bagh for a political rally. The Punjab was a particularly sensitive area because it had lost a large number of men in the Great War. Also it was both a Sikh and Muslim area, and there was concern amongst Muslims about the future of Islam following the downfall of the Ottoman Empire after the war. This concern led to a growing polarisation of Muslims within India, and to the consequent demand for partition which resulted in the emergence of Pakistan. But all this lay in the future, and on that fateful April day, as a speaker harangued the crowd in the Jallianwala Bagh in the shadow of the Golden Temple, the British army[9] drove through the narrow gateways and opened fire. 379 people were killed and 1,200 wounded: the relationship between Indians and British would never be the same again.

Two years later, in 1921, the Prince of Wales visited India in what was to be the last Royal visit before Independence. Perhaps inevitably, there was a different feel to this visit - the seat of government had moved from Calcutta to the vast new buildings designed by Edwin Lutyens and Howard Baker in New Delhi. Also, despite the pomp and circumstance of the Prince's reception in the Princely States, the larger cities such as Bombay and Calcutta gave him a mixed welcome, the arrangements being sorely hampered by the hartal. Nor had India forgotten Amritsar.

The Prince's main reason for visiting Calcutta was to open the Victoria Memorial. Conceived by Lord Curzon in 1902 as a fitting memorial to the late Queen-Empress, this great marble pile had taken until 1921 to complete, and was thought by some to be the Imperial answer to the Taj Mahal. Needless to say, Emerson's great white edifice on the Calcutta Maidan (which was now eclipsed by Lutyens' creation of New Delhi), fell far short of Shah Jehan's shimmering masterpiece. But there it stood, presided over by a statue of the late Queen herself, and there it remains, fulfilling its destiny as a dusty mausoleum to the Raj itself. But the opening ceremony was carried out with appropriate pomp.

The Prince of Wales' visit to Calcutta was recorded in *Pipalpati* early in 1922: "The children from all the schools, Indian and European, were given places in stands erected along the road by which H.R.H. went to the races on the 26th December and on the 28th when he went in State to open the Victoria Memorial." It was of course the school holidays and therefore fewer children were available, but a considerable effort was made to gather up as many as possible. "One of our Indian teachers who had gone to her home in the country for Christmas Day came back in time to join the procession which went from the Mission House to the Red Road on the 26th, headed by two girls carrying the Mission School banner." The day was not without disappointment: "The Prince was in ordinary dress on that day [26th], rather to the disappointment of the children who of course expected the *Rajah Sahib* not to look like other people." No doubt he considered ordinary dress to be more fitting for a day at the races! But he rose to the occasion two days later: "On the 28th they had the joy of seeing him in full military uniform with a bodyguard of soldiers, both Cavalry and Artillery, when he went in State to open the Victoria Memorial." (It was the Prince's father, later King George V, who, as Prince of Wales, had laid the foundation stone of the Victoria Memorial during his visit to Calcutta early in 1906).

The Sisters took a dim view of Gandhi's policy of non-co-operation especially regarding the Royal visit. The same issue of *Pipalpati* comments on it: "We regretted [the school holidays] all the more because the non-co-operators were doing their utmost to prevent people from going to see the Prince, and we as loyal subjects, should have been glad to take all our children to see their future King-Emperor, and to make our protest against non-co-operation. However we collected all we could of those who were in Calcutta."(10) But the hartal must have made life difficult for the Sisters, and certainly did so for their servants: "We had the experience of two hartals, the first on November 17th, the day the Prince landed in Bombay, and the second on Christmas Eve. The first was the most complete as the non-co-operators succeeded in terrorising the ghari-wallahs and shop-keepers to a great extent. Before Christmas Eve measures had been taken to withstand those who tried to interfere, and the hartal was only partially successful. Our servants were very loyal and did all their work though they were afraid to go outside the compound. Those who 'slept out' took the precaution of 'sleeping in' at least the night before, [and] in some cases for more than one night. The Pratt School cook had to bring his family with him to ensure their not being molested during his absence, as non-co-operation frequently means injuring a man's belongings while he is away. The wildest tales were circulated amongst servants to intimidate them."

The Sisters had another unexpected chance to see the Prince just before his departure: "The last sight the Sisters had of [the Prince] was at his departure for Rangoon which happened to be within an hour of the time we were expecting Sr Caroline Elizabeth and Sr Violet Grace to arrive at the same ghat from which he embarked. Some of those going to meet the Sisters went early enough to see H.R.H. depart. He received a very hearty 'send off' after a week of increasing heartiness on the part of the crowds who had recovered from their fear of the intimidators."

The original work of the Sisters - the Presidency General Hospital-continued to flourish. In addition to the vast new buildings opened in 1902, a large chapel[11] had been built by subscription and dedicated in 1916. This was situated behind the main block and was for the use of patients and staff. It had a marble altar and hanging rood and the Blessed Sacrament was reserved there for the sick. There was at this time a chaplain, regular services and a branch of the Guild of St Barnabas for the nurses. The hartal had affected the hospital as recounted by *The Times of India* on March 8th 1922: "The strike fever in Calcutta has extended to the servants of the Presidency General Hospital. These suddenly left work without giving notice. The staff has been reduced to a few faithful dressers, to the great distress of the patients. Although there have recently been increases of wages, the strikers have demanded more, but the authorities are determined to oppose their demand. St John Ambulance Missions, the Girl Guides, and Boy Scouts are carrying on the work. Colonel Walters, Inspector General of Hospitals, has appealed to the ladies of Calcutta to help, and many who have been trained in the War as nurses are coming forward willingly."

At the end of 1922 it was decided that the Community should withdraw from the Eden Sanatorium at Darjeeling. It had always been a difficult work, fraught with tension between the Community and the governing Committee. Whenever new work was undertaken by the Sisters, or their numbers were depleted, the Eden was always weighed in the balance. Sr Jane Frances would gladly have withdrawn from it on several occasions, but was dissuaded by the bishop. Now the decision was finally taken to withdraw as from Easter 1923. The existing records do not state a precise reason except that there had been a change in the management, so perhaps the Sisters had felt their position to be untenable. Also, the Community had sustained an unexpected loss in Sr Mary Editha who had been invalided home in November 1921. She had been Sister-in-charge of the Diocesan Girls' High School in Darjeeling and the high altitude aggravated a heart condition so that it was necessary for her to return to England. The loss of a Sister from so important a work as the High School might well have tipped the scales in favour of a withdrawal from the Eden. Whatever the reason, the Community adhered to their decision.

One door closes and another opens. During 1919 five of the village schools had been closed partly through lack of funds and partly because they were unsatisfactory. In one of these villages (Madhobpur), the villagers themselves took charge of the school, and it was hoped that the other four would be reopened. In fact they had all been reopened by the early part of 1921, and one had moved to better premises. But the village schools had what the Sisters called, "an up and down existence," and frequently closed and reopened according to the availability of teachers.

For a long time the Sisters had felt the need for some sort of base in the rice country from which they could visit the village schools quickly and easily. Sr Jane Frances and Margaret Robertson had thought nothing of the inconvenience involved in the rice country expeditions, but the Sisters who followed them in this work were sorely tried by the time it took travelling from one place to another. So the offer in late 1922 of a mission house and church belonging to the Society for the Propagation of the Gospel came like an answer to prayer. It was situated at Baruipur 17 miles from Calcutta towards Diamond Harbour, within easy reach of several of the schools. The Sisters would have the use of the mission house, and it was hoped that in due course two Sisters would be able to open a girls' boarding school. The S.P.G. would continue to run the boys' boarding school on the other side of the church, so they would maintain a presence.

This was an exciting offer, and the Sisters were very keen to take up the challenge, but it was difficult to summon up the same enthusiasm in England. This was partly because post-war deprivation was affecting all strata of society including those who had once generously supported the Sisters' work; and partly because the Sisters' supporters were getting elderly and were dying, and there were fewer, younger Associates to replace them. Also, the initial glamour of work in India had worn off - the Sisters who had worked there (with a few exceptions), fell in love with it, but after the Great War independence was in the air. People began to realise it was just a matter of time before the ending of British rule, and this affected peoples' perceptions of the Indian work. Perhaps the English Associates felt unwilling to financially support something which the Sisters would eventually leave behind. "We never know when we may have to withdraw from our work, and when we do so it may be without regret or anxiety if we know that there are those amongst the [Indian] people who will keep it up."(12) These words were spoken by Fr Manley of the Oxford Mission to a group of English Clewer Associates in 1922 regarding the future of the Sisters' work, and it sums up the changed attitude of both the Clewer Sisters and the Oxford Mission Brotherhood. They knew independence would mean their own withdrawal and were keen to establish something which would continue after their departure. But the lack of enthusiasm, and therefore of English funding, meant that the work at Baruipur did not get fully under way until 1928.

A number of deaths in the early 1920s further underlined the passage of time and of the old formative era of the Indian work. Firstly, as already observed in chapter 23 (footnote 2), Margaret Robertson died in her early fifties towards the end of 1922 after a long illness. Then on April 29th 1923, the death occurred of Canon A.N. Bannerjee, priest-in-charge of St Mary's, Bhowanipore since its opening at the end of the 1880s. This was the Bengali church next to the diocesan mission compound, and therefore closely associated with the Sisters and their work. He was buried next to the church and a large congregation of both Indians and Europeans gathered for the funeral.

Finally, Sr Jane Frances died suddenly on July 6th 1924. She died and was buried at Torquay whence she had retired for her health, the Sisters having several convalescent homes there. The Community *Annals* record that: "it was a Sunday and from her bed she had listened to the singing in chapel at Mattins, joining in the hymn, *Forever with the Lord*. Then as the Sisters were saying None the summons came and there was time just to reach her room, say a psalm and the last prayer, and she was gone in entire peace to her rest." The funeral took place on July 10th with a simple Requiem, Mother Evelyn, the Warden, Sr Laura Jane, Sr Katherine Maud, and her brother-in-law being present. At Clewer there was a Sung Requiem celebrated by the Sub Warden. Nor was she forgotten in her beloved India as the Community *Annals* relate: "The morning after the cable came there was a Requiem Mass at the [Lady] Canning Home and one also at the school in Darjeeling. On the 14th there was a Solemn Requiem at St Mary's church [Bhowanipore], Fr Holmes was the celebrant, Fr Shore the deacon and Fr Chakravarti sub deacon. The crucifer, thurifer, boat boy and acolytes were all Bengali. The bishop was present in a violet cope and gave his blessing. Fr Brown, Fr Douglass and Fr Pierson sat just below the bishop. It was the first Solemn Requiem ever sung in a Bengali church in Calcutta. Sr Honor played the organ and the Sisters sitting in the two front rows were responsible for the singing."

Sr Jane Frances would have been delighted at such a splendid service with so many members of the Oxford Mission Brotherhood taking part, and with Bengali servers too. But splendid though it was, it was not all. Prayers were said for her in Calcutta Cathedral and services were held in the rice country villages. There was also a Eucharist in Bengali attended by the teachers and pupils of the College and schools in the diocesan mission compound.

And then there were the tributes. Fr Holmes of the Oxford Mission wrote that: "Sr Jane Frances was one of God's great servants to Bengal and will long be remembered in the land where she was, to use the peoples' own phrase, 'a great spreading tree under whose shade many found shelter.'" Fr Shore described her as "a great figure in the ecclesiastical world of Calcutta." Bishop Copleston (bishop 1902-13), wrote to Mother Evelyn: "Sr Jane Frances was a heroic and saintly person whom I counted it a high privilege to know as I did, not only while I was Bishop of Calcutta, but for many years before when I became acquainted with her and her noble works in Bishop Johnson's time. May your Community long enjoy the fruits of her works and her example, and still more if it be God's will, of her prayers."

But the tributes were not just from high ranking Churchmen - the most heartfelt ones came from her own beloved Bengali's. Sister Olive wrote in *Pipalpati*: "Real sorrow was shown by the Indians... and many tears were shed. The remark was made by many, 'Oh she was such a holy person! Good people always die like that.' One or two said, 'My mother! Oh my mother's gone! She loved me so!' The thought that comforted [them] was that, 'now she and Miss Hoare were together.' On Rice Country Pay-Day following the news, a larger number than usual came up to the Mission House, 32 in all, for they had been told there would be a short service in St Mary's Church 'for Boro Sister's Soul.' Fr Chakravarti took the service - some prayers, a short reading, two hymns and a Litany for the Departed. Very heartfelt were the Amens and responses. Two hymns were sung: *Jesus' Victory* [with] Bengali rhythm and tune, and one of her favourites as they all seemed to know; the second *Forever with the Lord*, a special favourite with Bengalis at their funerals, and one she had herself sung the morning of her passing."

So one of the most dearly loved of the Clewer Sisters passed to her rest, and the irony is that she was buried in Torquay(13) which must have seemed much more like a foreign field than the Sisters' cemetery plot in Calcutta. But though her frail body died in England, she left her heart with the Indian people whom she had served so faithfully and heroically for nearly 30 years.

Footnotes

1. Bishop of Madras - Henry Whitehead (bishop 1899-1922), former Superior of the Oxford Mission.

2. Sr Alexandrina was admitted in June 1880 and professed in July 1882. She succeeded Sr Emily as Sister Superior of St Stephen's College Clewer in 1905, and in 1916 went to India and was invalided home after 2 years. In 1919 she was appointed Sister-in-charge of St John's Home, Clewer (a girls' orphanage) until its closure in 1932. She retired from active work owing to failing health, and lived in the Convent at Clewer until 1937 when she went into the Sisters' Infirmary. She died on February 26th 1938.

3. Sr Mary Victoria served in India from 1900-05; late 1905-08; late 1908-14; 1915-21. She left the Community in January 1923, having been invalided home in March 1921, after which she underwent major surgery - presumably her departure was connected with this.

4. Sr Jane Frances ' diaries have not survived.

5. Sr Jane Frances ' lack of conventionality was not restricted to the rice country. The oral tradition of the Community recalls how Sr Jane Frances arrived at Calcutta Cathedral one Sunday morning having forgotten her dentures. In due course a bearer arrived with the dentures on a velvet cushion; he solemnly processed up the aisle to the front pew where the Sister was sitting, who with equal dignity, removed them from the cushion and put them in her mouth!

6. The Clewer Sisters were closely associated with the Oxford Mission Brotherhood who acted as chaplains to them. Fr Brown, Fr Douglass, Fr Shore, Fr Hubback, Fr Manley, Fr Holmes, all of whom are mentioned in this chapter, belonged to the Oxford Mission. They were engaged in educational and mission work especially amongst boys, and even shared an Annual Report with the Clewer Sisters for several years before the Great War, so complementary was the work of the two Communities.

7. Bishop of Calcutta - Foss Westcott, who had been consecrated in 1919 in place of Bishop Lefroy who had died in office.

8. Sr Edith Emily - Sr Eudora tells a story of Sr Edith Emily ascending the stairs of the Presidency General Hospital quite unaware that she was being followed by a large brown bear! Numerous hospital servants endeavoured to warn her, but she took no notice until reaching the top she found herself face to face with the large beast, which presumably was retrieved by its owner. Exactly why the bear was there is unrecorded, but its trainer may have been a patient, or may have been visiting someone else.

9. British army - the officer in charge of the ill-fated operation was Brigadier-General Reginald Dyer who subsequently resigned his commission, but the soldiers who were obliged to fire at the crowd were mostly, though not exclusively, Gurkhas.

10. This was one of the few political statements recorded by the Clewer Sisters.

11. This once beautiful chapel is now abandoned and derelict.

12. Fr Manley would be gratified to know his prophetic words are true today.

13. It was Community policy that Sisters were buried where they died rather than returning to Clewer.

C S J B

I N D I A

-25-
FIDE ET AMORE - BY FAITH AND BY LOVE

During 1924 Sr Georgina, who had been Sister-in-charge of the Diocesan Collegiate School for several years, went home on furlough. Upon her return to India, early in 1925, she was transferred to the Diocesan Girls' High School in Darjeeling in one of those periodical "re-shuffles" which was necessitated by Sisters going on furlough or being invalided home. Her place at the Diocesan Collegiate School was taken by Sr Dorothy Frances who had to combine it with charge of the Diocesan College, due to the loss of Sr Mary Victoria. After a few months as second Sister at Darjeeling, under Sr Norah, the charge of the High School passed to Sr Georgina. She was to remain in charge of the school for the next 20 years, and because of the length of her tenure of office, she is still remembered fondly by former pupils who warmly recall their schooldays.

One of these pupils, Clarice [Clare] Walton, formerly Clarice Pereira, has written of her ten years at the school which began in March 1924: "My parents led my sister Doreen and myself up the drive from the Cart Road to leave us in the school. I well remember my first sight of the school, when, on looking up I beheld this enormous building looking down on us. It was a very warm day, even though it was only March, and two senior girls comforted us and gave us drinks of water. The focal point of the school was the central tower. The senior wing, with classrooms on the ground floor, and dormitories on the two floors above, jutted out from one side of the tower, and the junior wing and kindergarten, from another. A red roof covered this stone built structure, whose sides were supported by buttresses... This huge building nestled in a mantle of greenery... This was our home from March to November."

"The school had three departments - kindergarten, junior and senior. Each department had its own dormitories, classrooms and playgrounds, and also its own staff... Half term was in July, and our holidays were geared to the church festivals. St John Baptist and St Michael's days were special. They always started with Sung Eucharist, and were followed by House matches, concerts and dances during the day and evening... The Houses were named after the high peaks in the Himalaya which we could view most days from the school - Kinchinjunga, Janu, Pandim and Everest, which could only be seen from Tiger Hill - with luck."

"In March each year, two school batches of girls travelled from Calcutta to Darjeeling. Each batch of about 90 girls, on each of two days, was placed in the charge of teachers in groups of 7 or 8. These were comfortable journeys in sleepers with bathrooms attached to each compartment[1]. The overnight journey from Calcutta took about 11 hours across the plains of Bengal to Siliguri station in the foothills of the

Himalayas... Here we alighted with hand luggage to transfer to the Toy Train [i.e. the Darjeeling Himalayan Railway]. After settling our luggage in the small compartments, we all descended, in orderly fashion, to the restaurant to be served chota hazri [breakfast]. The Toy Train really was a toy in comparison with the giant Express on which we had spent the night... The engine was coal-fired, and to help the wheels grip, the track was fed with sand by two workmen sitting on the fender. This was a journey of about 50 miles, and the little engine chugged along to climb from about 1,500' to 7,200', passing through the Terai forest by a system of zig-zag shunting, and loops and tunnels... This journey took 5 to 6 hours and was not at all comfortable as we were 6 in a compartment with hand luggage, and the engine gave off an unpleasant smoke. Arriving at Darjeeling, we had a long walk by the Cart Road to school, but at the top of the drive was dear Sr Georgina and Miss Bell, our senior mistress, awaiting us."

"We had a very full and organised day:

6.45 a.m. Rising bell. (Later for the kindergarten, who had bread and milk in bed!)
7.30 a.m. Breakfast, followed by bed-making.
8.00 a.m. Prep, followed by a short walk.
9.00 a.m. Assembly, followed by lessons.
12.30 p.m. Lunch break.
1.15 p.m. Lessons.
3.30 p.m. Tea, followed by Games and walks.
5.30 p.m. Prep.
7.00 p.m. Chapel.
7.30 p.m. Dinner.
8.00 - 9.00 p.m. Prep for seniors.
10.00 p.m. Lights out.
A full day, by any standards."

"It was Lent when we arrived in school in March and this was a comparatively quiet period. I can remember "Refreshment Sunday" when we were allowed "stores" [tuck]. Then the reverence of Good Friday, when we all moved around in plimsoles to be quiet; and then the joyousness of Easter and a posy of pansies from Sister for each of us. At Whitsun we had a short break of 2 or 3 days from lessons. St John Baptist was a special feast day. A gym display was held in the morning for Mother Superior, [i.e. the Sister Superior] who had come up from the Mission House in Calcutta. Then matches in the afternoon against the "old" girls who may have been up on holiday, then a dance in the evening just amongst ourselves, when we all wore our long party dresses. So the first part of the year passed, with exams and a half-term holiday of a whole week. Sister was strict with us, but her responsibility for so many girls was very great. She insisted that we wore uniform when out, complete with hats, gloves and umbrellas, and that we always behaved in a ladylike manner - and no visits to the Bazaar!"

"After half-term we knew we were over the "hump," and school work and activities went along on an even keel till St Michael's Day... and the Pujah holidays with another week's break, when we had lots of leisure and less pressure. Then the days seemed to drag towards November, the final exams, Speech Day, and the last days when our trunks were brought down from storage to be packed. It was a joyous feeling. Elaborate labels were designed for our trunks, and two enormous "Homeward bound" posters painted to be hung on the engine for its arrival at Calcutta on each of the two days. School was locked away for three months. I can only remember 10 years of happiness though I must have been in trouble sometimes, but over nothing important."

"[Finally] a few thoughts of our lovely chapel. We always wore short veils for services, [and] the corridor leading to Chapel had a sign which read "Silence." A large picture of the "rich young ruler" hung in the corridor - the Sisters must have been faced with the same decision(2). The exhilarating services when the whole school assembled for feast days were a source of inspiration. The singing of anthems,... the Metropolitan of India Confirming us in chapel,... 'Lord dismiss us with thy blessing,' sung at our farewell service at the end of each year."

Concluding her recollections, Clare writes warmly of the Sisters and the fellowship which existed at the school: "The work and the effect of the Sisters was something intangible - it touched each of us in a different way. The Christian upbringing was the foundation for all of us. I have so benefited from all that was instilled into me at school, and Sr Georgina was my guiding star. The Sisters who cared for and nurtured us, and the staff over ten years, were always supportive of our welfare. The girls themselves were thoughtful, well disciplined and bound together in a certain comradeship and common purpose... We of St Michael's are now scattered in all parts of the world, but the spirit lives on and is part of us."

Happy memories, which are shared by a number of former pupils. As Clare herself comments, "I must have been in trouble sometimes," but when the overall times are good, the odd spot of trouble gets absorbed. But it would have been quite a different story if the regime had been unkind in any way. Such a regime could not have produced pupils who look back with such warmth on their formative years. There was strict discipline - the discipline of a good school, but there was love too. The school motto *Fides et Amore - By Faith and by Love* was lived out daily.

Even so, the school had its share of problems as Sr Georgina related in the Clewer *Associates' Newsletter* of March 1927: "Hill schools in India differ greatly from those in the plains because of their term arrangement, and also from the fact that they are practically all for Europeans and Anglo-Indians. Our school at Darjeeling is modelled on the lines of an ordinary good boarding school in England, but we cannot work at such steady pressure, and more has to be provided to relieve the rather unnatural arrangements of institution life for so many unbroken months." Indeed school photographs taken at the time bear out the image of an English boarding school. Gone is the motley assortment of dresses shown in a photograph of 1898, and orderly rows of smiling, white shirted girls wearing school ties and gym tunics, pose for the camera in the 1920s. It could have been anywhere in England.

Sr Georgina had high standards and clearly felt that the school had some way to go in attaining a satisfactory record. "Our best sides of work are music and art. Last year 40 pupils entered and passed (5 with honours), in the Associated Board of the R.C.M. and R.A.M. in its different grades. The Ablett exam results[3] keep up the school's reputation, while the work done in the studio is always a pleasurable sight when exhibited at the prize giving..." But academically Sr Georgina was more critical: "... The bookside needs to reach a higher standard and to bring out those valuable qualities of sustained effort and mastery of difficulties." But the reasons for this were complex and lay for the most part outside her control: "This [academic] advance is handicapped by the seeming indifference of many of the parents [who are] so different from Indians whose one idea is for their children to become mentally efficient. Also, the out of school prep has to be less than in a school in England which benefits by three broken up terms, instead of having the fatigue of one long period of time. The environment of India does not make for industry. The question a prospective parent asks of one whose children are already with us is never, 'Will my child get a good education?' but, 'Will my child be happy?' Of course there must be both possibilities - only it is disappointing to be continually up against the non-realisation that education means the formation of character, and that character cannot be formed unless children put their minds and wills to that which is difficult and sometimes even distasteful."

Having previously worked at the Diocesan Collegiate School in Calcutta, which catered for Indian children, Sr Georgina was now having to make the transition to a school for English and Anglo-Indian children, hence the very marked cultural differences. And just as one of the frustrations of Indian education was that girls were withdrawn from school and married at an early age, thus curtailing their progress, so in Darjeeling Sr Georgina found the English equivalent. "Another drawback is that so many of our girls leave us at 14 and 15 years to go and finish in England. We have tried to do the spadework; another school reaps the full blossoming. What we need at present is a domestic science and shorthand/typing course so as to keep on our girls who take the Cambridge School Certificate at 16 or 17. No one wants them for other work as young as that, and in India they only grow slack if they go home to fill up two or three years of waiting to begin their lifework. But for us to strike out in such a new line would mean money, and in these days of

Indianisation [i.e. nationalism], the European Educational Office has none to offer us and we ourselves have no surplus. Some girls are advanced enough to go on to the Cambridge Higher Certificate exam, but owing to its high and difficult standard few attempt it."

It was not all work and no play of course: "We really have made progress in Games for we now have a Physical Culture mistress from England who is responsible for the drill, gymnastics and games. The children play from 8-9.00 a.m. every day which is usually a fine hour even in rainy Darjeeling." Though she was a disciplinarian, Sr Georgina was clearly fond of the children in her care: "As I write, the calendar for March [painted by one of the art pupils] has just been sent to me. The painting consists of figures in school uniform with suitcases, racquets, dolls or teddybears returning to school... They certainly are most responsive and dear, and bear the long separation from home and parents with great equanimity. It is more than worthwhile for all of us when a parent writes, 'She is so sorry not to be returning, she has been so happy.'"

The proof of the happiness lay in that so many former pupils kept in touch and visited Sr Georgina to the end of her days. Writing of her in later years, Susanne Levi, a former pupil recalled: "Sister was a very strict disciplinarian, yet we also knew her as a loyal and trusted friend who really cared for us. We knew her smile and blush of pleasure and her voice of reprimand; her warm welcome to each one of us at the beginning of term, and her almost sad embrace at the end of the year. She has followed our careers since we left and shares whole-heartedly in all our joys and sorrows..."

The school had a number of secular teachers from England, and several of these arrived in the 1920s and served for many years. In her short history of the school(4) Sr Georgina recalled some of them. Miss Leslie [Lesley?] Melrose was the kindergarten teacher from 1921 until 1945, and only had three years absence during that time. Miss Mary Bell came in 1926 and taught history, English and French, as well as being school librarian. She left after 5 years, but returned and stayed until World War II during which she retired to Simla, and ended her days in England. Mrs Ridler was Matron to the juniors aged 5-9 from 1928-46. Miss Minna Shaw was herself a former pupil and returned to teach Art at the school following her training in England. She stayed with the school until it closed. "Wherever she was there was peace," wrote Sr Georgina.

Life in Darjeeling had its drawbacks as Sr Frances Clare discovered when on a break from her work in the mission house in Calcutta. Writing in *Pipalpati* in June 1926, she described how, accompanied by another Sister, she had taken a picnic to a dak bungalow five miles from Darjeeling: "From there we had a splendid view of the Diocesan School and the Governor's House. After enjoying the contents of the picnic basket we went for a walk through the forest. Everywhere were tall trees covered with moss and lovely white orchids, while the ground was carpeted with splendid ferns and large white begonias. After gathering a lovely handful of these and enjoying the beauty of it all, we were driven from the spot by the most insignificant of creatures. You have all heard the expression, 'to stick like a leech,' but I hope you may never know what it really means. We beat a hasty retreat to the bungalow and pulled off our shoes and stockings. One of the horrible creatures was having a good feast and could only be dislodged with salt. Three were ineffectually striving to force a way through my very thick stockings, and various others were crawling on us. At last when we thought all was safe and we had sat down peacefully, I felt a pricking on the side of my face and there was another squashy creature just beginning its wicked work." The Sister stoically concluded: "We lost our desire to wander in the forest after that, but it was only one of the trifles which add to the interest of life out here!... I am sure you would have enjoyed the day as much as we did, in spite of the leeches."

The 1920s saw further improvements to the school buildings, beginning with a complete renovation during the winter break of December 1926 - March 1927. Sr Georgina's pride in the work took a severe blow when the chaplain remarked that the wiring was so bad that he only hoped the place would not burn down! Heeding his warning, the work was put in hand and indeed the old wiring was found to be dangerous. Despite all the work which had been done, the school still had severe inadequacies as Sr Georgina explained in the January 1928 *Pipalpati*: "If mistresses are called both to teach and live in a large boarding school for nine consecutive months, of which three comprise incessant rains on iron roofs, they must find their nerves frayed to the thinnest edge if they are living sandwiched in between children's rooms on every storey." Therefore an enlargement was proposed in order to free the top floor for staff use and add extra bedrooms. "If the morale of the school is to be of the best," wrote the Sister, "the environment must be of the best that is possible, both for those teaching and those being taught. We must enable our staff to keep fresh. Nothing in England is similar to these trying hill school terms in India, so it is difficult to realize their demands on body and spirit." But it was to be the next decade before anything was done to enlarge the school along these lines.

Despite these difficulties, the end of the 1920s saw the school in good form. Two events in particular marked high points - the visit of the Clewer Sub Warden, and the re-naming of the school. The Sub Warden, the Revd Kenneth McMaster spent seven weeks in India in the latter part of 1928, and had visited all the Community work there. He was present at Darjeeling for the prize giving on All Saints Day. Writing in both the *Pipalpati* and the Clewer *Associates' Newsletter* for January 1929, he noted the, "sense of energy and eagerness on every side in spite of, or perhaps because of, the trunks and boxes protruding here and there on the upper floor, and hinting at the approaching end of the nine months term..."

Alluding to the still hoped-for extension he wrote: "Extension of school premises is the order of the day. New class rooms and dormitories are greatly needed for the little children. If these can be provided, the staff will enjoy in their times of leisure and repose, a little more privacy apart from the busy hum of school life." And then there was the worship in the school chapel: "I was greatly impressed with the devotion and beauty with which the Services were rendered - the Solemn Evensong on the Eve of All Saints and the sung Mass on All Saints and All Souls Day."

When the school had been rebuilt following the landslip, the new chapel had been dedicated to St Michael. "In times of stress and anxiety, as well as in times of joy, we have been so mindful of the guardianship of the Holy Angels", wrote Sr Georgina to the Associates. So in March 1929 the name of the school was officially changed to St Michael's Diocesan Girls' High School.

The 1920s had been a time of steady development for St Michael's under its new Sister-in-charge Sr Georgina, though, as we have seen, it was not without difficulty and disappointment. It was also a time when loyalties were forged which still exist, even though the school has long since closed - a casualty of the ending of Empire. And in Calcutta too, it was a time of great change, as old work struggled for survival, some came to an end, and new work began. So now it is time to return to the plains and take a closer look at the work there between 1925 and the Sisters' Golden Jubilee in 1931.

Footnotes

1. One of the gifts which British rule unquestionably brought to India was the railway system, and the map of India is still criss-crossed with railway lines like pre-Beeching England. But the luxury which Clare Walton describes from those far off days of 1924-34 now exists only in a number of specially re-furbished trains operating for foreign tourists. Most Indian trains are slow (even the so-called Expresses), and invariably run several hours late. For further details of my own Indian railway journey see chapter 31. Clare's description of the journey on the Toy Train [the Darjeeling Himalayan Railway] still rings true in the 1990s - even the rolling stock is the same! The only difference is the lack of refreshment facilities these days.

2. "... the same decision." Clare Walton is alluding to the fact that many of the Sisters had come from wealthy families, and their decision to embrace the Religious Life had meant renouncing worldly values of wealth and society.

3. Ablett exams - these were the exams of the Royal Drawing Society.

4. Sr Georgina CSJB *Past History of S. Michael's School, Darjeeling.*

Although Sr Georgina had worked at the Diocesan Collegiate School in Calcutta, she found her niche at St Michael's School, Darjeeling, and her name was to become inseparably linked with the latter school. Altogether she served five terms in India beginning in 1911, and ending in 1946 - Sr Georgina and Sr Lilian Mary were the last two Sisters to leave India (see chapter 30).

-26-
THE NEW PEOPLE

A decade after the bloodbath of the Great War, England attempted to forget the reality of unemployment, hardship and changing social values by mounting a spectacular tribute to Imperialism. The British Empire Exhibition was meant to be the greatest show on earth - at least since the Great Exhibition of 1851. It was the last chance to ride on the high tide of Imperialism before it finally ebbed away in another war and independence for the member countries. The site for this imperial extravaganza was Wembley, still surrounded by fields, but fast succumbing to new houses for city business men who could commute to the office on the underground railway.

The exhibition opened on April 23rd 1924 on a site covering 220 acres, divided by 15 miles of streets and pathways into pavilions and palaces, with a great central stadium, and surrounded by a railway to ease the feet of weary visitors. The opening ceremony was performed by King George V whose speech was broadcast by the British Broadcasting Company. Twenty seven million people visited the exhibition which cost £10 million, much of which was provided from industry and commerce; when it finally closed in October 1925 it had made a loss of £1½ million. But those who saw the exhibition never forgot it[(1)], and whilst many marvelled at the life-sized statue of the Prince of Wales made entirely of butter, others marvelled equally at the Queen's Dolls' House created by Sir Edwin Lutyens, architect of New Delhi. If the dolls' house was on a smaller scale than the Imperial buildings of New Delhi, the Indian pavilion should have reassured sightseers about the larger than life splendours over which the British flag still flew. The pavilion itself was housed in a replica of the Taj Mahal. Then there were carpets from Samarkand, silks from Kashmir, brasswork from Benares, silver, jade and ivory carvings, and carpet weavers from Baluchistan.

At Clewer, some of the Sisters were able to hear the broadcast of the King's opening speech at Wembley, and the Community *Annals* reported that the crowd listening in central Windsor spontaneously joined in the Lord's Prayer. But for all the pomp, Wembley was entirely cosmetic - as much a replica of the real thing as the mock Taj Mahal. The reality, as the Sisters knew well enough, was hard work which did not get easier as the years passed. As the Clewer Sisters approached the fifth decade of their work in India it began to feel like an increasingly uphill journey. There were a number of reasons for this - the demise of older supporters, the falling numbers within the Community, and new work elsewhere.

The loss of old supporters is demonstrated in the Hoare family who had continued to support the work of the Sisters by means of the Weald of Kent Association, and whose older members died during the 1920s. On July 21st 1925 William Hoare, Angelina's brother, died at Benenden following a major operation in May. He had founded the Weald of Kent Association in 1883 to support his sister's work, and after her death the support had been transferred to the Clewer Community, for their work in the rice country villages. At Easter 1927 Miss Veronica Hoare, one of Angelina's great nieces, visited the Sisters in Calcutta on her way to south India, and was thrilled at all she saw: "I had no idea that Aunt Ina's work had developed into such a truly tremendous enterprise, or that so many hundreds of Indian girls were being educated all in the original compound," she wrote to her aunt, Caroline Hoare(2). Her enthusiastic report must have cheered the members of the Association very much.

But 1929 saw the deaths of both Caroline Hoare and William Hoare's widow, both of whom had striven to keep the Association going and had spent much time and money in their endeavours. The rising generation had other priorities, as the October 1929 *Pipalpati* noted sadly: "Some of us hoped that Miss M. L. Hoare would take up the reins laid down by her mother, but she has only done this long enough to organise the future conduct of the Mission support here in the Weald. It was thought that the Association should be put on a wider basis. Up to now it has been rather a family Mission..." In fact, Miss Hoare's interests took her in a quite different direction as the members were to learn at the 1930 Annual Meeting: "This year we have lost to Kenya one whom the Secretary and Treasurer will miss badly. Miss M. L. Hoare has the keenness and energy of her mother and aunt, and shows it in all she takes up. We wish her well in her new work."

The Weald of Kent Association struggled on for a few more years, but in the meantime another old friend, Mrs Earle, had died. She had been Secretary to the other fund raising body, the St John Baptist Calcutta Mission Association, and had worked tirelessly to organise the Christmas gift boxes and other financial support. Her death in January 1928 left a gap which was increasingly hard to fill. But the falling numbers of supporters reflected a general trend within the Clewer Community after the Great War. Older Associates died and new ones did not always come forward in the numbers necessary to support such a large and diverse Community(3). And the Associates were themselves increasingly affected by the post-war economic depression which handicapped their ability to support charitable causes.

Another change following the Great War was the decline in Religious vocations (4). There was no single reason for this, nor was Clewer alone in experiencing this fall in numbers, but because it had once been so flourishing, the drop seems more dramatic. At first the Clewer Chapter failed to come to terms with this trend, although in the mid 1920s it had only just begun, and there was hope of a recovery. Until this time there had never been any problem about undertaking new work - if the offer of work was refused it was because it was unsuitable in some way, but not because there were too few Sisters. In April 1923 the Community *Annals* record a visit from Fr Stanton, vicar of St Mark's church, Barbados, who expressed the hope to Mother Evelyn that one day the Community would work there.

On November 2nd 1923, Mother Evelyn and Sr Susan left for a visit to Barbados where they were guests of the bishop. Clearly Mother Evelyn saw this as a new outlet for the Community at a time when it needed a new lease of life. It was not that she had grown tired of the Indian work, but there was in England, a growing sense of the impending loss of India. If the British withdrew from India then the Sisters knew that they must also, for the new Indian government would probably not welcome their continued presence. So the inevitable became more real, and though events such as the Wembley Exhibition tried to recapture the halcyon days before 1914, no one was deceived. Wembley may have made a memorable day out, but Britain was looking ever more ardently towards the Crown colonies, of which the West Indies formed part.

The Community *Annals* for February 6th 1925 have an entry tinged with irony: "A Notice [sent to the Sisters] said a Chapter would soon be held to consider for the first time our accepting work in Barbados, as the bishop is pressing for a reply. Also the question of the formation of an Indian Province will probably be brought forward." As noted before, Sr Jane Frances had first pressed the subject of Provincial status for India soon after her arrival, and had continued to make the plea, but it had been resolutely refused. The frustrating business of all decisions relating to India having to pass through the Clewer Chapter twice, had become particularly trying during the Great War when negotiations were being held about Kidderpore House. Now just a few months after Sr Jane Frances' death, it seemed as though her great desire was about to become a reality.

But alas, these hopes were to be dashed once more. The *Annals* record that on March 20th 1925 the first Chapter for Barbados was held; and the second was held on May 16th. The work was accepted, though there were reservations at both meetings, chiefly due to the question of shortages of Sisters. Branch houses in England were being closed because Sisters were not forthcoming - how was the work to be managed? Even so, the decision was made, and the bishop sent a telegram exclaiming, "Laus Deo." Then an undated entry, possibly late May 1925 records that, "a large number of Sisters stayed on for Chapter after the Retreat. The question of an Indian Province [was] considered, but the proposal was turned down, and a cable sent to India: 'Chapter Resolution unanimous. Unadvisable at present.' " A crushing blow both for governance and for the Sisters' morale.

Even so, India was not entirely forgotten. At the end of 1924 and the early part of 1925, i.e. a few months before this decision had been made by Chapter, the Warden of Clewer, the Revd G. H. Tremenheere, accompanied by his wife, had visited the Sisters in Calcutta and was greatly impressed by everything he saw. During his stay of two months the Warden saw all the work - the Presidency General Hospital, the Diocesan College and Collegiate School, the Milman Memorial School, the Vernacular Boarding School (formerly the Lower School), the Pratt Memorial School, and Kidderpore House, as well as visiting some of the rice country schools. His visit did not coincide with term time at Darjeeling so he did not go there, but met the Darjeeling Sisters amongst the 21 who made up the Indian contingent at this time.

1926 was the Golden Jubilee year of the Pratt Memorial School, the Sisters having taken charge six years after its foundation. In 1912-13 the school had been extensively enlarged, the work being completed in 1916, but it had been handicapped by debt ever since. Educational standards were well maintained, and by the Golden Jubilee a number of the teaching staff were former pupils either of the Pratt or of the Darjeeling High School. Also, several former pupils were studying medicine or nursing, and one was house surgeon at the Lady Dufferin Hospital in Calcutta. At this time there were about 100 boarders and 180 day girls; all boarders were required to be members of the Church of England[5], a condition not insisted upon for the day girls. The school still catered largely for Europeans and Anglo-Indians, and was European in its teaching methods. A girl could begin her school life in the large kindergarten department and progress through the school, eventually taking the Cambridge senior examination, or for particularly bright pupils, the Cambridge Higher Certificate. But it was uphill work because of the problems peculiar to the Anglo-Indian community, notably a sense of not belonging either to the English or the Indian population, a problem which was further exacerbated by the prospect of Indian self government. This, coupled with low income, lack of good housing conditions, and poor career prospects for many girls' parents, made the Sisters' work at the Pratt Memorial School very difficult. One of the side effects was that fees had to be kept low, and even then parents sometimes found difficulty in paying. This did not help the financial situation as the school was still burdened by the debt from the building fund and could only pay it through fees. But despite all the problems, the Pratt Memorial School entered its jubilee year with a spirit of optimism - and the hope of raising 25,000 rupees! Various fund raising events took place, and the celebrations were crowned by a visit from the new Vicereine, Lady Irwin, who presided over the annual prize giving.

The work of the Sisters was now being played out within an increasingly difficult political situation. Things would get worse, as the cultural gap widened not only between English and Indian, but also between Hindu and Muslim. This led to serious rioting in Calcutta as Sr Margaret reported in the August 1926 issue of *Pipalpati*: "In the Diocesan

Mission our first news of anything wrong was of a "golmal" [i.e. confusion] seen by Amodini, one of our Matrons, in one of the streets in the centre of the town on Easter Eve, followed by the unexpected return from the market of the "jhis" who had gone as usual to buy the children's food for the day. They saw a fight beginning in the market and hastily left their baskets of vegetables and returned bringing back the money but no food! The first outbreak lasted throughout Easter week, and then there was a lull followed by a worse outbreak, when most cruel assaults were made on individuals walking alone and unarmed. Daggers were used in barbarous fashion which caused wounds 'worse than war wounds' as one of the surgeons on the Medical College Staff described them. Moslems and Hindus seem to have been equally guilty as to this. Indian Christians and Europeans were untouched, but of course it produced a reign of terror amongst all others, and it was impossible to send servants out in any of the affected parts. It was difficult some days to get food; at Kidderpore, Sr Beatrice Mary had to appeal to the police to get a shopkeeper to open his shop and to stand over him while he got dhal and rice for the children. At the Mission House a fisherman was engaged to get fish from the tank. The shortage was entirely owing to fear and was overcome when convoys were organised by European volunteers to protect the butchers and produce vendors on their way to the markets."

The work at Kidderpore House had been steadily progressing, and by the mid 1920s was known as St Thomas' School. When the Sisters first took over it consisted of the kindergarten and junior classes, but by 1927 the whole age range from 5 to 18 was under the Sisters' care. This had been made possible through the sale of the old Free School buildings in Calcutta and the use of the proceeds (after much trouble on the property market), to build extra accommodation at Kidderpore. By 1927 180 children were at the school, most of whom were free cases as they came from extremely poor homes. Those whose parents could afford a fee paid 23 rupees a month. By the end of the decade a further building had been erected to give accommodation for 50 small boys who would eventually progress to St Thomas' Boys' School nearby. At this time the educational standard at St Thomas' was lower than at the Diocesan Collegiate School or the Pratt Memorial, but these were early days and there was a continuous improvement.

The work of the schools in the diocesan mission compound, notably the Diocesan College, Collegiate School and Diocesan Mission Boarding School (formerly the lower, or Vernacular school), went on fairly uneventfully during the latter half of the 1920s. The good standards were maintained and each issue of *Pipalpati* reported good exam results and satisfactory reports from the government inspectors. There was still a heavy dependence on help from England, and in spite of the loss of older benefactors such as the Hoare's and Mrs Earle, the Christmas gift boxes continued to arrive on time, packed to capacity with (mostly) useful articles for the prize givings. There were setbacks too, not least a difficult period in 1925-6 when two girls died from enteric fever. It had been an unhealthy year due to the late monsoon which gave rise to fevers and boils. Amodini, the matron of the Boarding School died from septicaemia from boils in July 1926. She was 42 yrs old and had first come to the mission as a pupil-teacher aged 13, and had remained there ever since. In 1920 she gave up teaching to become house matron and in 1926 became nurse matron. Her death was a great loss to the mission.

The most important development connected with the diocesan mission was the work at Baruipur. This centre had first been offered in 1922 by the Society for the Propagation of the Gospel who owned the property, but various problems, not least the lack of funds, but also changes in the S.P.G. secretariat, had mitigated against further progress. However, the situation had improved sufficiently by April 1926 for the Sisters to make an initial venture. This was at the time of the rioting, and the Sisters thought it a good idea to use the mission house at Baruipur as a base from which to visit the villages for the Bible Examinations.

But first they had to move in, as the account in the August 1926 *Pipalpati* relates: "On the morning of April 19th, a motor van arrived which had been 'wangled' by Sr Frances Clare from a neighbouring garage... Then began the packing. First and foremost the Altar, formerly in the European Orphanage Chapel[6], for the side chapel which had been prepared in the Church at Baruipur. Then followed prayer desks..., and a box containing Church things, tables, chairs, camp beds for the house, and last of all a live chicken in a 'moira', seated in front with the driver. Sr Frances Clare and her companions followed by train and found the van arrived and unloaded when they reached Baruipur. The first thing was to fit up the side chapel which looked very devotional when all was ready, and none of us who were there will forget the Holy Eucharist the next morning... The children and teachers who had come for the examination were all there... [They] spent the night in the building originally meant for the boys' school, and had such a good night free from mosquitoes that they told their parents when they went home that, 'God had driven away the mosquitoes now that the Sisters had come.' "

It was hoped that this small beginning would be followed by a gathering of Bible Women (women trained to give religious instruction to other women in the villages), and this duly took place during a fortnight in November 1926. The Sisters were greatly helped in this by Miss Gertrude Roy, a Bengali Associate, who early in 1926 had come to superintend the village work.

By 1928 the work had begun to bear fruit, and it became possible for a small boarding school to be opened at Baruipur. At first it was to be run by Miss Roy and three other Indian Associates, and 26 girls from 5-12 years were taken. They lived in the school house which had to double as classroom and dormitory, and tended their own garden as well as doing their own washing, cooking and cleaning, as they would at home. The teaching was very elementary, consisting chiefly of the 3Rs and the skills required for homemaking, for most of these girls would be married very early.

St Peter's Day (June 29th) 1928, was kept at Baruipur with great solemnity combined with festivity, for after so many years preparation and setbacks, the school and Sisters' house was blessed, together with the dedication of the new high altar in St Peter's church. Sr Margaret (the Sister Superior), and Sr Freda were present for Solemn Evensong which was presided over by Fr Balcomb of the S.P.G., and next morning there was a Eucharist. During the afternoon Sr Constance Ruth and two other Sisters arrived from the Presidency General Hospital, and Sr Frances Clare and several teachers came from the diocesan mission. At 3.00 p.m. the procession formed up in the church and wended its way around the adjacent buildings, which were all duly blessed. This was followed by tea for the adults and playtime for the children, together with the distribution of sweets by the Sisters. Sr Violet Grace (following her furlough in England from February until December 1928), and Sr Frances Clare, took up residence in the Sister's house, though in 1929 the latter returned to Calcutta to take charge of the Diocesan Mission Boarding School and was replaced by Sr Dorothy Florence.

1926 had seen the opening of the Lady Lytton block of nurses' quarters at the Presidency General Hospital. The Sisters were extremely relieved when the building operations came to an end as they related in the April issue of *Pipalpati*: "For the past year or more the south side of the compound [has been] more or less impassable by bullock carts in constant procession, and piles of bricks and mortar and slush all around the soaking tank [i.e. pond], which also served for the daily ablutions of all and sundry engaged in building. However, since Christmas the scene has been one of almost magic transformation as carpenters, painters and engineers completed the work, and an army of coolies loaded endless bullock carts with building refuse - cleared away the tank and remade the road." The new buildings were due to be officially opened by Lord and Lady Lytton on Friday February 26th, but Lady Lytton was ill and her place was taken by another family member. The new quarters provided accommodation for 90 nurses, a sign of how much the standards had improved since the arrival of the Sisters in 1881.

Another cause of thankfulness was the appointment of a full time hospital chaplain. Previously, one of the Cathedral staff had combined his duties there with the hospital chaplaincy, but there was an increasing need for a full time priest especially since the opening of the new chapel in 1916[7].

A number of Sisters were failing in health by 1928, which made it necessary to reorganise the staffing of the various works. But the greatest blow was the sudden death on August 29th after only a few days illness, of Sr Constance Ruth, who was 65. Professed in 1903, she had gone to India in 1906, and had been in charge of the nursing at the Presidency General Hospital since January 1919. Her death came just two months before the Sisters' withdrawal from the hospital in October 1928. This decision had been reached earlier in the year with great reluctance, for it was the original work of the Community in Calcutta. "But," wrote the Sisters, "the very growth and development of the work has led to the need for giving it up. When the Sisters took charge there were 17 nurses; now there are 84... As the nurses have become more highly trained the demands of hospital work have continually increased." And as it became increasingly difficult to find enough highly qualified Sisters to supervise the work, so it became necessary to withdraw from it. It was a tremendous wrench after 47 years, but the death of Sr Constance Ruth seemed to set the seal on the decision.

The wind of change was blowing in England too. Towards the end of 1928 Mother Evelyn resigned after 21 years as Mother Superior [8]. She had been a wise and kind Superior and had led the Community through the Edwardian heyday when numbers had peaked in 1911[9], thence through the war years and its aftermath. She had endeavoured to inject new life into the Community by accepting the work in Barbados, even though it was a controversial decision and one which, with hindsight, might be seen as ill advised. The Indian work inevitably suffered because, within a few years, Sisters were being withdrawn and sent to Barbados, a factor which did not help the morale of the Sisters in India. However, the decision to work in Barbados was made corporately by Chapter; it was not made by Mother Evelyn alone. Nor should the long term effects viewed from the safe distance of a later generation cloud Mother Evelyn's period of office.

November 27th 1928 saw the installation at Clewer of Sr Katherine Maud as Mother Superior. Professed in February 1899, Mother Katherine Maud had trained as a nurse at Guy's Hospital before being sent to work in the Presidency General Hospital in 1902. Upon returning to England in 1920 she took charge of St Andrew's Convalescent Home, Folkestone, and was still there when elected Mother Superior in 1928. Although she had been away from India for several years, she held the work close to her heart and was to make two visits during her seven years in office.

In addition to a new Mother Superior, Clewer had also gained a new Warden and Sub Warden. The relationship between the Sisters and the Warden, the Revd G. H. Tremenheere, had been fraught with difficulty. In May 1926 the Chapter had voted for his removal, an unprecedented step, and then made another break with tradition by electing the Bishop of Buckingham (the Rt Revd Philip Eliot), as their first non-resident Warden. The Revd Kenneth McMaster became Sub Warden in March 1927, and towards the end of 1928 he visited India.

His account, which was printed in both the Clewer *Associates'*

Newsletter of January 1929 and *Pipalpati,* was full of enthusiasm and joy which must have spread to Sisters and pupils alike. He particularly enjoyed the good atmosphere between the Hindu's and Christians and the way in which all mingled in the mission compound. Thus he wrote: "The compound hums with young and eager life. On one side you find yourself among Christian children in the Diocesan Mission school, with Bengali prayers, hymns and lessons, and Bengali teachers... Cross the compound and you are in the Collegiate School and College where teachers are some Indian and some English, the girls are some Christian and some Hindu, and lessons above Form IV are all in English. It is a panorama of youth from the children in the Kindergarten playing Montessori games on the floor, to the College girl, almost a B.A., studying Sanskrit with her pundit. Christians and Hindu's live in good fellowship together. Many of the Hindu girls attend the prayers with which School and College open daily, as well as the weekly lecture given in College by one of the Oxford Mission Fathers. You could see the affection in which the College was held by the number of old girls who turned up at the annual reunion on November 4th, making the compound gay with their beautiful and many coloured saris. A play of Tagore's was admirably acted in the evening. To watch the girls as they rendered this dreamy and elusive poem drama with the minimum of scenery, made one realise that the Bengali's are born artists and actors."

The mixture of Indian and Western cultures was obviously fascinating to him, especially regarding music: "It was a great treat one afternoon to hear the children sing Bengali hymns. They sat on the ground and sang without accompaniment. The tones and intervals are strange to European ears, reminding you a little of Highland music... The National movement has spread to the world of music. Exit piano and enter Indian instruments many and wonderful. It was a strange sight to see the Indian music master humming the air, whilst his pupils, seated opposite him, picked it out on the sitar or esraj." There was even music on the day he was taken by two Sisters in the Mission shalti to Jeydargote in the rice country: "It was music, music all the way, and garlands when we landed... We witnessed a Shankirtan [Gospel story in song and dance], were regaled with dab [cocoanut], and everywhere found joy and brightness in this Christian village, and overwhelming hospitality." Fr McMaster visited all the Sisters' work including Darjeeling, and the new centre at Baruipur. "Joy is the first word and the last," he concluded. "We are still the 'New people' as men called us long ago, and the new people are always at spring time."

The dawning of the 1930s brought a new chapter in the history of the Church of England in India. The passing of the Indian Church Measure at the end of 1927 gave autonomous status to the Church of India, Burma and Ceylon. The Constitution and Canons were ratified early in 1930, and on March 1st the Viceroy made the legal separation of Church from State; thus it was no longer part of the Church of England abroad.

Meanwhile politically, the new decade saw the escalation of Gandhi's campaign of civil disobedience. His famous "salt march," which challenged the government's monopoly on salt, signalled the start of another widespread disruption of public transport and services, and general inconvenience. Less peaceful members of the Indian community made life very difficult for Indian and English alike. Thus in the disruptions of April 15th 1930, several of the Diocesan College students almost missed taking their exams because the police would not permit them to travel across Calcutta. Eventually leave was given and a quick dash across the city, accompanied by Sr Dorothy Frances secured success! This particular rash of disturbance had been partly caused by the British themselves who, in 1927, had sought to review the Constitutional changes of 1919 by means of a Commission of Inquiry under Sir John Simon, but had failed to include any Indians. Such a grave omission could only lead to the sort of frustration which, failing to find a voice, resorted to civil disobedience.

1930 saw several changes in Sisters working in India, not least Sr Margaret who gave up as Sister Superior at the end of the year, after 12 years in office. She arrived home at the end of April 1931, and was succeeded by Sr Dorothy Frances who remained in office until she was recalled to Clewer to become Mother Superior in 1939. "Sr Olive's breakdown in health last year and Sr Frances Clare being away for rest have deprived us of two Bengali-speaking Sisters... Sr Edith Agnes has been in charge at Baruipur. Her work there was interrupted by nearly five months of illness and during most of that time one of our Indian Associates took charge of the school - we owe much to her," wrote a Sister in the October 1930 issue of *Pipalpati*. By the next issue things were still difficult, but with encouraging signs: "Sr Violet Grace had to go into Hospital during the September holidays and after leaving it, had to go away to recruit. We welcomed her back just in time for Christmas... We are looking forward now to welcoming back Sr Frances Clare who will take charge of Baruipur and all the village work. She is on her way now and with her is Sr Catherine Mildred, a trained nurse, who is coming out for the first time."

A welcome visitor at the end of 1930 was Mother Katherine Maud who left England on October 25th accompanied by Sr Lilian Maude, Sr Frances Anne and Sr Mildreda. The latter two Sisters boarded the *S.S. California* at Liverpool, but Mother and Sr Lilian Maude joined the ship at Marseilles. "It has been a great happiness and encouragement to have her with us," was the comment in the January 1931 *Pipalpati*. Though Mother Katherine Maud knew the Indian work very well, there were aspects which were new to her, such as Baruipur, which she visited more than once. She was also present for the endless round of prize givings, and the excitement caused by the arrival and unpacking of the Christmas boxes from England. The annual sale in the diocesan mission compound raised 1,000 rupees from the large number of old friends who came to see Mother Katherine Maud again. Also, some of the nurses from the Presidency General Hospital where she had worked for 18 years, made two dozen large cakes. These were quickly snapped up by Fr Brown of the Oxford Mission: "for his boys, and he was seen carrying away parcels of them assisted by Bishop Gore[10] who honoured us by coming to our sale."

December 8th 1931 saw the Golden Jubilee of the Sisters' work in India. It was marked by a High Mass in Calcutta Cathedral at which the Metropolitan of India, Bishop Foss Westcott, pontificated, and clergy from the Oxford Mission assisted, in the presence of a large congregation. "We took hundreds of children to the service at 7.00 a.m. and sang hymns in English and Bengali," wrote one of the Sisters in *Pipalpati*. The *Associates' Newsletter* of October 1931 reminded readers that: "Within a few days of the dedication of the Chapel [i.e. at Clewer] our first three Sisters, one of whom is still with us[11], sailed for Calcutta... Of the 78 Sisters who, following the three pioneers, have been dismissed from our Chapel to India, we rejoice in the thought that three were able to give 30 years of service... I would ask your prayers for the Sister Superior and the 14 Sisters and 4 Indian Associates who will be celebrating the Jubilee... Five Sisters have been laid to rest in Calcutta."[12]

The Indian work was beginning to show signs of aging. All the hospital work had gone; so too had the European Orphanage; the village work was re-focusing itself around Baruipur; and soon the Diocesan College would be under threat. Nationalism was accelerating; the days of the Raj were numbered. By 1931 the Wembley Exhibition was no more than a memory which small boys would take into old age. The butter statues and replica Taj Mahal had gone; the props stored away; the grand pavilions had become warehouses. Only the sports stadium remained; henceforth the cheers which echoed around it would be for different pursuits than the Imperial ideal. But for the time being the Sisters remained in India, and whilst their supporters, and indeed their own numbers, were diminished, their commitment remained steadfast. And so they proceeded into the next decade with those encouraging words of the Sub Warden still ringing in their ears - "Joy is the first word and the last... We are still the 'New People' and new people are always at spring time."

Footnotes

1. My father was 8 years old when he visited the Wembley Exhibition and he still had vivid memories of it in old age.

2. This was my own reaction too when I visited the present St John's Diocesan Girls' Higher Secondary School in the same compound in February 1995.

3. More details of the size and diversity of the Community of St John Baptist may be found in BONHAM, Valerie *A Joyous Service: The Clewer Sisters and their work* 1989.

4. Times were changing and women could now do so much more in secular life. Also, various charitable organisations were beginning to do social work which had hitherto been the exclusive domain of Sisters, so that women could do the same type of work without foregoing marriage and family life. Consequently, Religious vocations fell in the Communities which had always done welfare work, though they rose slightly in the enclosed contemplative Orders. The downward trend at Clewer was slight at first, but continued between the two world wars and never recovered. Thus in 1914, there were 214 professed choir Sisters which included those in India. By April 1921, this had dropped to 199; there was a dramatic drop to 189 by August 1922, several Sisters having left to join the Roman Catholic Church during this period. In 1939 there were only 123 professed choir Sisters, and numbers had fallen to 103 by 1944. Thus numbers of choir Sisters had halved in the 30 years between 1914 and 1944.

5. Until 1930 the Indian Church was still part of the Church of England.

6. An incomplete letter at Clewer from Bishop Foss Westcott of Calcutta, dating from 1944 refers to the European Orphanage Asylum moving to Ranchi, and the Clewer Sisters consequently being unable to remain in charge of it. No dates are given for this, but presumably the removal of the altar to Baruipur would suggest the orphanage had already closed. Because the letter has not completely survived, the recipient is unknown, but as the bishop refers to the Sisters as "they," it is unlikely to have been the Mother Superior. The Warden is a possibility.

7. One of these earlier Chaplains was the Revd Edward Francis Ainslie who was attached to the Presidency General Hospital in January 1919. His grand daughter, Joyce Keenan who was later both a pupil and a teacher at St Michael's, Darjeeling, writes: "He became a deacon in 1917 in St Andrew's Church, Darjeeling, [and] became a priest at Bhowanipur and was attached to the Presidency General Hospital in January 1919 as the Diocesan Chaplain for 4 to 5 years, and where he worked with the Clewer Sisters."

8. Having laid down her duties as Mother Superior, Sr Evelyn (as she now became), went to Torquay where the Community had other work, and remained there for the last 14 years of her life. But she did not opt out of Community life - in 1929 she visited the American Affiliation at Ralston in New Jersey, having previously been there in 1913. Upon returning to England she became Sister Superior of St Raphael's Home, Torquay. Her health began to fail in 1940, and she died at Torquay on May 25th 1942 and was buried there.

9. In 1911 the Community numbered 341 Sisters worldwide.

10. Charles Gore (1853-1932), had been Bishop of Oxford 1911-19, and therefore Visitor to the Clewer Sisters. He was already a sick man when he made this last visit to Calcutta, to see the Oxford Mission, in which he had long been interested.

11. This was Sr Anna Frances.

12. Those who had died in India were: Sr Mary Agatha; Sr Lucy; Sr Mary Christine; Sr Sophia; Sr Constance Ruth.

CSJB

INDIA

-27-
DEEP SORROW AND SORE TRIAL

The Golden Jubilee of the Sisters' arrival in Calcutta, which had been kept in December 1931, was a cause of joy and celebration both in Calcutta and in England, but there was also another Golden Jubilee which was observed in Calcutta on July 26th 1932. This was the 50th anniversary of Angelina Hoare's arrival at the house which became the Pipalpati mission house, and which eventually passed to the Sisters. Writing in the October 1932 issue of *Pipalpati*, Sr Violet Grace, who was in charge of the Diocesan Mission Boarding School, gave a lengthy account of the celebrations. "We read in Miss Hoare's writings that the month after she came to this house she began a school here. Therefore it fell to the lot of the Mission School which she began to have the honour and happiness of keeping her Jubilee."

A great deal of work went into preparing for the festivities which lasted a whole week, but there was a typically Indian hitch as the Sister recounted: "The little girls made paper chains and flags and it looked as if there was quite a mile of decorations heaped in readiness. Consternation was great when it was noticed that cockroaches were keeping festival and eating the paper. The children's minds were at rest when the chains were 'flitted' [i.e. sprayed with insecticide], and hung up where it was thought no harm would come to them." Despite these inconveniences, the school was made festive: "Great trouble was taken over the entrance and a large 'Welcome' in Bengali was put over the doorway[1] which one liked to think was the one by which Miss Hoare may have entered her house. Her large photograph, usually in the Sister Superior's room, was placed on a stand near the entrance with a Bengali inscription under it. A sari was draped over the portrait and pots of palms at the foot, and to crown it all, the picture was garlanded with such as Miss Hoare must often have been given. On the wall of the porch was a photograph of the original thatched school, a group of children with Sr Jane Frances taken some 15 years ago, and a picture of the old tank and bathing ghat."

At last the great day came and the Sisters and children attended Sung Eucharist at St Mary's Church early in the morning, Fr Chakravarti giving a short address. The afternoon saw a tea party for 'old girls' and their children followed by an entertainment. Guests numbered around 100 and there was much excitement: "A feature of the tea table was a three tier jubilee cake with fifty candles," wrote Sr Violet Grace. "At least we hope there were fifty, for when the cake-wallah who was arranging them said he had finished, thirty seven were counted on it! He then set to work to make up the deficit and it was thought well to take for granted that he had added thirteen more!" After tea there were the inevitable speeches, but the highlight was the speech made by Hemanto who had been at the Mission School for 47 years, firstly as a child looked after by Miss Hoare, then as a teacher, and for the last 18 years as matron. A group photograph followed which Sr Violet Grace declared had turned out well considering the difficulties of getting everyone together, duly posed and sitting still for long enough! The entertainment was also pronounced a success despite, "the very restless babies who held a concert of their own during the acting." The week's festivities had been both exhausting and rewarding, and like most things in India, never quite predictable. But summing up, Sr Violet Grace wrote: "It has been a week of great happiness... and we took down our paper chains and flags with the hope of a Diamond Jubilee in ten years time."(2)

The 1930s began well for the Sisters. They had kept the jubilees with gusto, and 1933 dawned with some good news: Sr Dorothy Frances was awarded the Kaiser-i-Hind gold medal for educational services to India. She was the fourth Clewer Sister to be thus honoured, Sr Jane Frances, Sr Mary Victoria and Sr Blanche Annie having previously received the silver medal. Sr Dorothy Frances spent most of 1933 on furlough at Clewer, Sr Blanche Annie having returned to India to take charge in her absence. This much needed rest soon ended, and on November 3rd Sr Dorothy Frances boarded the *Strathaird*, along with Sr Marian Edith (who was returning for a second term), and Sr Gladys going for the first time.

Only five Sisters died in India, but many were invalided home, and gradually the number of ex-Indian Sisters at Clewer diminished. The 1930s saw the deaths of Sr Mary Thekla on May 16th 1936, aged 85 (professed 49 years), formerly in charge of the European Orphanage: on January 4th 1938 Sr Mary Alethea died after many years at St Alban's Holborn, preceded by five years in India from 1890-95: and on January 19th 1939 Sr Honora died after many years as an invalid, but whose travels we followed in chapter 14.

Sister Dorothy Frances' term of office as Sister Superior had begun at a critical time: shortage of numbers, falling vocations and dwindling finances meant that the Sisters' resources were being stretched to the limits. The withdrawal from the Presidency General Hospital in 1928 had relieved some of the pressure, but now as the Community began its sixth decade on the sub-Continent, the strain began to show once more. High standards were the key to the Sisters' work, and if those standards began to fall then none were more dissatisfied than the Sisters themselves. They preferred to withdraw from a project rather than fall short. So it was that in the summer of 1932 the decision was made to close the Diocesan College in 1935.

Such a decision was not made easily or lightly, especially as the Commission on Christian Higher Education in India under the chairmanship of Dr Lindsay, Master of Balliol, had been very affirming towards the College. The Commission had a particular interest in Bengal, and its members had spent time at the Diocesan College. An entry in the Community *Annals* for February 1931 noted that: "the Committee [sic] has paid constant tribute to the place of the Diocesan College in the life of the community. As a residential Christian College for women, it has achieved a high standard of Christian character and professional ability, a standard Bengal has come to take for granted in the graduates of this College, scattered as they are in positions of leadership and responsibility in the home, school and college. This contribution to women's education the Committee [sic] are emphatic in desiring to see maintained."

The Commission had recommended that the missionary societies in England and America should co-operate in a scheme for a United Women's College in South Calcutta, but this had not been met with enthusiasm by the bodies concerned. In Calcutta, the Diocesan College had sustained a further blow in the loss of an annual grant for library books and laboratory equipment equivalent to £150 per year. Closure seemed inevitable, and the news was broken at the 1932 summer meeting in London of the St John Baptist Calcutta Missionary Association: "Our small buildings; our lack of endowment; the impossibility of development; the increasing pressure of University regulations, are all factors which weighed down the balance in favour of closing the College. The date was postponed at the desire of the Lindsay Commission for they hoped that their report would stir new interest and open new avenues of help."

But although the die was cast, the Sisters tried to be positive as the account in the July 1932 *Associates' Newsletter* shows: "The closing of the College will enable us to make use of the buildings for the Collegiate School which is sadly over-crowded and which gives us the care of the children from 4 to 18. Therefore it is of greater importance in moulding the character of their lives than in the case of the College students' course of 4 years. We hope and pray that in God's good Providence the work will not be allowed to drop, but that means may be forthcoming that it may be continued and developed under other auspices... This small College is the only Christian College for women in Bengal, indeed one of the two women's Colleges belonging to the Anglican Communion throughout India. For the sake of our Church one feels the vital importance of doing all that is possible to promote its continuity and increase."

There were still three years before the planned closure which enabled students already enrolled to complete their courses. But the College was not the only educational body having difficulties. In the summer 1932 issue of *Pipalpati*, Sr Dorothy Frances announced that the Milman Memorial School would be closed in December. The reasons were complex and tinged with political undertones beyond the Sisters' control. The school catered for Hindu girls who were traditionally married at 10 or 11, and the standard attained was therefore not highly academic but sufficient for basic literacy. But more recently, Hindu families had moved away from that tradition and now expected a higher grade of education: schools had mushroomed to meet the demand and the Milman had been left behind. Miss Basu, headmistress for the past 17 years was leaving at the end of 1931 and a former student of the Diocesan College, Mary Sarwan, had been invited by the Sisters to take charge during the following year.

This proved to be an unpopular decision as Sr Dorothy Frances explained in the summer 1932 *Pipalpati*: "We had not reckoned on the Bengali's hatred of change and his fear of the unknown. Miss Basu seemed a sheet anchor! When it was known that she was to leave, even though she had a year's notice, the parents believed and told their neighbours that the school would soon deteriorate, the next step... was that it was to be closed, that the staff would have to leave... Result, many parents took away their children and put them into a new school with Miss Basu on its staff - that it is unrecognised and in a bad building counted for nothing... The natural result of all this will be, I am afraid, that the Milman will have to be closed in December." In fact, the Milman school struggled on for another year but in the December 1933 issue of *Pipalpati* Sr Dorothy Frances wrote: "We have finally closed the Milman School and the premises will be let for two years, the rent will help us to pay off the debts incurred this year, and by 1934 or 1935 we may be able to make a final plan. Schools are springing up all around us and in a few years' time public opinion will perhaps swing back in favour of missionary schools."

January 15th 1934 saw a major earthquake in northern India which was considered one of the worst since that of 1906 in San Francisco. The epicentre of what soon became known as the "Great Indian Earthquake" was in Bihar, about 125 square miles being affected from Bhagalpore in the east, Gaya in the south, Patna in the west and Muzaffarpur and Darbhanga in the north, but further shock waves were felt from Allahabad to Darjeeling, and from Katmandu to Daltonganj. At first it was thought that casualties were slight, but soon the full horror was evident - over 7,000 lives lost; the city of Monghyr totally destroyed; hundreds buried alive at Muzaffarpur; devastation over 15,000 square miles. Relief funds were immediately set up by the Viceroy of India, the Mayor and Corporation of Calcutta, and major charities such as the Red Cross.

Very little damage was sustained in Calcutta, the most notable casualty being St Paul's Cathedral which had to be closed for a fortnight as the spire was damaged. It was later removed and replaced with a replica of Bell Harry tower at Canterbury which is why the building looks so familiar to English visitors! But although there was little damage, the shock waves were felt throughout the city and widespread panic ensued. The *Calcutta Municipal Journal* of January 20th 1934 reported that at 2.30 p.m. on Monday January 15th the city was rocked for eight minutes and that most of the clocks stopped. "It was at this juncture that alarm spread... Thousands of men, women and children rushed out of their houses and offices... and for several minutes, with the ground beneath their feet still heaving, the atmosphere was almost one of panic. In some quarters... many terrified residents [were] rushing shrieking into the streets, carrying with them such of their belongings as they could scramble together in the mad rush to get away from the swaying houses. Parks and open spaces were crowded and there were many who refused to re-enter their houses until long after nightfall." *The Times* reported the disaster over the next week as the growing scale of the tragedy unfolded. "The [Calcutta telephone] exchange was incommoded by a large number of people, who in the middle of their calls, threw down the receiver and rushed into the street." Similarly, there was panic in the Calcutta law courts: "The prisoners in the dock at one Court made a rush for the outside, as did most of the other persons in the Court, one prisoner getting clean away."

No serious damage was sustained by any of the buildings in the Sisters' care although further cracks appeared in the mission house (which was once more becoming dangerous), 15 years after the previous major appeal in which the bishop had urged a complete rebuilding. This had not proved possible at the time, and once again the Sisters were faced with major repairs to prevent the roof collapsing.

The early 1930s were particularly trying times for the Sisters' educational work. Not only was the College and the Milman School in difficulties, but there was also a growing problem with the village work centred at Baruipur. This had begun with a flourish in 1928 after a tentative start two years previously, and for several years *Pipalpati* carried enthusiastic reports. Numbers in the school gradually increased, educational standards were slowly raised to middle school level, despite the problem of girls suddenly being taken away for marriage and never being heard of again, and improvements were made to the buildings. But it was not ideal as a centre for the village work even though it was closer than Calcutta itself. Much of the trouble lay in the lack of Christians on the spot in the villages, the shortage of Bengali priests, and the difficulty of maintaining a disciplined life on the part of the Indian Christians. Furthermore, Baruipur was very unhealthy, malaria being endemic.

Pipalpati for October 1934 carried the news that: "Fr Balcomb is helping to solve the problems of the village work and Baruipur. He is resident at Canning where he has a boarding school for boys, and he tours constantly up and down the villages... He is gradually training men who will be more energetic priests, keen to help the scattered Christians in the best way. He has initiated many changes, and has won the confidence of the villagers in a remarkable way... He is very anxious to bring about a closer co-ordination between the work done by him and the few Bengali priests in the villages, and that done by the Sisters. He now meets Sr Frances Clare monthly. Baruipur is not conveniently placed as a centre for village work and his present idea is to put all the force we can muster into teaching the women." The next issue confirmed the ongoing nature of the problems: "It seemed best to close the school [at Baruipur] for a year. Malaria has not yet been conquered and three of the staff on whom we most rely have been victims… Fr Balcomb, an English member of St Andrew's Brotherhood,(3) who is Superintendent of the Sunderbuns S.P.G. work, hopes to keep the school going for a year which will give us time for further consideration. It was hoped that Baruipur would become a centre from which the work could be done in the villages, but this has not proved true, for Baruipur is really too far off and cannot even be used for the monthly pay day of teachers."

By the summer of 1935 the Sisters had decided that: "it has been found impracticable on many counts to return to Baruipur, but the school is being carried on and the Sisters visit from time to time." This was not the end of the Sisters' village work, simply a withdrawal from work which really stemmed from the S.P.G., and indeed the Society still owned the buildings. However, the summer 1937 issue of *Pipalpati* noted that: "the school which we had at Baruipur, which for the past three years has been under Fr Balcomb, has now closed for the malaria proved unconquerable. The township is very dirty and the people are unwilling to clear the stagnant ponds in which the mosquitoes breed."

On November 15th 1934, Mother Katherine Maud sailed for India accompanied by Sr Grace, in order to help solve the many problems surrounding the work there. After a good voyage aboard the P. & O. liner *Ranchi*, they arrived at Bombay and met Sr Hilda who was on her way home to England. On the way to Calcutta Mother caught a chill followed by a severe attack of dysentery. She had not recovered by the time she arrived in Calcutta, and after about two days was removed from the mission house to a hospital where several of the Sisters visited her. Afterwards, she was able to visit the village work at Thakurpukur and Canning, the other schools in Calcutta, and the Oxford Mission at Behala. Even at this eleventh hour efforts were still being made to save the Diocesan College by transferring it elsewhere and into other hands. The Oxford Mission Sisterhood of the Epiphany, who had recently opened a hostel in Calcutta for girls studying at the Bethune College, was very interested in women's educational work. Early in 1935 Mother Edith of the Epiphany Sisterhood approached the government of India requesting the use of Hastings House, for a women's College but was refused. In the event nothing could save the Diocesan College, but the buildings were taken over by the Collegiate School, following essential repairs.

So Mother Katherine Maud's visit failed to solve the problems surrounding the Diocesan College or to prevent its closure, but at a time when morale was low, her presence must have been an encouragement.

Mother Katherine Maud was popular within the Community; having worked in India for several years, she knew the problems at first hand, and she was always ready with a kind word for all the Sisters. The Sisters at Clewer little thought that when she left for India on November 15th they would not see her again. Christmas 1934 came and went, and although the post was late and the expected air mail letter from India did not arrive until December 27th, the Sisters in England received a cable on December 26th with the message: "All Christmas joy and blessing from Mother."

Mother Katherine Maud left Bombay accompanied by Sr Hilda Frances on February 16th 1935, but was taken ill again and had to go ashore at Port Sudan for emergency surgery. A cable was sent to Clewer informing them on February 22nd. The Community *Annals* record that: "further cables told of the success of the operation, but hopes were dashed when we heard that the surgeons considered Mother should get home as soon as possible for further advice and treatment." They arrived at Marseilles on March 18th where a nurse from St Bartholomew's Hospital was waiting to care for her on the overland journey. After arriving at Victoria station, they were met by an ambulance together with Sr Frances and Sr Evelyn Joan, and Mother was taken straight to St Bart's. Sisters visited frequently over the next three weeks and she seemed to be making progress. A further examination under anaesthetic on April 8th satisfied the surgeon that all was well and that she might go home after a further three weeks. All branch houses of the Community were cabled with the good news, but on April 9th she suddenly collapsed and never regained consciousness. She died peacefully next morning in the presence of Sr Frances, Sr Evelyn Joan, and her sister, Mrs Bartlett.

The funeral was at Clewer, the coffin being received and brought into the chapel early in the evening of April 12th. A vigil was kept until 8.00 p.m. by the novices, and the night vigil by the Sisters. A Requiem Mass was said at 7.00 a.m. by Fr Browne, one of the Chaplains, followed by the Solemn Requiem at 8.30 a.m. at which the Warden, the Rt Revd Philip Eliot (Bishop of Buckingham) pontificated. Others present included the Rector of Clewer, the Vicar of Clewer St Stephen, and members of the Council of the House of Mercy. The burial in the Sisters' cemetery in Hatch Lane followed at 10.30 a.m. in the presence of the Community and many guests, including the Abbot of Nashdom, the Rt Revd Dom Martin Collett. The Community *Annals* record that: "the day was full of sunshine and there was a great sense of peace. The letters received were a testimony to her widespread influence." In Calcutta, a Requiem was held on the same day as the funeral in England, Fr Shore of the Oxford Mission presiding and preaching. It was well attended, and the congregation included the matron and a nurse from the Presidency General Hospital where Mother Katherine Maud had worked as a young Sister many years previously.

On July 23rd 1935 Sr Frances was elected Mother Superior and was duly installed on July 25th. The Community *Annals* summed up the year 1935 with the sad words: "so closed for the Community a year of deep sorrow and sore trial. May it fulfil the purpose of God in the year to come."

Amidst all the difficulties there were signs of hope. During Mother Katherine Maud's visit to Calcutta an Indian postulant had been admitted. The Easter 1935 issue of the Clewer *Associates' Newsletter*, noted that: "We have long been hoping and praying for the development of an Indian order of Sisters under the care of our Community, and this was the happy inauguration, as we trust, of a fulfilling of that hope in God's good time. Dipika Bejborea is a new Christian, so that the step she has taken has meant an entire severance from her family which has cost her much." She had been admitted on January 25th 1935 and in October arrived at Clewer to serve her noviciate there. Dipika had been Baptised in November 1932 at St Mary's Church, Bhowanipore, and was Confirmed shortly before Easter 1933. She was on the staff of the Diocesan Collegiate School having previously been a student at the College. Following her novitiate in England Sr Dipika returned to Calcutta where she was professed on December 23rd 1939, the Bishop of Calcutta receiving her vows. Sr Dipika was not the only Indian woman to offer her life in the Clewer Sisterhood - the future Mother Susila of the Christa Sevika Sangha, was at this time a pupil at the Pratt Memorial School, and her story will follow in a later chapter. Meanwhile, at the same time as Dipika was preparing for Baptism, a former pupil of the Diocesan College had become a novice with the Oxford Mission Sisters of the Epiphany at Barisal, and another was hoping to join the St Denys' Sisters in new work at Itki.

St Michael's School, Darjeeling, was in good spirits during the 1930s despite the ever present financial concerns. The decade had begun with plans for an extension to the buildings, not to take in extra numbers but to give better accommodation to the 170 pupils and staff. The estimated cost was the colossal sum of £7,500, but a number of institutions and well wishers in England gave generously. Looking back Sr Georgina recalled: "During 1931 the steel frame work of the extension was begun by multitudes of coolies whom no height intimidates, hauling into place huge steel girders with no other machinery than bamboo poles and ropes. Before the rain broke the roof was on and the much required building was ready for March 1932."[4] The new building was blessed at the start of the nine month school term in 1932, using the same order of service as that used at the blessing of the rebuilt school in 1904.

Sr Georgina's optimism probably helped offset the very real anxiety about money which underlay the work at St Michael's. Even so, a tremendous effort was made to pay off the debt so that the Sister could report in the winter 1934 issue of *Pipalpati* that it had been cleared. The money had been raised piecemeal by means of sales and entertainments, and the situation had been helped by the Indian builder who was prepared to receive payment by instalments. But this was only part of the ongoing financial burden of running the school, as Sr Honor explained in the winter 1933 issue of *Pipalpati*: "Owing to a very big cut in the Government grant, the financial aspect has caused grave anxiety... The fees as compared with English boarding schools are about half the cost, so unless our numbers are very big, as there is no endowment, fees alone do not nearly cover the cost of running the school. We are hoping next year will bring us a big increase of pupils." Meanwhile the Sisters tried to economise by staff and salary cuts, but were constantly inundated by requests from parents (many of whom were Anglo-Indians), for reduced fees.

St Michael's escaped relatively unscathed from the great earthquake of January 1934 which severely damaged two other schools nearby, as well as Government House. But parents were slow to enrol their children at the Darjeeling schools during the coming year because they considered it to be an unsafe area. This was an added burden at a difficult time. Another factor lay in the growing number of Roman Catholic schools with large numbers of Sisters: "It is not possible for us to compete," wrote Sr Georgina in the winter 1935 *Pipalpati*. "They have so many trained Nuns that they practically dispense with secular staff altogether."

1936 was the jubilee year of the foundation of St Michael's School, and an appeal was launched to provide a tennis court (which the Sisters considered to be much needed as all the other schools had one). Response from England was very poor, but the Indian Church Aid Association was generous. Thus St Michael's continued much as before, constantly struggling to keep solvent, and somehow managing to maintain a consistently high standard of education against all the odds.

During the 1930s the Pratt Memorial School, like St Michael's, was trying to maintain a good standard of education whilst struggling with the particular socio-economic problems surrounding the Anglo-Indian community, many of whom were unemployed - victims of the economic depression. In response to their plight the Sisters had reduced the school fees as far as they could, but many parents were behind with their payments, and indeed some children left the school with their fees in arrears and little hope of payment. Also, children were being sent to school clearly under-nourished and ill clad. The Sisters were constantly appealing for money to help clothe the children, or for good cast-off clothes. Indeed every report from the school in *Pipalpati* throughout the decade was preoccupied with the economic and social problems which beset its progress. However, a good educational standard was maintained, and a strong sense of loyalty fostered amongst the pupils, so that many would look back at their schooldays with affection.

Throughout the 1930s the Sisters were working against an increasingly difficult political background. They had been invited to India by the

British government, but had never been involved in the politics of India, although by implication they were caught up in the "Englishness" of it. But whilst they were undeniably endeavouring to bring non-Christian Indians to faith in Christ, the fifty or more years they had spent there had fostered a deepening respect for Indian life and culture. So while negotiations for self government continued throughout the 1930s, the Sisters went about their business as best as they could knowing that the final outcome of independence would be their own withdrawal. It is true that the strikes in Calcutta, and other forms of civil disobedience were inconvenient, but it was all part of the unpredictability of life in that country, and they took it in their stride. But perhaps it was inevitable that at some stage the political situation would come home in an unacceptable way. The early 1930s saw two incidents, both of which brought deep shame and embarrassment to the Sisters.

Firstly, the Clewer Community *Annals* record the following entry on February 6th 1932: "An attempt was made on the life of the Governor of Bengal [Sir Stanley Jackson] by Bina Das[5], a former student of the Diocesan College, staying at the College at this time for a few weeks. The action was quite contrary to the spirit of the College whose members all subsequently signed a letter expressing their sorrow at what had been done. The affair was of course a very great shock and blow to Sr Dorothy Frances and to all the Sisters, but the behaviour of the other members of the College was beyond praise." As already noted, the College was struggling for existence and this incident, coming just a few months before the decision was made to close it, did not help morale, although it did not have any influence on that decision.

The second incident occurred while Sr Dorothy Frances was home on furlough in 1933 and was reported by Sr Hilda Frances in the October issue of *Pipalpati*: "The College is passing through a very difficult time. At the beginning of August, owing to the theft of some money from a student, a search of the dormitory was instituted, and in one girl's bed loaded firearms were found. The police were called and the girl was arrested, and is at this moment undergoing her trial. She is one of our best students and has always been most docile and well behaved. The tragic part of these cases, which are by no means infrequent in the Colleges, is that young men and girls are being made the tools of the unscrupulous men behind them... A book on Bolshevism was found in this girl's locker... From essays, remarks made in class and so forth, I find that the great majority of the students, probably all the non-Christians, think that the end justifies the means. Several students have left the [College] Hostel in consequence of this affair, and I intend to get rid of one or two others whose influence I feel to be bad. This makes our financial position even more difficult than it was before."

Despite their horror at both these incidents and the slur thus attached to the last days of the Diocesan College, the Sisters did not abandon the erring students. In the summer 1934 issue of *Pipalpati*, Sr Dorothy Frances recounted her efforts to keep in touch with the girls: "I was given leave to see Bina Das and Banalata Das Gupta this last month, and am hoping to see Jyotikana Datta next week. None of them is in Calcutta now. The interview takes place in the presence of warders, so that is unsatisfying. One can only hope that it proves our friendship to the prisoners." The news was better in the October 1935 issue when Sr Dorothy Frances was able to report that: "To our great joy Jyotikana Datta was released unconditionally by the Governor for she had shown a fine spirit of courage and obedience in prison. She has gone to England to relatives." In fact she was released in time to travel to Clewer with Sr Grace, and from thence was fetched by her relations who took her home to Bristol where she hoped to study medicine.

1935 was a crucial year on the wider political front for it saw the passage of the Government of India Act. This had been a difficult birth coming as it did in the wake of Gandhi's salt march protest, followed by the Round Table talks in London between the British Government and the Congress Party, which lasted four years. Throughout this period the civil disobedience campaign continued unremittingly in India, agitated by the effects of the economic depression, and frequently spurred into violence by less peaceful men than Gandhi. The 1935 Act gave each of India's eleven provinces an autonomous government responsible to a parliamentary body elected by Indians. The Indian electorate was raised from seven million to over thirty million, and after much hesitation, the Congress Party decided to participate - and won in eight of the provinces. The British Governor in each province was reduced to no more than a figurehead symbolising the power that was fading. The main stumbling block to the success of the Act came from the Princely States which covered two-fifths of British India, and had remained largely autonomous. The new Act created a federal framework designed to absorb the Princely States as well as the eleven provinces, but the princes failed to agree and wasted precious time. Furthermore, the overwhelming success of the Congress Party in the elections had left the Muslims with simmering grievances. As will be seen later, those grievances came to boiling point with disastrous results before the final withdrawal of the British.

The mid 1930s saw a confusing number of name changes within the Sisters' work, but the winter 1936 issue of *Pipalpati* sheds a little light on it. The chief culprit was the Lower or Vernacular School which in recent years had become known as the Diocesan Mission Boarding School, then the Middle English School and now became St Elizabeth's Middle English School. The Diocesan College had finally closed in 1935, and its buildings were immediately taken over by the Diocesan Collegiate School which by the end of 1936 was becoming known as St John Baptist School. By the end of the decade it was correctly known as St John's Diocesan Girls'

High School[6]. The mission itself had changed from being the Pipalpati mission house in the days of Angelina Hoare, and was latterly known as the Diocesan mission house, but as Sr Dorothy Frances pointed out, the name was misleading because the house and grounds were held in trust by the Diocese of Calcutta, but it did not give any financial support to the work. And so it was thought logical to change the name to St John Baptist Mission which became effectual from 1936.

The demise of the work at Baruipur largely through the prevalence of malaria, had not brought the village work to an end. Both the Sisters and Fr Balcomb were still endeavouring to teach the Christian faith in the rice country villages despite overwhelming odds. But the style of the work had changed from the days of Angelina Hoare and Sr Jane Frances who would spend days at a time travelling from one village to another. The Community no longer had Sisters to spare for such protracted visits, hence the choice of the ill-fated mission centre at Baruipur. By 1935 the Sisters' village work had consolidated itself into several centres: Thakurpukur where there was an S.P.G. girls' school; Kaurapuker where there was a London Mission School - the missionaries allowed the Sisters to hold Confirmation classes in the school; Kharriberia, a settlement of Christians; Mograhat, another Christian village where Fr Balcomb had secured a rest house for the visiting Sisters; Kalagachi, a very inaccessible rice village; Jeydargote, where Fr Balcomb had built another rest house for the Sisters; and there was still a girls' boarding school at Baruipur which the Sisters visited from time to time.

By the mid 1930s it became increasingly logical for the Sisters to work alongside Fr Balcomb and the S.P.G. rather than independently. After all, the experiment at Baruipur had worked well - it was the mosquitoes which had defeated everyone's endeavours. Fr Balcomb was based at Canning where there was a flourishing boys' school and a church, but he regularly visited the rest of the area south of Calcutta which was divided into five districts each with an Indian priest. As will be seen from the centres listed above, there was a large degree of co-operation between the Sisters and the S.P.G. Writing in the October 1936 *Pipalpati*, Sr Dorothy Frances envisaged further work together: "S.P.G. gives a grant to the girls' boarding school but otherwise only helps the men's work and priests' salaries. It may be that as our private contributions grow less and therefore our power to develop diminishes, that it would be well to pool our resources with those of S.P.G. and become handmaids of that great and wise society. Where the Weald of Kent Association could give £195 in 1926, in 1933 it gave £89, and since that [time] less. S.P.G. is supporting a Community in another part of the mission field, and the Society recognises that it is almost impossible for any small body of people to raise funds in these difficult days."

By the end of 1937 Sr Dorothy Frances was able to report a further strengthening of the bonds with S.P.G. Some extra land had been acquired by Fr Balcomb at Thakurpukur and on it he had built a new school for the boys, and was proposing to open a girls' boarding school in the existing buildings. He had invited the Sisters to supervise the girls' hostel and appoint the staff for the school which would cater for girls from the rice country villages. Thus the seed sown and nurtured at Baruipur was being transplanted, and the Sisters entered the new work with enthusiasm.

As the world escalated towards another major war the Community of St John Baptist was rocked by changes, some of which were held in common with the rest of the Empire, and others which were internal. But all were to affect their work in India in the long term. May 1935 had seen the silver jubilee of the King-Emperor George V, and he had been deeply moved by the great show of affection accorded to him. At Clewer the household had listened to the wireless broadcast of the thanksgiving service at St Paul's Cathedral, and had tuned in again in the evening to hear the King's speech to his people. Just seven months later, in January 1936, the King had died at Sandringham and the Empire mourned his passing. Sr Dorothy Frances wrote in the *Pipalpati* magazine of summer 1936: "The expressions of sorrow on the news of the King-Emperor's death were most genuine and deep. Hostility and criticism vanished, for all felt the power of the simple devotion of the King to his Empire."

On July 25th 1935, a few months before the King's death, Sister Frances had been installed at Clewer as the seventh Mother Superior. Her fairly brief term of office was marked by the Indian work becoming a separate Province at last. As noted before, this had been brought before Chapter at various times and had always been turned down. However, during Mother Katherine Maud's last visit to India a Chapter had been held there, and no doubt the difficulties of not having Provincial status had been discussed. November 1936 saw the Clewer Chapter discussing it once more, and again at its May and November meetings in 1937. By this time agreement had been reached and the Constitution was being worked out - but it was too late to be of any major significance. The days of Empire and thus of the Sisters, were waning fast.

Throughout 1936 England was in the grip of a major Constitutional crisis over whether the uncrowned King-Emperor Edward VIII could come to the throne if he married a divorcee. As Prince of Wales, Edward had visited India in 1921 and had opened the Victoria Memorial in Calcutta. As news of the crisis in England filtered through to India the Sisters waited anxiously. The Clewer Community *Annals* carried the bland entry: "December 10th, King Edward VIII abdicated. December 12th King George VI proclaimed." The Coronation of the last King-Emperor took place on May 12th 1937: at Clewer the household were able to hear both the service and the King's broadcast to the nation in the evening.

February 19th 1938 saw the arrival from India of Sr Dorothy Frances for several months furlough. During her stay the triennial election for the office of Mother Superior was due. There were three nominations - Sr Frances, Sr Leila (Assistant Superior), and Sr Dorothy Frances. Mother Frances had consented to be nominated again, but warned the Community that if re-elected she would not be able to visit the branch houses as her rheumatism was getting worse. Despite this warning, the Community re-elected her, and she was re-installed on November 12th 1938. A few days previously on November 9th, Sr Dorothy Frances was appointed Mother Provincial for India, and she left for her return journey on November 17th accompanied by Sr Elizabeth Mary.

Just three months later, on February 17th 1939, the Warden sent a letter to all choir Sisters informing them that: "the Mother General [Mother Frances], through increasing physical weakness has, in the interests of the Community, asked to be released forthwith from the responsibilities of her office. I have no option but to accede to her request." So for the first time in its history Clewer was without a Superior - an abdication crisis indeed! On May 5th 1939 a Chapter of Election was held with two nominations - Sr Leila and Mother Dorothy Frances. The latter, who had only just returned to India, now found herself elected and recalled to Clewer. On May 25th 1939, Sr Hilda Frances was installed as Mother Provincial by the Metropolitan of India. Meanwhile, Sr Dorothy Frances managed to secure a passage back to England on June 1st and arrived at Clewer on the evening of the Nativity of St John Baptist (June 24th), after an uncomfortable voyage. She was installed as Mother General on July 7th 1939 by the Warden, the Bishop of Oxford being unable to attend due to illness.

So it fell to the lot of Mother Dorothy Frances who was heart and soul in the Indian work, to eventually supervise its closure. But that lay a few years ahead. Meanwhile the Community *Annals* recorded the brief entry for September 3rd 1939: "11.00 a.m. War declared. All listened to the King's speech at 6.00 p.m." And in the October issue of *Pipalpati* Mother Hilda Frances remarked: "All our thoughts are filled with the war, and here in India our minds turn homewards even more than usual... With the cloud of war hanging over us the future is very uncertain."

Thus ended a period of deep sorrow and sore trial, and the next decade saw the Sisters immersed in the clouds of war, the threat of invasion and the uncertainty of what Independence would bring. But the 1930s had not been all darkness. In December 1933 a young, newly professed Sister had left Clewer for India - she fell in love with it and has written warmly of her time in Calcutta and Darjeeling. The next chapter comprises Sr Eudora's memories of what she describes as the most vivid years of her life.

Footnotes

1. When I visited St John's Diocesan Girls' Higher Secondary School in February 1995 similar greetings had been placed over the doorways for me.

2. Diamond jubilee - Sr Violet Grace would be gratified to know that her school's successor has now passed its Centenary.

3. St Andrew's Brotherhood was begun c1907 by Fr Mohendra Chakravarti as an Indian brotherhood on Franciscan lines, which grew out of the Oxford Mission Brotherhood. In 1923 Bishop Foss Westcott asked Fr Chakravarti to take charge of St Mary's Church, Bhowanipore, next door to the diocesan mission. He later returned to the Brotherhood. Fr Arthur Balcomb had joined the Oxford Mission Brotherhood in 1920, but later left to take up work with the S.P.G. He is mentioned in *A Hundred Years in Bengal: a history of the Oxford Mission 1880-1980*, but his membership of St Andrew's Brotherhood is not mentioned.

4. Sr Georgina CSJB *Past History of S. Michael's School, Darjeeling.*

5. Since Independence, Bina Das has been regarded as a heroine in the struggle for self government.

6. It is now known as St John's Diocesan Girls' Higher Secondary School.

C S J B

I N D I A

-28-
UNFORGETTABLE DAYS: A SISTER REMEMBERS

The early 1930s saw the usual comings and goings of Sisters from Clewer to India and Barbados, and in spite of the fall in numbers, novices were being received, some of whom were duly elected for Profession. The Community *Annals* record that on July 24th 1931, five months before the Golden Jubilee of the Indian work, four novices were clothed - Sr Eudora, Sr Annys, Sr Rosemary and Sr Elizabeth Helen. Of these, all of whom were eventually professed, Sr Eudora and Sr Rosemary were to work in India, and Sr Annys was to become Mother Superior at Clewer (from 1958-78). Sr Eudora and Sr Rosemary were professed on October 24th 1933: just over a year before this, on September 17th 1932, Sr Gladys had been professed. She too would work in India, and like Sr Eudora, would be impressed by it for the rest of her long life(1).

During much of 1933 Sr Dorothy Frances was on furlough at Clewer. Upon her departure for India in November she took with her Sr Marian Edith who was returning after several years in England (she was one of the Sisters whose ship had been torpedoed in April 1918), and Sr Gladys, who was going out for the first time. Just 10 days before Sr Dorothy Frances left England, Sr Eudora was professed at Clewer: two months later on December 29th she sailed for India with Sr Celia.(2)

"I well remember the voyage to Bombay, sailing from Tilbury on the P.& O. steamer *Moldavia*; the misery of the Bay of Biscay; the first smell of the east at Port Said; the Red Sea and the Southern Cross;... leaning over the side [in the Indian Ocean] and being told that the sea there was five miles deep," writes Sr Eudora(3). "Persuading Sr Celia to leave the ship at Bombay was a major operation, but finally we landed. Having missed the night train to Calcutta we threw ourselves on the mercy of the All Saints Sisters ... and there spent the night and most of next day. After a hot and hectic day seeing (and smelling) something of the teeming city, including a visit to the Cathedral, we caught the night train to Howrah station in Calcutta. It was very early in the morning but several Sisters, in white habits, were there to meet us. I felt stunned with the noise and clamour of the station - coolies in their puce coloured livery, and was thankful for the comparative quiet of the ghari in which we drove to the Mission House. Sr Dorothy Frances welcomed us with great kindness and warmth."

So began five years which Sr Eudora has described as the most vivid of her life - newly professed, and yet treading a path which so many others had trod before her. Her journey coincided with the great earthquake, but it does not feature in her memoirs because she was still en route, and as noted in chapter 27, the damage in Calcutta was very slight compared with Bihar. It must have been daunting to arrive in a new country amongst Sisters who were virtual strangers, but she took it in her stride: "In due course I learnt that my destination was to be the Pratt Memorial School in Lower Circular Road. Sr Irene was the Headmistress - she had left the novitiate just before me so I did not know her at all well. I was to be second Sister, besides a large staff of teachers and matrons. Mercifully for me, English was spoken, with Hindi as the second language... The weather was glorious, and a good breaking in for newcomers to the otherwise villainous Bengal climate. I found that I was to teach R. E. throughout the school apart from the kindergarten and the Cambridge [matriculation] class taken by Sr Irene."

Sr Eudora soon became accustomed to the routine at the Pratt Memorial School and to working in India, although there were spells of homesickness. But she has recalled the two highlights of each week to which she eagerly looked forward: "Firstly, driving on Saturday mornings to the mission compound for the Community Mass, followed by chota hazri [breakfast], and a general get-together. In this way I got to know at least the names of the other Sisters then working in the plains[4]; also, since it was the long vacation for our school in the hills (St Michael's, Darjeeling), I learnt too, that the great days of 30 and more Sisters working in India were no more... What with illness and leaves, 11 was to be the norm during my time. Secondly, the weekly visit of Sr Dorothy Frances to the 'Outhouses'[5]. She usually came on a Tuesday to the Pratt. This meant an interview which sometimes went well and sometimes didn't. But unless there was an emergency, and there were plenty, she did her level best to come, and never shall I forget her goodness and loving-kindness."

"There are plenty of reminiscences of Pratt Memorial School," writes Sr Eudora, "and of the delightful and very naughty little Anglo Indians, plus 10% of Indians. It was there that I was knocked flat by an outsized monkey who sat on my chest - Sr Irene held her breath. She thought he was going to bite me. There too I lost my ring and was well scolded by Sr Violet Grace, Sr Irene being on furlough. It was found by one of our faithful servants who I suspect had wrested it from a not so faithful one by threatening him with terrible punishments if he kept a 'holi' thing. Being left in charge one year during the Puja holidays, someone put the bright idea into my head of getting the River Police to lend a launch so that I could take the children left behind [at the school] for a picnic. Except for passing the burning ghats, we had a wonderful trip." Mother Susila of the Christa Sevika Sangha was a pupil at the Pratt Memorial School along with her three sisters, and recalls Sr Eudora teaching the Angelus to a little crowd of girls in the school playground.

During these early days, Sr Eudora was still finding her way around Calcutta: "All this time I was finding my way about the incredible, cosmopolitan city of Calcutta, and imbibing more and more of its atmosphere of terrible contrasts - of appalling smells and sickening sights

- of lordly sahibs and cringing coolies - of Khalighat and the fanatical pilgrimages - of the ubiquitous leper with his hollow cry and tin can." It was very much the way Sr Jane Frances had reacted to this city which she came to love so deeply. Sr Eudora was also still getting to know the other Sisters. "Being so recently professed, I only knew Sr Gladys at all well. She had come out a few months earlier. In those early days we shared our sorrows and rubbed along pretty well, considering how different we were. She was always kind, but blunt."

Sisters working in Calcutta were sent for rest periods to Darjeeling. Sr Eudora recalls such times with pleasure: "We wore black habits and felt cold at an altitude of nearly 8,000 feet. It was not the best time of year for seeing the snows, but what unforgettable days when the mists lifted and that incomparable range revealed itself peak upon peak crowned by Kanchenjunga at a height of 27,000 ft. One thought nothing of creeping out at 4.00 a.m. to climb the hillside behind the school in order to see the sunrise on the snows. One memorable morning Sr Freda and I saw an electrical storm at one end while the sun rose on the other. Everest is about 50 miles away as the crow flies and we made an overnight expedition to Tiger Hill to see the sunrise - staying in a dak bungalow and thinking nothing of being eaten by leeches!"

On at least one occasion both Sr Eudora and Sr Gladys were resting at Darjeeling: "Sr Georgina was in her element caring for the resting Sisters and was constantly thinking out new delights; but for me the best times were those of exploring the surrounding countryside with its villages and tea gardens, temples and monkeys! Sr Gladys and I had a unique experience of these one day. We were saying our Office out of the old pocket Office books with thin India paper. We were sitting overlooking a vast valley... Far below us, yet crystal clear in that rarified air, we saw a family of brown monkeys lined up on the branch of a tree. We held our breath and were entranced to see mother systematically grooming the family, beginning with father and going along the line to the youngest of the tribe. Then we saw mother change places with father who began to groom her, - a light breeze rustled a page of that India paper, and although they were far below us, they heard and were gone in the twinkling of an eye."

It was on one of those rests at Darjeeling that Sr Eudora went on a lone expedition, the memory of which still gives her pleasure even though she was sternly reprimanded! "From the school verandah I had often studied the dry bed of the Tieesta River several thousand feet below, and secretly vowed to get there one day," she recalls. "This came to pass the year that Sr Georgina was on furlough [1937], and Sr Violet Grace was deputising for her. I was sleeping in the bungalow below the school and started my trek from there, dropping down through the tea gardens, meeting no one apart from one [tea] Planter who seemed surprised to see me alone in those parts, but I paid no heed... I saw banana trees again and began to feel uncomfortably hot in my black clothes, but otherwise quite happy, for the Tieesta was getting ever nearer. It had been a drop of over 3,000 feet so no wonder I was getting prickly heat again! The mighty Tieesta was reduced to a mere trickle in the midst of great boulders; quite an adventure leaping from one to another before finally settling down to eat my lunch."

"I was quite comfortably eating lunch under my white umbrella until I noticed some fresh panther spoor all too close to my boulder! It seemed sensible to get out of that locality at once! This I did, postponing the conclusion of the expedition to Phulbazar and cravenly doubling back on my tracks. I made for home. But climbing **up** 3,000 feet of wild terrain was no easy matter, and at times I had to go hand over hand up a dry gully with my heart bursting out of my ribs. At last I was able to take some rest in a Hindu village beneath a pipal tree. Here I said [the Office of] None. By this time a hill thunderstorm was well under way and I was glad enough to join forces with a Bhutian woman who by the conical basket on her back was going up to the Darjeeling bazaar. We couldn't communicate with each other, but she with charming courtesy gave me her large 'babu' umbrella that was all spokes and no cover! Thus we stumbled and crawled, getting soaked to the skin but finally arriving, I to my hut and she to the bazaar to sell her small store of sweet potatoes and little yellow tomatoes. I knew the *ayah* [maid] would have left hot water in my bathroom and would presently bring me a teatray. I was most respectably tucked up in bed when Sr Violet Grace descended upon me. She was not amused at my account having already heard (I suspected from the Planter), and lectured me on propriety and a lot of other things. I'm sure I deserved it, and it was all very good for my soul - yet I still look back on that escapade with pleasure."

One of the highlights of the year was the festival of St John Baptist on June 24th. In India, as in England, this was kept both as a holy day and a holiday. Sr Eudora recalls that: "We gave over our posts lock, stock and barrel to the secular staff and joyfully made our way to the mission house for the Festival Mass celebrated in my time by Fr Shore, the Superior of the Oxford Mission - a great rock in a stony land. There followed a luxurious day of just being together, and of taking full advantage of the St John's Day tradition of doing what you like. Once Sr Dorothy Frances took me with her to the New Market to buy sweets and cakes. We had Baal sherbert in the morning, and afternoon tea at tastefully arranged small tables in the Community room. On my first St John's Day, Sr Gladys solemnly took me at 4.00 p.m. to see a brace of fluffy yellow ducks happily quacking away in a round basket. She then told me I should be eating them at 8.00 p.m.!"

This was entirely in keeping with Sr Gladys' dry humour which she retained into old age. Whilst in India she had an eye for the amusing and unusual, and her work in the village schools gave her plenty to laugh about. Writing an account of the work in the summer 1936 issue of

Pipalpati, she concluded: "We pass two restaurants side by side on a main road - one is called The Epicure's Inn, and the other The Glutton's Inn! Here is an advertisement which cheers us - 'The Calcutta Cycle Emporium, all kinds and parts of Bicycles and Music."

Whilst at first Sr Eudora knew Sr Gladys best of all, she soon came to know the other Sisters equally well, and still recalls those with whom she worked: "Sr Freda was the House Sister [at the Diocesan mission house], as well as being in charge of the Church Workroom and the Sisters' clothes. Besides being Sister Superior, Sr Dorothy Frances was also Head of the Diocesan College [until its closure] and the Collegiate School with Sr Honor, and Sr Hilda Frances. St Elizabeth's Boarding School for Bengalis in the villages was staffed by Sr Frances Clare and Sr Gladys. These two also supervised the village schools in the Sunderbuns. Sr Dorothy Florence worked in the villages from the Mission House. Sr Caroline Elizabeth and Sr Lilian Maude were at St Thomas' Kidderpore; Sr Irene and I were at the Pratt Memorial School. Sr Georgina was in charge of St Michael's Darjeeling with I think, Sr Marian Edith, Sr Hilda and Sr Lilian Mary."

Sisters came and went to and from India, some home on furlough, others home for good, so that the record of who was working where, at any given time is difficult to maintain. But the Sisters listed above were working in those particular places at some stage during Sr Eudora's time (early 1934-1938). They were however, subject to being moved around to fill up vacancies left by illness and furlough. Thus more than once Sr Eudora found herself at the Diocesan mission house, as she recalls: "I found myself one January working in the Mission Compound filling a gap in the High School for Bengali girls. This was devastating for me as I knew no Bengali. My first task was that of collecting books from the Bengali book list for the year. Ayesha Roy came to my rescue and earned my undying gratitude. Somehow I painfully rubbed along, filling in what gaps I could... [but] many and bitter were the tears I shed... It was a great day for me when my Scripture Division of 15 Bengali girls really took me to their hearts. I have to this day the list of their names." It may have been at this time when, hurriedly responding to a commotion in the mission compound, Sr Eudora discovered Sr Frances Clare emerging from the large tank [pond] dripping wet and covered in slimy greenish mud and algae! The unfortunate Sister had been returning from her work in the villages when the ghari had accidentally driven straight into the tank. Of the two Sisters, Sr Frances Clare was not amused!

On another occasion: "Sr Freda's mantle fell on me when she left for her furlough and I spent the best part of a year in the Church Workroom. Two very skilled Indian girls worked there and turned out beautiful work. We were kept pretty busy with orders, and one in particular stands out in my memory. The new Bishop of Nagpur asked us to make his Enthronement Cope and Mitre. I had a marvellous time buying cloth of gold in the bazaar and glorious blue brocade from Bokhara." Never having made a mitre before, the Sister borrowed Bishop Foss Westcott's from Calcutta Cathedral and used it as a pattern! The new bishop was delighted and sent a postcard declaring: 'Magnifical. Alleluia'."

Following Sr Freda's return, Sr Eudora moved to St Thomas' School, Kidderpore, where Sr Rosemary was in charge. "Here I found myself doing much what I had done at the Pratt Memorial School only in pleasanter surroundings - a change from the vociferous Lower Circular Road with the Muslim Girls' School on one side of the compound at St James' Church and its environs on the other. St Thomas' spacious compound was well cared for by a host of *malis*, [mallees, i.e. gardeners], and was flanked by the Lieutenant Governor's House [the Belvedere], and Kidderpore zoo, and the cantonment church of St Stephen. Sr Rosemary and I being twins,[6] managed to have fun together as well as working very hard in the usual understaffed situation. She herself came of Baptist missionary stock, was born in India and loved it, though it had taken its toll of her health. Together we had some lovely picnics with and without the children, often going up the river to Diamond Harbour where we would camp under the casurinas and coconuts. It fascinated me to watch her (the delicate one), consume a whole cold chicken (admittedly an Indian one)! Since by this time India was well and truly in my blood, I lapped up all Sr Rosemary's many Indian tales, including her psychic ones, more especially concerning the hauntings of Kidderpore House." One of Sr Rosemary's experiences was the sighting of a ghostly horse and carriage drawing up to the house and a woman in brown getting out of it. On another occasion the children said they could see angels at night in the dormitory, though they did not seem in the least bit afraid of this spectacle. Investigations revealed that the ceiling was riddled with white ants and was in imminent danger of collapse!

As 1938 dawned, Sr Eudora could have little idea that this would be her last year there. "1938 was a happy time although Sr Dorothy Frances was in England on furlough and the news from Europe was pretty grim," she recalls. A note of regret always enters Sr Eudora's voice when she recalls that, "Gandhi was at the height of his popularity and he had a refuge in Elgin Road where I *nearly* saw him as I passed on my way to Chowringhee, but I never got a glimpse of him." Elgin Road was just round the corner from the Diocesan mission house, and Sr Eudora always hoped she would catch a glimpse of Gandhi, whom she admired.

The chapel at St Thomas' school was surrounded by classrooms and was therefore rather noisy, so Sr Rosemary and Sr Eudora made a shelter of reed mats on the flat roof and used it for their times of private prayer. "Towards the end of April [1938] I was watching the spectacular sunset when, 'you are going to Barbados,' leapt into my mind for no apparent reason," writes Sr Eudora. "We [in India] got next to no news from the West Indies and of course I immediately forgot it - for about two weeks, and then, one Saturday morning at the mission house I heard Sr Lilian

Maude tell Sr Rosemary that she had better return to St Thomas' alone as she wanted to see me. Somewhat alarmed but quite in the dark, I followed her into the office and was told to sit down as I might have a shock. At that moment I remembered - and astounded her by saying, 'I am going to Barbados.' She then read me part of the airmail letter from Mother Frances [at Clewer] telling of the collapse of Sr Mary Joyce and of her fear of leaving only three Sisters there. In short she would have to rob India and send me! This was a severe blow and the shock sent me to bed with Dengue fever, something I had never had. However, preparations had to be made at once and a passage booked. In May, the hottest month of the year, I crossed India again and sailed from Bombay on the *S.S. Strathaird*." Sr Eudora, travelled alone and arrived back at Clewer on May 28th 1938: she left for Barbados on October 1st.

Sr Eudora was in India at a momentuous time which coincided with Mother Katherine Maud's last visit and death in 1935; and with the final deliberations of the Clewer Chapter during 1937 about granting Provincial status to the Indian work. Politically, there was the continuing move towards Independence following the passage of the Government of India Act. And in England, the death of the King-Emperor was followed by the Abdication crisis. Sr Eudora has described India as: "a land of heat and frustrations, mosquitoes and a thousand other miseries," but also writes that: "India is in my heart." The heyday had passed - much of the Indian work had been given up by the mid 1930s, and other parts were struggling. Within 10 years of Sr Eudora's departure it would all be left behind. And yet Sr Eudora's experience of India was so vivid that it has remained an integral part of her life, and defies any negative feelings about the Sisters' work at this time. "I stayed long enough to glimpse what commitment could look like," she writes. That the commitment remained as firm in those last days as it was in the heady days of the 1880s when it was all new and exciting, cannot be seriously challenged.

Footnotes

1. Sr Gladys served two terms in India - from the end of 1933 until the end of 1938; and from early 1940 until early 1945.

2. It was Sr Celia who had accompanied Sr Jane Frances on her last voyage back to England in the summer of 1919.

3. Sr Eudora *Personal and Private Memoirs* 1975.

These were written by Sr Eudora at the invitation of Mother Annys and were never intended for publication, but for the use of the Community. I am indebted to Sr Eudora for allowing me to use the Indian chapter from her memoirs and to quote from it. The material has been augmented by further conversations with her. Sr Eudora died on March 11th 1997 shortly before her 96th birthday.

4. The plains - anywhere which was not a hill station.

5. Outhouses - all the work of the Community outside the Diocesan mission compound.

6. Twins - Sisters who were professed together.

-29-

DAYS OF GREEN AND GOLD: A POSTSCRIPT TO THE 1930s

Before leaving the 1930s with all its problems, it may be well to look through the eyes of a schoolgirl at that troubled decade. Sr Eudora has already given a Sister's view of the period, and while the Community had passed its heyday, there was still plenty of work to do, and the Sisters applied themselves to it with an indomitable sense of purpose. Similarly, life in the schools went on against all the odds, and the girls in the Sisters' care were given a solid start in life which many look back at with affection and gratitude.

Helen Wala (nee Lucas), was seven years old in 1931 when she became a pupil at the Pratt Memorial School, having previously attended a private school in Shillong, Assam: "Although it is a faint memory, I recall my father taking me to the school where I had to be tested for reading skills, and I was accepted. The Principal then was dear Sr Caroline Elizabeth.(1) She was a motherly presence to us little ones. However, I was quite unhappy for a time because the Pratt was so different from my previous school. Sr Caroline Elizabeth left in 1932 and Sr Irene, previously the senior Sister, took her place. She was very strict indeed! But she was very interested in her pupils and was to remain as Principal until the Sisters left [the school] in 1940. So she knew us very well and was a great influence on us. She was always very interested in me in a special way, encouraging me a great deal and always expected the best of us."

Over the past sixty years the school buildings have been extended several times, but the main building remains the same as Helen Wala's description: "The Pratt School was a very large building, three stories high, in an inverted L shape with a long gravel entrance and portico. There were two large dormitories, one for the juniors (7-12), and the other for the seniors (13-17). At any given time there must have been 130-50 boarders, the rest were day scholars. The classrooms were on all three floors and there was a very large hall with a stage where morning and afternoon assemblies were taken, classes starting promptly at 9.00 a.m. and ending at 3.15 p.m. The hall was also used for gym and other leisure activities including school plays. The main wooden staircase was like a miniature art gallery with many fine reproductions and other artefacts on display. We used the main staircase at all times except to reach the dormitories which were accessible by the stone stairs."

Chapel attendance was an important feature of school life: "We had a lovely chapel at the far end of the building above the refectory. The rules were quite strict - senior girls attended chapel in the morning and for

Evening Prayer, and helped in the sacristy on Saturdays (we had a roster). On Sundays we went to morning services and Holy Communion at St James' church adjacent to the school. There was a boys' school also called St James,' and the properties were separated by the boys' playing field walls and the rectory grounds. When we became seniors we went to Evensong. One rector was the Revd Matthews; he prepared us for Confirmation. Later we had a very shy, quiet rector whose wife was most kind to us senior girls and had us to Sunday tea and gave us outings, and we helped her with Sunday School classes."

"On Saturdays we had a good deal of free time. The windows had wide ledges and we used to like to sit on them to read our library books. I loved to read and was always in trouble with the Sister or teacher on duty for reading in "line" and I got many a book confiscated! The school system was based on houses - we had four named after British heroes. There was fierce competition between them both academically and in sports. We had a head girl and four prefects. I was head girl in 1941. All meals were taken in the refectory and breakfast was in silence as the Sisters were in chapel [directly above]. Tea time, of course was the best, as we were allowed to bring tuck boxes and could have treats with our tea."

The Sisters always aimed at a high standard in their schools, and despite all the problems encountered at the Pratt Memorial in the 1930s and referred to elsewhere, they seem to have achieved that standard both with their own teaching and with the secular teachers employed there: "We had a good teaching staff," writes Helen Wala, "many of whom I remember very well for the great interest they took in us, and particularly encouraging my best in history and literature. We had art and music as well, and I recall I tried to get out of taking art by appealing to Sr Irene. She very sternly, but in a kindly voice, told me I should go on, as 'Miss Smith could teach a caterpillar to draw!' We took examinations through the Royal Academy of Art, and a few of us also learned piano and took the Royal School of Music examinations. We had a good training in musical appreciation, and Miss Woodward, head of music, had a junior and senior choral group, and we occasionally gave concerts for parents and also performed at the Calcutta College of Music. Once a year a huge art display of all the work done by the various forms was held. In 1936 Miss Bullock involved the entire school in a marvellous production of the 'Pied Piper'. It was open to the public and was a great success."

Looking back across the years, Helen Wala remembers several other Sisters: "Sr Lilian Mary, Sr Honor, Sr Elizabeth Mary and Sr Violet Grace. The latter[2] was the Principal for a year in 1936 when Sr Irene took a year's leave. Discipline was strict, but we had many activities and a good deal of fun. Sr Honor played the piano for us to dance to on 'hall nights.' School plays were the great thing - I loved being in them and my closest friends in school were in them too." But it was not all music and drama - as with all good boarding schools, sports was an important feature of the curriculum and Helen Wala recalls: "two large grass playing fields. Basketball was the main game, though we had badminton too. There were school sports of the usual sort, and also sports with other schools."

"The Sisters instilled in us great sportsmanship, discipline, love of learning, qualities of fairness. Our school motto was *Nil Desparandum* and the school colours were green and gold.[3] We wore navy uniforms with ties and waist cords in the school colours; with panama hats (worn to church), and navy felt in the winter, with bands in the school colours. On special occasions we were allowed to dress up and wear our own frocks."

"There were Girl Guides and Blue Birds too - Lord Baden Powell visited Calcutta for a very big jamboree, and the Pratt School was represented. But I dropped out of the Guides because my best friend wasn't interested - it was not compulsory to join. Sr Irene gave us another task - we were put in charge of mixing up the blue ink and filling all the inkwells in the classrooms. We considered ourselves set apart and quite important!"

School friendships can be very enduring and in some cases prove lifelong, as did this one between Helen and Gwynneth[4] formed over the inkwells at the Pratt Memorial School. "Gwynneth and I both enjoyed plays, and Sr Irene once allowed her to put on scenes from 'The Rivals' which we were then studying. None of the staff were involved. She did all the casting, production and direction. Gwynneth was Lydia and I played Mrs Malaprop. We borrowed furniture and got help with the costumes. It was the highlight of our 15th year!"

By this time the Empire was again at war, and in 1940 the Sisters found it necessary to withdraw from the Pratt Memorial School. Miss Ena Lawrence became the Principal and did much to maintain the school's traditions and standards. In 1941 Helen Lucas (as she was then), left the school having completed the Cambridge Senior School Certificate, and Miss Lawrence was instrumental in getting her admitted to a teacher training college. She left college in 1943, and came back to the Pratt Memorial where she taught from 1944-5 before teaching at St Michael's School Darjeeling from 1945-6 under Sr Georgina. It was at St Michael's that she met another teacher, Joyce Keenan, herself a former pupil of St Michael's, and another enduring friendship was forged.

Writing in the *Pipalpati* magazine early in 1940, Sr Irene concluded her report of the school's activities with the prophetic comment: "A real love for the school is becoming more and more apparent amongst the children. During the past year more than one older girl has declared that in after years she is determined to come back and serve her old school. Whether that be so or not, we can but trust that some of what the school has striven to inculcate will remain, and bear fruit somewhere, to the glory of God."

Footnotes

1. Sr Caroline Elizabeth left the Pratt Memorial School in 1932; Sr Eudora, recalling the period from 1934-38, remembers her at St Thomas' Kidderpore.

2. Sr Violet Grace acted as Principal at the Pratt Memorial School while Sr Irene had her furlough in 1936, and then went to Darjeeling to deputise for Sr Georgina in 1937.

3. The school colours are still green and gold.

4. Gwynneth now lives in Wales, and Helen in the USA, but they still correspond and meet from time to time. But this was not the only lasting friendship formed in those far off school days. Back in England, the Clewer Sisters had another successful girls' school - St Stephen's College, then at Folkestone. One day Sr Irene asked Helen if she would like a pen pal in England as two girls at St Stephen's College had expressed an interest: "One of the girls quickly dropped out, but the other one, Jean, became a lifelong friend and now lives in Vancouver, Canada. We wrote to each other from 1937, right through the war years and met for the first time when I came to England in 1948. We felt as though we had always known each other - and we still write letters!"

St Stephen's College was at Folkestone between the wars; it was evacuated to Taplow Court during World War II, and then moved to Broadstairs. The Sisters withdrew from teaching there in 1965, but maintained links until the school's closure in 1991. For a detailed history of St Stephen's College see: BALSTON, Jenny *The story of St Stephen's College 1994.*

CSJB

INDIA

-30-
EARTH'S PROUD EMPIRES

When Britain went to war against Germany in September 1939, the Empire followed suit as it had in 1914 - but with greater reservations. A quarter of a century previously, King George V had declared war on behalf of the entire Empire, but times had changed, and in 1939 the legislatures of Canada, Australia, New Zealand and South Africa all had the right to decide whether to fight alongside Britain. They chose to do so - no one seriously thought they would not. But despite all the constitutional reforms which purported to prepare the way for self-government in India, it was the Viceroy, Lord Linlithgow, who decided without consulting any Indians that the sub-Continent would go to war for King and Empire. Such supreme tactlessness further muddied the already murky political waters and helped set India on the collision course leading to Partition.

In retaliation against the British insult, the Congress Party demanded immediate independence in return for India's support; this was refused and so the Congress provincial governments resigned. But Britain needed India as a fighting force as India knew well enough, and months of hard bargaining followed only to be crushed at British Cabinet level. Muhammad Ali Jinnah, leader of the increasingly powerful Muslim League, had already pledged his party to backing the British, and the resignation of the Congress dominated provincial governments strengthened his hand. Increasingly, he was being brought into negotiations alongside Gandhi and Nehru. The situation took a further critical turn after the fall of Singapore in February 1942. The invasion of India seemed imminent, the protection of the Empire was crucial, but Britain's newest ally, the USA, was by its very nature opposed to imperialism. It was after all fighting the imperialist ambitions of Japan, and indirectly of Germany and Italy, and Roosevelt had no sympathy with protecting the British Empire in the long term. Thus Britain came under increasing pressure from her own allies to make concessions to India.

Sir Stafford Cripps, on behalf of the British government, laid down an offer of independence after the war in return for immediate help. Now at last India had the reality of independence within its grasp. Even so, the process was extremely delicate and was further complicated by the "Quit India" campaign during 1942 which resulted in the imprisonment of Gandhi and other leaders, as well as some 60,000 party activists. As with most of Gandhi's peaceful protests there were plenty of participants who resorted to violence. And now Jinnah was pressing his case for partition: within months of the war beginning he had presented his

Lahore Resolution, which coined a new name - Pakistan[1]. Cripps' declaration had laid down that after the war any province wishing to opt out of the independent Indian Union and form its own government could do so. No one except Jinnah recognised the potential of this loophole; it was the hoop through which Pakistan would leap. While all these talks had been going on behind the scenes, thousands of Indians were already fighting for the British. In 1939 there were 189,000 Indian troops, and by the end of the war the numbers had risen to two and a half million - all volunteers.

Despite the outbreak of war the Sisters continued their work, although they must have felt the odds were increasingly against them. "We find it difficult to concentrate on our ordinary tasks, but schools must go on, and *Pipalpati* must appear before term closes," wrote Mother Hilda Frances in the October 1939 issue. It had not been possible to send the Christmas gift boxes from England, but a faithful group of English supporters organised a sale and sent the proceeds.

The Sisters withdrew from two of their Calcutta schools early in the war - St Thomas' Kidderpore and the Pratt Memorial. These withdrawals were not so much casualties of the war as of the changing circumstances in India. "Owing to the shortage of Sisters who can go to the climate of Bengal we have been obliged to give up the charge of St Thomas' Kidderpore," began the account in the January 1940 *Associates' Newsletter*. "We have worked there for about twenty years, a period which has brought about drastic and fruitful changes, so that an old fashioned charity school with girls in hideous long uniform frocks has become a happy, up-to-date school with healthy, gay children in coloured tunics." But there was another reason which hastened the Sisters' decision as Mother Hilda Frances explained in the October 1939 issue of *Pipalpati*: "The Governors of the school have decided to move the Boys' School from the centre of the town to Kidderpore, in close proximity to the girls. We consider that this is most undesirable in itself and would make it quite impossible for us to continue in charge of the Girls' School, so we shall be giving up that work at Christmas, our withdrawal being hastened by the shortage of Sisters, accentuated by Mother Dorothy Frances' recall to England.[2]

The Sisters' work at Kidderpore ended on a high note with a visit from the Viceroy, Lord Linlithgow, who presented the prizes to both the girls' and boys' schools. Recalling the event in *Pipalpati*, Sr Lilian Maude wrote that: "Tea was provided for the Viceroy and the distinguished guests in the school hall, which had to be redecorated for the occasion, an added trial involving the bespattering of whitewash over everything within a radius of 200 yards!... At the end of this momentous day the Staff requested our presence in the Kindergarten Hall, where we found the whole School assembled to say goodbye." It wasn't quite goodbye - not until December 28th when the new Principal, Mrs Halliday arrived.

But that final leave-taking was in Sr Lilian Maude's words, "a trying ordeal."

The withdrawal from the Pratt Memorial School was announced in the October 1940 issue of the Clewer *Associates' Newsletter*: "We expect to retire from the Pratt Memorial School at the end of the year, regretfully, yet it is probably time that we left the work to those we have sought to train. Many old pupils are competent, well equipped, enthusiastic teachers, and it is for them to rise up now and carry on those principles and traditions which have been established." In fact those hopes have been fulfilled beyond the Sisters' greatest expectations.

St Elizabeth's Middle English School was struggling for existence at this time and was sorely hit by the financial strictures of the war. The deficit was increasing at an alarming rate because so many English subscriptions were no longer forthcoming. On December 6th 1938 morale at the school had been boosted by a visit from Lady Brabourne, wife of the Lieutenant Governor of Bengal. She had visited both St Elizabeth's and St John's Diocesan Girls' High School (formerly the Diocesan Collegiate School), and afterwards sent a cheque for 250 rupees to help with repairs. The Brabourne's had proved very popular in Bengal but their term of office was curtailed by the sudden death of Lord Brabourne on February 24th 1939.

Memories of Sisters being shipwrecked in the Mediterranean during the Great War must have been uppermost in everyone's minds as the new conflict got under way. At first travelling was not too difficult; Sr Gladys and Sr Rosemary finally sailed on December 22nd 1939, having met the worst hazards of the journey at Southampton where thick fog had prevented the ship's departure for four days. But as the war escalated, and especially after Italy declared war on England and France in June 1940, crossing the Mediterranean became virtually impossible. Just before that, in March 1940 Sr Caroline Elizabeth, Sr Lilian Maude, Sr Dorothy Florence and Sr Violet Grace arrived back in England after a very good voyage of less than three weeks. A thanksgiving service for a safe passage had been held on board before everyone disembarked. This was the last time Sisters would be able to travel to or from India until 1944.

The European theatre of war was 8,000 miles away and, except for the U-boat threat in the Mediterranean, the reality was difficult to imagine. But far closer was the growing threat from Japan. That threat assumed an immediacy on February 15th 1942 with the fall of Singapore. Stoically the British saw it as a temporary setback, but the reality was the spread of Japanese occupation up through Burma, drawing ever closer to the backdoor of India. The Clewer Community *Annals* for February 21st 1942 record that: "a cable from India said that orders had been given to close St Elizabeth's [Middle English] School and send the children home. Also the lower classes of St John's [Diocesan Girls'] High School were sent home. The upper classes were sent to St Elizabeth's buildings as the government had commandeered the High School buildings for their own use." A further entry on April 16th revealed that: "an airgraph was received from India telling us that by order of the government both schools were closed down in Calcutta. The Japanese had made such rapid gains in Burma, and established a certain control in the Indian Ocean that the threat of invasion had drawn very near, and it seemed wisest that the Indian children should be under the care of their relatives." On April 27th a cable from India arrived at Clewer saying that the Bishop of Calcutta advised evacuation, 3 Sisters were to go to Naini Tal, 3 to Chanda and Mother Hilda Frances to Darjeeling. But two days later, on April 29th, another cable was received saying "Evacuation deferred."

The May 1942 issue of the Clewer *Associates' Newsletter* bore the slightly contradictory news that: "both the Calcutta schools are closed and part of the Mission compound walled off to make an A.R.P. centre. So far the few Sisters there have not been ordered to leave. By their presence they help and encourage the Bengali Christians living near them. An 'alert' sounded during the Three Hours Service at St Mary's church which adjoins the compound, but the congregation remained splendidly calm. There would probably have been 300 people there." By August Mother Hilda Frances was able to write that she had been allowed to open a few classes for St John's High School in St Elizabeth's building: "a very difficult arrangement but she is anxious to keep some of the work going for the sake of the children." St Elizabeth's Middle English School was able keep functioning by evacuating to Thakurpukur, where the Sisters had care of the hostel to the girls' school which was run by the S.P.G.

Just about the only part of the Sisters' work which assumed any semblance of normality at this time was St Michael's School Darjeeling. Nancy Leslie started in the infants' section in 1941, moving into the junior school a year later. No matter how anxious the Sisters were about the war at home and the threat of invasion, school life went on. Thus Nancy Leslie writes that: "school started at 9.00 a.m. with register, and then prayers in the hall, marching in by forms and height. The marching was to music and I remember Georgie, as we called Sr Georgina, sometimes got a bit 'uptight' over the marching and we had to do it until it reached her standard! Only the staff had benches to sit on, the children sat or knelt on the wooden floor. Prayers were over by 9.30, and generally the first lesson was Religious (Old Testament, New Testament and 1662 Prayer Book Catechism). There were three lessons before break at 11.15 until noon, and then five lessons afterwards, finishing at about 2.45." Like all boarding schools "prep" featured a good deal, and Nancy recalls two sessions a day which were supposed to be conducted in silence, but she recalls: "we learnt the deaf alphabet to communicate and hoped not to be caught!"

The chapel was a central feature of school life and there was a worship manual for the girls' use. There was a service early each evening and the girls would process in by houses wearing their white veils. During the war there was a special litany for peace. On Fridays the whole school attended choir practice in the school hall when the hymns for the Sunday Eucharist would be practiced. Some of the senior girls were allowed to attend St Andrew's parish church on Sunday evenings. Nancy recalls that: "Confirmation was an annual event with the Bishop of Calcutta using the 1928 service. Generally you were Confirmed on reaching Form IVA, but I remember my mother thought 13 was too young - a letter from Georgie changed her mind. It was a new white dress and special veil occasion, with a day off school, not to mention a bath the night before! I think we had a cake, and I am not sure whether or not first Communion about ten days later was treated in the same way."

"On Easter Day, St John Baptist Day, Sr Georgina's birthday and St Michael's Day, we had to go individually to Sister's room to wish her a happy Easter/feast/birthday/feast. At other times going to Sister's room was not a pleasant occasion except when you were being prepared for Confirmation", writes Nancy. She recalls that: "discipline was strict. We had school dances, for the staff and girls only, but towards the end of my time there were a couple of occasions when either the boys of St Paul's were invited, or we were invited there." At the end of the nine month term there was a dance, "and a special dinner afterwards when everyone ate together - and Georgie bidding us goodnight with tears."

Academic standards were rigorous too, and each Saturday brought not only lessons but also a written test. Marks were awarded during lessons and the monthly marks read out to the whole school, "a humbling experience," as Nancy recalls. But it was not all work and no play. Whilst some pocket money had to be reserved for Sunday collection and replacing lost rulers and rubbers, there was usually something left over to spend on the sweetman who came to the school on Saturdays (but not in Lent). "He sold a variety of sweets, buns and chapattis. One year he tried to put the price up, and Georgie sent him packing. He was back the next week - I suppose 100 girls spending their money was not to be sneezed at."

Whatever deprivation the rest of India was suffering, the food at St Michael's does not seem to have been affected. The same public school stodge seemed to be served there as elsewhere throughout the Empire! Nancy writes that: "tea was after lessons and consisted of bread and butter, except on Tuesdays and Thursdays (outside Lent) when tuck boxes were allowed, although they had to be shared." Two walks a day (after breakfast and tea), ensured a degree of fitness.

Clearly Sr Georgina was not going to be easily persuaded to close the school buildings and evacuate, as she later recalled in her history of the school: "The Educational Department ordered all the Darjeeling schools to make arrangements for evacuation to a safer part of India, and to have notices printed to send round to parents of the plans made. St Paul's had accommodation arranged in the Bombay direction, but they had none for a girls' school. Can you not imagine the anxious disturbance that would be aroused in parents' minds by such an announcement? Anyhow we did not upset our parents and, as you know, Darjeeling was quite safe." So the school stayed on, and apart from adhering to blackout restrictions, life went on as before - for a handful of years at least.

Meantime the Sisters in Calcutta were still working at the village centre at Thakurpukur, and by this time St Elizabeth's Middle English School had also been evacuated there. The Clewer *Associates' Newsletter* for August 1942 announced that the Sisters had enlarged the day school there for Bengali village girls. Two or three of the Sisters were living there so that they could continue the work in the villages. Sr Frances Clare, Sr Gladys and Sr Dipika laboured on stoically, but kept a sense of humour as their account of a Confirmation showed: "We had hoped that some of the candidates would have come to Thakurpukur for a few days when we had our Refresher Course there in May, but there was some mistake about letting them know, so they did not turn up. When the time of the Confirmation drew near, Bishop Tarafdar[3] was laid up with malaria, so that it was not till June 25th that we all finally collected at Thakurpukur for the great event. Bishop Tarafdar arrived half an hour before the time and there was rather a delay getting the women into order according to their names. They had all taken their places on the floor and answered to any name that the senior Bengali padre, who did not know them, called out! However, at last we were all ready and had a reverent, dignified service... It was a great joy to see so many illiterate women confirmed. Some of them had received teaching for two or three years. One had walked two miles with a bad fever, and others had come the night before so as to be in time."

In 1943 Bengal was seized in the grip of famine. Newspapers showed photographs of women and children dying of hunger in the Calcutta streets and the Bengal death toll exceeded the five-yearly average by 689,000. In his book *The men who ruled India*, Philip Mason attributes the famine to: "a failure of the administration in transition." He notes that under the old system of government, famine had been recognised as endemic, and there were contingency plans which could be put into effect as soon as shortages began. In 1942 the monsoon had not failed nor had the rice crop, there being only a shortfall of three weeks supply. With a proper system of rationing this could have been overcome. But the war had complicated things. Rice from Burma had always been a reserve to fall back upon but by 1943 Burma was occupied by Japan. Furthermore, boats and wheeled vehicles had been removed from coastal areas of Bengal because of the fear of invasion and this hampered the relief operation.

The situation was complicated even further by the increasing complexity of government. The Indian government in New Delhi was pre-occupied with the war effort despite the Imperial death knell having been tolled in London. The provincial governments were pre-occupied with internal wranglings and power struggles, and were reluctant to admit the need for help, or to ask for it. As the situation worsened, prices rose from 80 pounds of rice at 3 or 5 rupees before the war, to 10-14 rupees in January 1943, to 30 rupees in May 1943. In October the new Viceroy, Lord Wavell, went to Calcutta to see for himself and spent three days there: "round the streets by night to see how the destitutes were sleeping and by day to see them being fed... Three pretty hectic and distressing days. I wonder if my intervention will do any good."[4] Wavell ordered the army to distribute supplies.

The pivotal factor surrounding this particular famine was panic buying. Philip Mason puts it succinctly: "At a time when the administration was strained by war and weakened by political experiment, a harvest rather below average started a rise in price. In ordinary times it would have lasted a few weeks and then rice from somewhere else would have come in. But now there was nowhere else for rice to come from and the air was full of rumours; the Japanese were coming, the English were going, Calcutta was being bombed, all the ships on the sea were being sunk, Burma and its rice were lost, it would soon be every man for himself. To everyone who had money, it seemed that it would be a good thing to buy rice. And a great many people had money. There had been war contracts and compensation had been paid for carts and boats taken up as a precaution against Japanese invasion. Much of that compensation went into rice. And as prices rose, panic increased and more and more rushed to buy... In Bengal, there was little grain in the markets and that at a price too high for any but the rich. The rice growers had enough; the rich had enough. Most of the town middle classes had seen what was coming in time and bought early. The industrial worker had grain supplied him by his factory. But the casual labourers who bought day by day had nothing; landless labourers from the villages sometimes had nothing and flocked to the towns. It was an urban famine, and that was one thing that made it so shocking; the casualties were concentrated where they could be seen."[5]

The Sisters were themselves caught up in the plight of the famine victims as recounted in the October 1943 issue of the Clewer *Associates' Newsletter*: "One of the Sisters in Bengal writes, 'Fancy being thrilled at being able to buy rice at seven times its usual price!' The Calcutta Cathedral congregation has established a free food depot at Thakurpukur, the village to which our St Elizabeth's School is evacuated. 15,000 had come [for relief] in one day... Many who come are already so ill that the food (rice and lentils), is too strong for them. We used to read in the geography books 'the staple food is rice', but I imagine that we thought it took the place of bread or other cereals which we use. We did not grasp that 'staple' is almost synonymous with 'sole' in the villages."

The May 1944 issue of the Clewer *Associates' Newsletter* carried a sombre announcement: "We have to tell you that it has become inevitable that we should withdraw. You will all sympathise with us, for the needs of 'Mother India' appeal to all alike. The climate of Bengal is, as you know, a peculiarly trying one, so that only those with good health can be sent out, and that means that unless we have a good supply of young and strong Sisters we cannot keep up the supply of workers. At present we are not able to send out Sisters to take the place of several who must return for good, and so it has become clear that the work must pass into other hands."

The Community *Annals* shed further light on the returning Sisters - Sr Honor, Sr Freda, Sr Irene and Sr Rosemary. On March 9th 1944 a notice was sent round the Community saying that: "at the end of January four Sisters left Bombay to return to England. They had spent some days at Mazagon with the All Saints Sisters so as to be on the spot in Bombay to secure passages at a moment's notice if required." The entry on March 24th noted that: "a telegram arrived to say that the Sisters expected to be at Euston on Saturday morning. As we did not know the time of the train, and were unable to glean any information by telephone, Sr Eudora[6] went up to London in the evening to try to find out. She spent the night with the St Alban's Sisters[7] and incidentally had a trying time as there was rather a bad raid in the night. The next morning she discovered that the Sisters would not arrive until the evening."

The *Annals* continue on March 25th: "Sr Eudora met the travellers at Euston at 6.50 p.m. They managed to catch the 8.44 from Waterloo to Windsor, and when the train had started Sr Mary Rachel [from St Alban's Holborn] telephoned that they were on their way. We had not been able to get a taxi in Windsor because of the 'blackout' so Miles brought round the laundry van and took Mother and Sr Evelyn Joan to the Southern station to meet the travellers. They and all their luggage arrived at the Convent about 10.15 p.m. and after a hot drink in the Retreat Room they gladly went to bed. Owing to a case of smallpox on board ship they were under government orders to be kept in quarantine for three days, which they spent in bed recovering from the strain of their journey."

Sr Rosemary returned from India already terminally ill. On May 7th 1944 she was admitted to King Edward VII Hospital, Windsor, but was discharged on May 13th and went into the Sisters' Infirmary. The *Annals* noted sadly that: "The doctors can do nothing to help her and probably she will not be with us for very long." She died at 11.30 p.m. on June 22nd, "after a period of great weakness and discomfort," and was buried in the Sisters' cemetery at Clewer on June 26th.

These final years saw the deaths of several Sisters who had once worked in India - Sr Kate Mary died in April 1939 having been the Secretary of the Indian work at Clewer for the past 19 years, and before that had been in India for almost 30 years; Sr Gertrude Emma who died on October 1st

1943 had worked at the Presidency General Hospital during Sr Lucy's time but had returned to England on health grounds, and had later worked amongst the families of the Brigade of Guards[8]; on April 1st 1944 Sr Edith Helen died; and Sr Celia died on August 16th 1947. Also, two former Mothers Superior died - Sr Frances and Sr Evelyn. Sr Frances had lived in the Infirmary ever since her resignation in February 1939, and had become increasingly helpless. She died on November 10th 1940 and was buried three days later. Sr Evelyn died at Torquay on May 25th 1942 and was buried there, having led a very active Community life after resigning as Mother Superior (see chapter 26, note 8).

One of the great disappointments sustained by the Sisters was the lack of Indian vocations. It is true that Sr Dipika had been professed on December 23rd 1939, but the numbers the Sisters had hoped for were not forthcoming. As independence grew nearer, they realised that the future for the Religious Life lay in indigenous Communities, which would combine Indian culture with the Christian faith. Perhaps in earlier times when the Empire seemed secure, this idea had not been fostered. It is difficult to know from a distance of nearly a century, and this is one question which the archives fail to address. Nor is it likely that Indian Sisters would have been regarded as truly equal with the English Sisters[9] - it was an idea which would have run contrary to imperial culture. Certainly it would be true to say that while the Sisters affirmed Indian culture and customs in some of the schools in the Diocesan mission compound, they made no concessions to it in their own lives, apart from adapting their diet, wearing a white habit, and learning Bengali. They remained an *English* Religious Community abroad, and so too did other Communities at this time. And the lack of Provincial status meant that not only were all decisions made via the Clewer Chapter, but any Indian postulants would have been sent to Clewer to serve their novitiate. Indian women, such as Sr Dipika, who asked to join the Clewer Sisterhood, were faced with a complete change in culture in addition to the rigours of the novitiate. It is hardly surprising that Indian vocations were not forthcoming.

In 1940 a note in the Clewer *Associates' Newsletter* had observed sadly that: "The Church in India has not yet brought us vocations, and it does not yet preach the Religious Life as a life to be valued and considered as a vocation. We were told on one occasion in Calcutta at a public meeting with Sisters present, how necessary Sisterhoods and Brotherhoods were for their cheapness!... It is to the indigenous Communities that the Church of India, Burma and Ceylon will look to sow the good seed in the hills, valleys and plains of India, ploughed and prepared to some extent by those in the West."

Now it was too late to begin fostering Indian vocations, because independence would mean the final return to Clewer, and the Community could not commit itself to receiving Indian women - after independence what would they do? It would be unfair to expect them to live in England, but to leave them in India would be like abandoning them. This was the dilemma facing the Community, for within a year or two of Sr Dipika's profession, Sir Stafford Cripps had committed Britain to the final withdrawal.

But as noted in chapter 27, Sr Dipika was not the only person seeking to join the Clewer Sisters. There was also Susila, and it was through her rather than Sr Dipika, that the future indigenous Community was to evolve. Susila had a long history with the Sisters. One of four sisters, and Tamil by racial origin, Susila came to Calcutta as a small child because her father was on the staff at Bishop's College. The four girls all went to the Pratt Memorial School; Susila started in the kindergarten and then entered the main school in 1929. She recalls Sr Caroline Elizabeth, "taking me onto her lap", also Sr Irene, Sr Lilian Mary, Sr Lilian Maude, Sr Honor and Sr Eudora. In 1936 Susila's father went to Bangalore and so she became a pupil at the Bishop Cotton School there, but her youngest sister stayed at the Pratt. Towards the end of 1937 Susila returned to Calcutta as a student at St John's Diocesan Girls' High School, and after matriculating in 1940 went to Thakurpukur. In 1939-40 Susila decided she wanted to join the Clewer Community - after all, Sr Dipika had just been professed and there was much talk about Indian vocations. At this time also she became one of the handful of Indian Associates. But Mother Hilda Frances felt that Susila was too young, and doubtless the uncertainty of the future loomed large in her mind. The Community gave her financial assistance in order to go to college in south India. Upon completing Intermediate Arts she returned to Calcutta to Lady Brabourne College, staying in the meantime with the Sisters in the St John Baptist mission compound.

By 1944 Susila was still feeling called to the Religious Life, but by this time the Clewer Community had made the decision to withdraw. Therefore Mother Hilda Frances advised her to go to the Oxford Mission Sisters of the Epiphany at Barisal because they would be staying on. After taking her Honours Degree she joined that Sisterhood in 1950. But the idea of an indigenous Community was still very much part of Sr Susila's vocation, and in 1970 she was given permission to live at Jobarpar in what is now Bangladesh, with three Bengali women who aspired to the Religious Life. This Community, which has been fed and nurtured by seeds sown by Clewer and the Oxford Mission, has now passed its silver jubilee. Called the Christa Sevika Sangha (Handmaids of Christ), the Sisters work in Jobarpar supervising boys' and girls' hostels and a play centre for small children, and also helping in St Gabriel's School; and at Barisal, where they supervise St Mary's Asroi (Home). So the Clewer Sisters' cherished hope for an indigenous Community has been fulfilled.

Another indirect influence on the Sisters' decision to withdraw was the Church of South India scheme. This was a proposed scheme of reunion between four dioceses of the Church of India, Burma and Ceylon (Anglican), the South India Provincial Synod of the Methodist Church, and the South India United Church which was itself an amalgam of Presbyterians, Congregationalists and other non-episcopal bodies. It immediately provoked controversy in England because of the non-episcopal nature of all but the Anglican partners, and when the details were first revealed in 1943 it sent shock waves through the Anglo-Catholic wing of the Church of England. Societies such as the Annunciation group were formed to uphold traditional faith and order, and the Religious Communities were petitioned to pray about the scheme. Thus the Community *Annals* for December 9th 1943 record that: "The Council for the Defence of Christian Principles has asked the prayers of the Community, 'that the Church may attain to the unity of the faith,' and for guidance for those making proposals for union with other Christian bodies, with special reference to the South India re-union scheme which is exercising us all at the present time."

In spite of all efforts to thwart it, the united Church of South India became a reality in 1947, but there was still opposition in England. The non-Anglican clergy had not been re-ordained, but all the bishops shared in the Anglican succession, and future clergy were to be ordained by a bishop. The question which now exercised people in England was what kind of relationship should the Church of England have with the new body? It was not until 1955 that the Convocations of Canterbury and York discussed the matter and a relationship of "growing intercommunion" was decided upon. But this did not provide for non-episcopally ordained ministers of the C.S.I. to celebrate the Eucharist in the Church of England.

Fifty years on, and several reunion schemes later, it might be easy to dismiss the South India scheme as a storm in a tea cup, but at the time it caused many people to ask questions about the meaning of authority and episcopacy. This present ecumenical age might see South India as pioneering and prophetic, perhaps even ahead of its time, but that only serves to underline its importance - and its gravity. The diocese of Calcutta was not involved in the 1947 scheme, although it is now part of the Church of North India, similarly constituted in 1970. But both the Clewer Sisters and the Oxford Mission Brothers were deeply anxious about the South India scheme, although Clewer had already made the decision to leave before the new Church was inaugurated. The Oxford Mission, after much soul searching, accepted both schemes and worked within the new system.

Having announced to the Clewer Associates their intention of withdrawing from India, the Sisters explained in the *Associates' Newsletter* of May 1944 what would happen to the remaining work: "The village work, begun by Miss Hoare and supported mainly by the Weald of Kent Association, has been definitely and closely connected with the S.P.G.

36. Welcoming party at St John's Diocesan Girls' Higher Secondary School, Calcutta, February 1995.
Left to right: a senior student, Valerie Bonham, Joyce Sampson, Mrs Rosita Chrestien (Lady Principal).

37. Senior students from St John's dancing to welcome us, February 1995.

38. The former Diocesan College, now St John's Diocesan Girls' H. S. School, February 1995.

39. The former Diocesan Collegiate School, now part of St John's Diocesan Girls' H. S. School, February 1995.

40. *Pratt Memorial School, Calcutta, February 1995.*

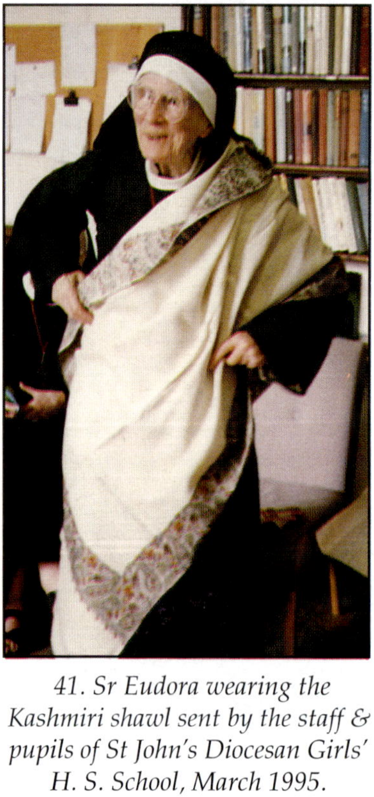

41. *Sr Eudora wearing the Kashmiri shawl sent by the staff & pupils of St John's Diocesan Girls' H. S. School, March 1995.*

42. *Sr Eudora in the garden at Clewer, 1996.*

That Society supports the Superintending Missionary who lives in the rice country. Since he became resident in the district a new epoch has begun. Great and hopeful changes have taken place [lately] and the Sisters have rejoiced to see some definite fruits of their labours." St Elizabeth's School was also working well from its evacuated site at Thakurpukur and the Sisters were able to report that: "it is now carrying on steadily without a resident Sister. The staff consists almost entirely of former pupils who have worked with the Sisters long enough to learn what Christian education and discipline mean."

The Sisters were very concerned about the future of St John's Diocesan Girls' High School. Writing in May 1944 they noted that the school: "is nearing a new epoch in its history, for we suppose that after the war when the buildings are freed, these will have to be greatly improved and enlarged, and the school will very likely have to become entirely Bengali speaking. The school was permitted to remain a special school for a time when University changes were made in recent years (i.e. the upper classes continue to be taught in English, and Matriculation was to be taken in English). But as the University authorities view this exception with disapproval, it is almost certain that it will be withdrawn before long. Yet parents have learned to value the tone and the high standard of work and conduct demanded from the children, and this tradition will live, for the old girls valued it, and the staff is largely composed of those who have been taught there. We hope that one of our own Christian old girls will be appointed Head Mistress."

These were also the last days at Darjeeling, although St Michael's was the final work to be given up. As noted in chapter 29, Joyce Keenan joined the teaching staff at St Michael's from 1945-6 at the same time as Helen Lucas, the latter having previously taught at the Pratt Memorial School. Joyce had long connections with St Michael's having been a pupil there herself during the 1930s. Her mother had also been a pupil in the original school destroyed by the great landslip in 1899, so between them they spanned most of the school's existence. "St Michael's will pass into other hands," wrote Mother Dorothy Frances in May 1944. "The Diocese is responsible for the school and the Metropolitan is President of the Governing body. He is anxious to find another Religious Community to take up the work when we leave."

Foss Westcott, Bishop of Calcutta and Metropolitan of India since 1919, was greatly distressed by the prospect of the Sisters' withdrawal as a letter written in 1944 to an unknown recipient shows: "...The notice of their withdrawal from India was a cause of profound distress to me and to all who have known of the invaluable work which they have carried on in this diocese for the past 64 years. It is impossible to over estimate the example and influence of such a Community working among the population of a great city, and the measure of our appreciation of all that they have done... is also the measure of our sorrow at the circumstances which have compelled them to withdraw... But I shall entertain the hope that numbers of their novices will again rise in the near future and will enable them once more to renew their work in the diocese which now mourns their departure."[10]

The beginning of the final withdrawal took place early in 1945. The Community *Annals* for January 22nd record that: "we received a cable from India telling us that the five Sisters who had been waiting at Mazagon for passages had sailed from Bombay. We were not allowed to know the date, but they had left round about the time they had hoped to do which meant that they had not had a very long wait at Mazagon." On February 14th Mother Dorothy Frances received an airgraph written at sea on February 1st by Mother Hilda Frances saying they were very comfortable and had a cabin to themselves. February 22nd saw Mother Dorothy Frances receiving a telegram from the Sisters saying they hoped to be in London next day. Sr Mary Rachel from St Alban's Holborn met the travellers in London and telephoned Clewer once they were safely on the train. Several Sisters and three taxis were at the Southern railway station to meet them and they were greeted at the Convent by the Sisters assembled in the Lodge and in order to celebrate the occasion the Lodge bell was rung for the first time since the outbreak of war. They had travelled on board a troopship which had docked at Glasgow and the Commanding Officer had been very kind to them. The *Annals* take up the account: "He found them a reserved carriage on the train from Glasgow, and they were taken from St Pancras to Waterloo with all their luggage free of charge in an army lorry."

The five Sisters who arrived in England on February 23rd 1945 were Sr Hilda, Mother Hilda Frances, Sr Frances Clare, Sr Elizabeth Mary and Sr Gladys. Sr Dipika had chosen to remain in India - she did not join one of the indigenous Communities, but lived alone for the rest of her life. There now remained just two Sisters at St Michael's School, Darjeeling, which was due to be given up at the end of 1945. And so for the time being Sr Georgina and Sr Lilian Mary stayed on.

Peace came to Europe in May 1945 and Darjeeling joined in the rejoicing as Sr Georgina recalled in her history of St Michael's School: "British, Americans, Indians, Chinese, hill people, everyone added his quota to the Victory spirit. There was no thought of superiority or boastfulness, only deep thankfulness that it was all over." It wasn't quite all over - even though British forces had entered Rangoon on May 3rd 1945 the war in the Far East was still a grim reality. But for a brief spell the hill station allowed itself to forget, and became immersed in the festivities. "At St Michael's there was an air of cheer and goodwill pervading the atmosphere," continued Sr Georgina, "... and at the morning Assembly an unmistakeable quiver went through the school as with one accord in the National Anthem it lifted up heart and voice to Him who has given us the Victory. Then the entire school massed on the playground for its own celebration. The Kindergarten led by Miss Melrose, marched in proud and triumphant procession, waving allied flags, beating drums, clashing cymbals and cheering. The rest of the school then sang, 'There'll always be an England' and 'England Mine,' and staff and children continued in community singing. That night Darjeeling was bejewelled and gemmed with hundreds of little coloured electric lights hanging from the trees and buildings. Government House looked like a coloured picture from Arabian Nights. Our elder girls were invited to a Victory Dance at St Paul's School and they looked upon it as the crown of their various rejoicings. Most unfortunately it rained and it was nearly a three mile walk all uphill, but nothing daunted, they trudged up in mackintoshes by 5.00 p.m. Supper was at 6.30 and all ended by 10.00 p.m. It was then pouring with rain and a much bedraggled and tired but happy party arrived quite ready for a second supper before going up to bed after a more than strenuous evening."

August 6th 1945, the Feast of the Transfiguration, saw the dropping of an atomic bomb on Hiroshima and on Nagasaki three days later. On August 14th the Japanese surrendered - the war was finally over.

Peace may have been celebrated at St Michael's School, Darjeeling, to the strains of, "There'll always be an England," but the reality was that the Raj was over. So too was Churchill's wartime leadership; just before Hiroshima a Labour Government took office under Clement Atlee, the Socialist old boy of Kipling's Haileybury. At the end of the European war the Congress leaders had been released from prison and immediately refused to co-operate with Jinnah in a coalition government. In the 1945 Indian elections the Congress Party won in Hindu areas and the Muslim League wherever Islam was the majority religion. Gandhi's mantle seemed already to have descended upon Nehru with whom Jinnah refused to work, and he called for a day of Direct Action by Muslims. The riots which raged in Calcutta for 10 days resulted in almost 3,500 deaths and the drafting in of 45,000 troops to enforce peace. Talks between the Indian leaders in London resulted in stalemate, while India escalated towards civil war. In February 1947 Wavell was recalled in favour of Lord Louis Mountbatten, whose task as the last Viceroy was to steer India to independence by no later than June 1948. Mountbatten achieved a rapport with Nehru and Gandhi, but Jinnah remained intransigent. Already the Punjab was in the grip of civil war, the worst affected places being Lahore and Amritsar - the latter was already a scar on the record of British rule. It was in this climate of increasing bloodshed and deadlock that Mountbatten decided unilaterally that independence would come at midnight on August 14th 1947, the second anniversary of the Japanese surrender.

And so it did. As the Union Jack was lowered over Government House in New Delhi, so the Star of India was raised in its place. As Nehru and Mountbatten shared drinks with distinguished guests at the Viceroy's

House, now the Rashtrapati Bhawan, two of the principal players were missing. Mahatma Gandhi, soon to fall under an assassin's bullet, was in Calcutta deeply distressed that his great dream had been turned by other hands into the means of dividing his beloved country. And the suave, Westernised Jinnah was in Karachi, capital of his newly founded country of Pakistan inaugurated 24 hours earlier. Mountbatten, hearing of a Sikh plot against Jinnah's life, had travelled by his side in the procession to lessen the chance of the car being bombed - a sad irony for a man who, 30 years later, would die by a terrorist's bomb.

The last two Sisters had already come home. There had been various hopes and plans for the future of St Michael's, and at one stage there was a strong possibility that the Wantage Sisters would take over, but this was not feasible. According to Sr Georgina's history, the Sisterhood of the Epiphany offered to help during 1946 until the Community of Jesus the Good Shepherd[(11)], whose mother house was at West Ogwell in Devon, could send two Sisters. In October 1946 the Sisters from West Ogwell left for Darjeeling. Their time there was shortlived, for within a few months of their taking charge, the new Metropolitan of India ordered the school to be closed. It had vast debts, and the diocese refused to help claiming that no funds were available. Thus passed the prestigious St Michael's - the now ramshackle buildings only hint at what it once was.

On April 6th 1946 the Sisters at Clewer received a cable stating that Sr Georgina and Sr Lilian Mary had sailed from Bombay in the *Andes*. They had been waiting for a passage for nearly three months and had been staying with the Wantage Sisters at Poona. On April 20th (Holy Saturday), news reached Clewer that the Sisters were expected at Southampton in the afternoon, so Sr Annys, who was at Bournemouth, went to meet them. Alas, the ship did not berth until 6.00 p.m. and no passengers were allowed off until next day. The *Annals* note that: "Sr Annys could do no more than wave from the dock!" Next day, which was Easter Sunday, word came through to Clewer that the Sisters would leave Southampton during the afternoon. An Associate drove Sr Grace and Sr Hilda Frances to the railway station at 5.00 p.m. and the travellers eventually arrived at 7.00 p.m. The voyage had been very quick - only 13 days, which in all those 64 years must have been a record.

When Mother Dorothy Frances had written to the Associates in May 1944 telling them of the decision to withdraw she finished with these words: "Whatever has been creative under God's guidance will grow and bear fruit. The time is ripe for Bengali Christian women to witness to the power of their faith." These were wise words and prophetic ones, for much of the educational work in Calcutta has not only survived the Sisters, but still thrives.

In 1993-4 St John's Diocesan Girls' Higher Secondary School kept its Centenary. In her address at the Centenary ceremony on June 18th 1993, the Principal, Mrs Rosita Chrestien, spoke warmly of Angelina Hoare founder of the Pipalpati mission, and of the Clewer Sisters who took it over from her. "During the time when the school was run by St John's Sisters, the reputation of the school was at its zenith, for the Sisters worked with the utmost devotion, untiring efforts and profound wisdom. Sr Hilda Frances, the last English Principal of this school was awarded the Kaiser-i-Hind for her contribution to women's education... I strongly believe that St John's Diocesan, founded as it is on the extraordinary and selfless efforts, profound wisdom, untiring patience, love, and caring of the [past] generations of people, will maintain its past glory in the years to come, and will continue to illuminate young minds in the same way as it has done in the years gone by. What we build today is based upon the foundation of love, service and dedication of all those who have gone before us, and any success we achieve now is our gift to those of the past, and our contribution to the present. Hence we hope to continue the glorious traditions of this school, follow the ideals set by our predecessors, and instil in our students the values which have been passed down to us."(12)

Footnotes

1. The acronym Pakistan was made up from the names of the following Muslim dominated areas in north west India - P (Punjab), A (Afgania, formerly the North-West Frontier Province), K (Kashmir), S (Sind) and TAN (BaluchisTAN). The scheme had originally been devised by a group of Muslim students at Cambridge in 1932-3 who dreamed of a Muslim homeland. In Urdu "Pak" means pure, and "Stan" means land, so "Pakistan" means land of the pure.

2. The boys' school at St Thomas' Kidderpore is still nextdoor to the girls' school.

3. The Right Revd S. K. Tarafdar, a Bengali, had been Assistant Bishop of Calcutta since 1935.

4. Wavell The Viceroy's Journal ed. by Penderel Moon. 1973

5. MASON, Philip *The men who ruled India* (this edition 1987) pp. 384-5.

6. Sr Eudora had finally returned to England from the United States in November 1943 after an eventful time. After India, she had been working in Barbados where, in March 1941, she and Sr Marian made Community history by being the first two Sisters to fly. They flew from Barbados to Trinidad in an hour and a quarter, a journey which would have taken 16 hours by sea. Sr Eudora also visited St Vincent where the islanders decided she was a German spy disguised as a nun and had to return hastily to Barbados, which she managed to do aboard a troopship by signing on as the ship's cook! The war prevented her returning to Clewer, but she managed to get a passage to America where she stayed with the Clewer Sisters in New York and shared in their work.

7. St Alban's Sisters. The Clewer Sisters worked at St Alban's, Holborn from 1869-1955.

Recalling that night at St Alban's, Holborn, Sr Eudora recently remarked that, "Yes, it was an extremely trying night - the St Alban's Sisters spent the night on the roof fire-watching, but they made me stay in chapel praying!" "Not the whole night in chapel, Sister," I replied. "Oh no, not all night, but even so, I wanted to be up there on the roof with them - it was very exciting." Exciting or not, the fire-watching was important - St Alban's church had been badly damaged in the Blitz.

8. An important work in former years had been amongst the families in the married quarters at the Guards Barracks in London and Windsor.

9. If a large number of Indian women had shown an interest in joining the Community it is likely that the Sisters would have established a separate Indian Community. As noted in chapter 27, the Easter 1935 *Associates' Newsletter* had mentioned the Sisters' great desire for: "the development of an Indian order of Sisters *under the care of our Community*" (my italics). This remark was prompted by the admission as a postulant of Dipika Bejborea, who was related to the poet Tagore.

10. This typescript copy of part of a letter from Bishop Foss Westcott dated 1944, is in the Clewer archives, but the recipient is unknown. The earlier part, which I have not quoted, gives a resume of the Sisters' work as if to suggest that the recipient was unfamiliar with their history in India. I have used this extract because it underlines Westcott's genuine grief at losing the Sisters, something which he described earlier in the letter as, "the most distressing event which has happened during my tenure of the office I at present hold." Westcott had held that office (Bishop of Calcutta and Metropolitan of India), since 1919 and resigned it in 1945.

11. The Community of Jesus the Good Shepherd, West Ogwell also took over the Clewer work in Barbados. In 1996 the Community decided to leave West Ogwell - Mother Ann Verena and three Sisters have moved to Clewer and now live alongside the Clewer Community, sharing their life and worship, whilst maintaining their own Community identity. Two other Sisters have gone to other Communities.

12. Principals of St John's Diocesan Girls' Higher Secondary School since the Sisters left have been: Miss Charulata Das, a former student 1944-60; Miss Molina Mukherjee 1960-77; Miss Jaya Shome 1977-78; Miss Nilima Pye 1978-80; Mrs T. Samuel Raj 1985-90; and in 1990 Mrs Rosita Chrestien, the present Principal took office.

CSJB

INDIA

-31-
HOMECOMING - RETURN TO CALCUTTA

"You cannot possibly write a book about India without going there." This was Donald Allchin's reaction when, at the start of work on this trilogy, I went to discuss the project with him. It seemed sensible enough but I felt very apprehensive as I had never travelled abroad before and India seemed like jumping in at the deep end. Even so, the further I progressed with the research and the more I came to "know" Sr Jane Frances through her letters and other writings, so I became keener to go. And then there was Sr Eudora - still at Clewer, though fast failing in health, but still in love with India nearly 60 years after leaving it. I had clearly fallen under the same spell that most of the Sisters who worked in that great country had fallen under. So I resolved to go, but there were still friends who thought I was crazy as exemplified by the incredulous remark of one of them: "But Valerie you have never been further east than Cromer!"

Having resolved to go, there needed to be some plan - what did I want to do? I decided that time would not allow me to research archives (even if any had survived), so it would be a case of following the steps of the Sisters, tracking down and photographing the hospitals and schools where they had once worked in Calcutta and Darjeeling - always assuming the buildings still existed. "Keep your sense of humour, but above all, expect the unexpected," was the sound advice given me by another friend a few days before I left for India. So it was that on February 8th 1995, I left England accompanied by a friend from Windsor, Joyce Sampson, who knows the Sisters well. We flew to Delhi intending to spend a week touring northern India en route to Calcutta. The Sisters had faced a variety of perils and adventures as the earlier chapters of this book will have shown, and our week long journey across India turned out to be something worthy of the heyday of Sr Jane Frances!

My first impression of Delhi was of a large sprawling city, a place of contrasts between the grand Mughal architecture of Shah Jehan's Red Fort (which we did not have time to see around), and Lutyens' stately but sterile Imperial buildings. And everywhere the noise of car horns, choking exhaust fumes, leperous beggars, street children tugging at one's sleeve, heat and dust, but also a surprisingly leafy, tree-lined city. A perilous ride as passengers on a cycle rickshaw took us through the bazaar area of Old Delhi - too narrow for any other vehicle. Here we saw real Indian life - colourful and very basic, but maintaining a dignity over and above the poverty and deprivation. Our hotel overlooked the massive, pink coloured Jantar Mantar, an astronomical observatory built by Sawai Jai Singh in the 18th century - one of five of which the one at Jaipur (which we also saw), is the largest.

Next day we flew to Jaipur where we spent two nights in the luxurious Jai Mahal Palace Hotel. After Delhi, which was very much the capital city, Jaipur with its pink coloured buildings and bustling streets, was every bit an Indian city, untouched by relics of British rule, having remained a Princely State all through the Raj period. Here the usual goods transport is by camel or bullock cart, and elephants with painted heads and trunks are a common sight at the end of the day gently lumbering home from transporting tourists up to the Amber fortress. We got caught in a solid traffic jam consisting of rickshaws, camel carts and bullock carts. Of course there is motorised transport - motor scooters, Ambassador cars (based on the Morris Oxford), and heavy trucks painted all over in bright designs, but these have to vie with the animal transport. Also, cows wander at leisure, sitting down in the road wherever they please, and they have the right of way because in Hinduism they are sacred. A visit to the fortress at Amber (partly by elephant), and a tour of the City Palace, gave us a good taste of Jaipur. It was a place from which I had to tear myself away rather than leave of my own free will, but we had to move on.

Early on the Sunday morning we left Jaipur to drive to Agra with a diversion to Fatehpur Sikri, a city built in the 16th century and only inhabited for 14 years, after which the wells dried up. Thick fog made for a hair-raising drive with large trucks looming head-on (no one uses lights). Four major traffic accidents held us up and reminded us of our mortality. But when trouble seemed inevitable there was always a cheery smile from our guide or driver and the often exasperating assurance of, "Don't worry: no problem: I fix." Our first experience of this was on arrival at Fatehpur Sikri when the guide did not turn up. Our driver darted around frenetically and within a few minutes had produced an understudy who gave us a whistle-stop tour of the place in just under an hour. (It usually takes an hour and a half).

Fatehpur Sikri is a splendid place with breath-taking architecture, but an eerie atmosphere; rather like walking on a deserted filmset (although in fact there were a lot of other tourists around). By now the sun had broken through the fog and it was hot, but our arrival in Agra was behind schedule. Even so, the morning's journey had been fascinating, and we had passed through villages where the market places were teeming with life; villages built of mud huts with straw roofs and dung cakes for fuel drying by the roadside. We had passed some boys with three performing bears, a man smoking from a hookah, a snake charmer with a cobra, as well as camel and bullock carts, and an elephant dangerously lumbering along in the fog. One village was entirely given up to ornamental stone cutting - the men were sitting by the roadside carving the most intricate patterns in the same style as we had seen at Fatehpur Sikri and would see at the Taj Mahal.

By mid afternoon we arrived at Agra having left Jaipur at 7.00 a.m. and we had not eaten, though we had stopped for coffee at a rather grubby rest house during the morning. A cheese sandwich made at the hotel and hastily eaten in the car had to suffice if we were to get to the Taj Mahal before the admission fee went up from 2 rupees to 100 rupees at 4.00 p.m. (cashing in on the sunset!). Agra itself is dirty and squalid, a place no one would want to visit were it not for the Taj Mahal. 1.5 million people live in this sprawling city, and in recent years an even more unsightly suburb has grown up around the luxury hotels. It is ironical that an object of such supreme beauty should be surrounded by such degradation. I had half expected to be disappointed by the Taj Mahal - so often in tourist guidebooks the camera is selective about what is shown. But it is even more breathtaking than I had imagined, and on such a vast scale too - it is indeed the epitome of all that is beautiful beyond words. It makes all our cathedrals seem clumsy and basic, shimmering as it does in the sunlight with its whiteness reflected in the water below, and subtly changing colour with the rising or setting sun. Only the east could produce it and only India, which is such a land of contrasts, could contain it.

Next morning (Monday), we left our hotel at Agra to fly to Varanasi, better known as Benares, the holiest city in Hinduism. It was a two hour flight which would leave us plenty of time to explore before leaving on the Tuesday night train to Calcutta. That was the theory, but my prophetic friend's words, "expect the unexpected" were to ring true. Agra airport is shared with the military, so when our flight was delayed we little realised that civil flying time was fast ticking away. We waited in the mid-day heat (+80 degrees Fahrenheit) for ages before it was announced that the flight was cancelled, and that the next one would be on Wednesday - two days away. Our guide assured us that replacement transport would be provided by Indian Airlines who eventually agreed to take 14 of us to Varanasi by coach. Meanwhile, we were taken to a nearby hotel, given lunch and told that a coach would arrive in an hour. At 7.00 p.m. we finally left in a ramshackle bus with smooth tyres and no air conditioning, each of us clutching a packed supper, which was the only food we were to see for 24 hours!

After two hours at snail's pace the bus blew a tyre, and replacing it took another hour during which we were standing by the roadside inhaling choking exhaust fumes, emitted by the heavy trucks passing by. Back on the road we tried to sleep, but the road surface was full of pot-holes and we were shaken from limb to limb. Also, we kept having to stop at roadblocks manned by armed guards. By 7.00 a.m. we had been driving for 12 hours, and the driver had not had a break except for about 20 minutes at a roadside rest house where he had a cup of tea - but no rest. Our travelling companions were a white South African couple, and an extended family of Sri Lankans, some of whom now lived in Australia, and who were on a pilgrimage to Buddhist shrines. The Sri Lankans knew the coach driver's dialect and he told them we would not reach Varanasi until mid-day. Then we began to pass stationary trucks - about 100 of them - and discovered that a truck had shed its load, and that another had overturned trying to get past it. The road was blocked and would not be cleared for two days! The driver did not seem very concerned about this, but the Sri Lankans were not at all happy and tried to persuade him to take another route. He was very reluctant, saying there were no proper roads, only mud tracks, and we would get stuck miles away from anywhere. Meanwhile, nature called, and several of us wandered down a mud track in the same direction as people from the nearby village. Suddenly I heard a terrific commotion: two of the women, looking for some privacy, had gone behind a mud wall not realising it was somebody's backyard! The village women were furious and chased the unfortunate (and profoundly embarrassed) members of the group away with brooms and colourful language.

Meanwhile one of the village men had told the driver about another route which would bring us back to the main road beyond the accident. It was only a mud track, very uneven and narrow in places, but by this time a large number of vehicles were using it. All seemed well despite a hold-up of 40 minutes at a level crossing while three immensely long trains went through. Then we went on again for several miles until a large oncoming truck forced us off the road into the muddy ditch, and we became firmly stuck. It was just what the driver had feared. At that point if anyone had said "No problem: I fix," I think **we** might have fixed **him**, but no one did.

We were in a village and everyone crowded round to see the spectacle. Some of the boys helped, pulling up armfuls of weeds and grass to put under the wheels, whilst others ran and fetched shovels. Every attempt to drive out sent us further into the ditch. The driver was adamant that we should all stay in the bus, but it was listing very badly with every abortive attempt to drive out of the ditch. There began to be a real danger that it would turn over - and it was leaning towards the door. We decided to get out while we could; it was the only time in the whole episode that I felt frightened. Finally, and with some difficulty we got out of the bus, ankle deep in thick mud and just stood there rather helplessly. "Keep your sense of humour," my friend had said. In fact that wasn't difficult; the villagers were highly amused, and laughter transcends language. So we stood and laughed together as we slid around trying not to fall over. By now it was late morning, it was raining quite steadily, the mosquitoes were having a banquet. And then I looked up and saw vultures circling overhead!

Suddenly a bright red tractor appeared as if from nowhere, or at least as if from an agricultural show in middle England! At first no one seemed to have any rope, but eventually something was produced. "Heave-ho" sounds much the same in any language, but to no avail. The tractor strained forward and went flying into the opposite ditch where it got stuck, the rope snapped, and the bus retreated backwards. All this time there had been vehicles passing us, including an army lorry full of soldiers who hurled insults and abuse and flatly refused the driver's plea for help. These were the only unhelpful people we encountered in the whole of our visit to India. The tractor episode had completely blocked the road both ways, and so there was a stream of traffic waiting to get past us including a little three-wheeled auto-rickshaw. The South African couple hired this rather dubious transport to take them to Varanasi (Benares), and invited Joyce and I to join them. With help from the villagers (in return for baksheesh), we retrieved our luggage from the bus and sallied forth hoping our luck had changed.

The auto-rickshaw had no springs and we were shaken from limb to limb; there was only a canvas roof, so we were exposed to the rain, flying mud, and choking fumes, which the vehicle's motor cycle engine belched forth. The exhaust pipe runs alongside the front wheel and emits its fumes over the passengers; my respiratory system was lined with black for several days! After a few miles we reached Cawnpore of Indian Mutiny fame); where the driver suddenly staged his own mutiny and refused to go any further because his licence would not permit it. No amount of persuasion or baksheeh would make him change his mind, and we felt at a complete loss, not knowing where we were, what to do, or how far we were from Varanasi. We momentarily regretted leaving the Sri Lankans.

Then suddenly a guardian angel appeared! On the road we had passed a motor cyclist wearing a turban, and with a Sikh-style beard. He had waved at us and we had waved back. Now, he appeared once more, and recognised us standing forlornly in the muddy street vainly trying to bargain with the rickshaw man. He stopped, parked his machine, came over to us, and in immaculate English asked if he could help. We told him our problem and he immediately went across the road and hired another auto-rickshaw. He settled the price with the driver and told us not to pay a single rupee more. He helped us load the luggage, waved goodbye, and then he was gone - we never saw him again. I think that angels *sometimes* look like Sikhs riding motorbikes!

The second driver took us to Allahabad, but instead of going to the military airport, he drove straight past it, together with all those rows of Ambassador taxis waiting to be hired. When he finally stopped, having circuited the city, there was nothing for hire except a rather ancient looking jeep. Faced with no other choice, we hired it to take us the 100 miles to Varanasi. One of the frustrating things about the whole day was that at 7.00 a.m. when we first encountered the traffic jam on the blocked road we were about 150 miles from Varanasi, and now at about 3.00 p.m. we were still 100 miles away.

The jeep was even less roadworthy than the auto-rickshaw, and it proved to be yet another "white knuckle ride." At Allahabad we had our first sight of the sacred Ganges which was a curiously moving experience. Here is the confluence between the Ganges and the Yamuna, and all along the river banks there were literally thousands of tents. Several million Hindu pilgrims had gathered for the Kumbh Mela, a gathering held every few years, the culmination of which is the ritual bathing in the sacred river. Just as Christian shrines like Lourdes and Walsingham attract religious shops, so too the streets of Allahabad were filled with holy shops cashing in on peoples' piety.

A few miles out of Allahabad we passed a colourful procession of Sadhu's (Hindu holy men), travelling from the Mela to bathe in the sacred waters at Varanasi. Certainly it was a slice of Indian life we would not have otherwise seen. The procession was headed by naked acrobats who somersaulted and danced vigorously. Next followed some splendidly dressed men in scarlet and gold tunics, and turbans with long flowing sashes, wielding great curved swords, who became very aggresive when they saw our cameras. Several carts followed, loaded with all their household equipment. On another, there was a venerable looking holy man with flowing beard and white hair, very similar in appearance to one we had seen earlier who had greeted us in the middle of the muddy street at Kanpur. A splendid bull elephant with silver tipped tusks, horse drawn carts and camel carts, all followed on. We were going through a small town with a busy market place and the traders were selling straight from the pavement. As he passed a pile of greengrocery the elephant stretched out his trunk and helped himself to a free meal! The poor trader hastily removed the rest out of reach, but the elephant was a fast mover and had taken a large helping.

The jeep was very cramped and uncomfortable. Also it had faulty brakes, no side windows just a flapping canvas cover, loose steering, no windscreen wipers, and most seriously of all, no horn. In India everyone drives by sounding their horn, before pulling out and overtaking, irrespective of oncoming traffic. With no horn we were very vulnerable. By Indian standards it was a very good road - Number 2 Highway running from Delhi to Calcutta, and called in the days of the Raj, the Grand Trunk Road. It was not as rough as many of the roads we had been on, or at least not in the middle which was where our driver chose to go, missing oncoming vehicles by a whisker (and a prayer).

We arrived at our hotel in Varanasi at 7.00 p.m. exactly 24 hours after leaving Agra in the ill-fated bus. A relieved travel agent met us having been waiting all that time with no idea of what had befallen us, except that we had left Agra by bus. We were fast learning that one of the pitfalls of independent travelling, as opposed to an escorted tour, is that the agent will wave goodbye to you at the airport or station and another will be at the destination to meet you; but if anything goes wrong en route there is no means of letting the agent know. Delayed flights and trains can be traced, but a bus stuck in a ditch miles from anywhere is lost until it turns up. All the agent can do is wait, and ours was at his wits end when we turned up in the disreputable jeep, wet, dirty, and covered in mud. We were running exactly 24 hours late, and were supposed to be leaving by the night train to Calcutta in exactly half an hour's time: "The train is running late; there is time to catch it; no problem," the agent optimistically declared! We stood our ground feeling in no fit state for another journey.

Next morning (Wednesday), we rose early and went by boat along the sacred Ganges. There had been a thunderstorm during the night and it was still raining, so fewer people than usual were bathing, praying and cremating their dead. In contrast to my first sight of the Ganges at Allahabad which had moved me deeply, I now felt as though I was intruding. There is something voyeuristic about tourists watching these devout Hindus at their morning devotions, which I found distasteful and vaguely troubling. Before returning to the hotel for breakfast we walked through the narrow streets of the old town past the pilgrim shops and the golden temple, avoiding sacred cows wandering in the narrow alleys. Later we visited the Buddhist temples at Sarnath, a very holy spot being the place where the Lord Buddha preached his first sermon 500 years before the birth of Christ. There was an atmosphere of peace and prayer at Sarnath which was very powerful and moving. The place was crowded with a large number of Buddhist monks, some of whom were small boys. Here too we met our Sri Lankan friends and fellow passengers from the bus, who said it had been recovered from the ditch soon after we left, but they had not reached Varanasi until the evening. Even so, it was good to know they were safe and well, and able to resume their pilgrimage.

By this time I was really looking forward to reaching Calcutta. We were due to catch the 5.00 p.m. night train - the Amritsar-Howrah mail. The travel agent managed to obtain two berths in the air-conditioned sleeper compartment at very short notice, as we had missed last night's train. All the way along we had been told not to buy water from wayside stalls, and when we were assured by the agent that food and drink would be available on the train, we foolishly made no contingency plans. We resisted the temptation to buy bottled water from the platform in case it was impure and only had with us two 500ml bottles of mineral water bought at the hotel.

After we had been standing on the crowded platform for nearly 3 hours the train finally arrived at 7.00 p.m. During that time we had felt increasingly vulnerable with small children tugging at us for alms, crowds surging around, announcements being made in a language we did not understand, trains arriving and leaving, and the nagging doubt as to whether we should be on the one which was pulling out. And nowhere to sit down! Eventually the train came in and our agent settled us onto it, securing our luggage to the seat with a padlock and chain. When the food arrived it was inedible, there was no pure water, and the bedding for which we paid 15 rupees looked filthy - people were putting on extra clothing! At midnight the so-called express train stopped for two hours, and then proceeded very slowly indeed until dawn, punctuated by frequent lengthy halts. No doubt the arduous journey to Varanasi had taken its toll and dehydration had already begun, but by the morning both Joyce and I were feeling very unwell. During the early hours of the morning the Conductor told me that the train was now running $6^{1}/_{2}$ hours late and would not arrive in Calcutta until after mid-day. I was beginning to feel very worried about our shortage of water, and dare not drink what I had for fear of running out completely. A Hong Kong Chinese family were sharing our compartment; they were on their way to visit relatives in Calcutta, and they were very kind to us. As soon as they knew we were short of water they shared theirs with us, which helped considerably. Chai (tea) vendors passed up and down the carriage frequently, dispensing their strong, sweet brew from large dirty looking kettles. In the end I decided I might die anyway, so risked the chai and was none the worse for it.

Towards the end of that train journey I had grown very despondent and feared that if it went on much longer I would collapse. The train felt increasingly tomblike, the journey never ending. I tried to take an interest in the countryside of Bihar, which would have been very familiar to those pioneering Clewer Sisters. Rice was growing and people were busy in the paddy fields planting out the green shoots. It must have been very similar to the rice country in the Sunderbuns so beloved by Sr Jane Frances. I thought of the Easter carol, "Now the green blade riseth from the buried grain." The nearer we got to Calcutta the larger the villages became, and gradually the villages gave way to large colonial style houses. Then as we approached Howrah, the porters leapt onto the train and started carrying heavy cases away on their turbanned heads! We arrived at Howrah station across the river Hooghly from Calcutta at 1.30 p.m. on Thursday February 16th - the journey had taken $18^{1}/_{2}$ hours and we were $6^{1}/_{2}$ hours late. We had been told to wait on the train for the travel agent, and as we left the train and tried to get past the beggars blocking our path, he said, "There are some ladies here to welcome you." There on the platform were four teachers from St John's Diocesan Girls' Higher Secondary School (formerly run by the Clewer Sisters), with a large banner proclaiming, "Mrs Bonham and Mrs Sampson - Welcome."

I had written to Mrs Chrestien, the Lady Principal, to say I was visiting Calcutta and would like to visit the school. About 18 months earlier she had written to Sr Eudora, and they had been in touch ever since. But I had no idea that anyone would be waiting to greet us, or I would have sent a message through the travel agent - the welcoming party had been to meet every train from Varanasi for the past 24 hours. They had beautifully scented red and white floral garlands made from tube roses which they placed round our necks, and which smelt like flowers from heaven. After the horrendous journey it was an Easter experience, a passing from death to life, like stepping out of the tomb into the garden. For me, the women at the tomb in the Gospel will always be those four women at Howrah station.

I had read a great deal about Calcutta, and was familiar with it through research. But that first drive from Howrah station across the great Hooghly bridge, skirting Eden Gardens and the Maidan (Calcutta's great open space), past the Raj Bhavan formerly Government House, with a sighting of the Victoria Memorial and a glimpse of St Paul's Cathedral - was like a homecoming. All those letters home which Sr Jane Frances and others had written; all those descriptions of flag waving receptions on the Maidan for visiting Viceroys and other grandees; all those familiar addresses on letter headings - it all came flooding back. And here I was right in the middle of it 50 years after the last Sister sailed home, feeling as if I was revisiting somewhere I had been before and knew very well.

This was especially so next day when we arrived at St John's Diocesan Girls' Higher Secondary School. Before leaving our hotel, Mrs Banerjee and her colleagues had given us an invitation from Mrs Chrestien to visit the school. They collected us next morning and we were driven through the city which is probably quite different from how it was in the Sisters' time. There are more high rise buildings mostly post-Raj, and the heavy traffic fills the atmosphere with choking exhaust fumes. But the school has not changed: the buildings are substantially the same, and were instantly recognisable from the archive photographs, especially those which formerly housed the Diocesan College and Collegiate School. The sense of homecoming when I got out of the car and saw those familiar buildings was really overwhelming - I knew exactly where I was! Only one thing was different - the bronze statue of St John Baptist unveiled by Mother Teresa at the school's centenary in 1993 and looking very similar to that in the Sisters' chapel at Clewer.

And then there was the welcome! We were quite unprepared for it, and tremendously moved by it. The whole school was assembled outside; the Bishop of Calcutta was present; and as we walked along with Mrs Chrestien, flower petals were scattered in our path and girls clad in beautiful saris danced before us. Even the playgrounds were decorated in traditional Bengali patterns with carefully laid out flower petals. We were led to a covered area where speeches of welcome were made. Joyce and I both replied, Joyce speaking of her work as a governor in several Windsor schools, and I speaking of the Clewer Sisters and how much they still thought of India. Sr Eudora's name had been mentioned by Mrs Chrestien, and it was good to be the bearer of messages from Sr Eudora herself, to the school she still holds dear. More dancing and displays followed, and then we were each given a bouquet and gifts which had been made in the school. The names of the Sisters who had worked in Calcutta were read out, and I was presented with a gift to take back to Clewer for Sr Eudora. The ceremonies ended with the school anthem, "Make me a channel of your peace."

A tour of each classroom followed, punctuated by lunch prepared for us by some of the teachers. The school is flourishing with 3,000 girls from 3+ to 18 years, and 75 teachers. It is a fee-paying school, although the fees are modest; lessons are in English, Hindi and Bengali. There is a great sense of "family" and commitment - many of the teachers are former pupils, and some have their own daughters there as teachers. Teaching methods are geared to blackboard and easel work, with spelling, dictation, mental arithmetic etc, but there is also a science laboratory and a computer room. Good results are achieved, and many of the girls progress to university. There is a long list in the Centenary Book of former students who have distinguished themselves in professional and public life. Classes are numerically larger than in England, but there was a good atmosphere in the school which seemed well disciplined without being too restrictive. The classroom tour was rather hurried because everyone wanted to see us and time was limited, but the overall impression was of happy children smartly dressed in their simple white uniforms with blue belts and ribbons, who seemed interested in their lessons and keen to work. Perhaps the Indian schools now have something to teach us in England!

Mrs Chrestien and her staff very kindly organised the rest of our stay in Calcutta, taking us to the other schools, and to the hospitals, and also to the Oxford Mission. Because we had arrived in Calcutta 24 hours late, it had been necessary to rearrange our schedule with the travel agents. We had originally planned to leave Calcutta by the Monday night train en route to Darjeeling, and transfer next morning to the Toy Train from Siliguri. After the previous train journey, neither Joyce nor I felt we could face another, and so we decided to stay in Calcutta until Wednesday and then fly to Bagdogra, from whence a car would take us to Darjeeling. In this way we were able to recover some of our lost time - eventually we needed every minute of it.

On the Saturday morning we had a tour of Calcutta organised by the travel agent, slightly amended to take in some of the sights familiar to the Sisters. Thus we went to St John's Church, St Paul's Cathedral (where we found the memorial brass to Angelina Hoare), the Victoria Memorial, the Lower Circular Road Cemetery (of which more later), and the National Library, formerly the home of the Lieutenant Governor of Bengal. We also drove past Dalhousie Square now called B.B.D. Bag, the bazaar area known as Bow Bazar and along College Street past the second hand bookstalls and the crumbling Medical College Hospital. Oddly, it is illegal to photograph government buildings such as the National Library, the Raj Bhavan (formerly Government House), or the Shahid Minar (formerly the Ochterlony Monument), all of which are most impressive, and are just the sort of photographs that tourists love to take!

On Saturday afternoon Mrs Chrestien and some of her staff took us to see the Presidency General Hospital, now renamed the Seth Sukhlal Karnani Memorial Hospital (S.S.K.M.), but still widely known as "the P.G." Before going there Mrs Chrestien said she would first take us to the inter-schools sports event on the Maidan to see the prizes being presented. As soon as we arrived Joyce and I felt decidedly under-dressed, being clad in casual summer clothes complete with scruffy sunhats. My sunglasses were held together by a safety pin, having fallen apart during one of our difficult journeys! Within minutes of arriving, we were being welcomed over the public address system and invited to present some of the prizes to the winning students. This was a great honour, and standing there on the dais on the Calcutta Maidan hanging medals round the necks of athletic young men and women, made me feel like the Vicereine of India! This was the sort of task Lady Dufferin would have performed - but she would have been dressed for the occasion, as indeed so would Joyce and I, had we known what was in store!

After leaving the Maidan we then went to the Presidency General Hospital where the great main block with its 550 foot frontage still looks just as it did in the Sisters' time; so too does the Woodburn block a bit further away in the same compound. I could not identify the Lady Canning Home, although I did not go all the way over to the present day nurses' quarters, so it might still be there behind the newer buildings. There were crowds of people milling around, and I feared someone would challenge me as I was taking photographs. But no one did, which was odd given the official attitude about photographing government buildings, and the P.G. is a government hospital. Or maybe I was lucky and didn't get caught! We did not go inside the P.G.; the outside was enough. Although the main block is structurally unchanged, and still impressive, it is a sorry sight. The window openings were covered in filthy looking hessian with piles of rubbish stuffed in between; there was an open ditch all round the outside full of foul smelling water. We were taken behind the main block to see the chapel, now derelict and padlocked. The altar and reredos is still in place, but the chairs were piled up and books strewn over the floor. It had not been used for years. A large room to the right of the chapel, was full of people living there in the worst over-crowded conditions, but with a large coloured television dominating the room. Sadly, we made our way back to the car, skirting the wild hungry looking dogs which circled around us, much to my dismay.

On the Sunday we attended the Sung Eucharist at St Paul's Cathedral just five minutes walk from our hotel. Crossing the road in Calcutta is almost a ticket to eternity. There are pedestrian crossings and traffic lights but no one takes any notice of them, and the taxi drivers seem to delight in driving straight at pedestrians. On several occasions we ended up asking local residents to help us cross the road, and received help every time. After such an eventful time over the previous week it was a great relief to have the opportunity of attending a Eucharist. Calcutta Cathedral is the oldest colonial cathedral and is now part of the United Church of North India, whose Communion rite was used, along with *Hymns Ancient and Modern*. It was a very "English" service despite the celebrant, servers and choir being Indian, almost like going into a time warp back to the Raj. Even so, it was an enjoyable service, and we were made very welcome by the congregation at coffee afterwards. The Cathedral is a beautiful building, like a white wedding cake outside and full of colour inside. The sanctuary area is decorated with mosaics and paintings, and there are many fascinating memorials throughout the building. But it is not very photogenic, the dark seating and numerous fans always seeming to dominate everything else. It is one of Calcutta's hidden gems. If time had permitted we could have visited some of the work in the bustees being done by the Cathedral Relief Fund established by Hazel Platts, the English born Cathedral Warden, who told us all about it. But time was so short that we had to decline.

On Monday morning, Mrs Kaveri Banerjee and Mrs Dipika Biswas took us to the Pratt Memorial School on the Lower Circular Road. This is now a very busy thoroughfare with heavy traffic, but once inside the school gates it is all forgotten. Like St John's Diocesan School, the Pratt Memorial School is bursting with enthusiastic students, and it looks exactly as it did when Sr Eudora taught there. Even the school colours - green and gold - are the same. Driving through the gates there is the main building in its inverted L shape, and at the time of our visit it was looking very smart, having just been repainted externally with gleaming white walls and green window shutters. We were taken round the school by Mrs Veronica Ghosh, Principal since 1980, and who is herself a former pupil. There are 2,000 girls at the school and 68 teachers. After the war the school (which had been evacuated to Nagpur), was able to return to its own buildings. Mrs Ghosh has recently revived the boarding section for pupils coming from a distance, of whom there are about 70. We had less time here than at St John's but came away with good impressions. In recent years there have been extensive new buildings, so that the present school is much larger than in the Sisters' time.

The last of the Sisters' schools which we visited in Calcutta was St Thomas' Kidderpore, and we had even less time there than at the Pratt Memorial, and did not see in any of the classrooms. But walking around the compound and talking to the Principal, Mrs Chattya Ghose, gave us a good idea of the school's ethos. Mrs Ghose greeted us warmly and was sorry we had so little time. She is a former pupil of St John's Diocesan School, is Vice-President of St John's School Management Committee, and remembers Sr Hilda Frances, Sr Dorothy Frances, Sr Honora and Sr Eudora. There are still two parallel schools at St Thomas' - the boys' and girls', each with their own Principal. The main disappointment of the day consisted in discovering that Kidderpore House, once owned by Warren Hastings, had been demolished about 20 years previously. The girls' school has 2,000 pupils, of whom 150 are boarders, and there are 65 teachers. Altogether, 7,000 girls are educated in the three schools once run by the Sisters, all of which endeavour to maintain high standards of education within a Christian context, thus continuing the ethos established by the Sisters.

Mrs Chrestien arranged for us to visit the Oxford Mission at Behala and we were duly taken by Mrs Banerjee and Mrs Biswas. By this time the Mission was reduced to two Brothers who, with secular help, looked after "street boys" and orphans, giving them a basic education, and teaching them life skills such as carpentry, weaving, electrical wiring and maintenance of two wheeled vehicles. We were shown around the Mission compound by Br Amit Biswas, including the chapel and Mission House before looking round the boys' school and workshops. At the time of our visit, the Mission was still trying to assess its future following the deaths of the last two English Brothers, Fr Peter Thorman (professed 1937), and Fr Theodore Mathieson (professed 1946). In particular, Fr Mathieson had exercised a special ministry amongst the boys by bringing out their considerable musical talents. He had founded the Mathieson Music School which was struggling to continue since his death. Br Amit then took us across the road to see Sr Florence of the Sisterhood of the Epiphany, who had opted to remain in India when the last few members of her Community returned to England. She was delighted to see us, and as soon as we mentioned Clewer said, "How is Sr Eudora!" Unfortunately we missed meeting Mother Susila of the Christa Sevika Sangha by about two hours, but I subsequently met her in England during her 1996 visit.

There was something very moving about the Oxford Mission which defies expression, so it was all the more sad to learn that the Mission as we saw it, has virtually ended. Br Amit was recovering from a kidney transplant at the time of our visit, and has since had to leave the Brotherhood on health grounds. It was not viable for the remaining Brother to stay under these circumstances, and so he has been released by the Mission. But the work at Behala will continue under a secular priest, the Revd James Stevens, who will act as Administrator and Spiritual Director.

Having experienced the squalor of the Presidency General Hospital, we were glad to have the balance redressed by seeing a modern private hospital. This was south of the city in the area bordering the rice country, and known as the 24 Perganas. Mrs Chrestien, Mrs Mitra and Mrs Sen, the hospital administrator, took us by jeep (a better one, thankfully), on an interesting journey which took us past one of the bustees which is very close to one of Mother Teresas's hostels, and past the tanneries. We thought of the kind Hong Kong Chinese family who shared their water with us on the train, and whose relatives worked in the tanneries in the Chinese quarter. The driver went extremely fast and the ever present slow cows wandering around or lying down in the middle of the road made for some interesting and hair-raising manoeuvres. The object of our excursion was to see the Peerless Hospital & B. K. Roy Research Centre which was opened in 1994, and is sponsored by the Peerless hotel group. The hospital has the latest facilities and technology and could stand alongside anything in the West. But such is the depth of poverty that most of the poorer people would not afford the quite reasonable fees, which is why government hospitals like the P.G. are so overcrowded.

On our travels around Calcutta, both by car and on foot, we saw poverty, - people living on the streets, and in the bustees (shanty settlements). Calcutta was always a place with grinding poverty, but refugees from Bangladesh in the 1970s have compounded the problem. But Calcutta is not alone - Delhi and Bombay are probably worse now. In Calcutta the situation has improved over the last few years, and Mother Teresa's influence is everywhere. It is not until you attempt to walk in the Calcutta streets that the extent of the poverty comes home, not that we saw people dying on the streets, but simply trying to cope with living. And one could not help being moved by the quiet and gentle dignity of those meagre attempts at living - washing at standpipes; sweeping the mud floor from under the canvas shelter which served as home; eking an existence from a bowl of rice. India changes one's sense of values.

We made two visits to the Lower Circular Road Cemetery in the hope of finding the Clewer Sisters' burial plot, but were unsuccessful. Armed with a 1920s photograph, I thought the task would be fairly easy - the plot seemed to be in a corner by a wall which should have been easily recognisable. We found neither wall nor graves, and afterwards I had a nagging feeling that we had gone to the wrong cemetery! Since returning home I have discovered that we did. The Clewer archives had suggested that the Sisters were buried in the Lower Circular Road area, but never made it clear which of several cemeteries contained the burial plot. The famous South Park Street Cemetery was closed before the Sisters' arrival, so I did not go there. Instead I concentrated in vain on its neighbour in Lower Circular Road. But speaking about it to Sr Eudora elicited the information that the Sisters were buried in the "military cemetery," although she could not remember exactly where it was. By means of a lengthy correspondence with the British Association for Cemeteries in South Asia, the site of the burial plot has been traced in the old military cemetery at Alipore, known as the Bhowanipore Cemetery. This is not far from the Presidency General Hospital where the Sisters began their work, and is at the south end of what was formerly Lower Circular Road. However, time has not been kind. A great deal of neglect and vandalism took place after 1947, and while the cemetery is now maintained and kept in good order, many memorials have been lost sight of. It would have been good to have found that particular corner of a foreign field which is forever Clewer, and the outcome of the quest has saddened me, but though I failed to find the graves of dead Sisters, I found instead their work still living and flourishing.(1)

In addition to visiting the schools, the hospitals and the Oxford Mission, we also had a sight of St Barnabas' Kidderpore now in a Muslim area; St James' Church next to the Pratt Memorial School; St Stephen's Kidderpore next to St Thomas' School; and St Mary's, Bhowanipore next to St John's School. Time did not permit us to go inside these churches, but it is good to know that they are still in use and bearing witness to the Christian faith more than a century after their foundation.

Visits to see the new suspension bridge over the River Hooghly, opened in 1994, and lunch at the exclusive Tollygunge Club, completed our touring around Calcutta. On the night before we left for Darjeeling Mr and Mrs Chrestien took us out for a Bengali meal which we enjoyed greatly and which was a splendid ending to our stay in Calcutta.

It was with great reluctance that we left Calcutta - we had been very much at home, and could have spent much longer there had time permitted. On the way to Dum Dum Airport we made a diversion to the Medical College Hospital which we had previously only glimpsed from the road. The great classical building with its columned portico is now derelict and looking decidedly dangerous, but the former Eden Hospital in the same compound is still in use and recognisable, though extended and built around. There are many other new buildings in the hospital compound, which like the P.G. is a government institution.

Our flight to Bagdogra was uneventful - a relief after all our adventures. We were met at the airport by the travel agent and continued the journey up to Darjeeling by car, arriving at about 7.00 p.m. The road wound its way up the foothills of the mountains snaking around in hairpin bends with sheer drops. There were plenty of warnings of the perils of driving too near the edge, such as: "Too near the side means suicide." As we increased in altitude we began to pass tea gardens, the bushes clinging to the hillsides, but elsewhere the bareness of the hills testified to the increasing deforestation which is having serious effects on the environment. I had been disappointed about not taking the Toy Train, but still did not feel like a seven hour journey when we could travel by car in three hours. Therefore I was pleased to discover that the Cart Road which we were taking, runs parallel with the railway, and in fact they cross and re-cross each other frequently. So we did get a flavour of the journey the Sisters would have made, and we were able to stop and photograph the train as it came chugging past. The other pleasant surprise was discovering the railway loop below Tindharia looking exactly as it did in an 1890s photograph in the Clewer archives.

Our hotel proved to be a great disappointment - a cold room (no heating until the fires were lit in the evening), damp beds, frequent power cuts (a common problem throughout the town), and faulty plumbing (one day the toilet flushed boiling water, and the shower produced something like liquid rust)! It was also about 40 degrees Fahrenheit colder than Calcutta, and the throat infection which I had already begun, the legacy of traffic fumes no doubt, now came on with a vengeance. Next morning we arose before dawn and were taken by jeep on an extremely cold and bumpy journey to Tiger Hill to watch the fabled sunrise over the Himalayas. I would like to know how many of the thousands of tourists who get wrenched from their beds at an untimely hour actually **see** anything except thick clouds and lowering, angry skies! Certainly that is all we saw throughout our entire sojourn until just as we were leaving the hotel early on the Saturday morning to start our homeward journey. At that moment the sky cleared, the sun came out, and the snow-clad Himalayas revealed their beauty, souring and towering above the cloud bank below. That single moment made the discomforts of the past two days worthwhile.

After the disappointment of the non-sunrise at Tiger Hill, our guide took us around the town, and we found that the so-called "Queen of the Hill Stations" now wears a very tarnished crown, having been subject to the influx of refugees from Tibet and Sikkim in recent years. The Eden Sanatorium, once run by the Sisters was visible from our hotel and looked exactly the same except that there are now buildings all around it. Now officially called the "Sahid Durga Malla (Eden) Hospital", it is usually still known as the Eden, and is a government hospital. It is very shabby in appearance with peeling paint and political slogans daubed over parts of it. Joyce later realised that her father had been a convalescent patient there during or just after the Great War when the Sisters were still in charge.

Our guide also took us to the once prestigious St Michael's Diocesan Girls' School which is now a government training college and part of the Indira Gandhi National Open University. Our visit was really quite alarming because the main door was bristling with very unfriendly looking armed guards. The college term had not begun and no one seemed to know anything about the letter I had written asking to see the place. Our guide asked permission for me to take photographs - the guards were not well disposed to this. Then we were told to come back later when the Principal would be there. I guessed that their time-keeping would be different from mine and that we stood in danger of wasting many hours. We were standing outside the main entrance in the former playground. All around us were tents where people were living, and they were viewing the whole scene with curiosity. Then there was a breakthrough: one of the guards agreed that we could speak to the administrator in his office. We were taken up the main staircase, now so shabby that Sr Georgina would have wept. Another frosty reception followed until I produced Mother Jane Olive's letter of introduction plus some old photographs of how the school used to look. The ice melted and from that moment the administrator couldn't help enough, but I thought that asking to see around inside might be asking too much. Also what I had already seen was quite enough. So we took our photographs of the crumbling edifice and left fairly briskly, down the drive and through the slogan daubed gateway.

The rest of our time in Darjeeling was occupied with a visit to the botanical gardens during which we were caught in a hail and thunderstorm, and a short trip on the Toy Train to Ghoom where we visited the Buddhist monastery which was in the process of a major restoration. Then early on the Saturday we began the long journey home: by road to Bagdogra; by air to Delhi; and then after several hours wait, the long flight from Delhi to Heathrow. The final panic happened at Delhi where, as a result of my spare batteries showing up on the security screens, not only were they confiscated but my boarding pass too! This was almost too much and I spent almost an hour in a cold sweat worrying whether I would get home after all. A helpful Indian passenger tried his utmost to persuade the security guard to let me have the boarding pass and finally declared that he would not board the plane until Joyce and I were safely on board. All was well eventually, but they made the three of us wait until last!

And so we came home with a host of traveller's tales. My friend had certainly been right about expecting the unexpected, and there can be no doubt that Cromer is definitely safer, but infinitely duller! Even so, apart from the train journey to Calcutta, I enjoyed the whole experience, and we certainly saw much more of India than we had expected. Having been there I can see why the Clewer Sisters fell in love with it, and why once you have been to India you are never quite the same again. We encountered such helpful and kind people, and there were times when it was really humbling. But above all, Mrs Chrestien and her staff from St John's School went to such lengths to make our time in Calcutta comfortable and enjoyable. Since we returned home Mrs Crestien has visited Clewer and was able to meet Sr Eudora and see around the Convent.

After giving up the Indian work the Sisters' final words were these: "If the work done in the different spheres in Bengal has been **rightly** done then we should be wrong to doubt that it will bring forth fruit in due season." Fifty years later, not only is their work bringing forth fruit in Indian Christian schools, but also the Sisters themselves are still remembered with deep affection. That is probably the greatest testimony of all to the quality of their work, and to the depth of the relationship they forged with India and its people. Empires rise and fall - only love remains.

Footnote

1. The Clewer Sisters hope to erect a plaque near where the Sisters' grave crosses once stood, and this possibility is being looked into as this book goes to press.

APPENDIX 1

MOTHERS SUPERIOR OF CLEWER AND SISTERS SUPERIOR OF INDIA, 1880-1947

Mothers Superior of Clewer:
M. Ellen 1875-81
M. Jane Frances 1881-89
M. Betha 1889-1907
M. Evelyn 1907-28
M. Katherine Maud 1928-35
M. Frances 1935-39
M. Dorothy Frances 1939-58.

Sisters Superior of India:
Sr Lucy 1881-89
Sr Jane Frances 1889-1919
Sr Margaret 1919-31
Sr Dorothy Frances 1931-39 (Mother Provincial from 1938)
Sr Hilda Frances (Mother Provincial) 1939-45.

APPENDIX 2

BISHOPS OF CALCUTTA, 1814-1945

Thomas Fanshaw Middleton, 1814
Reginald Heber, 1823
John Thomas James, 1827
John Matthias Turner, 1829
Daniel Wilson, 1832
George Edward Lynch Cotton, 1858
Robert Milman, 1867
Edward Ralph Johnson, 1876 (resigned 1898)
James Edward Cowell Welldon, 1898 (resigned 1901)
Reginald Stephen Copleston, 1902 (consecrated 1875, resigned 1913)
George Alfred Lefroy, 1913 (consecrated 1899)
Foss Westcott, 1919 (resigned 1945).

APPENDIX 3

VICEROYS OF INDIA, 1880-1947

Lord Ripon, 1880-84
Lord Dufferin, 1884-88
Lord Lansdowne, 1888-94
Lord Elgin, 1894-99
Lord Curzon, 1899-1905
Lord Minto, 1905-10
Lord Hardinge, 1910-16
Lord Chelmsford, 1916-21
Lord Reading, 1921-26
Lord Irwin, 1926-31
Lord Willingdon, 1931-36
Lord Linlithgow, 1936-43
Lord Wavell, 1943-47
Lord Mountbatten, 1947-50

APPENDIX 4

SISTERS IN INDIA

Sister	Left England	Arrival Back In England
Lucy	November 4th 1881 S.S. Myra	died in India April 18th 1889
Fanny Gertrude (1st time)	ditto	January 25th 1885 S.S. Capella
Anna Frances (1st time)	ditto	February 24th 1887 S.S. Myra
Eleanor Isabel (1st time)	April 18th 1882 S.S. Myra	October 8th 1886 S.S. Kaiser-i-Hind
Sophia (1st time)	ditto	March 29th 1890 S.S. Golconda
Blanche (1st time)	October 12th 1882 S.S. Myra	March 24th 1889 S.S. Capella
Cuthbert (1st time)	ditto	April 20th 1886 S.S. Ballarat
Mary Agatha	ditto	died in India September 24th 1884
Annie (1st time)	February 3rd 1883 S.S. Myra	March 29th 1890 S.S. Golconda
Sibyl (1st time)	ditto	April 12th 1888 S.S. City of Cambridge
Christian (1st time)	January 31st 1884 S.S. Khedive	February 24th 1887 S.S. Myra
Honora (1st time)	January 24th 1885 S.S. Myra	October 3rd 1887 S.S. Capella
Sophie (1st time)	January 11th 1886 S.S. Myra	May 30th 1891 S.S. Mombasa
Carolina (1st time)	November 19th 1886 S.S. Governor	December 20th 1889 S.S. Oceana
Mary Thekla (1st time)	ditto	March 11th 1893 S.S. City of Cambridge
Gertrude Emma (1st time)	January 16th 1887 S.S. Clan Matheson	April 6th 1892 S.S. Manora
Mary Angela (1st time)	January 16th 1887 S.S. Clan Matheson	April 6th 1892 S.S. Manora
Mother Jane Frances (visit)	December 29th 1887 S.S. Mongolia & Clyde	April 12th 1888 S.S. City of Cambridge
Anna Frances (2nd time)	ditto	March 11th 1893 S.S. City of Cambridge
Fanny Gertrude (2nd time)	January 25th 1888 S.S. Capella	May 30th 1891 S.S. Mombasa
Muriel (1st time)	November 14th 1888 S.S. City of Venice	March 28th 1895 S.S. Simla
Sibyl (2nd time)	January 21st 1889 S.S. Myra	March 22nd 1894 S.S. Khedive
Jane Frances (as Sr Superior)	November 14th 1889 S.S. City of Chios	June 4th 1898 S.S. Victoria

Sister	Left England	Arrival Back In England
Blanche (2nd time)	ditto	March 11th 1899 S.S. City of Vienna
Mary Alethea (1st time)	January 18th 1890 S.S. City of Bombay	November 26th 1895 S.S. Chusan
Mary Isabel (1st time)	ditto	December 25th 1894 S.S. Chusan
Mary Christine (1st time)	January 23rd 1890 S.S. Chusan	died in India October 29th 1891
Sophia (2nd time)	January 29th 1891 S.S. Rewa	died in India February 8th 1894
Florence (1st time)	ditto	March 2nd 1897 S.S. Malta
Gertrude (1st time)	January 15th 1892 S.S. Manora	March 17th 1897 S.S. Sumatra
Gertrude Emily (1st time)	ditto	March 2nd 1897 S.S. Malta
Bethia (1st time)	ditto	December 22nd 1897 S.S. Caledonia
Sophie (2nd time)	November 22nd 1891 S.S. Rewa	January 19th 1897 S.S. Simla
Rose Marian (1st time)	December 31st 1892 S.S. Rewa	April 11th 1898 S.S. City of Cambridge
Kate Mary (1st time)	ditto	March 11th 1899 S.S. City of Venice
Laura Jane (1st time)	January 27th 1894 S.S. Dunera	ditto
Margaret (1st time)	October 12th 1894 S.S. Chusan	May 18th 1900 S.S. Arabia
Honora (2nd time)	November 30th 1894 S.S. Oriental	March 15th 1900 S.S. Ballarat
Sibyl (3rd time)	January 4th 1895 S.S. Simla	February 14th 1901 S.S. Rewa
Mary Pauline (1st time)	ditto	March 15th 1900 S.S. Ballarat
Muriel (2nd time)	November 8th 1895 S.S. Simla	February 14th 1901 S.S. Rewa
Susanna (1st time)	January 25th 1896 Vincenza Lorenzo	April 13th 1901 S.S. Jelunga
Mary Thekla (2nd time)	January 1st 1897 S.S. Sumatra	April 12th 1902 S.S. Manora
Blanche Annie (1st time)	ditto	February 21st 1903 S.S. Sumatra
Edith Clara (1st time)	ditto	December 17th 1904 Caledonia & Macedonia
Mary Lucilla (1st time)	ditto	February 22nd 1902 S.S. Manora
Florence (2nd time)	January 14th 1898 Victoria & Malta	December 14th 1902 S.S. Persia
Catherine Bridget (1st time)	ditto	February 21st 1903 S.S. Sumatra

Sister	Left England	Arrival Back In England
Elisabeth Kate (1st time)	ditto	March 2nd 1904 S.S. Golconda
Jane Frances (2nd time as Sr Sup.)	October 21st 1898 S.S. Palawan	May 18th 1905 S.S. Scindia
Emily Elizabeth (1st time)	January 27th 1899 S.S. Golconda	March 11th 1902 S.S. City of Cambridge
Grace Ancilla (1st time)	ditto	January 24th 1904 S.S. Caledonia
Edith Gwendoline (1st time)	ditto	June 21st 1901 S.S. Arabia
Mary Victoria (1st time)	January 19th 1900 S.S. Borneo	May 18th 1905 S.S. Scindia
Kathleen Honora (1st time)	ditto	March 18th 1905 S.S. Manora
Edith Rachel (1st time)	ditto	October 19th 1901 S.S. Sicilia
Margaret (2nd time)	November 29th 1900 S.S. Caledonia	October 2nd 1905 S.S. Caledonia
Kate Mary (2nd time)	ditto	March 3rd 1906 S.S. City of Corinth
Edith Emily (1st time)	ditto	ditto
Mary Frances (1st time)	January 15th 1901 Oceana & Caledonia	April 30th 1906 S.S. Gurkha
Sybil (4th time)	September 20th 1901 S.S. Peninsular	March 26th 1907 S.S. Syria
Muriel (3rd time)	ditto	March 18th 1905 S.S. Muttra
Mary Pauline (2nd time)	January 17th 1902 S.S. Sunda	March 26th 1907 S.S. Syria
Helena Maria (1st time)	ditto	ditto
Katherine Maud (1st time)	ditto	February 11th 1907 S.S. Egypt
Mary Etheldreda (1st time)	January 16th 1903 S.S. Somali	January 19th 1908 S.S. Persia
Frances Anne (1st time)	ditto	March 13th 1909 S.S. Namur
Laura Jane (2nd time)	January 28th 1903 S.S. Maliana	January 19th 1908 S.S. Persia
Florence (3rd time)	November 26th 1903 S.S. Mongolia	December 20th 1908 S.S. Egypt
Mary Thekla (3rd time)	January 16th 1904 S.S. Sardinia	March 13th 1909 S.S. Namur
Blanche Annie (2nd time)	ditto	December 20th 1908 S.S. Egypt
Gertrude Emily (2nd time)	December 16th 1904 S.S. Oriental	September 30th 1907 S.S. Egypt
Mabel Theresa (1st time)	January 17th 1905 S.S. Sunda	March 16th 1910 S.S. Simla

Sister	Left England	Arrival Back In England
Beatrice Mary (1st time)	ditto	ditto
Annica (1st time)	March 18th 1905 S.S. Muttra	February 19th 1911 S.S. City of Sparta
Edith Clara (2nd time)	September 15th 1905 S.S. Persia	June 14th 1911 Baldina
Jane Frances (3rd time)	October 31st 1905 S.S. Scindia	May 11th 1914 S.S. Scindia
Mary Victoria (2nd time)	ditto	January 19th 1908 S.S. Persia
Constance Ruth (1st time)	January 6th 1906 S.S. Avoca	February 19th 1911 S.S. City of Sparta
Florence Mary (1st time)	ditto	April 22nd 1910 S.S. Golconda
Kate Mary (3rd time)	December 28th 1906 Bohemia	December 23rd 1911 S.S. City of Paris
Mary Frances (2nd time)	ditto	April 23rd 1914 S.S. City of Benares
Muriel (4th time)	January 25th 1907 S.S. Arabia	April 22nd 1910 S.S. Golconda
Edith Emily (2nd time)	ditto	December 23rd 1911 S.S. City of Paris
Mary Pauline (3rd time)	September 7th 1907 S.S. Nubia	March 21st 1914 S.S. Persia
Sr Helena Maria (2nd time)	ditto	February 16th 1913 S.S. City of Benares
Katherine Maud (2nd time)	December 5th 1907 S.S. Persia	March 10th 1913 S.S. Maidan
Catherine Bridget (2nd time)	February 27th 1908 S.S. Oceana	ditto
Mary Editha (1st time)	ditto	February 16th 1913 S.S. City of Benares
Mary Victoria (3rd time)	October 20th 1908 S.S. Caledonia	May 11th 1914 S.S. Scindia
Mary Etheldreda (2nd time)	January 8th 1909 S.S. City of Glasgow	March 10th 1913 S.S. Maidan
Kathleen Honora (2nd time)	ditto	March 13th 1910 S.S. Caledonia
Emily Barbara (1st time)	ditto	November 16th 1913 S.S. Maloja
Mother Evelyn (visit)	December 1st 1909 S.S. Arabia	March 13th 1910 S.S. Caledonia
Florence (4th time)	ditto	March 8th 1915 S.S. Karmala
Mary Thekla (4th time)	January 8th 1910 S.S. Malta	ditto
Mary Evelyn (1st time)	ditto	February 1st 1916 S.S. Caledonia
Sibyl (5th time)	April 13th 1910 S.S. Persia	May 3rd 1913 S.S. Poona

Sister	Left England	Arrival Back In England
Frances Anne (2nd time)	October 8th 1910 S.S. Jelunga	February 1st 1916 S.S. Caledonia
Beatrice Mary (2nd time)	January 7th 1911 S.S. Simla	March 29th 1916 S.S. Kaiser-i-Hind
Katherine Hope (1st time)	ditto	December 17th 1916 S.S. Caledonia
Mabel Theresa (2nd time)	February 1st 1911 S.S. City of Paris	February 1st 1916 S.S. Caledonia
Georgina (1st time)	October 3rd 1911 S.S. City of Glasgow	December 17th 1916 S.S. Caledonia
Marian Edith (1st time)	January 6th 1912 S.S. Simla	April 20th 1918 Warwickshire (torpedoed)
Constance Ruth (2nd time)	ditto	April 12th 1915 S.S. Kashgar
Olive (1st time)	October 11th 1912 S.S. Caledonia	June 10th 1919 S.S. Scindia
Edith Emily (3rd time)	January 13th 1913 S.S. City of Benares	February 27th 1919 S.S. Nankin
Edith Alice (1st time)	ditto	June 10th 1919 S.S. Scindia
Celia (1st time)	ditto	July 3rd 1919 S.S. Thongwa
Edith Helen (1st time)	ditto	April 20th 1918 Warwickshire (torpedoed)
Blanche Annie (3rd time)	January 9th 1914 S.S. City of London	February 20th 1920 S.S. City of London
Mary Editha (2nd time)	ditto	ditto
Helena Maria (3rd time)	ditto	March 7th 1920 S.S. Sardinia
Dorothy Frances (1st time)	ditto	February 26th 1921 S.S. Kaiser-i-Hind
Jane Frances (4th time)	November 21st 1914 S.S. Caledonia	July 3rd 1919 S.S. Thongwa
Kate Mary (4th time)	ditto	June 25th 1920 S.S. Nankin
Norah (1st time)	ditto	April 7th 1920 S.S. Maidan
Mary Victoria (4th time)	January 9th 1915 S.S. Medina	April 14th 1921 S.S. Nyanza
Honor (1st time)	January 9th 1915 S.S. Medina	January 8th 1921 S.S. Khyber
Katherine Maud (3rd time)	February 27th 1915 S.S. Arabia	April 7th 1920 S.S. Maidan
Alexandrina (1st time)	December 4th 1915 S.S. Caledonia	April 20th 1918 Warwickshire (torpedoed)
Dorothea (1st time)	ditto	Left Community while in India - November 1918
Mary Frances (3rd time)	January 1st 1916 S.S. Kaiser-i-Hind	March 11th 1922 S.S. City of Poona

Sister	Left England	Arrival Back In England
Kathleen Prisca (1st time)	ditto	February 11th 1922 S.S. Nankin
Beatrice Mary (3rd time)	January 1st 1917 S.S. Namur	ditto
Mary Evelyn (2nd time)	ditto	December 29th 1921 S.S. City of Calcutta
Margaret (3rd time)	December 4th 1918 S.S. Nagoya	May 9th 1925 S.S. Kaiser-i-Hind
Constance Ruth (3rd time)	ditto	November 26th 1923 S.S. Mooltan
Ursula (1st time)	ditto	February 21st 1925 S.S. Malda
Georgina (2nd time)	January 6th 1919 S.S. City of Marseilles	February 1st 1924 S.S. Madura
Margaret Monica (1st time)	ditto	ditto
Katherine Hope (2nd time)	January 30th 1919 S.S. City of Cairo	February 21st 1925 S.S. Malda
Helen Kathleen (1st time)	ditto	November 26th 1923 S.S. Mooltan
Frances Clare (1st time)	ditto	February 1st 1924 S.S. Madura
Mabel Theresa (3rd time)	January 16th 1920 S.S. Nevasa	February 24th 1924 S.S. Mulbera
Helen Muriel (1st time)	January 16th 1920 S.S. Nevasa	February 16th 1926 S.S. Malda
Isabel Jean (1st time)	ditto	ditto
Edith Emily (4th time)	March 12th 1920 S.S. Margha	February 21st 1925 S.S. Malda
Edith Alice (2nd time)	ditto	October 18th 1924 S.S. Kaiser-i-Hind
Celia (2nd time)	ditto	February 21st 1925 S.S. Malda
Olive (2nd time)	ditto	ditto
Blanche Annie (4th time)	December 31st 1920 S.S. Kaiser-i-Hind	March 23rd 1926 S.S. Manora
Mary Editha (3rd time)	ditto	December 29th 1921 S.S. City of Calcutta
Norah (2nd time)	February 11th 1921 S.S. Nellore	February 16th 1926 S.S. Malda
Caroline Elizabeth (1st time)	December 1st 1921 S.S. City of Poona	January 22nd 1928 Genova
Violet Grace (1st time)	ditto	February 8th 1928 S.S. Morvada
Helena Maria (4th time)	January 9th 1922 S.S. City of York	January 15th 1927 S.S. Ranpura
Mary Rachel (1st time)	ditto	February 16th 1924 S.S. Mulbera

Sister	Left England	Arrival Back In England
Dorothy Frances (2nd time)	February 4th 1922 S.S. Morvada	January 15th 1927 S.S. Ranpura
Beatrice Mary (4th time)	January 5th 1923 S.S. Manela	January 22nd 1928 Genova
Kathleen Prisca (2nd time)	ditto	February 8th 1928 S.S. Morvada
Mary Evelyn (3rd time)	September 8th 1923 S.S. Novara	February 26th 1927 S.S. Malda
Frances Anne (3rd time)	October 27th 1923 S.S. Talma	March 8th 1930 S.S. Margha
Honor (2nd time)	ditto	February 22nd 1929 S.S. Margha
Helen Mildred (1st time)	January 5th 1924 S.S. Merkara	December 30th 1924 Nevasa & Madura
Edith Helen (2nd time)	November 15th 1924 S.S. Nellore	December 9th 1930 S.S. California
Frances Clare (2nd time)	ditto	February 1st 1930 S.S. Manela
Constance Ruth (4th time)	November 4th 1924 S.S. Caledonia	died in India August 29th 1928
Freda (1st time)	ditto	December 9th 1930 S.S. California
Helen Kathleen (2nd time)	January 3rd 1925 S.S. Mantola	November 22nd 1928 S.S. Manora
Margaret Monica (2nd time)	ditto	February 1st 1930 S.S. Manela
Georgina (3rd time)	January 17th 1925 S.S. Merkara	February 26th 1931 S.S. Britannia
Margaret (4th time)	December 4th 1925 S.S. Kaiser-i-Hind	April 28th 1931 S.S. Manolia
Edith Emily (5th time)	ditto	December 29th 1928 S.S. Razmak
Edith Alice (3rd time)	ditto	February 26th 1931 S.S. Britannia
Ursula (2nd time)	ditto	return not recorded - left Community
Olive (3rd time)	January 9th 1926 S.S. Nagoya	June 21 1929 S.S. City of Calcutta
Isabel Jean (2nd time)	January 21st 1927 S.S. Rawalpindi	November 22nd 1928 S.S. Manora
Edith Agnes (1st time)	ditto	December 8th 1931 S.S. California
Dorothy Frances (3rd time)	November 25th 1927 S.S. Kaiser-i-Hind	February 10th 1933 S.S. Strathaird
Helen Muriel (2nd time)	ditto	March 26th 1929 S.S. Manora
Beatrice Mary (5th time)	December 14th 1928 S.S. Rajputana	January 23rd 1934 S.S. Victoria
Caroline Elizabeth (2nd time)	December 26th 1928 S.S. Ranchi	ditto

Sister	Left England	Arrival Back In England
Violet Grace (2nd time)	ditto	February 9th 1934 ship not recorded
Grace (1st time)	January 26th 1929 S.S. Mashobra	January 12th 1934 S.S. Strathnaver
Dorothy Florence (1st time)	ditto	February 9th 1934 ship not recorded
Honor (3rd time)	October 19th 1929 S.S. Mantola	February 8th 1935 S.S. Strathnaver
Kathleen Prisca (3rd time)	ditto	January 2nd 1932 S.S. Strathnaver
Hilda (1st time)	ditto	December 21st 1934 S.S. Kaiser-i-Hind
Hilda Frances (1st time)	ditto	March 20th 1935 accompanied Mother Katherine Maud on her 1935 homeward journey when the latter died.
Katherine Maud (penultimate visit)	October 25th 1930 S.S. California	February 26th 1931 S.S. Britannia
Frances Anne (4th time)	ditto	January 23rd 1934 S.S. Victoria
Lilian Maude (1st time)	ditto	March 6th 1936 ship not recorded
Mildreda (1st time)	ditto	October 28th 1932 S.S. Margha
Frances Clare (3rd time)	January 2nd 1931 S.S. Britannia	January 24th 1936 S.S. Maloja
Catherine Mildred (1st time)	January 2nd 1931 S.S. Britannia	February 10th 1933 S.S. Strathaird
Georgina (4th time)	October 20th 1931 S.S. California	January 22nd 1937 S.S. Strathaird
Freda (2nd time)	ditto	ditto
Lilian Mary (1st time)	ditto	ditto
Blanche Annie (5th time)	November 4th 1932 S.S. Strathaird	January 12th 1934 S.S. Strathnaver
Irene (1st time)	ditto	May 4th 1936 S.S. Strathmore
Dorothy Frances (4th time)	November 3rd 1933 S.S. Strathaird	February 19th 1938 S.S. Mooltan
Marian Edith (2nd time)	ditto	ditto
Gladys (1st time)	ditto	January 20th 1939 S.S. Mooltan
Celia (3rd time)	December 29th 1933 S.S. Moldavia	March 6th 1936 ship not recorded
Eudora (1st time)	ditto	May 27th 1938 S.S. Strathaird

Sister	Left England	Arrival Back In England
Caroline Elizabeth	November 2nd 1934 S.S. Strathnaver	March 6th 1940 ship not recorded
Dorothy Florence (2nd time)	ditto	ditto
Rosemary (1st time)	ditto	January 20th 1939 S.S. Mooltan
Katherine Maud (last visit)	November 15th 1934 S.S. Ranchi	left India Feb 16th 1935; ill en route; taken to St St Bart's; died 10.4.35.
Grace (2nd time)	ditto	October 4th 1935 S.S. Maloja
Violet Grace (3rd time)	December 28th 1934 S.S. Moldavia	March 6th 1940
Honor (4th time)	November 29th 1935 S.S. Kaiser-i-Hind	March 25th 1944
Hilda (2nd time)	ditto	February 23rd 1945
Frances Clare (4th time)	November 13th 1936 S.S. Narkunda	February 23rd 1945
Irene (2nd time)	ditto	March 25th 1944
Lilian Maude (2nd time)	January 8th 1937 S.S. Maloja	March 6th 1940
Georgina (5th time)	October 29th 1937 S.S. Strathaird	April 21st 1946
Hilda Frances (2nd time)	ditto	February 23rd 1945
Freda (3rd time)	December 30th 1937 S.S. Stratheden	March 25th 1944
Lilian Mary (2nd time)	ditto	April 21st 1946
Dorothy Frances (5th time)	November 17th 1938 S.S. Narkunda	June 24th 1939 S.S. Rajputana
Elizabeth Mary (1st time)	ditto	February 23rd 1945
Gladys (2nd time)	December 22nd 1939 S.S. Strathmore	February 23rd 1945
Rosemary (2nd time)	ditto	March 25th 1944

APPENDIX 5

A DAY IN THE RICE COUNTRY

This letter was sent from Calcutta by Sister Jane Frances to the Sisters at Clewer and was reproduced in the Easter 1891 issue of the *St John Baptist Magazine.* There is also in the Clewer archives a manuscript version of which this is a transcript. It was on a visit such as this one that Sr Jane Frances was photographed - see cover.

December 12th 1890. Lady Canning Home, Calcutta.

Dearest Sisters,

I have had four such interesting and curious days in the rice country, a little to the south of Calcutta accompanying Miss Hoare on a little circuit among the rice country village schools. During these days I did not see European or Eurasian or hear a word of English or even Hindustani, nothing but Bengali, and have been in the midst of simple Bengali Christian life which has impressed me very favourably. They are such gentle people with a certain natural refinement, that is very attractive.

The object of this expedition was to examine some of the little village schools in their religious knowledge. During the course of some 12 years work Miss Hoare has planted about 30 of these schools in as many of the scattered rice country villages, specially where there are groups of native Christian families. Mrs Wheeler, the Bengali lady who came to Clewer on Commemoration Day, visits these schools as Government Inspector and gives them their passes under the educational code but the religious examination has to be separate.

We made our headquarters at one of the larger villages where there is a pretty large school of 80 girls, 50 of them Christians. In rural Bengal, where female education of any sort is quite a new idea, this means a good deal. We put up at the Christian teacher's house which though only built of clay and bamboo was quite a superior one, and Miss H has a room there where she puts up on these missionary expeditions. The arrangements are all most primitive but everything remarkably clean. It was very amusing to be right in the midst of the simple family life. There were 6 little girls of 10 or 11 but not all *sisters,* but relations of one degree or another who are studying up for Bengali primary scholarships. I had the amusement of hearing them going over their Genesis in Bengali, sitting in the verandah off the room where we had our meals, under the guidance of the old master. They were charming little girls and seemed to be very bright scholars. Two mornings were taken up in examining the children of this school, the rest of the time in visiting other similar but smaller schools within reach of them.

Now as to the country. Too flat certainly to be beautiful, rice fields stretching for miles and miles. Just now until the hot season, I believe always some two feet of water or more. In parts the ripe rice hung down so that the grains dipped into the water. In other parts it had been cut, and here rice stalks stood *out* of the water. No hedges as visible divisions, instead of paths through cornfields, narrow water paths through which long narrow flat bottomed boats are punted along with poles. Two passengers can go in a boat with comfort. You sit in the bottom of the boat, one behind the other, and a little thatched roof open at the sides protects you from the sun. It is very slow locomotion, but pleasant, the water in the rice fields is very clean, you slip along among the rustling grain which often dips into the boat. Instead of cornfield weeds there are curious wild water plants, the most abundant a pretty water convolvulous with large pink flowers. But like the poppy at home this means no good to the rice plants. Here and there a white *lotus* or water lily lifts up its head to the sun, or another of a delicate lilac. These look so lovely and have such an air of distinction, one can understand their being the favourite poetical image for everything beautiful; they do not *float* on the water like our pond lilies bit stand right up on stalks out of the water, and in the early morning sunlight when freshly opened looked as if they had come straight from heaven and were gazing up into heaven again. Here and there from these stretches of watery fields rise little bits of higher ground like islands from the sea of rice fields. On these grew picturesque groups of different kind of palm trees and among them are the little villages of the rice cultivators, and in some where there is a sufficient number of Christian families to make a nucleus, are Miss H's little day schools chiefly for girls.

From this larger centre I visited *six*. All places have the same general character, but each some special feature as well, and the schools of course varied in quality. I want more practice to speak Bengali fluently, but can understand it now easily when it is not spoken very fast as in very slipshod fashion, and could take my share in the simple examination with great interest. There were different standards corresponding to those of the government code, and besides Creed, Lord's Prayer and 10 Commandments, I heard a certain elementary Catechism through and through till I felt as if I could have said it in my sleep. It is drawn up for the instruction of Hindoos and has such questions as, "Is the soul a part of God?", "Shall we be born again after death?" and various other curious things. They learn by heart very easily and the amount they knew was very creditable. Two books of coloured Scripture prints, one of Old and the other New Testament make a very good course of Bible history. The smallest classes begin with 5 pictures only. The bigger ones could explain the whole series from beginning to end very well indeed. Clearly it is an excellent way of fixing facts in their minds.

Sunday we spent at another village where the accommodation was not so good, as service was to be held there and not at the larger place. The church was simply a small clay and bamboo structure with a few mats spread inside. But there was a good and reverent congregation and a whole series of religious functions, administration of Holy Communion, Matins, sermon, 4 Baptisms, a Churching, all attended by regular Bengali hymns. Not as in Calcutta with *A & M* tunes to Bengali translations, but real weird Bengali tunes with continually recurring refrains. When one gets a little used to them and hears them sung with great fervour to original Bengali hymns they are very touching. This little mud church stood on a kind of promontory with weedy water on each side. A clear space was made in the weeds, the old native padre stood in a boat and the congregation on the bank. All the candidates were children but only one an infant. We took over 2 nice little girls with us for Baptism, one of whom is added to my list of godchildren. These 2 were not Hindoos but neglected Christian children. They were immersed (with their clothes on) and fresh garments put on after. I have omitted to say that a little portable altar is carried about in a box by the old padre with a nice frontal and veil. It gave a respectable look to the place.

We had more school examinations in the afternoon, and Evensong and Bengali hymn singing just at sunset in one of the rice sheds, not in the little church, a row of Hindoos listening to the singing apparently with admiration. I saw the 6 little girls set to work at arithmetic problems written out in the most delicate Bengali writing by the old pundit, and they set about each with her little inkpot under the palm trees to work these trial papers and they did very neatly too. These rice field people are more like peasant farmers or proprietors than like our agricultural labourers, so of a higher type they cultivate their own lands paying dues to government and to the zemindas" [i.e. zamindas - landlords].

Your ever loving, Jane Frances , Sr Supr, CSJB

CSJB

INDIA

SOURCES AND BIBLIOGRAPHY

PRIMARY SOURCES: Archive material or other unpublished sources

(There is much archive material at Clewer, but it is not organised systematically. Such cataloguing as exists has largely been done by the author in connection with writing this trilogy. Therefore the phrase *Clewer Archives* does not imply the existence of an organised working collection: it merely relates to certain documents belonging to the CSJB which have provided primary sources for the three books).

1. CLEWER ARCHIVES: Manuscript, or unpublished sources

Unless stated otherwise in the text, all letters quoted are at Clewer either in original MS/ typescript form or as copies. Also, some were edited and reproduced in *St John Baptist Magazines* or the *Associates' Newsletters*. Most of the MS letters and copies are kept together in a portfolio with the following file headings:

i. Presidency General Hospital - letters from Isabella Wilson; Bishop Edward Johnson of Calcutta; Bishop J.F. Mackarness of Oxford; Sr Lucy; various officials from the Calcutta Hospital Nurses' Institution.

ii. Sr Jane Frances - letters to Clewer from India.

iii. Angelina Hoare - miscellaneous writings on her rice country work; letters from Sr Jane Frances to Clewer about Miss Hoare's work; letters from Sophia L. Hoare to Mother Superior at Clewer; letters from Bishop Johnson to Sr Jane Frances.

iv. Medical College and Eden Hospitals - official letters from government concerning CSJB withdrawal 1909-10.

v. European Orphanage - letters between Sr Lucy and Mrs Kitchin concerning terms under which CSJB would work at the Orphanage.

vi. Diocesan Girls' High School, Darjeeling - letters from Sr Jane Frances; letter from Bishop Johnson to T.T.Carter; letters from Bishop Foss Westcott to the Mother General at Clewer 1944-5.

vii. Eden Sanatorium, Darjeeling - from Secretary of Committee to Sr Jane Frances concerning terms under which CSJB would work; letter from Bishop Johnson; letter from Sr Jane Frances.

viii. Kidderpore House - letters from Secretary to Mother Superior at Clewer concerning terms under which CSJB would work; letters from Sr Jane Frances in reply and also to Clewer; letters from Bishop of Calcutta to Clewer.

2. OTHER UNPUBLISHED PRIMARY SOURCES:

i. Community of St John Baptist, Clewer Community *Annals* 1881-1947.

ii. Sister Eudora, CSJB : *Personal and Private Memoirs*. Written for the Community in 1975 at the request of Mother Annys.

iii. Letters to the author from: Clare Walton, Joyce Keenan, Nancy Leslie (all from St Michael's Darjeeling); Helen Wala (Pratt Memorial School).

iv. BONHAM, Valerie *Diary of an Indian Journey, February 8th-26th 1995* Unpublished MS 108 pp.

v. Community of St John Baptist: List of Sisters in India. MS list kept by the Sister Secretary at Clewer.

3. PUBLISHED PRIMARY SOURCES

i. *St John Baptist Magazine* Easter 1882-1907

ii. *Associates' Newsletter* 1909-48

iii. *Pipalpati* 1904-41

iv. Sr Georgina, CSJB *Past History of S. Michael's School, Darjeeling.* undated typescript .

v. Community of St John Baptist Clewer *Our work in Bengal* April 1939 23pp.

vi. St John's Diocesan Girls' Higher Secondary School 1894-1993. Centenary celebration book. Calcutta 1993.

vii. Newspapers:

Calcutta Municipal Journal

Friend of India

Statesman - Record of the great Indian Earthquake 1934

Times

Times of India

Times of India Overland Weekly

SECONDARY SOURCES

BAYLY, C.A. *The Raj: India and the British 1600-1947* (Exhibition catalogue) National Portrait Gallery 1990.

BENCE-JONES, Mark *The Viceroys of India* Constable 1982.

Bengal Directory 1882

BHANJA, K.C. *Darjeeling at a glance* Darjeeling: Oxford Book & Stationery Co. not dated but probably 1930s.

BOWLE, John *The Imperial Achievement* Secker & Warburg 1974.

BRADLEY, John, ed. *Lady Curzon's India: Letters of a Vicereine* Weidenfeld & Nicolson 1985.

The Churchman's Missionary Atlas S.P.G. 4th ed. 1922

COTTON, H.E.A. *Calcutta Old and New: A Historical & Descriptive Handbook to the City* Calcutta: W. Newman & Co. 1907.

CURZON OF KEDLESTON, MARQUIS *British Government in India* Cassell 1925 2 vols.

DAVIES, Philip *Splendours of the Raj: British Architecture in India, 1660-1947* Penguin 1985

DUFFERIN AND AVA, Marchioness of *Our Viceregal Life in India: selections from my Journal 1884-8* John Murray 1889 2 vols.

EDWARDES, Michael *Raj: the story of British India* Pan 1969 (first published by Sidgwick & Jackson 1967 as *British India 1772-1947*).

ELLIS, Royston *India by Rail* 1989.

FABB, John *Royal Tours of the British Empire 1860-1927* Batsford 1989.

FARRELL, J.G. *The Seige of Krishnapur* 1973 (a novel about the Indian Mutiny).

FOWLER, Marian *Below the Peacock Fan: First Ladies of the Raj* Penguin edition 1988.

GARDNER, C.E. *Life of Father Goreh* Longmans, Green & Co 1900

GILMOUR, David *Curzon* John Murray 1994.

Here and there with the S.P.G. in India 3rd series SPG 1905.

(HOARE) *Life of Angelina Margaret Hoare* by her sisters and Mrs Walter Hoare Gardner, Darton & Co. 1897

A Hundred Years in Bengal: a history of the Oxford Mission 1880-1980 Delhi 1979

Imperial Gazeteer of India. Calcutta 1909. Vol 1 Provincial Series Bengal. Vol II 1909 Darjeeling.

JAMES, Lawrence *The Rise and Fall of the British Empire* Little, Brown & Co. 1994.

KINCAID, Dennis *British Social Life in India 1608-1937* 1938.

KIPLING, Rudyard *From Sea to Sea and other sketches Vol. 2 The City of Dreadful Night* MacMillan & Co 1914

LAPIERRE, Dominique *City of Joy*.

LAPPING, Brian *End of Empire* Granada: Channel 4. 1985

LONGRIDGE, George *A History of the Oxford Mission to Calcutta* Mowbray 1910

LOSTY, J.P. *Calcutta - City of Palaces* British Library/Arnold 1990

MacMILLAN, Margaret *Women of the Raj* Thames and Hudson 1988

MASON, Philip *The Men who ruled India* Pan Books in association with Jonathan Cape Ltd. This ed. 1985. (original ed. 2 vols. 1953-4)

MILMAN, Frances Maria *Memoir of the Rt Revd Robert Milman, D.D...* John Murray 1879.

MOORHOUSE, Geoffrey *Calcutta* Penguin 1974

MOORHOUSE, Geoffrey *India Britannica* Paladin 1984

MORRIS, Jan *The Pax Britannica Trilogy: Pax Britannica* 1968; *Heaven's Command* 1973; *Farewell the Trumpets* 1978. Faber (later editions Penguin)

MORRIS, Jan *Spectacle of Empire.*

MORRIS, Jan with Simon Winchester *Stones of Empire: the Buildings of the Raj* O.U.P. 1986.

NEILL, Stephen *A History of Christian Missions* Pelican 1964

NICOLSON, Nigel *Mary Curzon* Weidenfeld & Nicolson 1977

PEARSON, R. *Eastern Interlude: a social history of the European Community in Calcutta* Calcutta: Thacker, Spink & Co. 1933

SCOTT, Paul *The Raj Quartet* 1966-75

SHELLIM, Maurice *The South Park Street Cemetery* BACSA 1986

South Park Street Cemetery, Calcutta: Register of graves and standing tombs from 1767. London: BACSA 1992. (This updates the information in the register of 1900).

SPEAR, Percival *A History of India* Vol. 2 Penguin rev. 1978.

STEEL, Flora Annie & GARDINER, G. *The Complete Indian Housekeeper and Cook* new ed. 1898.

Thacker's Indian Directory, Calcutta 1890 & 1899.

THEROUX, Paul *The Great Railway Bazaar: by train through Asia* Penguin edition 1977.

THEROUX, Paul & McCURRY, Steve *The Imperial Way: making tracks from Peshawar to Chittagong* Hamish Hamilton 1985.

TROLLOPE, Joanna *Britannia's Daughters: Women of the British Empire* Pimlico edition 1994 (originally published by Hutchinson 1983).

TULLY, MARK *No Full Stops in India* Penguin edition 1992.

WAVELL *The Viceroy's Journal* ed by Penderel Moon. O.U.P. 1973

WESTLAKE, Graeme D. *An introduction to the Hill Stations of India* Indus 1993.

WILSON, C.R. ed. *List of Inscriptions on Tombs or Monuments in Bengal possessing historical or archaeological interest* (Lists monuments in St Paul's Cathedral, Calcutta). 1896.

WORSWICK, C. & EMBREE, A. *The Last Empire*

YULE, Henry & BURNELL, A.C. *Hobson-Jobson: The Anglo-Indian Dictionary* 1886.

INDEX

D

E

N

O

P

Q

R

S

T

U

V

W

Z